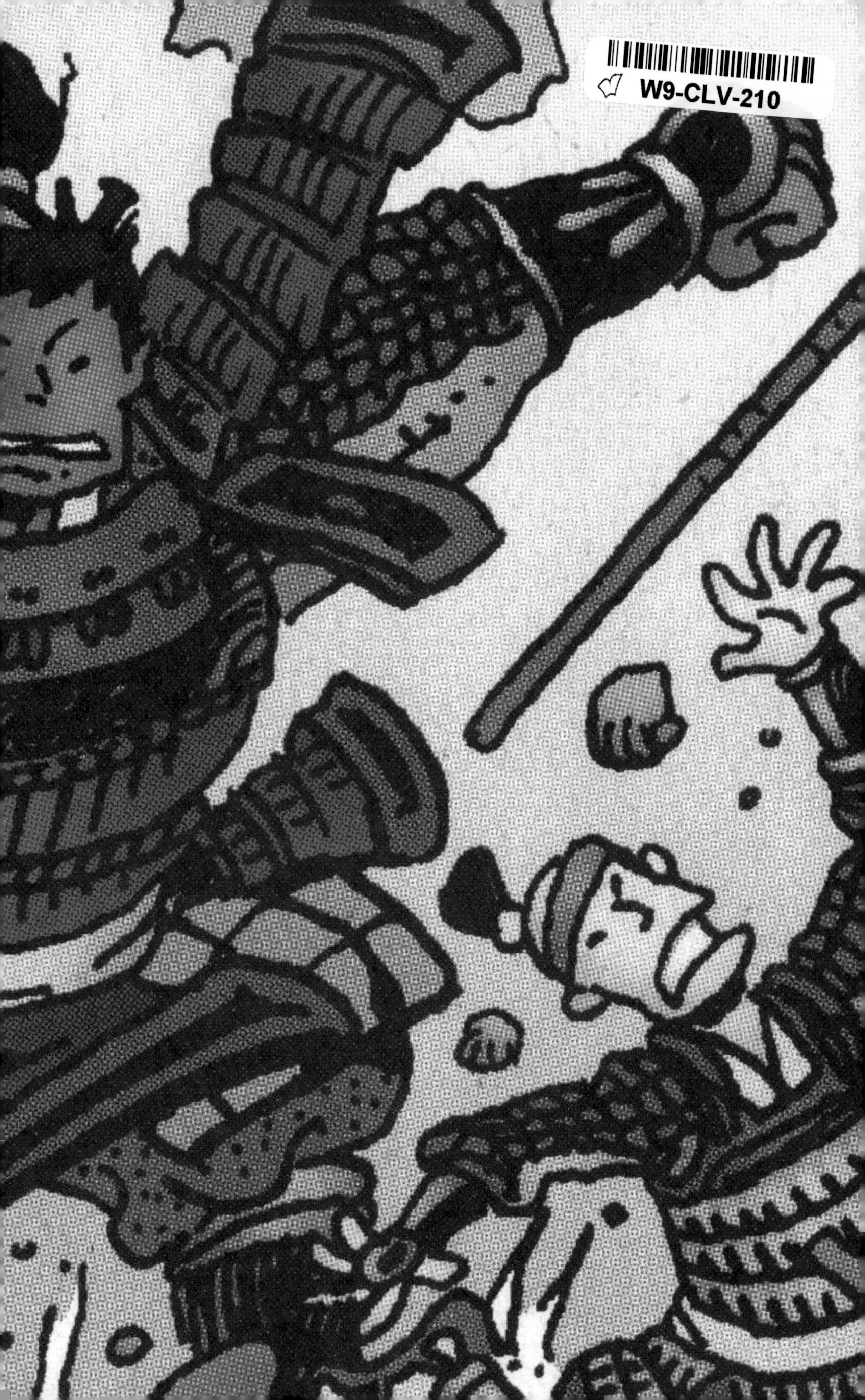

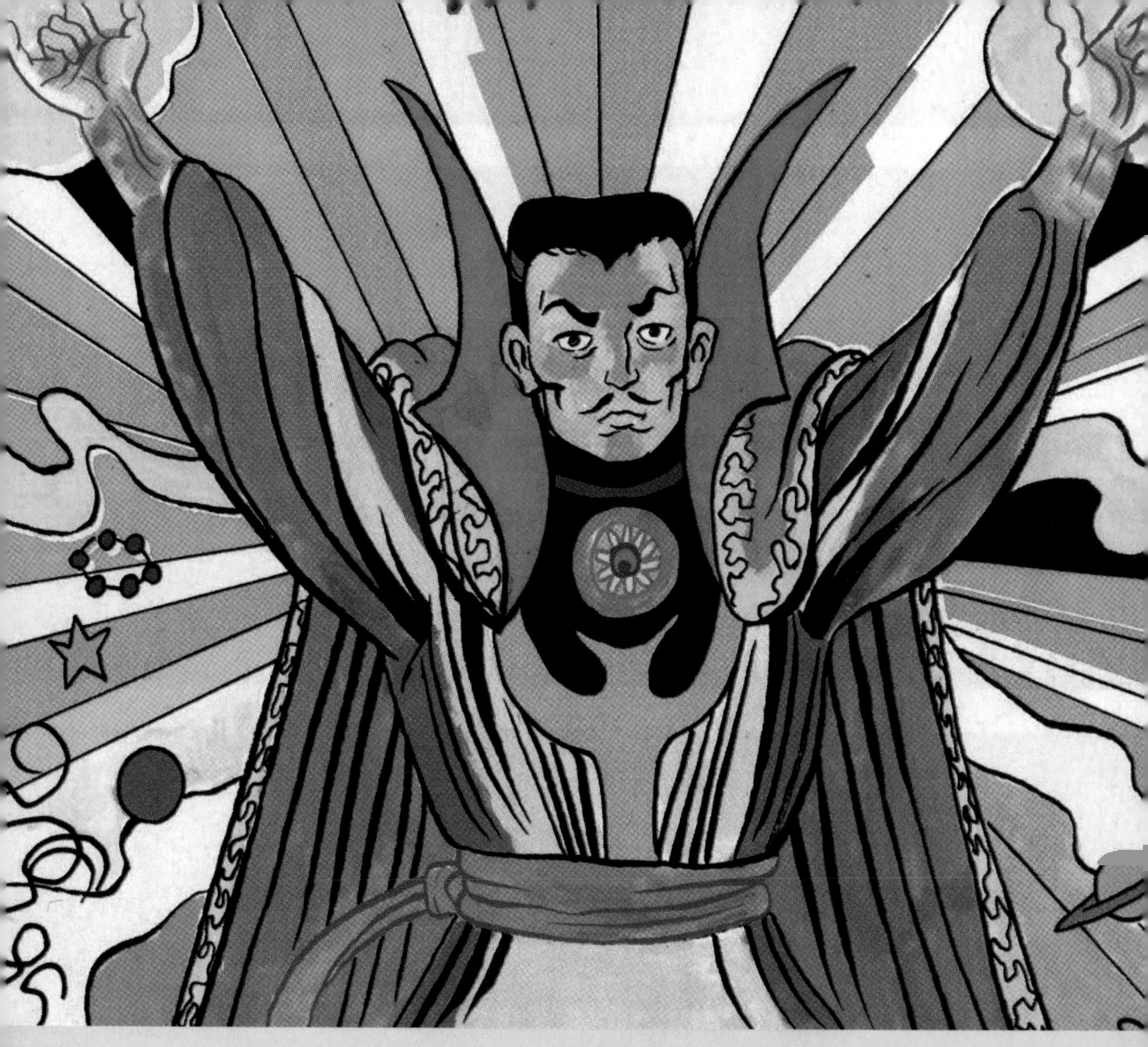

SERIES EDITORS: JODY LEHEUP, AUBREY SITTERSON, JOHN BARBER & AXEL ALONS

Special thanks to Eric Reynolds, Sean T. Collins & Victor Ochoa

Cover Design: Chip Kidd

Collection Editor: Jennifer Grünwald
Assistant Editor: Alex Starbuck
Associate Editor: John Denning
Editor, Special Projects: Mark D. Beazley
Senior Editor, Special Projects: Jeff Youngquist
Senior Vice President of Sales: David Gabriel
Production: Jerry Kalinowski

Editor in Chief: Joe Quesada
Publisher: Dan Buckley
Executive Producer: Alan Fine

STRANGE TALES. Contains material originally published in magazine form as STRANGE TALES #1-3, STARTLING STORIES: THE MEGALOMANIACAL SPIDER-MAN and ALL SELECT COMICS 70TH ANNIVERSARY SPECIAL. printing 2010. ISBN# 978-0-7851-4626-1. Published by MARVEL WORLDWIDE, INC., a subsidiary of MARVEL ENTERTAINMENT, LLC. OFFICE OF PUBLICATION: 417 5th Avenue, New York, NY 10016. $29.99 per copy in the U.S. (GST #R127032852); Canadian Agreement #40668537. **Printed in the U.S.A.** ALAN FINE, EVP - Office of the President, Marvel Worldwide, Inc. and EVP & CMO Marvel Characters B.V.; DAN BUCKLEY, Chief Executive O and Publisher - Print, Animation & Digital Media; JIM SOKOLOWSKI, Chief Operating Officer; DAVID GABRIEL, SVP of Publishing Sales & Circulation; DAVID BOGART, SVP of Business Affairs & Talent Management; MIC PASCIULLO, VP Merchandising & Communications; JIM O'KEEFE, VP of Operations & Logistics; DAN CARR, Executive Director of Publishing Technology; JUSTIN F. GABRIE, Director of Publishing & Editorial Operations; SU CRESPI, Editorial Operations Manager; ALEX MORALES, Publishing Operations Manager; STAN LEE, Chairman Emeritus. For information regarding advertising in Marvel Comics or on Marvel.com, please contact Ron Ster of Business Development, at rstern@marvel.com. For Marvel subscription inquiries, please call 800-217-9158. **Manufactured between 1/11/10 and 2/10/10 by R.R. DONNELLEY, INC., SALEM, VA, USA.**

10 9 8 7 6 5 4 3 2 1

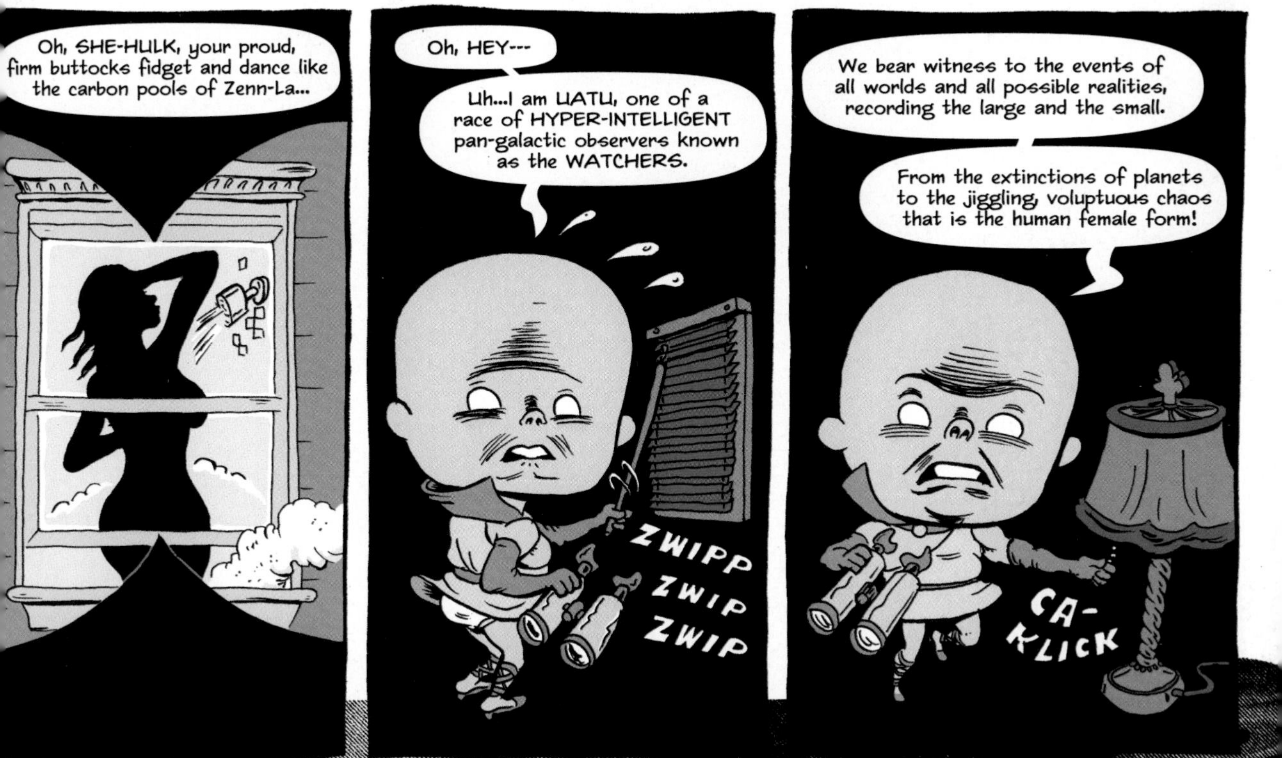

Oh, SHE-HULK, your proud, firm buttocks fidget and dance like the carbon pools of Zenn-La...
Oh, HEY---
Uh...I am UATU, one of a race of HYPER-INTELLIGENT pan-galactic observers known as the WATCHERS.
ZWIPP
ZWIP
ZWIP
We bear witness to the events of all worlds and all possible realities, recording the large and the small.
From the extinctions of planets to the jiggling, voluptuous chaos that is the human female form!
CA-KLICK

..., A Watcher!" by Nick Bertozzi, colored by Chris Sinderson

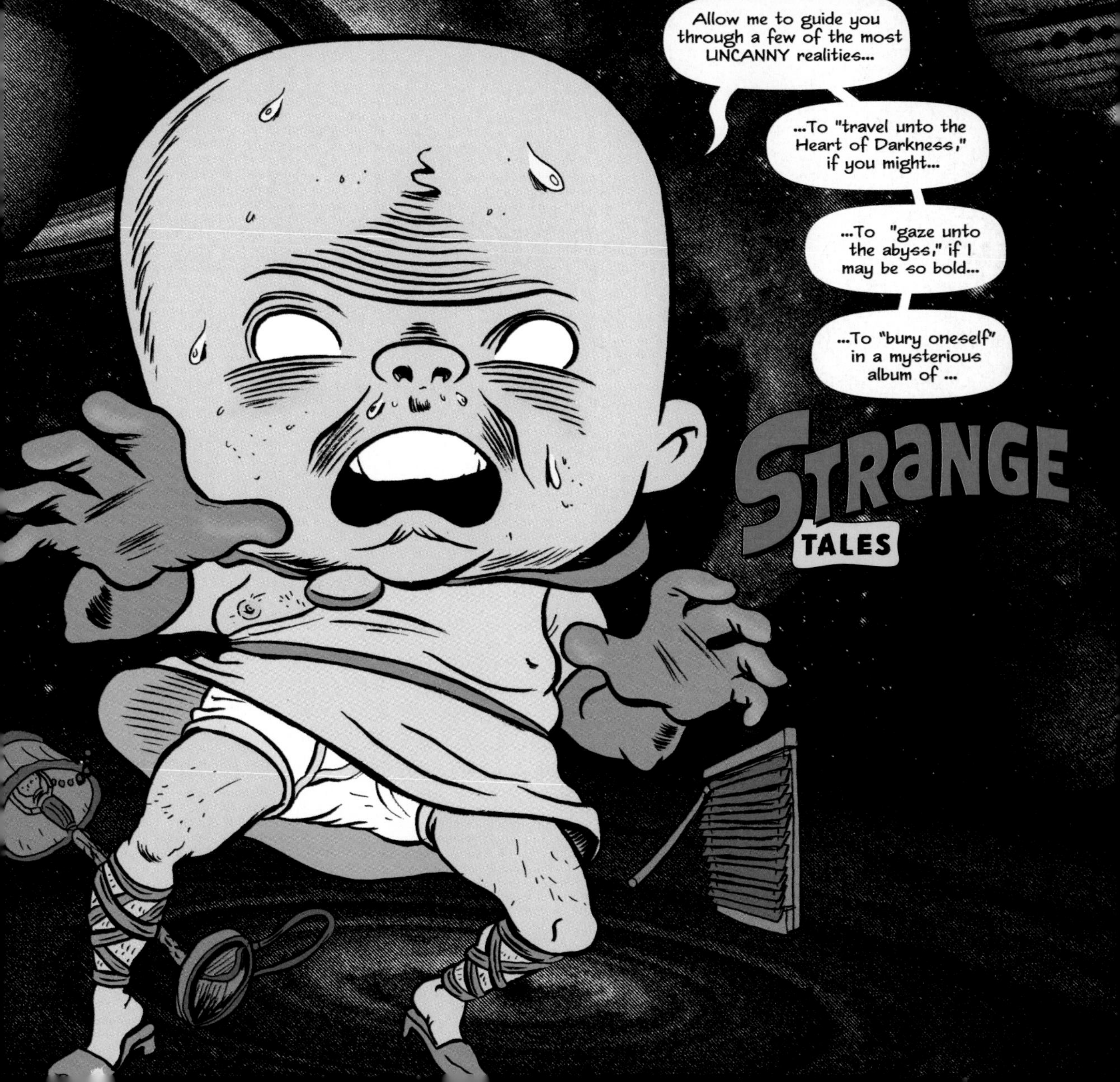

Allow me to guide you through a few of the most UNCANNY realities...
...To "travel unto the Heart of Darkness," if you might...
...To "gaze unto the abyss," if I may be so bold...
...To "bury oneself" in a mysterious album of ...
STRANGE TALES

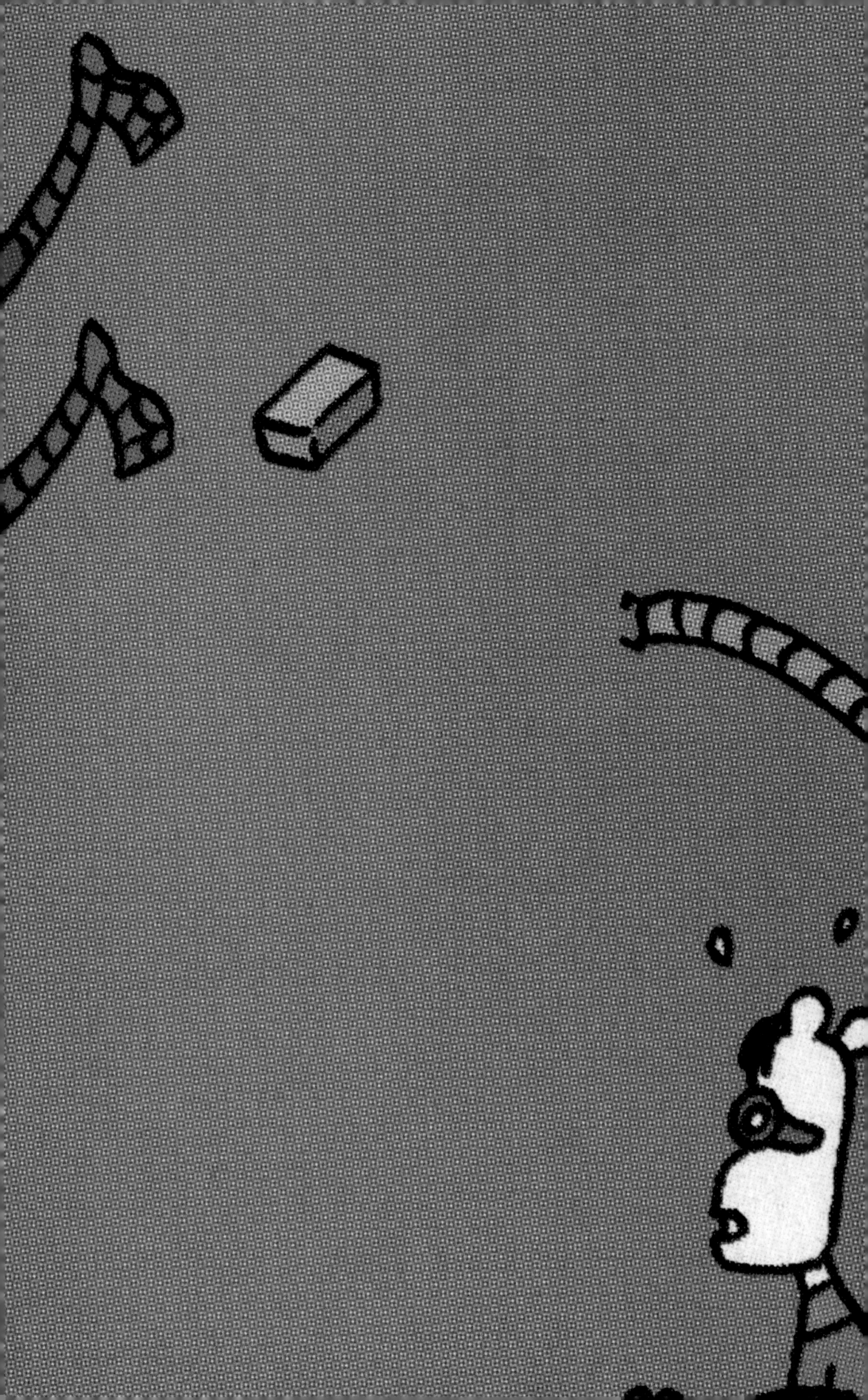

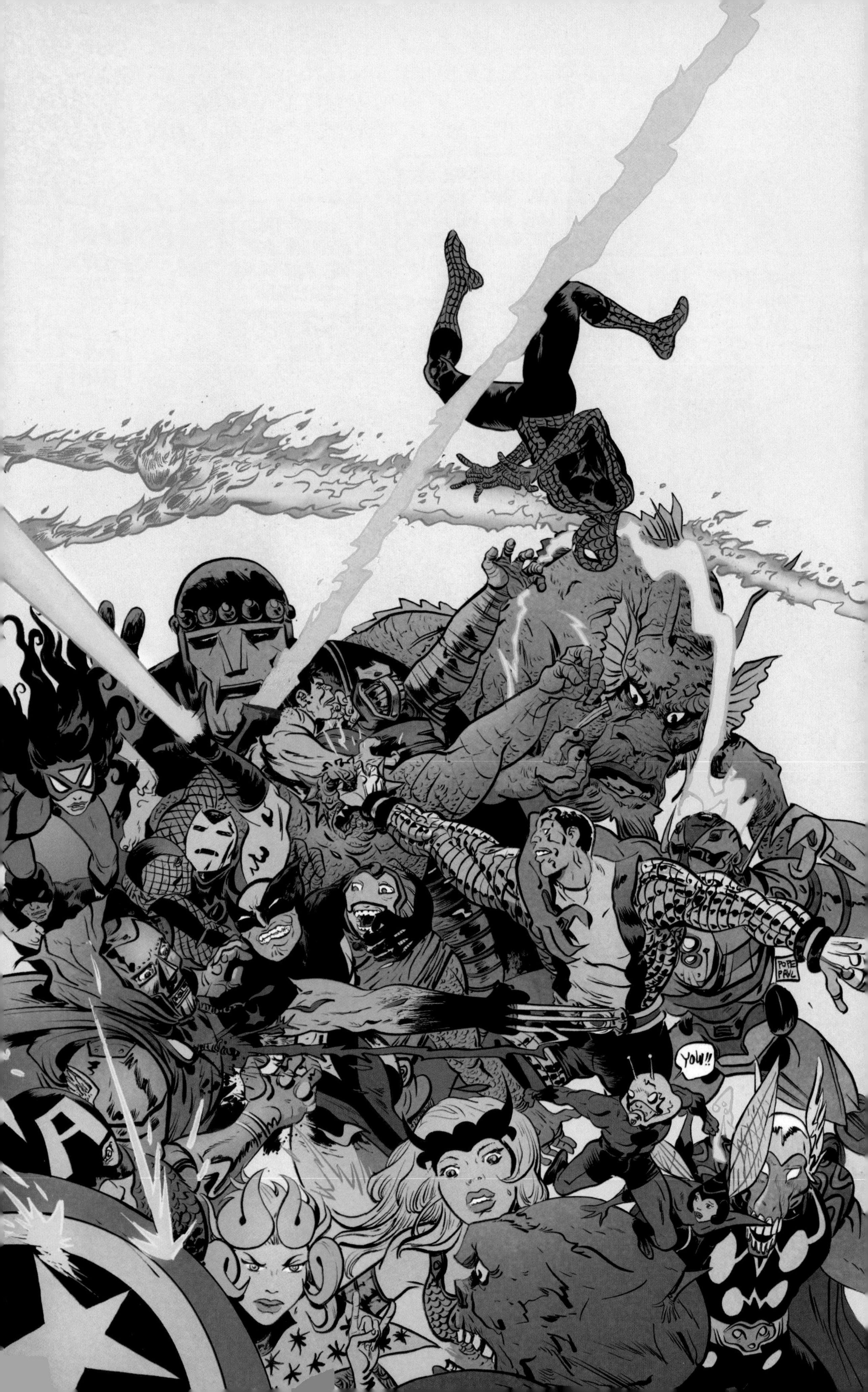
POPE
PAUL
YOW!!

GORGON! MEDUSA! BLACK BOLT! KARNAK! TRITON!

THEY ARE NOT A MENAGERIE OF MERRY MUTANTS, THEY ARE NOT A GANG OF ADOLESCENTS BY RADIOACTIVE INSECTS! THEY ARE *SUPER-BEINGS* WHO HAVE HARNESSED THE SECRETS *STRANGE SCIENCES!* TOGETHER, THEY ARE A FABULOUS FAMILY OF... *INHUMANS!*

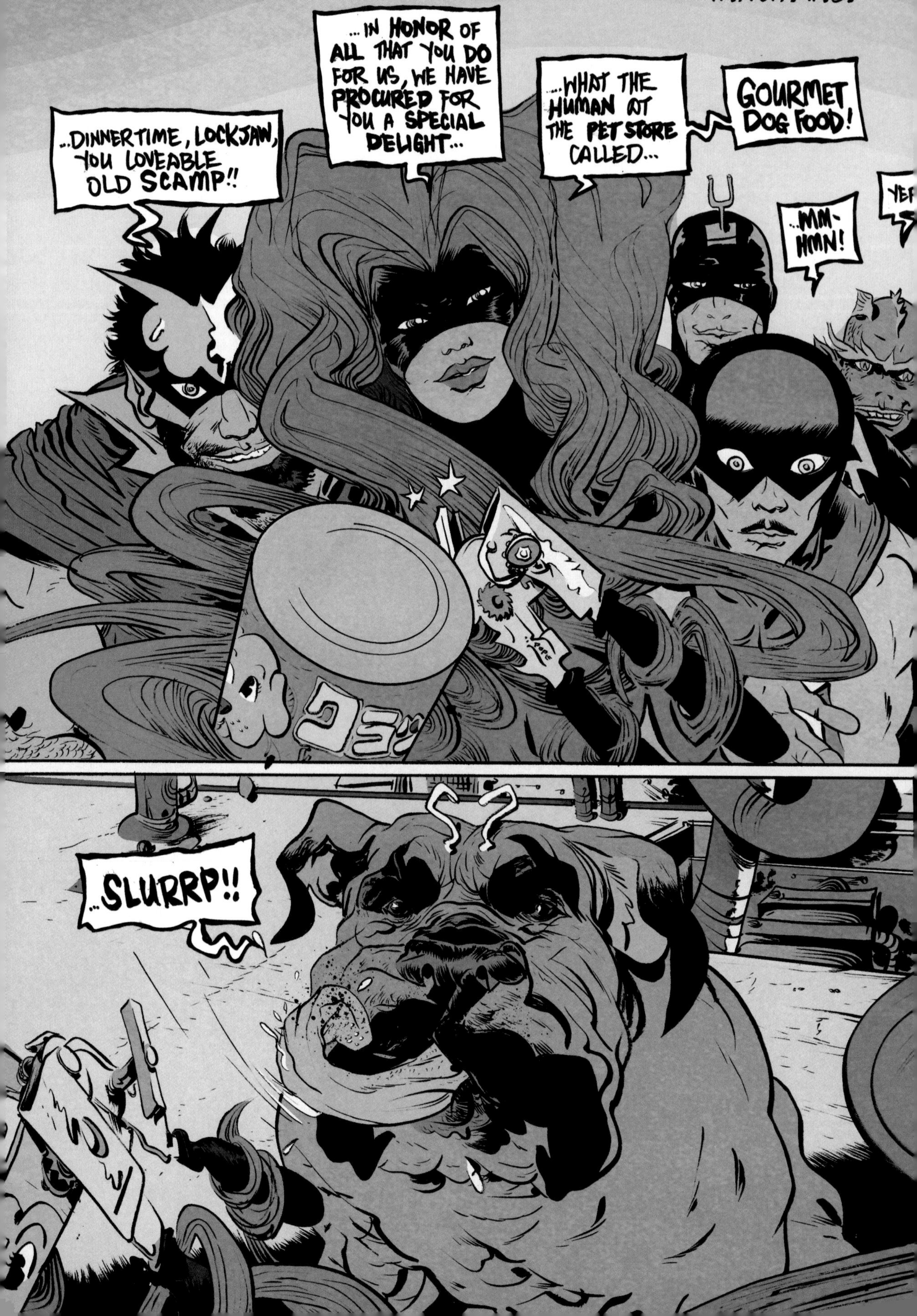

...DINNERTIME, LOCKJAW, YOU LOVEABLE OLD SCAMP!!
...IN HONOR OF ALL THAT YOU DO FOR US, WE HAVE PROCURED FOR YOU A SPECIAL DELIGHT...
...WHAT THE HUMAN AT THE PET STORE CALLED...
GOURMET DOG FOOD!
...MM-HMN!
...SLURRP!!

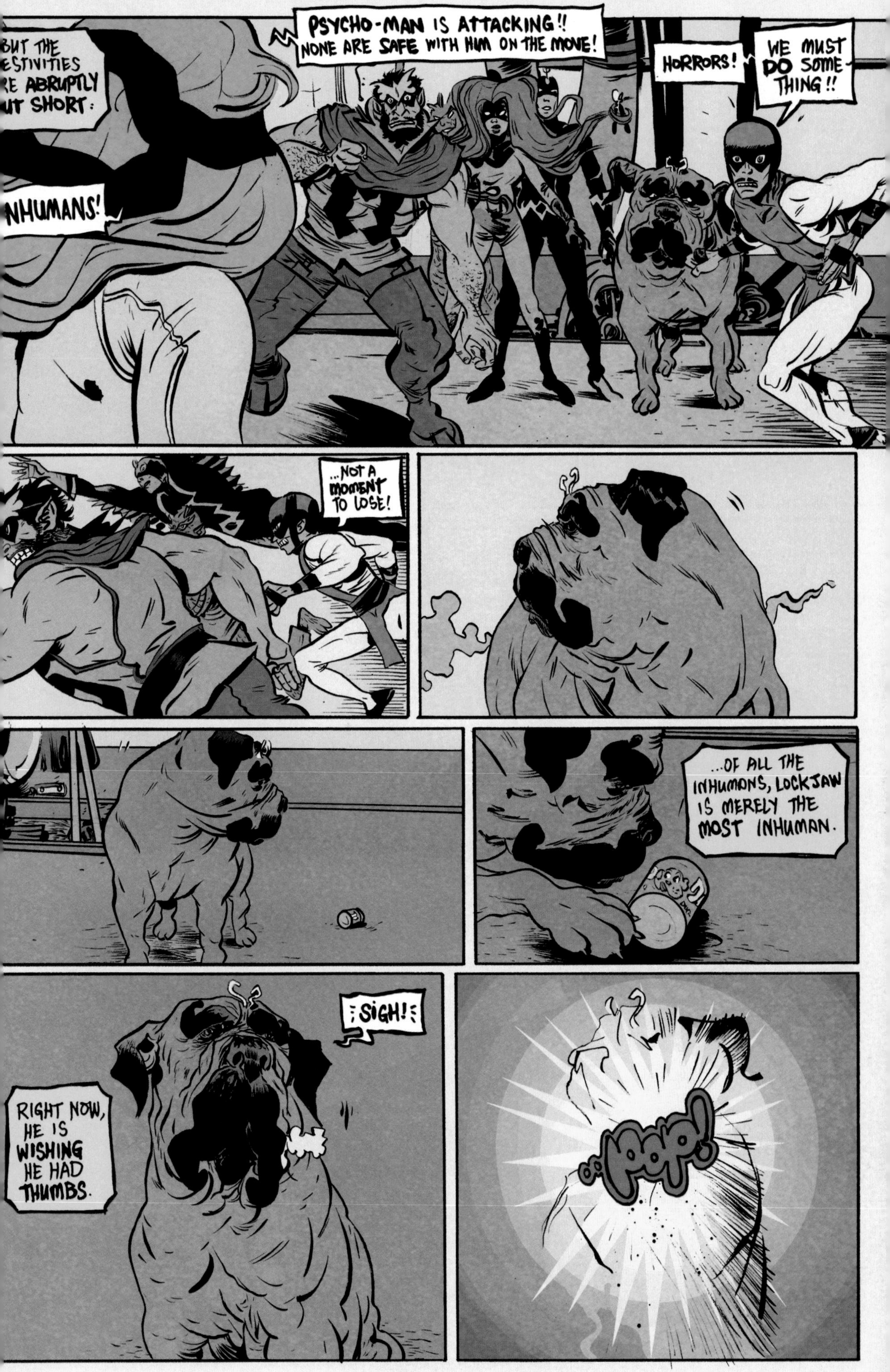
BUT THE ESTIVITIES RE ABRUPTLY UT SHORT:
PSYCHO-MAN IS ATTACKING!! NONE ARE SAFE WITH HIM ON THE MOVE!
HORRORS!
WE MUST DO SOMETHING!!
INHUMANS!
...NOT A MOMENT TO LOSE!
...OF ALL THE INHUMANS, LOCKJAW IS MERELY THE MOST INHUMAN.
SIGH!
RIGHT NOW, HE IS WISHING HE HAD THUMBS.
POP!

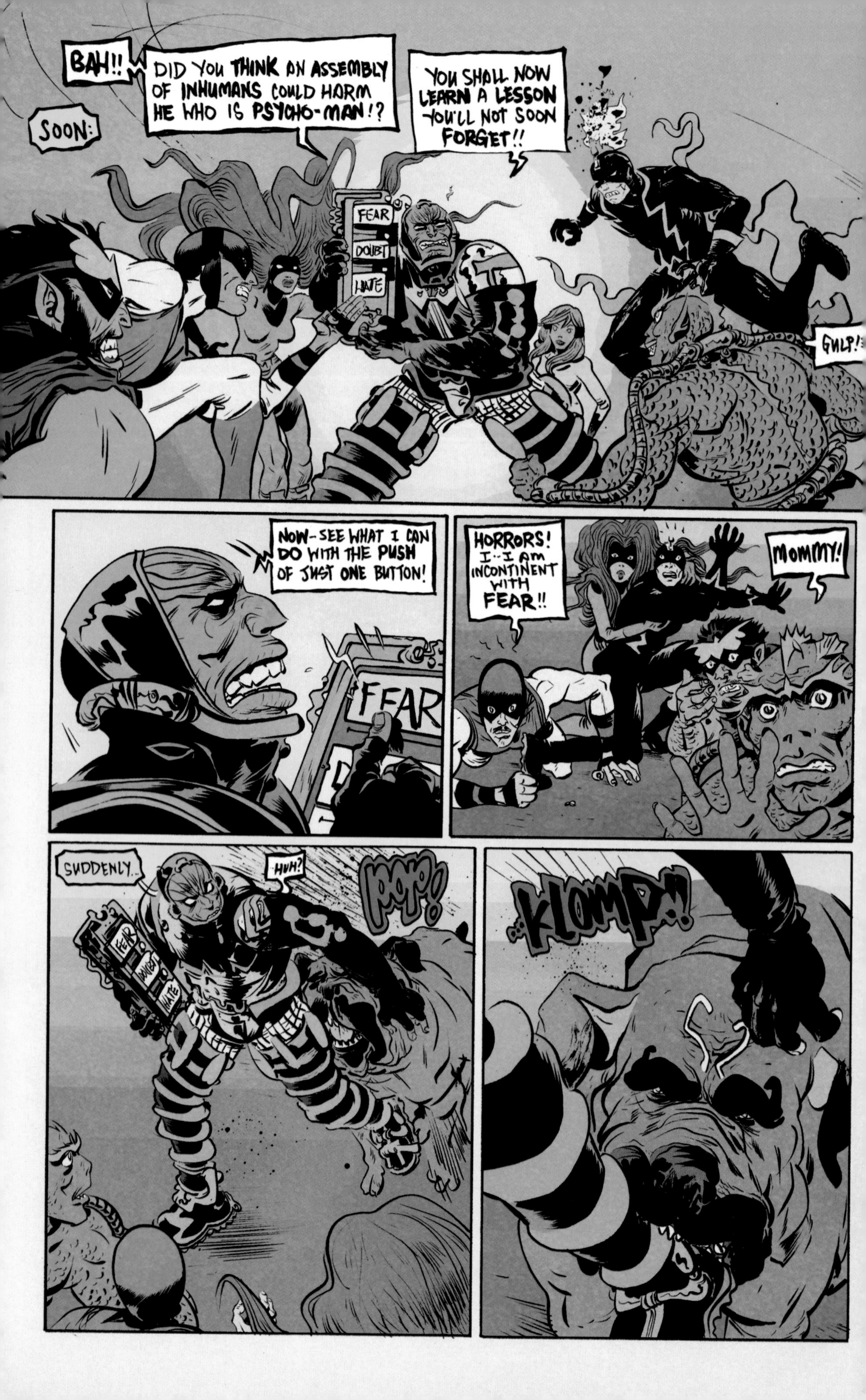
SOON:
BAH!!
DID YOU THINK AN ASSEMBLY OF INHUMANS COULD HARM HE WHO IS PSYCHO-MAN!?
YOU SHALL NOW LEARN A LESSON YOU'LL NOT SOON FORGET!!
FEAR
DOUBT
HATE
GULP!
NOW-SEE WHAT I CAN DO WITH THE PUSH OF JUST ONE BUTTON!
FEAR
HORRORS! I--I AM INCONTINENT WITH FEAR!!
MOMMY!
SUDDENLY...
HUH?
POP!
KLOMP!

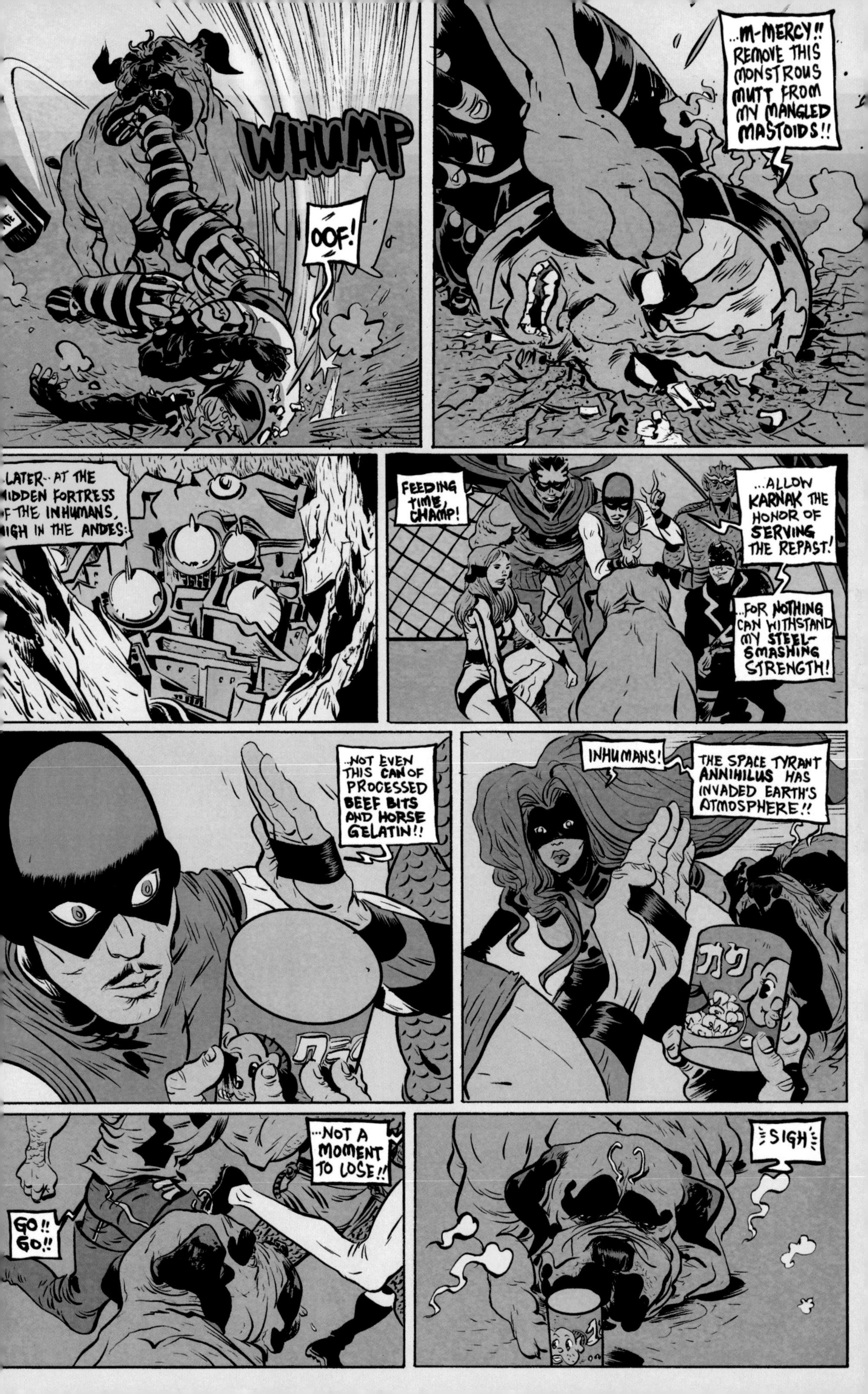
WHUMP
OOF!
...M-MERCY!! REMOVE THIS MONSTROUS MUTT FROM MY MANGLED MASTOIDS!!
LATER... AT THE HIDDEN FORTRESS OF THE INHUMANS, HIGH IN THE ANDES:
FEEDING TIME, CHAMP!
...ALLOW KARNAK THE HONOR OF SERVING THE REPAST!
...FOR NOTHING CAN WITHSTAND MY STEEL-SMASHING STRENGTH!
...NOT EVEN THIS CAN OF PROCESSED BEEF BITS AND HORSE GELATIN!!
INHUMANS!
THE SPACE TYRANT ANNIHILUS HAS INVADED EARTH'S ATMOSPHERE!!
...NOT A MOMENT TO LOSE!!
GO!! GO!!
SIGH

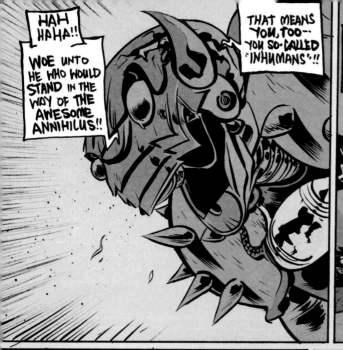

HAH HAHA!! WOE UNTO HE WHO WOULD STAND IN THE WAY OF THE AWESOME ANNIHILUS!!

THAT MEANS YOU, TOO-- YOU SO-CALLED 'INHUMANS'!!

YOU ARE NO MATCH FOR MY FLYING GUN-SHIP! ITS SPEED AND POWER ARE UNMATCHED IN ALL THE UNIVERSE--!!

YOU HAVE M[Y] PERMISSION TO GROVEL

BY THE GRUFF OF MY CHINNY-CHIN-CHIN!! HE'S RIGHT HERE ALL BUT DOOMED!!

COULD THIS BE THE END?!

...NO ONE CAN SAVE YOU NOW!

POP!!

--UT!!

GRR RH!!

::GAAHH!!: AMBUSH FROM ABOVE!! A-A GIANT DOG!?

ANNIHILUS SURRENDERS! ANNIHILUS CRIES UNCLE!

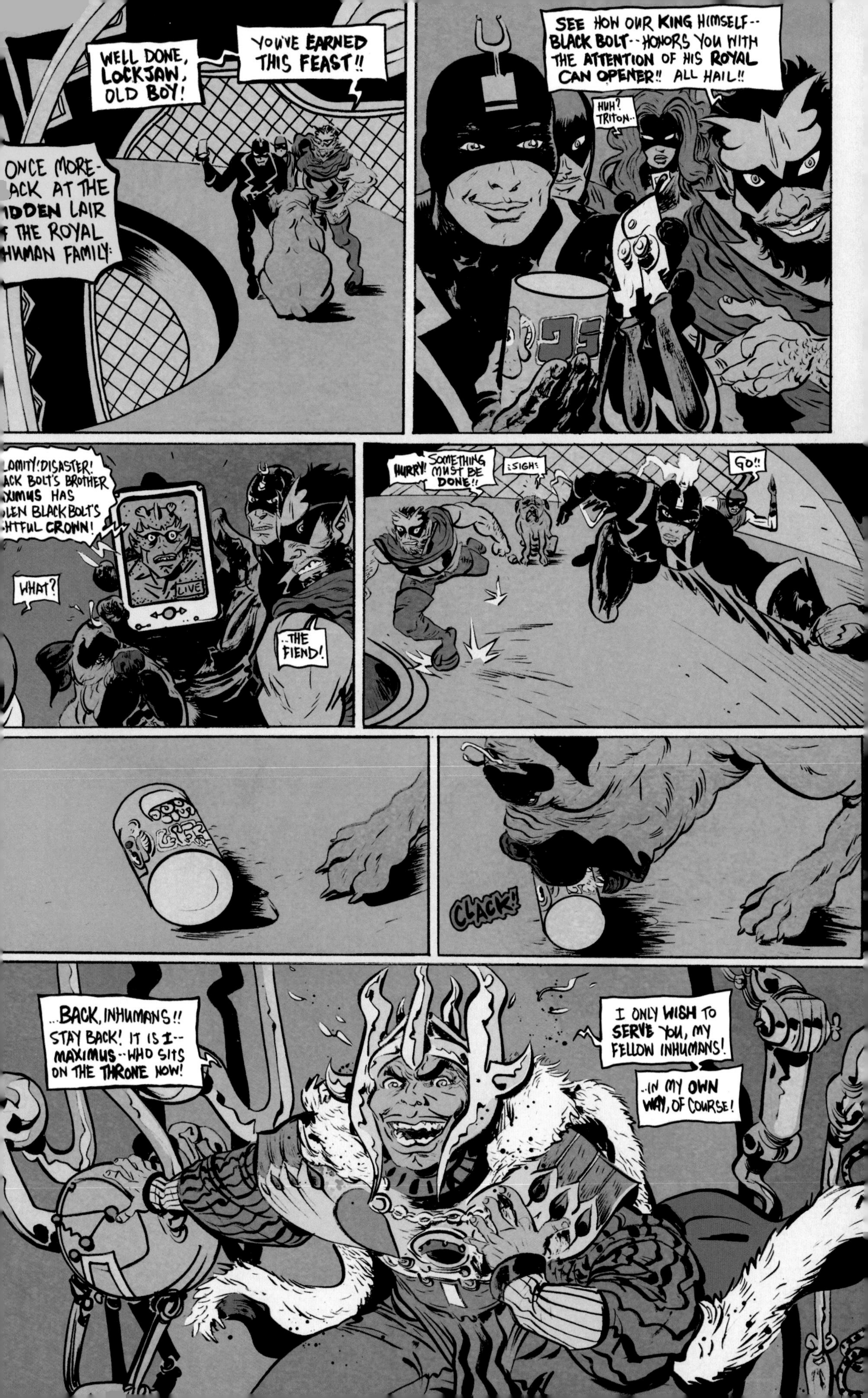

ONCE MORE- ACK AT THE IDDEN LAIR F THE ROYAL HUMAN FAMILY:
WELL DONE, LOCKJAW, OLD BOY!
YOU'VE EARNED THIS FEAST!!
SEE HOW OUR KING HIMSELF-- BLACK BOLT-- HONORS YOU WITH THE ATTENTION OF HIS ROYAL CAN OPENER!! ALL HAIL!!
HUH? TRITON..
LOMITY! DISASTER! ACK BOLT'S BROTHER XIMUS HAS LEN BLACK BOLT'S HTFUL CROWN!
LIVE
WHAT?
..THE FIEND!
HURRY!
SOMETHING MUST BE DONE!!
SIGH
GO!!
CLACK!
...BACK, INHUMANS!! STAY BACK! IT IS I-- MAXIMUS-- WHO SITS ON THE THRONE NOW!
I ONLY WISH TO SERVE YOU, MY FELLOW INHUMANS!
..IN MY OWN WAY, OF COURSE!

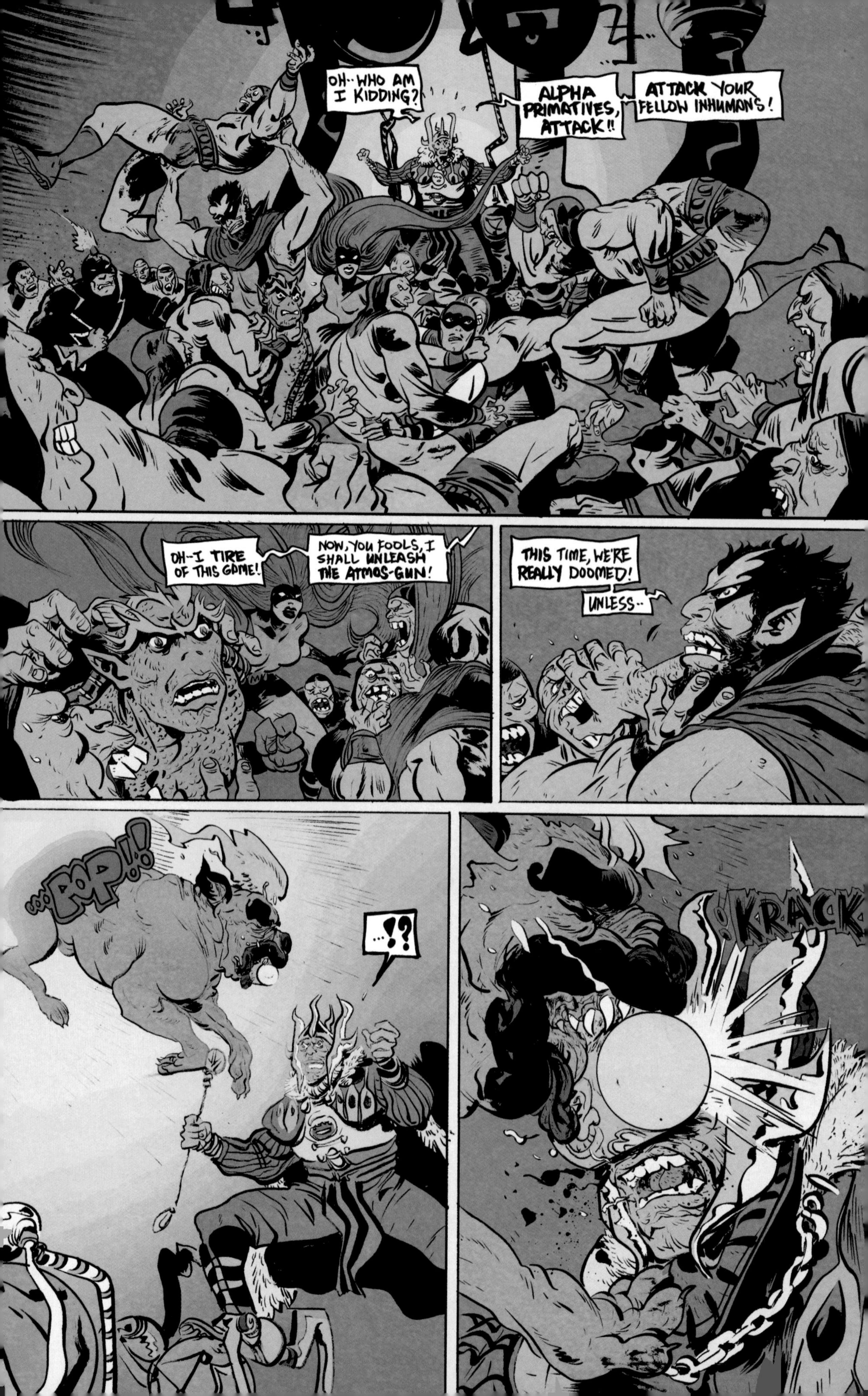
OH-- WHO AM I KIDDING?
ALPHA PRIMATIVES, ATTACK!!
ATTACK YOUR FELLOW INHUMANS!
OH-- I TIRE OF THIS GAME!
NOW, YOU FOOLS, I SHALL UNLEASH THE ATMOS-GUN!
THIS TIME, WE'RE REALLY DOOMED!
UNLESS--
...POP!!!
...!?
KRACK

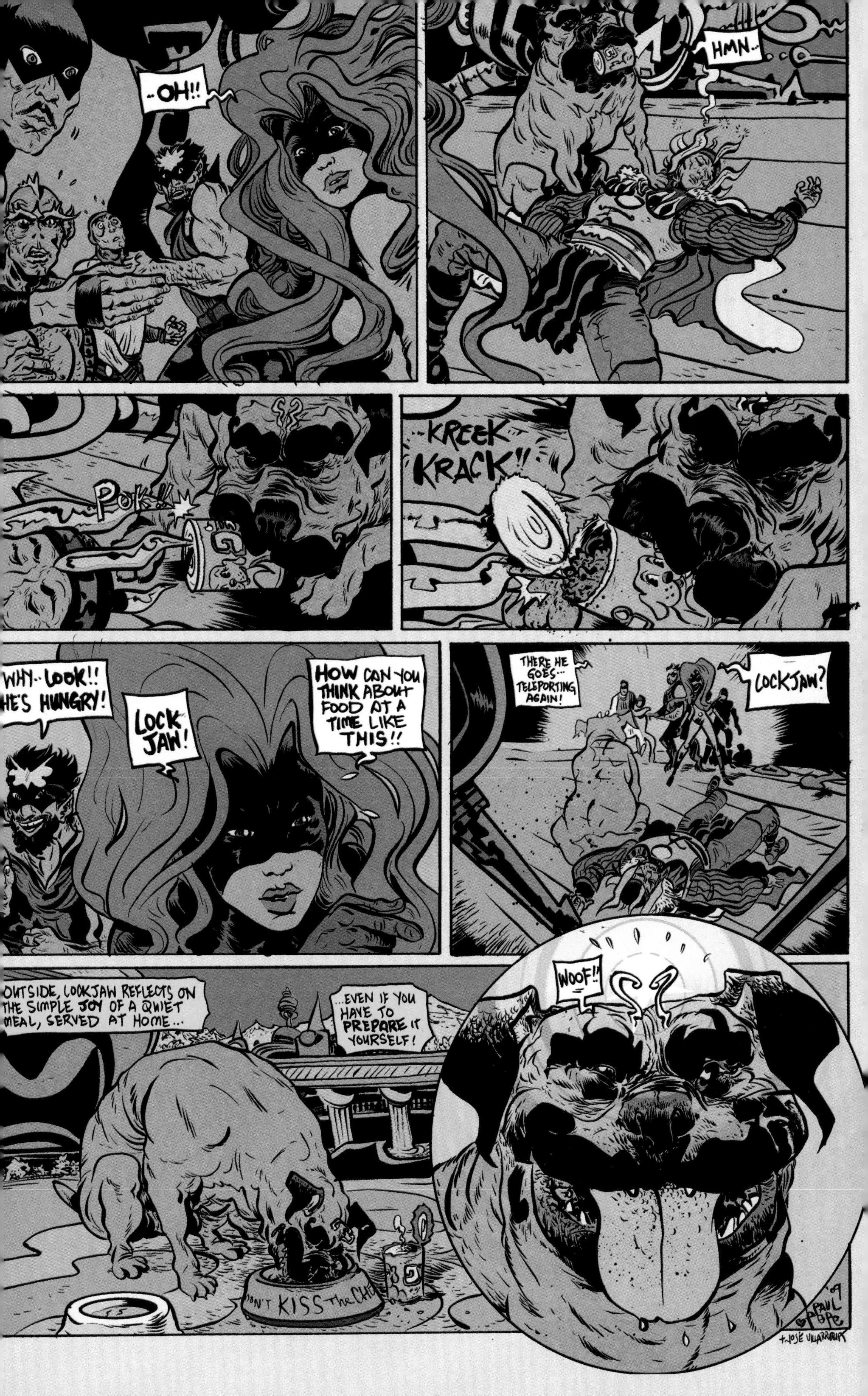
..OH!!
HMN..
POK!!
..KREEK
KRACK!!
WHY.. LOOK!! HE'S HUNGRY!
LOCKJAW!
HOW CAN YOU THINK ABOUT FOOD AT A TIME LIKE THIS!!
THERE HE GOES... TELEPORTING AGAIN!
LOCKJAW?
OUTSIDE, LOCKJAW REFLECTS ON THE SIMPLE JOY OF A QUIET MEAL, SERVED AT HOME...
...EVEN IF YOU HAVE TO PREPARE IT YOURSELF!
WOOF!!
DON'T KISS the CH
'09 PAUL POPE
+ JOSÉ VILLARRUBIA

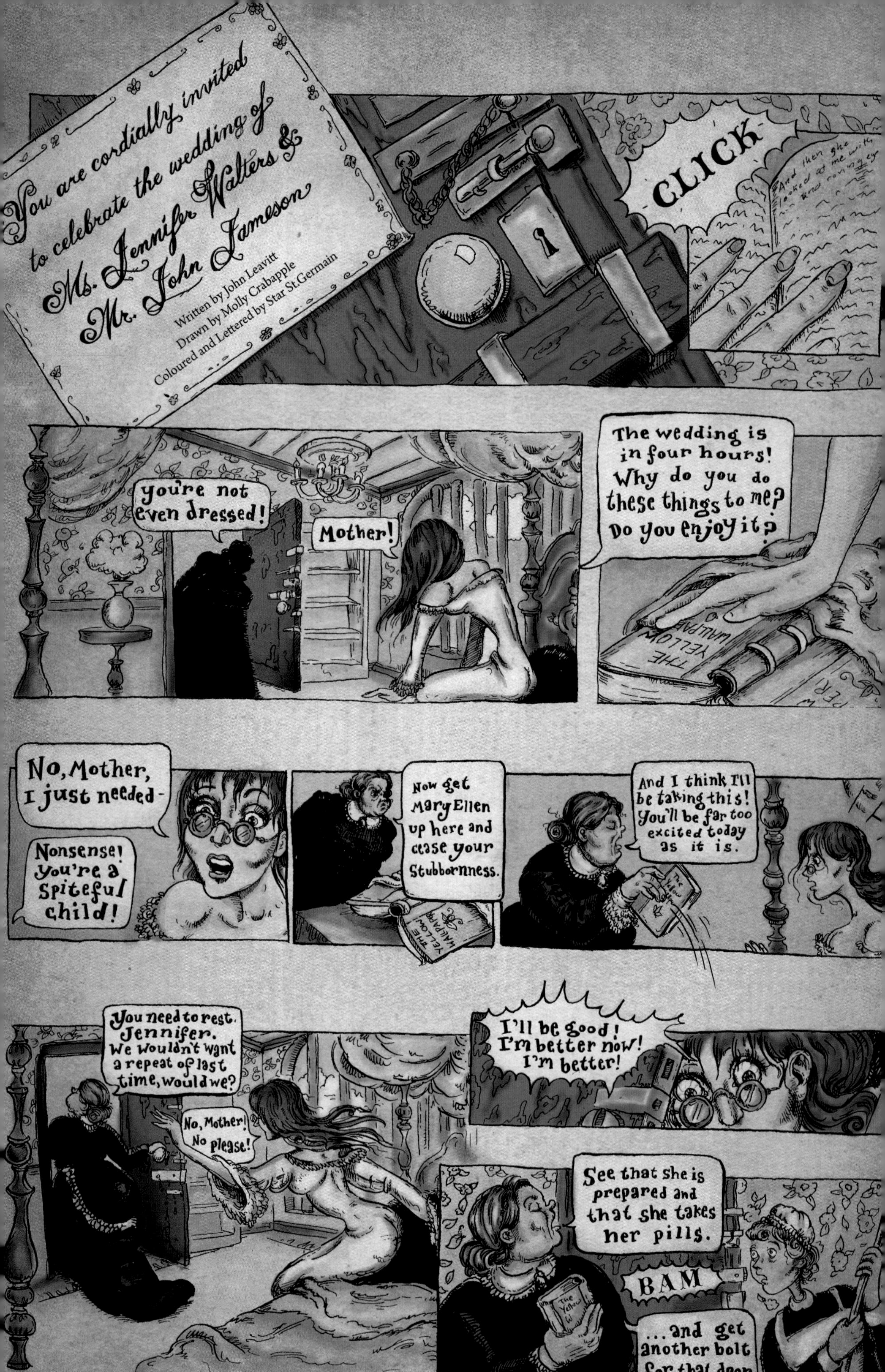
You are cordially invited to celebrate the wedding of
Ms. Jennifer Walters &
Mr. John Jameson
Written by John Leavitt
Drawn by Molly Crabapple
Coloured and Lettered by Star St.Germain
CLICK
You're not even dressed!
Mother!
The wedding is in four hours! Why do you do these things to me? Do you enjoy it?
THE YELLOW WALLPA
No, Mother, I just needed-
Nonsense! You're a spiteful child!
Now get MaryEllen up here and cease your stubbornness.
THE YELLOW WALLPAPER
And I think I'll be taking this! You'll be far too excited today as it is.
You need to rest, Jennifer. We wouldn't want a repeat of last time, would we?
No, Mother! No please!
I'll be good! I'm better now! I'm better!
See that she is prepared and that she takes her pills.
BAM
...and get another bolt for that door.

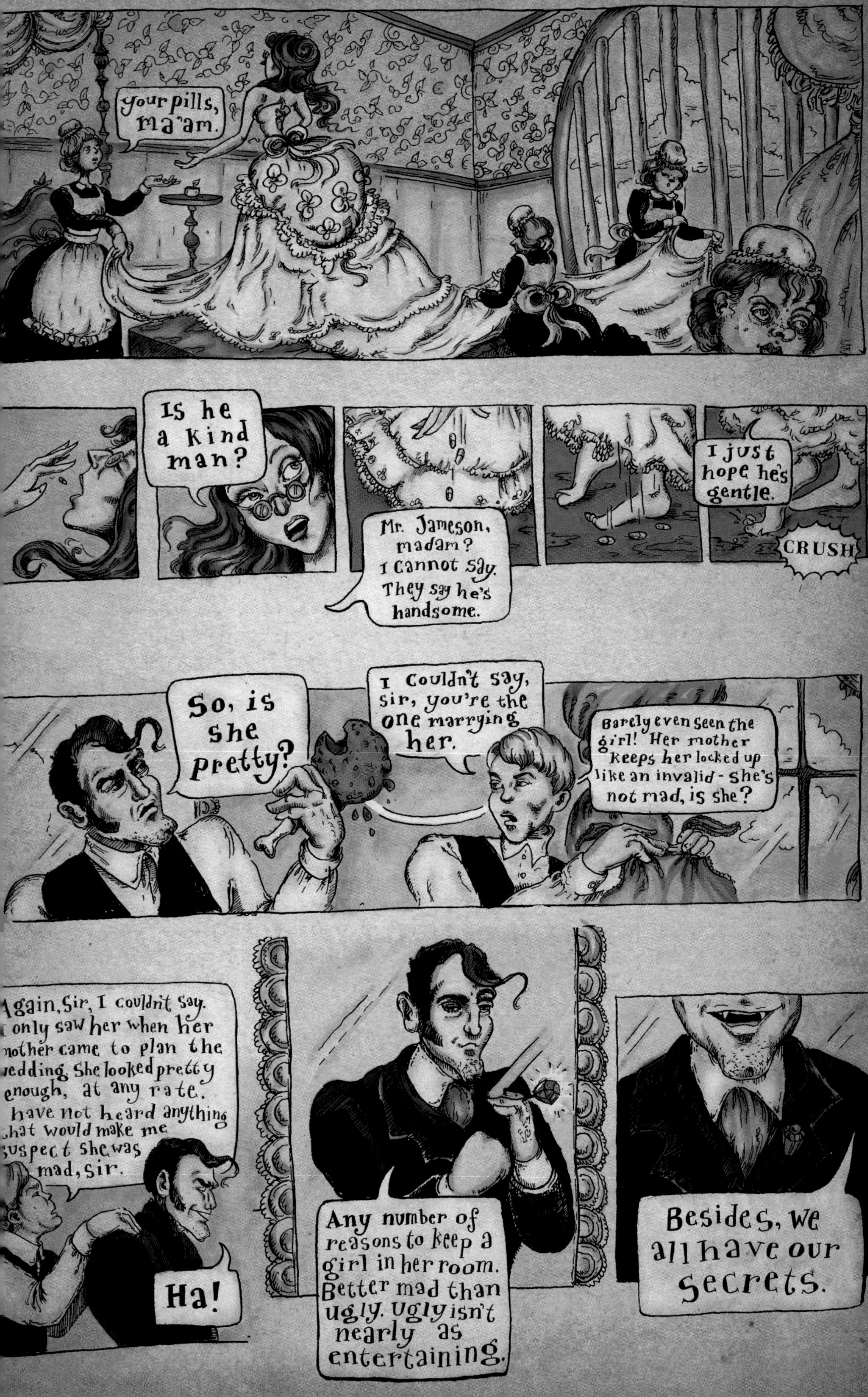
Your pills, ma'am.
Is he a kind man?
Mr. Jameson, madam? I cannot say. They say he's handsome.
I just hope he's gentle.
CRUSH
So, is she pretty?
I couldn't say, sir, you're the one marrying her.
Barely even seen the girl! Her mother keeps her locked up like an invalid - she's not mad, is she?
Again, sir, I couldn't say. I only saw her when her mother came to plan the wedding. She looked pretty enough, at any rate. I have not heard anything that would make me suspect she was mad, sir.
Ha!
Any number of reasons to keep a girl in her room. Better mad than ugly. Ugly isn't nearly as entertaining.
Besides, we all have our secrets.

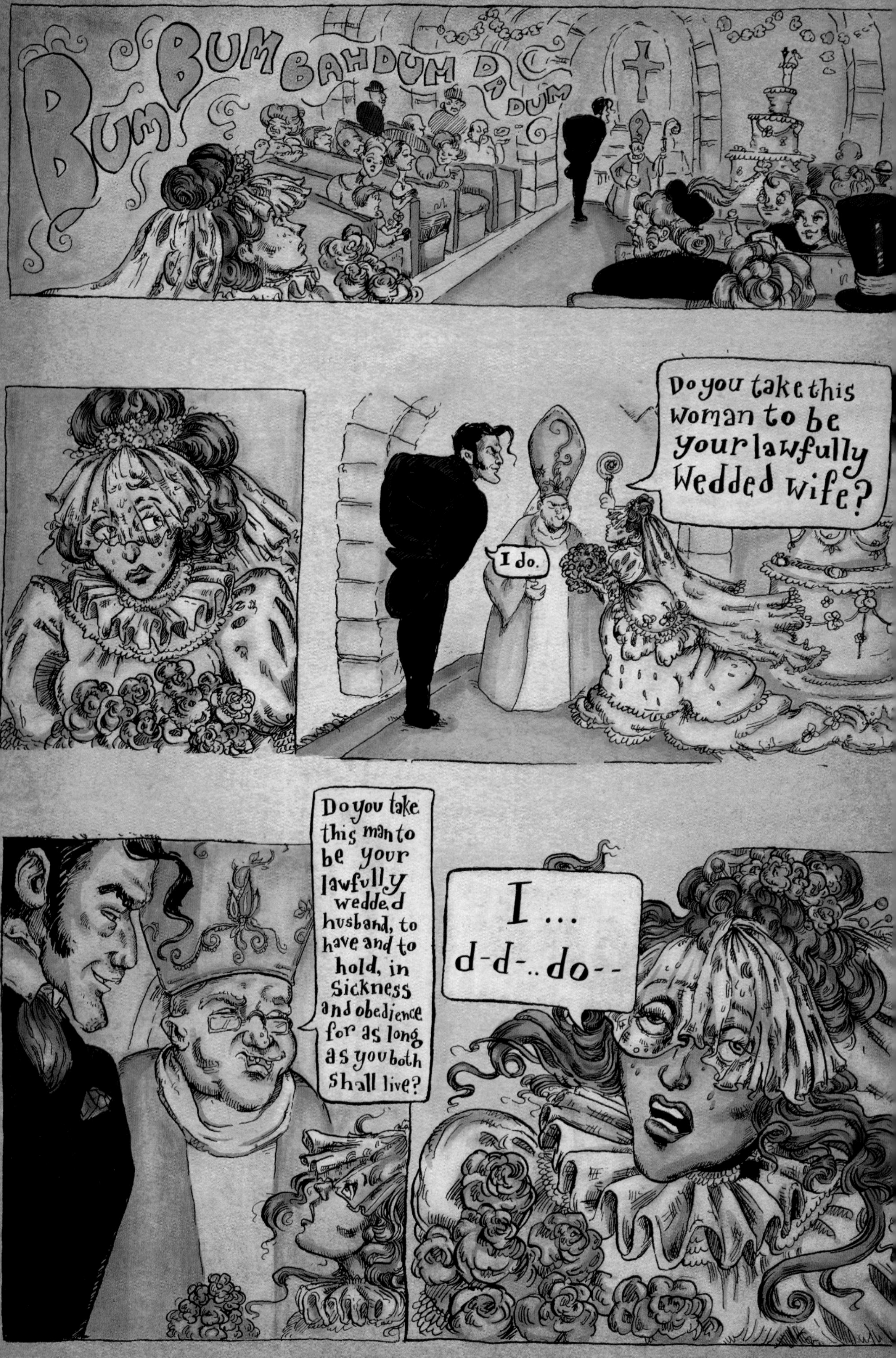
BUM BUM BAHDUM DA DUM
Do you take this woman to be your lawfully wedded wife?
I do.
Do you take this man to be your lawfully wedded husband, to have and to hold, in sickness and obedience for as long as you both shall live?
I... d-d-..do--

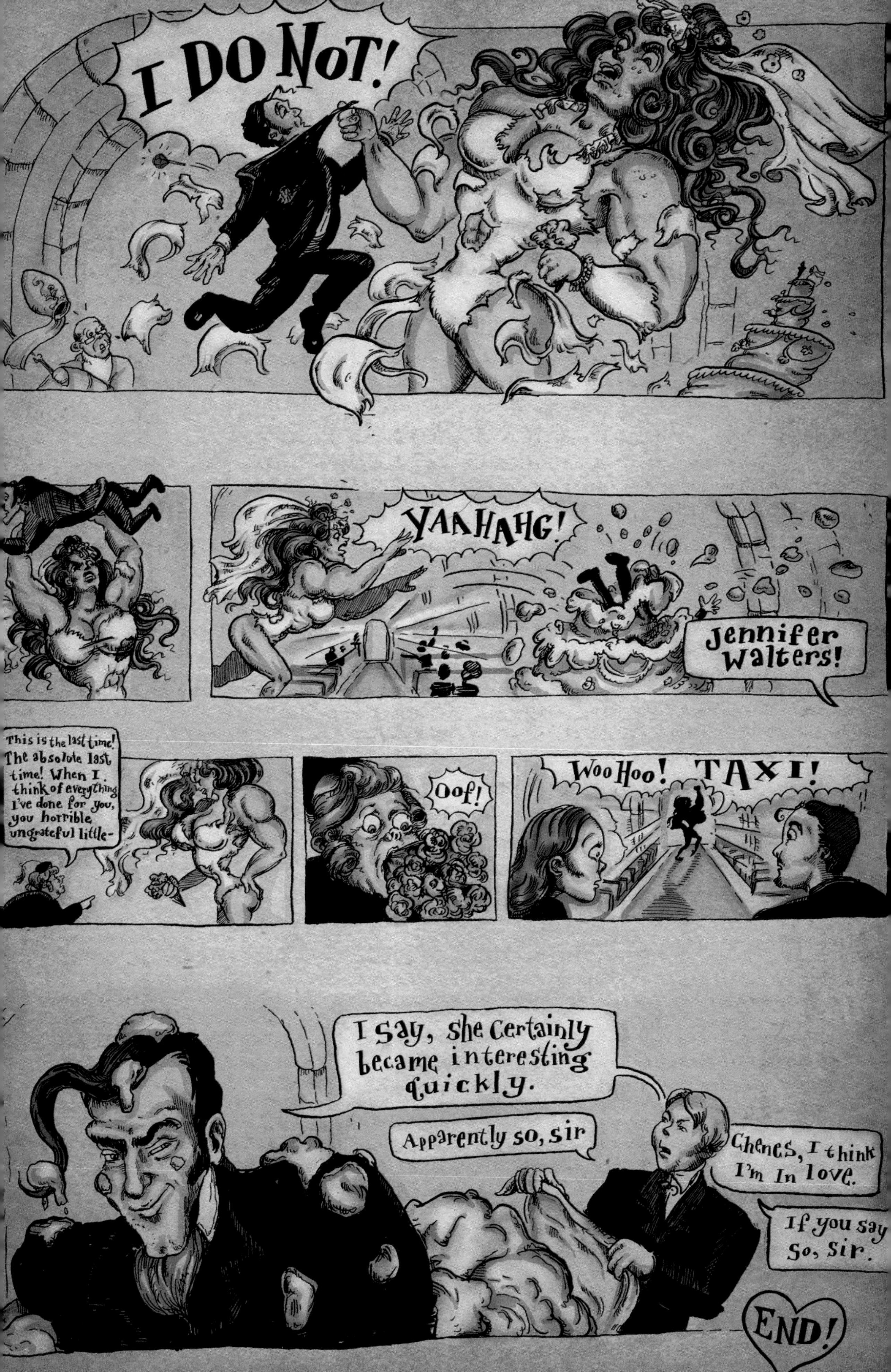
I DO NOT!
YAAHAHG!
Jennifer Walters!
This is the last time! The absolute last time! When I think of everything I've done for you, you horrible ungrateful little-
Oof!
WooHoo! TAXI!
I say, she certainly became interesting quickly.
Apparently so, sir
Chenes, I think I'm in love.
If you say so, sir.
END!

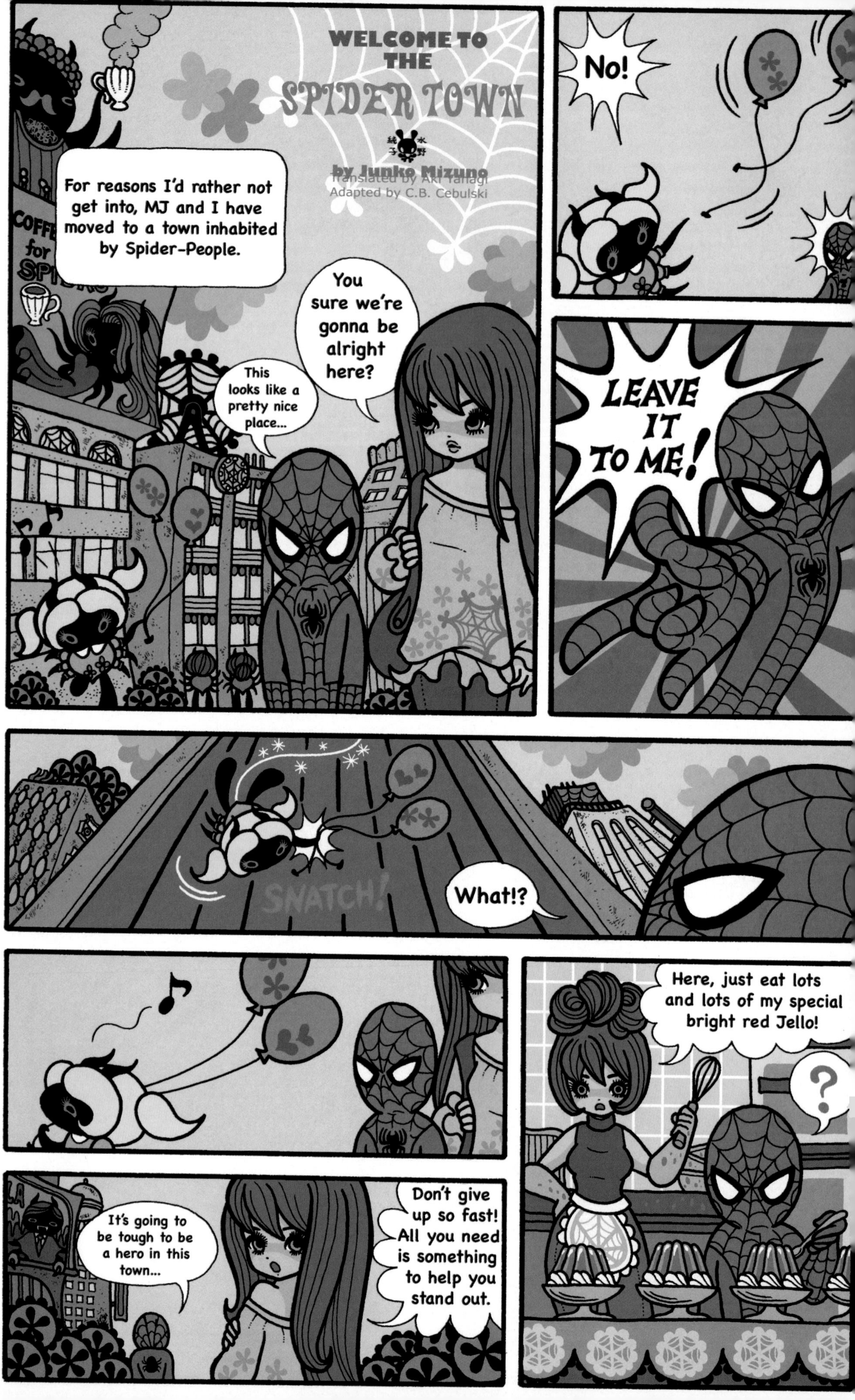
WELCOME TO THE
SPIDER TOWN
by Junko Mizuno
Translated by Aki Yanagi
Adapted by C.B. Cebulski
For reasons I'd rather not get into, MJ and I have moved to a town inhabited by Spider-People.
This looks like a pretty nice place...
You sure we're gonna be alright here?
No!
LEAVE IT TO ME!
SNATCH!
What!?
It's going to be tough to be a hero in this town...
Don't give up so fast! All you need is something to help you stand out.
Here, just eat lots and lots of my special bright red Jello!
?

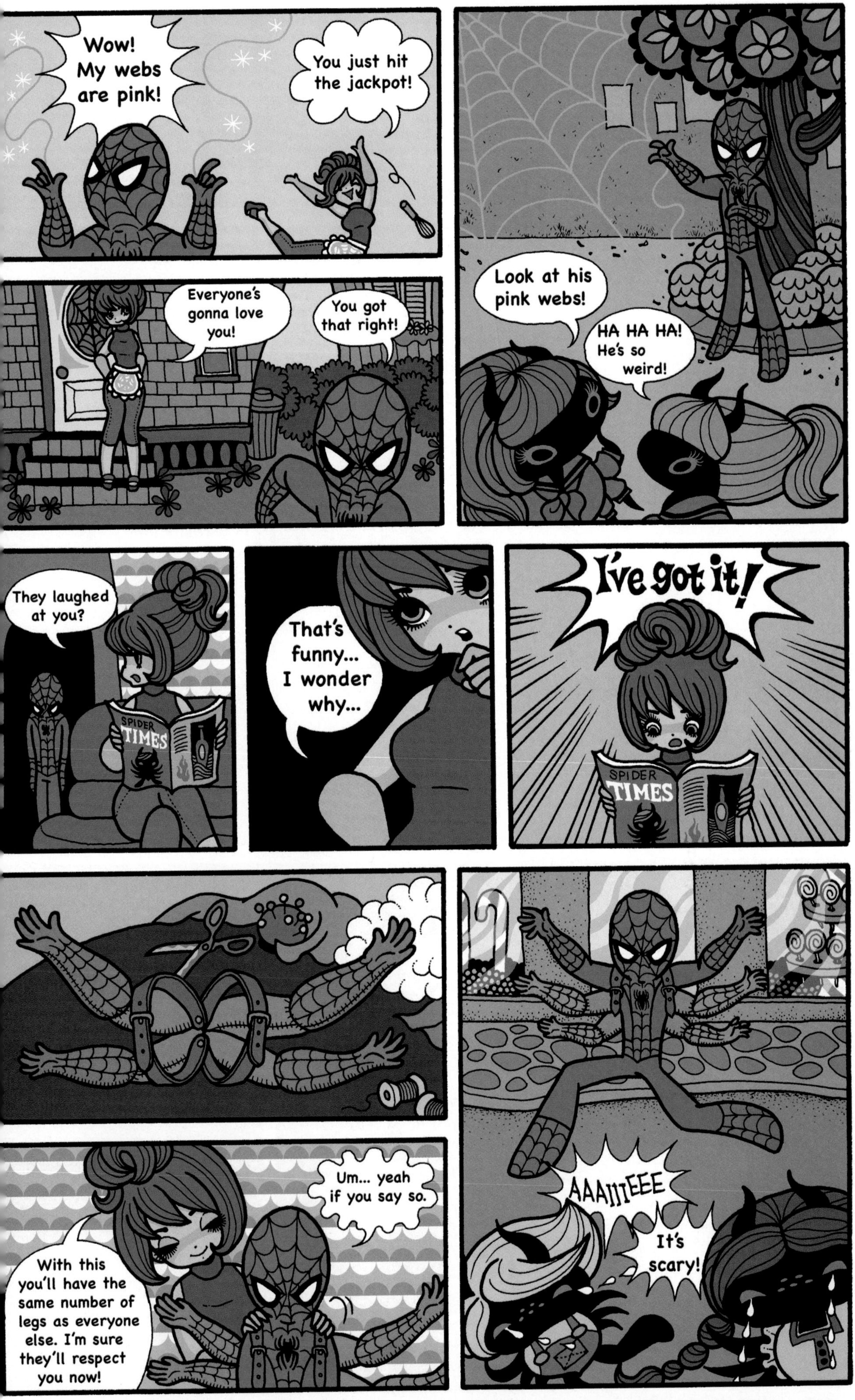
Wow! My webs are pink!
You just hit the jackpot!
Everyone's gonna love you!
You got that right!
Look at his pink webs!
HA HA HA! He's so weird!
They laughed at you?
SPIDER TIMES
That's funny... I wonder why...
I've got it!
SPIDER TIMES
With this you'll have the same number of legs as everyone else. I'm sure they'll respect you now!
Um... yeah if you say so.
AAAIIIEEE
It's scary!

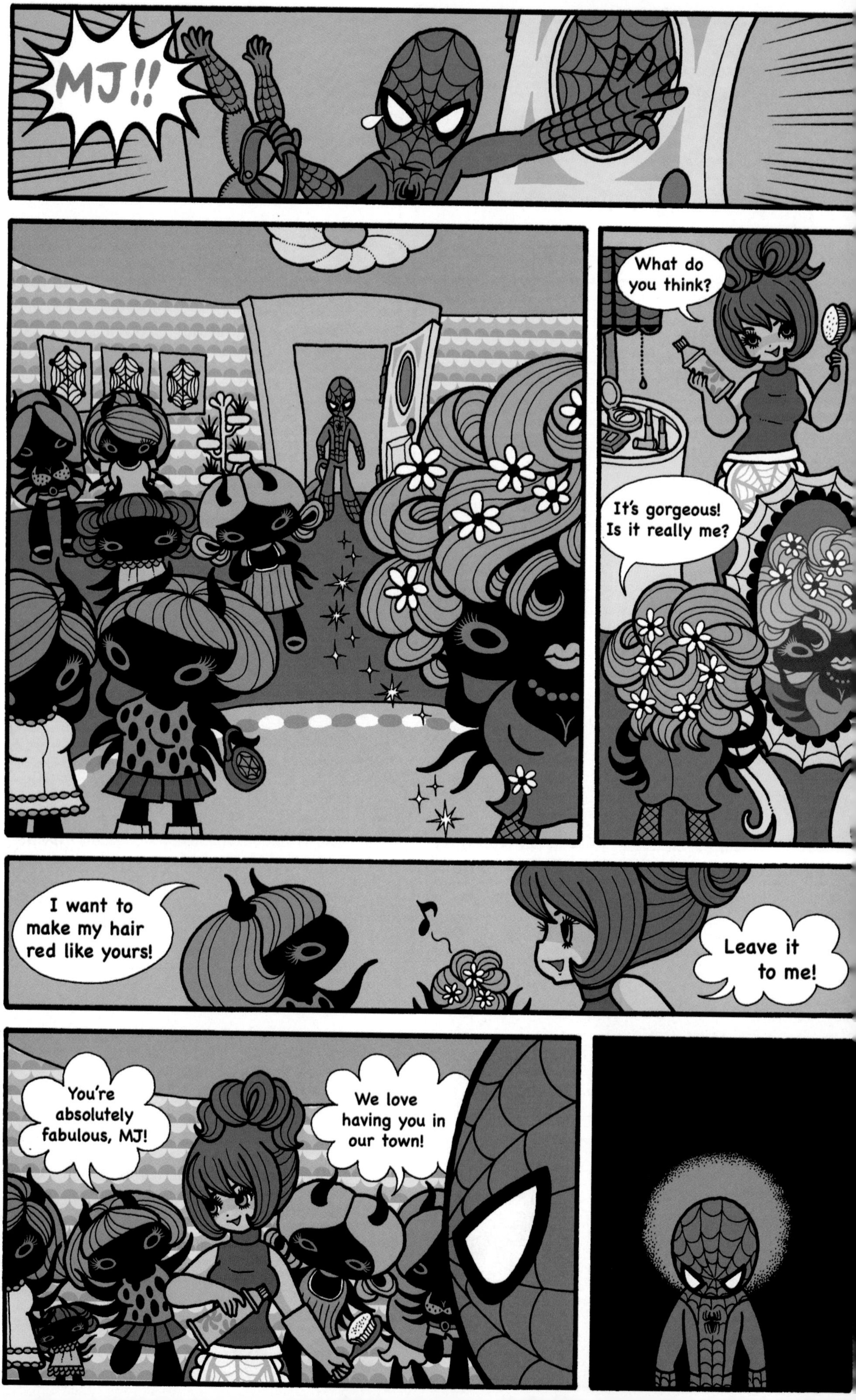
MJ!!
What do you think?
It's gorgeous! Is it really me?
I want to make my hair red like yours!
Leave it to me!
You're absolutely fabulous, MJ!
We love having you in our town!

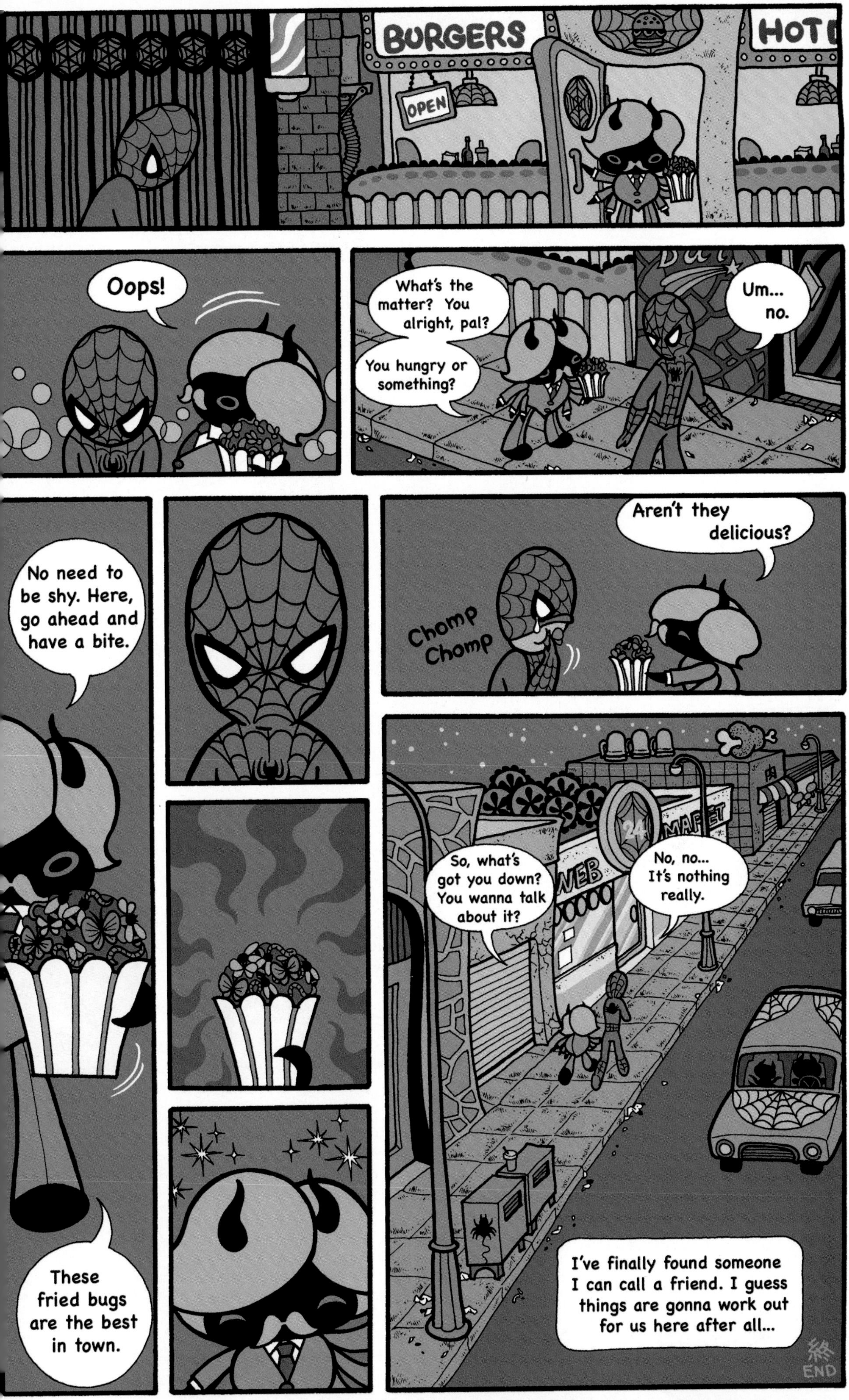
BURGERS
HOT
OPEN
Oops!
What's the matter? You alright, pal?
You hungry or something?
Um... no.
No need to be shy. Here, go ahead and have a bite.
These fried bugs are the best in town.
Aren't they delicious?
Chomp Chomp
24
MARKET
WEB
So, what's got you down? You wanna talk about it?
No, no... It's nothing really.
I've finally found someone I can call a friend. I guess things are gonna work out for us here after all...
終
END

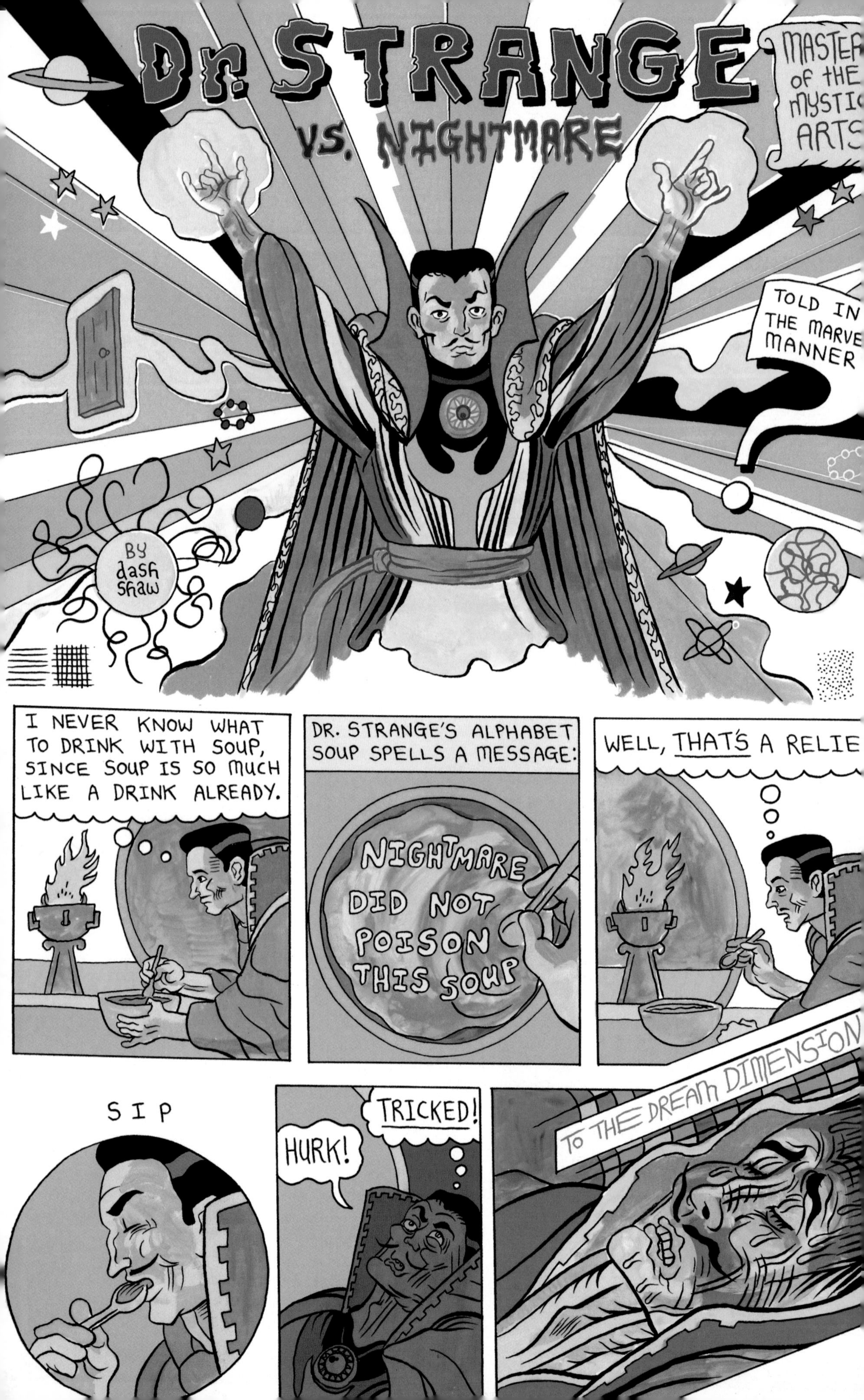
Dr. STRANGE
MASTER of the MYSTIC ARTS
VS. NIGHTMARE
TOLD IN THE MARVE MANNER
BY dash shaw
I NEVER KNOW WHAT TO DRINK WITH SOUP, SINCE SOUP IS SO MUCH LIKE A DRINK ALREADY.
DR. STRANGE'S ALPHABET SOUP SPELLS A MESSAGE:
NIGHTMARE DID NOT POISON THIS SOUP
WELL, THAT'S A RELIE
SIP
HURK!
TRICKED!
TO THE DREAM DIMENSION

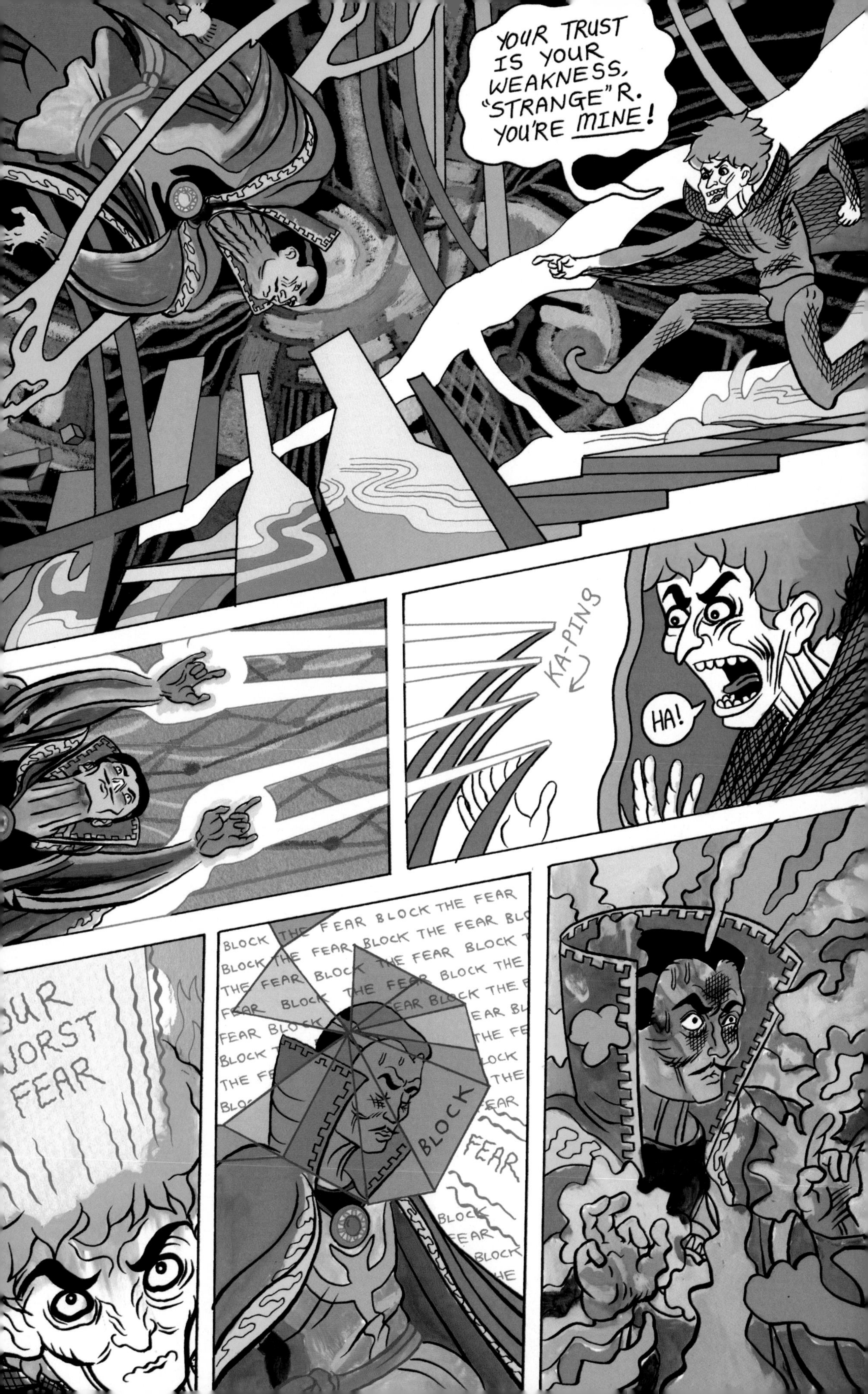
YOUR TRUST IS YOUR WEAKNESS, "STRANGE"R. YOU'RE MINE!
KA-PING
HA!
OUR WORST FEAR
BLOCK THE FEAR BLOCK THE FEAR BLOCK THE FEAR
BLOCK
FEAR
BLOCK
FEAR
BLOCK

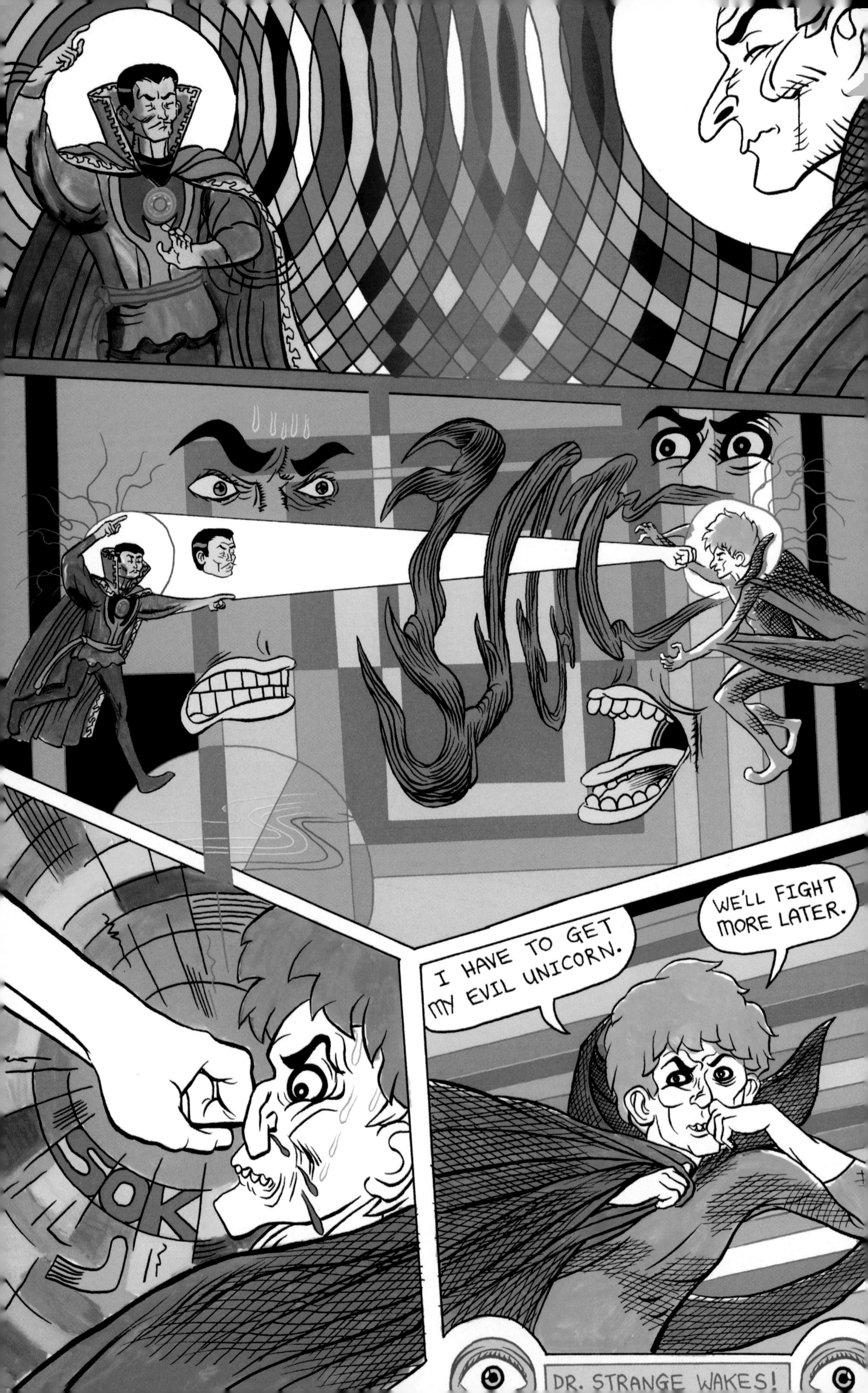
SOK
I HAVE TO GET MY EVIL UNICORN.
WE'LL FIGHT MORE LATER.
DR. STRANGE WAKES!

I MUSTN'T SLEEP, OR ELSE NIGHTMARE MAY STRIKE AGAIN.

THEREFORE: BLACK AS INK.

SMALL TEAR. MUST BE VERY GOOD YAWN.

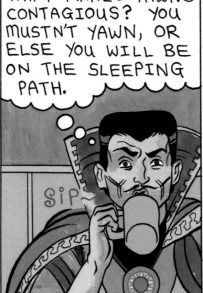

WHAT MAKES YAWNS CONTAGIOUS? YOU MUSTN'T YAWN, OR ELSE YOU WILL BE ON THE SLEEPING PATH.

SIP

HE'S YAWNING LIKE A NEWBORN. BIG, WIDE YAWNS. THE KIND YOU SMACK YOUR LIPS AFTER.

DON'T YAWN! YOU MUSTN'T! NEVER!

BITING LIP.

ah.

ANOTHER BATTLE WON BY DR. STRANGE.

A TEAM OF EXPERIMENTAL HULK CLONES CREATED B THE GOVERNMENT FOR ONE PURPOSE: TO HUNT DOWN AND DESTROY THE HULK!
Dwee!
HULK SQUAD, SMASH!
BY JAMES KOCHALKA
BLARG.
BWAM

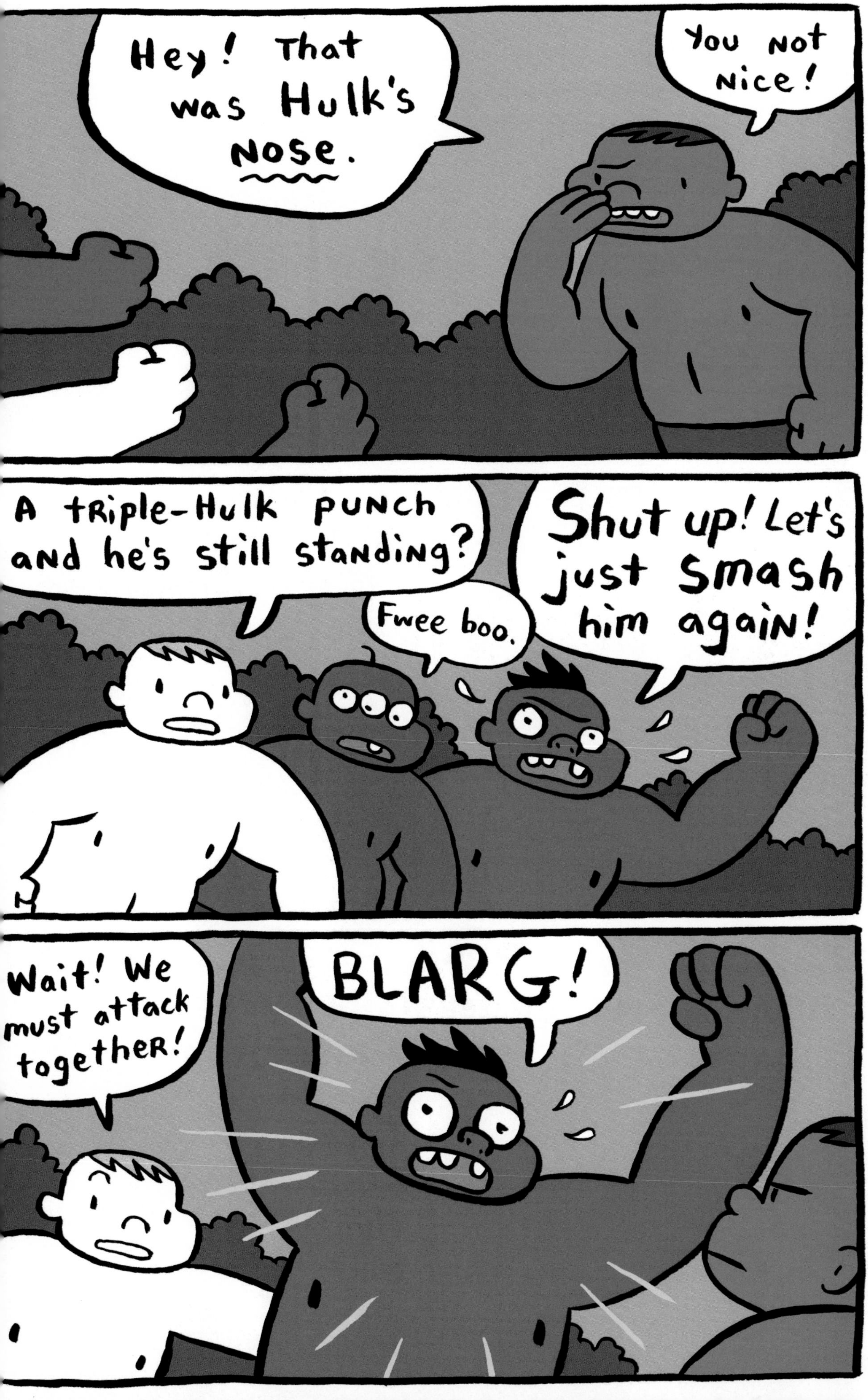

Hey! That was Hulk's NOSE.
You not Nice!
A tRiple-Hulk puNch aNd he's still standiNg?
Shut up! Let's just smash him agaiN!
Fwee boo.
Wait! We must attack togetheR!
BLARG!

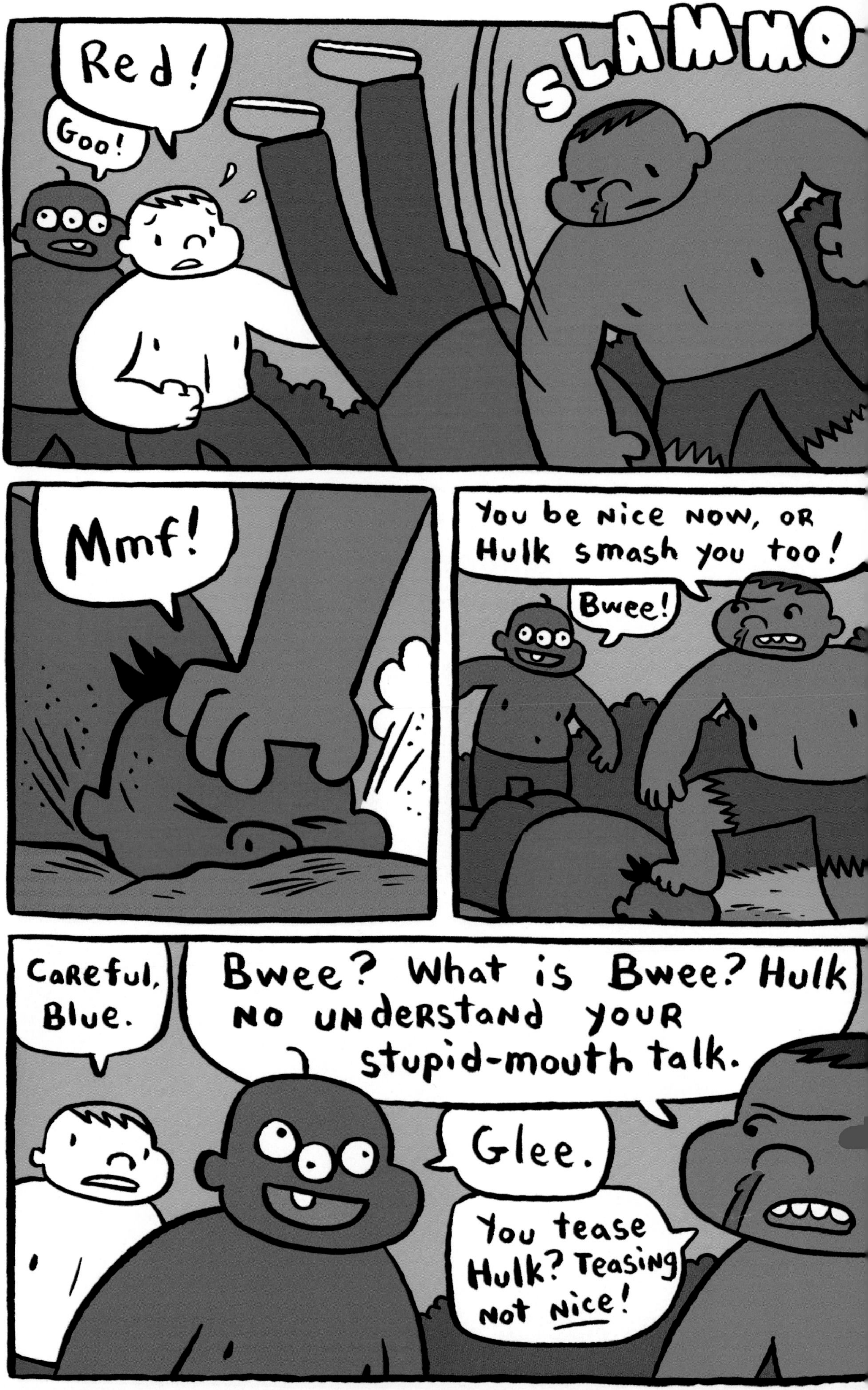
Red!
Goo!
SLAMMO
Mmf!
You be nice now, or Hulk smash you too!
Bwee!
Careful, Blue.
Bwee? What is Bwee? Hulk no understand your stupid-mouth talk.
Glee.
You tease Hulk? Teasing not nice!

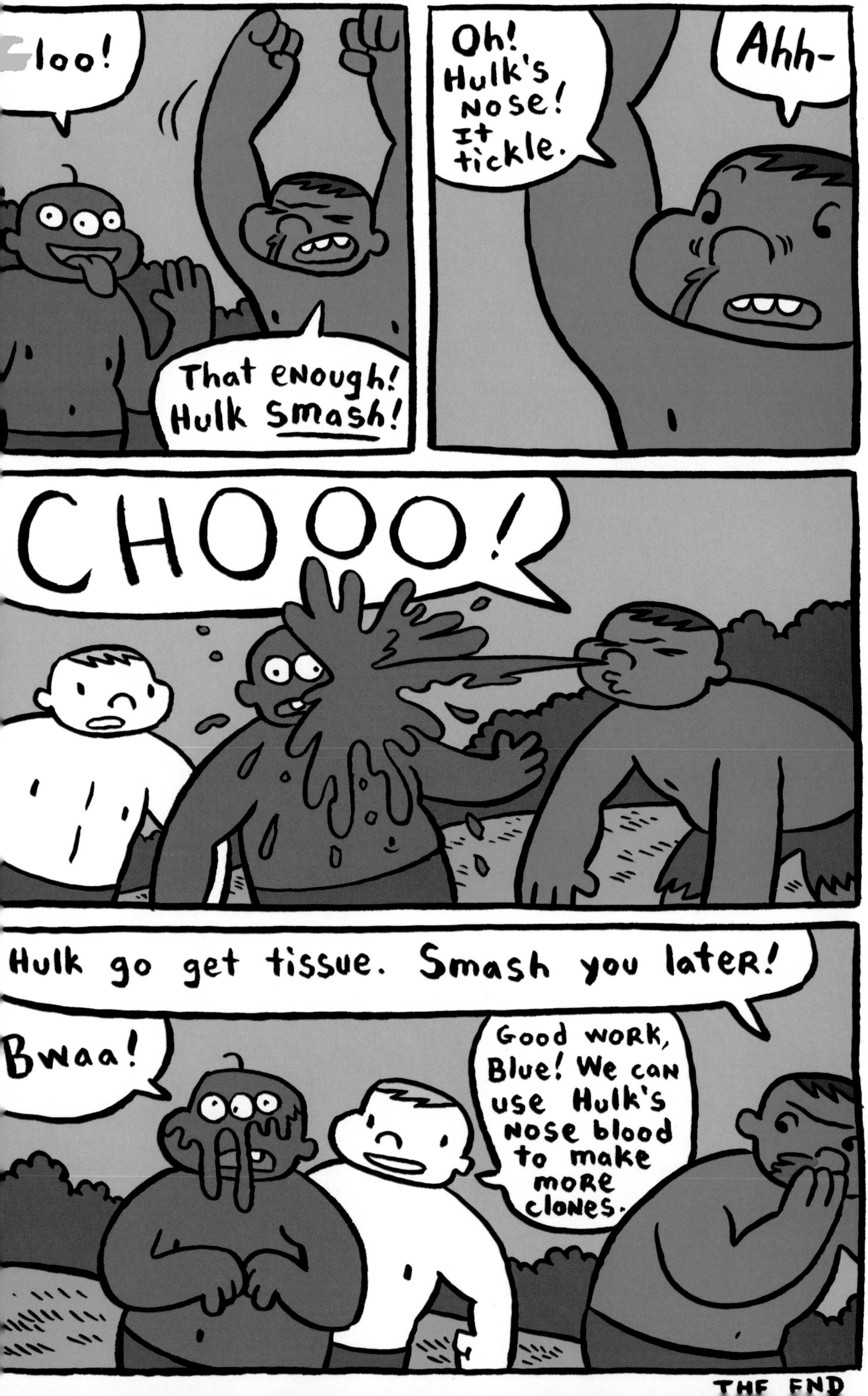

loo!
That eNough! Hulk Smash!
Oh! Hulk's Nose! It tickle.
Ahh-
CHOOO!
Hulk go get tissue. Smash you later!
Bwaa!
Good WORK, Blue! We can use Hulk's Nose blood to make more clones.
THE END

MARVEL'S MOST EMBARRASSING MOMENTS

BY JOHNNY RYAN

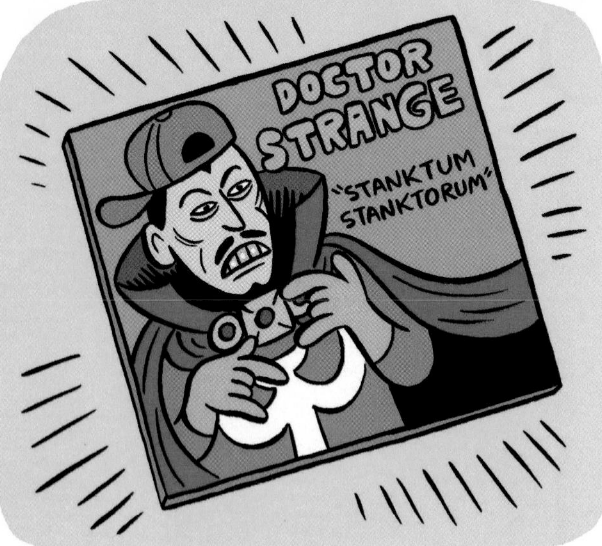
DOCTOR STRANGE
"STANKTUM STANKTORUM"

IN 1985 DR. STRANGE MAKES A RAP ALBUM.

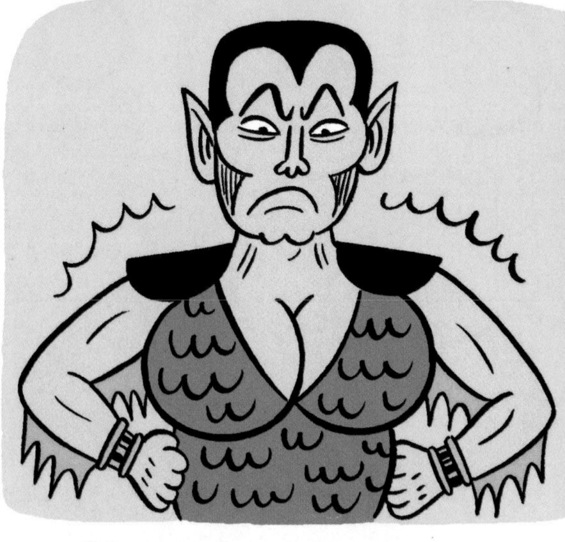

PRINCE NAMOR LOSES A BET AND HAS TO GET BREAST IMPLANTS.

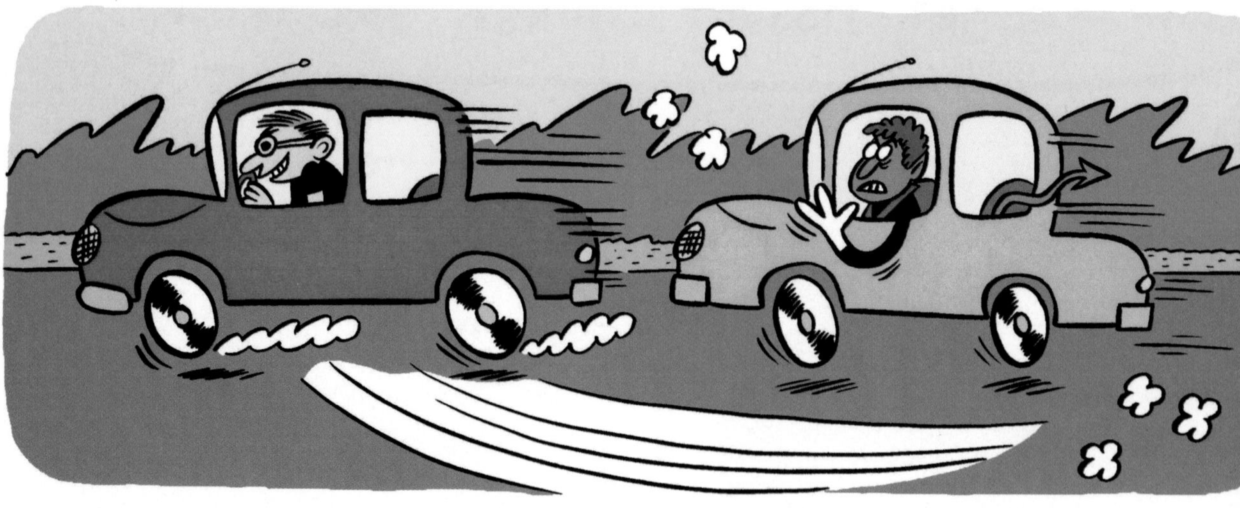

AFTER BEING CUT OFF, NIGHTCRAWLER IS UNABLE TO FLIP THE "BIRD".

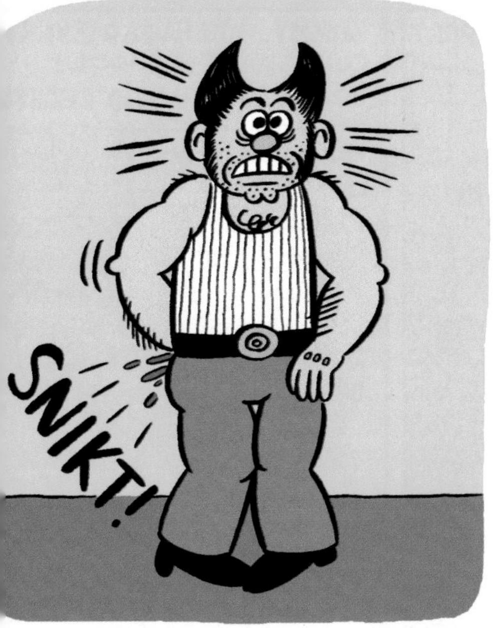
SNIKT!

WOLVERINE HAS AN ACCIDENT WHILE PICKING A WEDGIE.

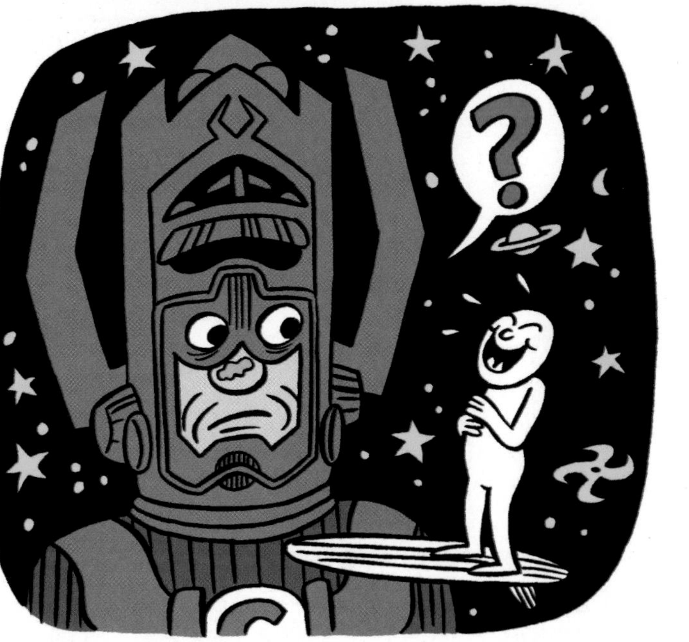
?

THE TIME GALACTUS HAD A BOOGER STUCK ON HIS NOSE.

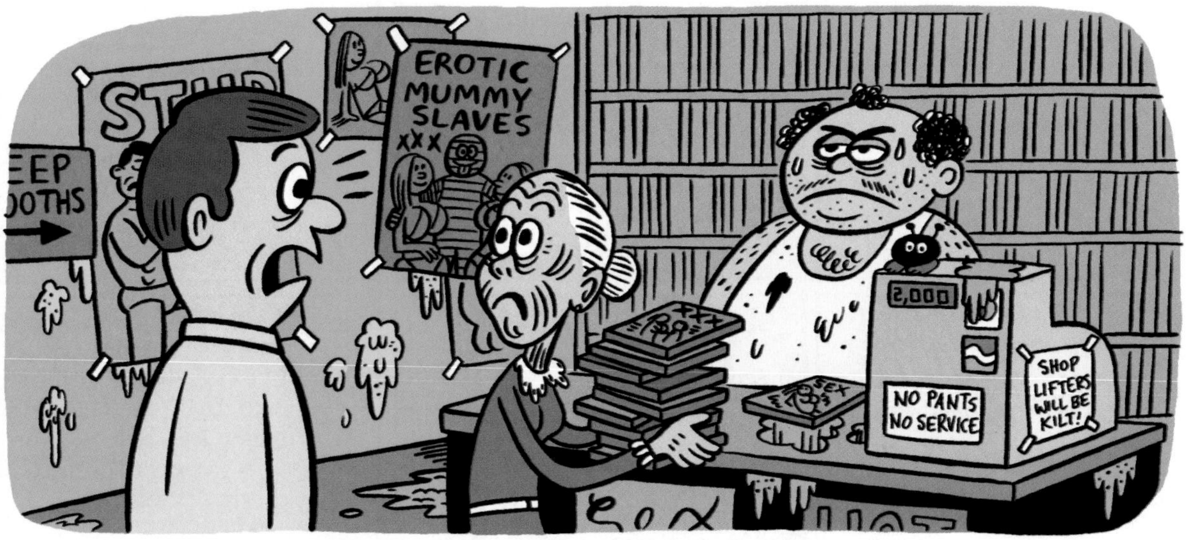
EROTIC MUMMY SLAVES XXX
2,000
NO PANTS NO SERVICE
SHOP LIFTERS WILL BE KILT!
SEX

PETER PARKER CATCHES AUNT MAY BUYING PORNO.

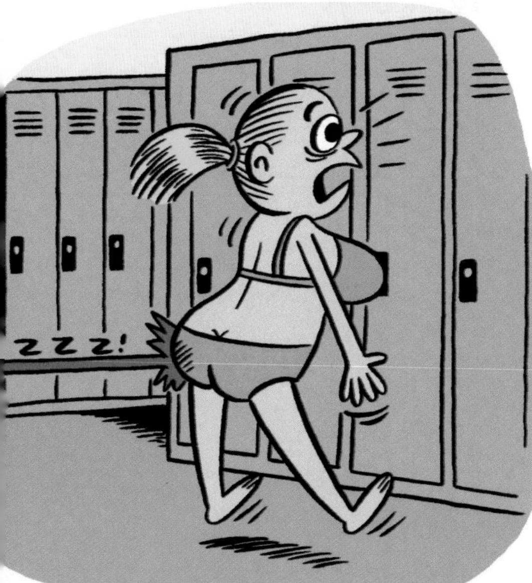
ZZZ!

CYCLOPS IS CAUGHT PEEPING IN THE GIRLS LOCKER ROOM.

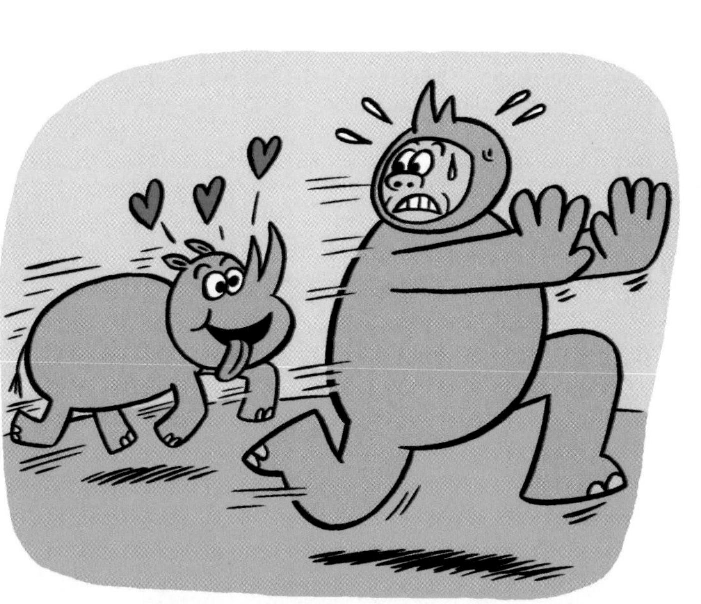

A REAL RHINOCEROS FALLS IN LOVE WITH THE RHINO.

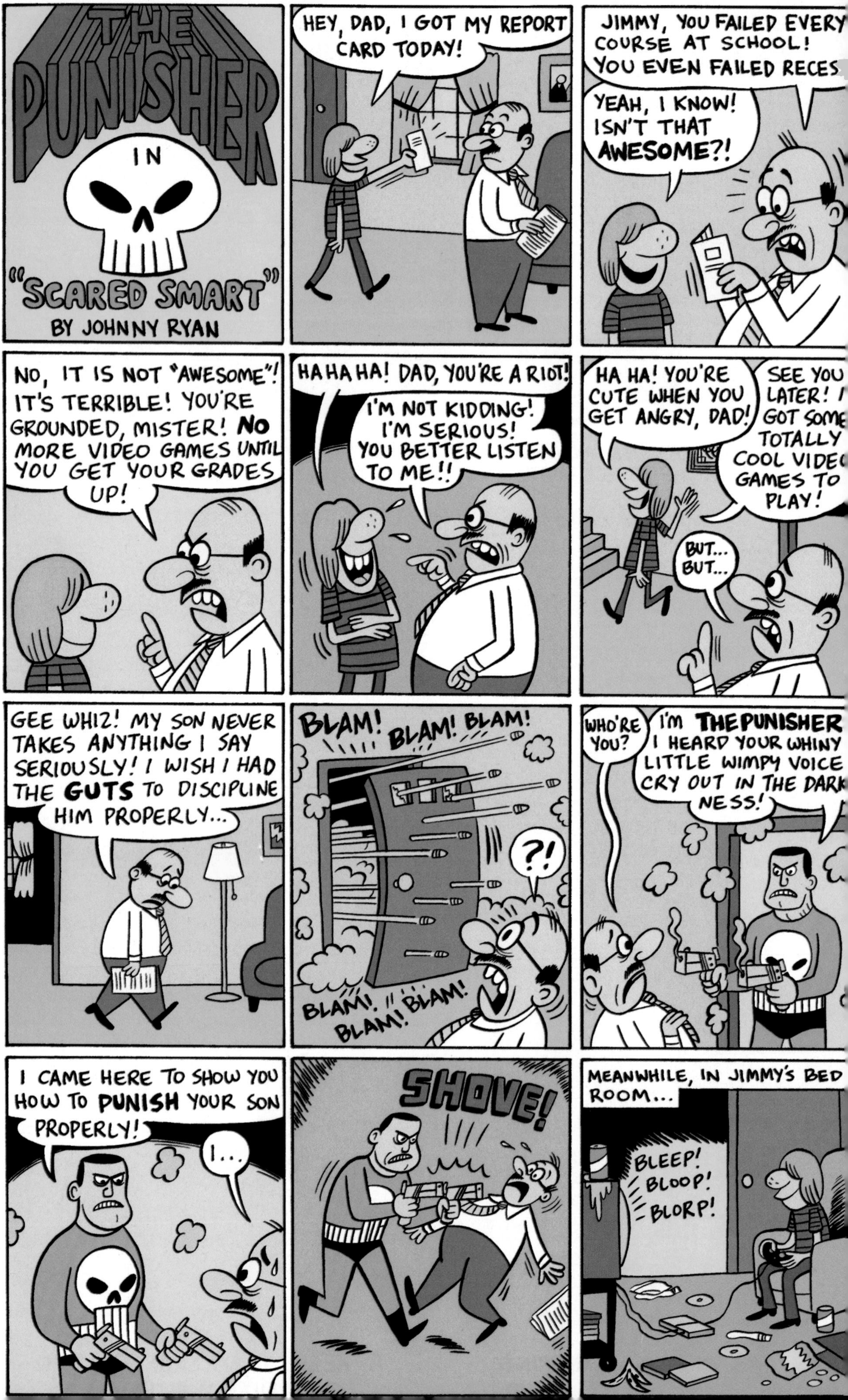

THE PUNISHER
IN
"SCARED SMART"
BY JOHNNY RYAN
HEY, DAD, I GOT MY REPORT CARD TODAY!
JIMMY, YOU FAILED EVERY COURSE AT SCHOOL! YOU EVEN FAILED RECES
YEAH, I KNOW! ISN'T THAT AWESOME?!
NO, IT IS NOT "AWESOME"! IT'S TERRIBLE! YOU'RE GROUNDED, MISTER! NO MORE VIDEO GAMES UNTIL YOU GET YOUR GRADES UP!
HA HA HA! DAD, YOU'RE A RIOT!
I'M NOT KIDDING! I'M SERIOUS! YOU BETTER LISTEN TO ME!!
HA HA! YOU'RE CUTE WHEN YOU GET ANGRY, DAD!
SEE YOU LATER! I GOT SOME TOTALLY COOL VIDE GAMES TO PLAY!
BUT... BUT...
GEE WHIZ! MY SON NEVER TAKES ANYTHING I SAY SERIOUSLY! I WISH I HAD THE GUTS TO DISCIPLINE HIM PROPERLY...
BLAM! BLAM! BLAM!
?!
BLAM! BLAM! BLAM!
WHO'RE YOU?
I'M THE PUNISHER I HEARD YOUR WHINY LITTLE WIMPY VOICE CRY OUT IN THE DARK NESS!
I CAME HERE TO SHOW YOU HOW TO PUNISH YOUR SON PROPERLY!
I...
SHOVE!
MEANWHILE, IN JIMMY'S BED ROOM...
BLEEP! BLOOP! BLORP!

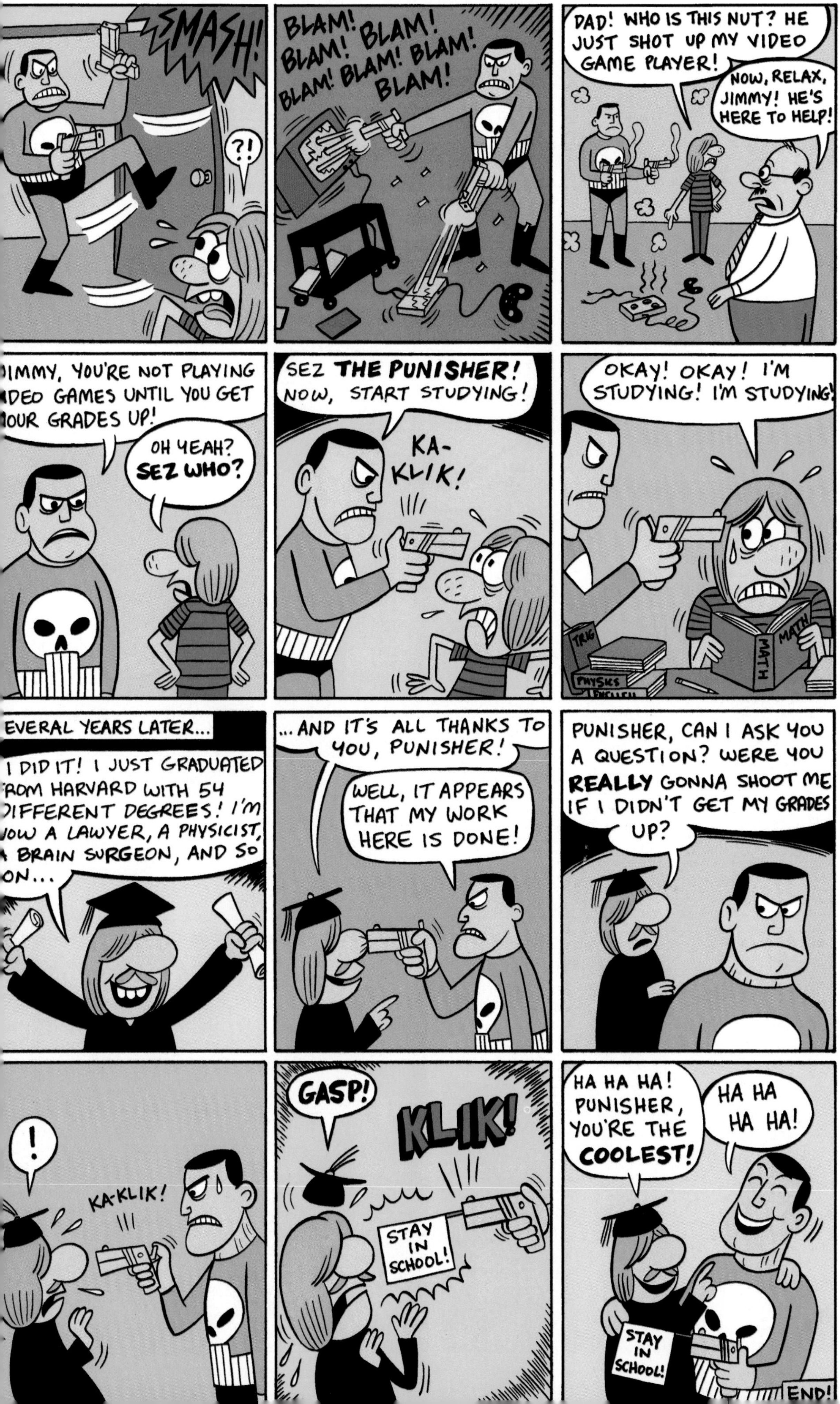
SMASH!
?!
BLAM! BLAM! BLAM! BLAM! BLAM! BLAM! BLAM!
DAD! WHO IS THIS NUT? HE JUST SHOT UP MY VIDEO GAME PLAYER!
NOW, RELAX, JIMMY! HE'S HERE TO HELP!
IMMY, YOU'RE NOT PLAYING IDEO GAMES UNTIL YOU GET OUR GRADES UP!
OH YEAH? SEZ WHO?
SEZ THE PUNISHER! NOW, START STUDYING!
KA-KLIK!
OKAY! OKAY! I'M STUDYING! I'M STUDYING!
TRIG
MATH
PHYSICS
EVERAL YEARS LATER...
I DID IT! I JUST GRADUATED FROM HARVARD WITH 54 DIFFERENT DEGREES! I'M NOW A LAWYER, A PHYSICIST, A BRAIN SURGEON, AND SO ON...
...AND IT'S ALL THANKS TO YOU, PUNISHER!
WELL, IT APPEARS THAT MY WORK HERE IS DONE!
PUNISHER, CAN I ASK YOU A QUESTION? WERE YOU REALLY GONNA SHOOT ME IF I DIDN'T GET MY GRADES UP?
!
KA-KLIK!
GASP!
KLIK!
STAY IN SCHOOL!
HA HA HA! PUNISHER, YOU'RE THE COOLEST!
HA HA HA HA!
STAY IN SCHOOL!
END!

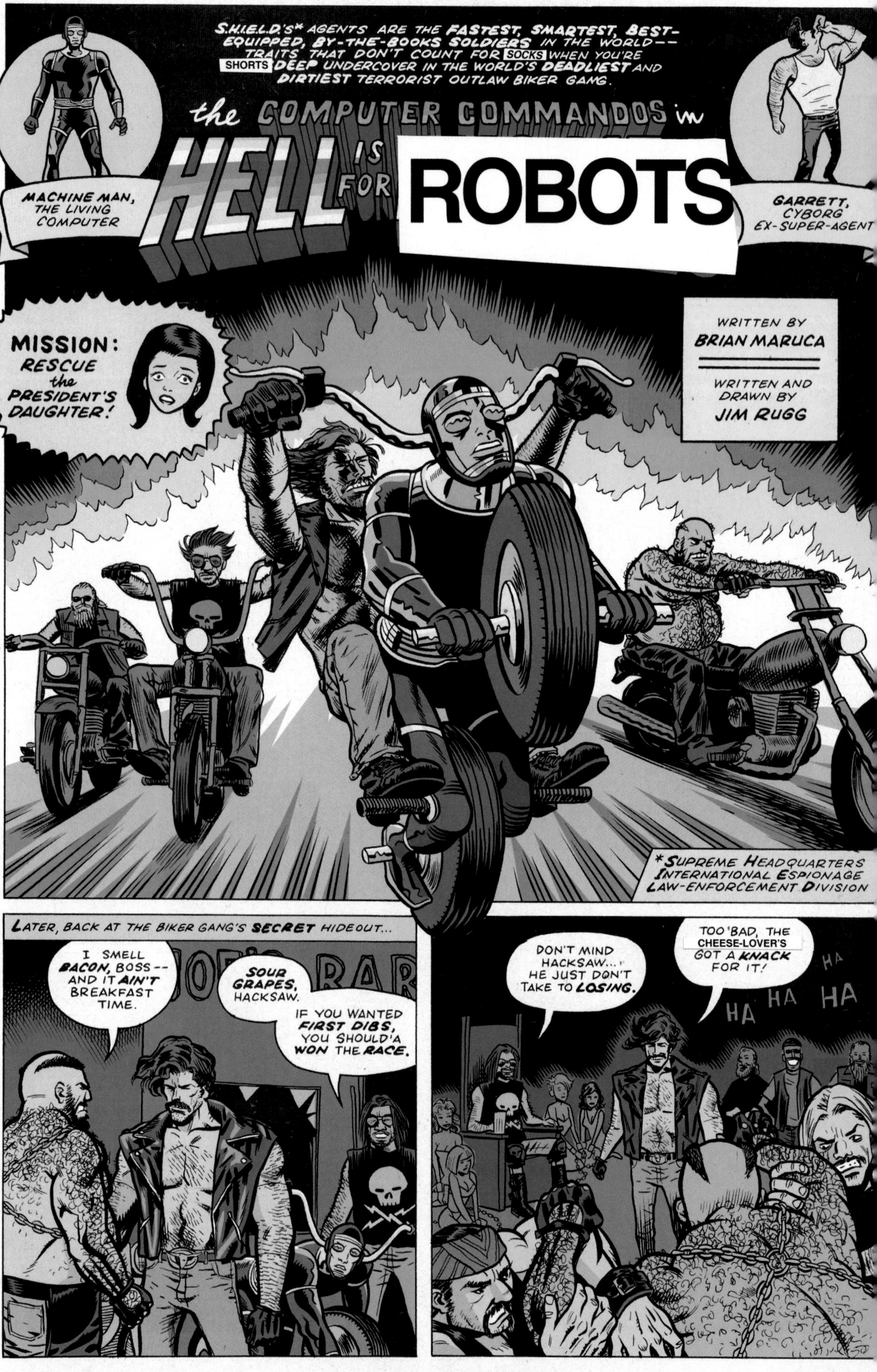

S.H.I.E.L.D.'s* AGENTS ARE THE FASTEST, SMARTEST, BEST-EQUIPPED, BY-THE-BOOKS SOLDIERS IN THE WORLD-- TRAITS THAT DON'T COUNT FOR SOCKS WHEN YOU'RE SHORTS DEEP UNDERCOVER IN THE WORLD'S DEADLIEST AND DIRTIEST TERRORIST OUTLAW BIKER GANG.
the COMPUTER COMMANDOS in
HELL IS FOR ROBOTS
MACHINE MAN, THE LIVING COMPUTER
GARRETT, CYBORG EX-SUPER-AGENT
MISSION: RESCUE the PRESIDENT'S DAUGHTER!
WRITTEN BY BRIAN MARUCA
WRITTEN AND DRAWN BY JIM RUGG
*SUPREME HEADQUARTERS INTERNATIONAL ESPIONAGE LAW-ENFORCEMENT DIVISION
LATER, BACK AT THE BIKER GANG'S SECRET HIDEOUT...
I SMELL BACON, BOSS-- AND IT AIN'T BREAKFAST TIME.
SOUR GRAPES, HACKSAW.
IF YOU WANTED FIRST DIBS, YOU SHOULD'A WON THE RACE.
DON'T MIND HACKSAW... HE JUST DON'T TAKE TO LOSING.
TOO BAD, THE CHEESE-LOVER'S GOT A KNACK FOR IT!
HA HA HA HA

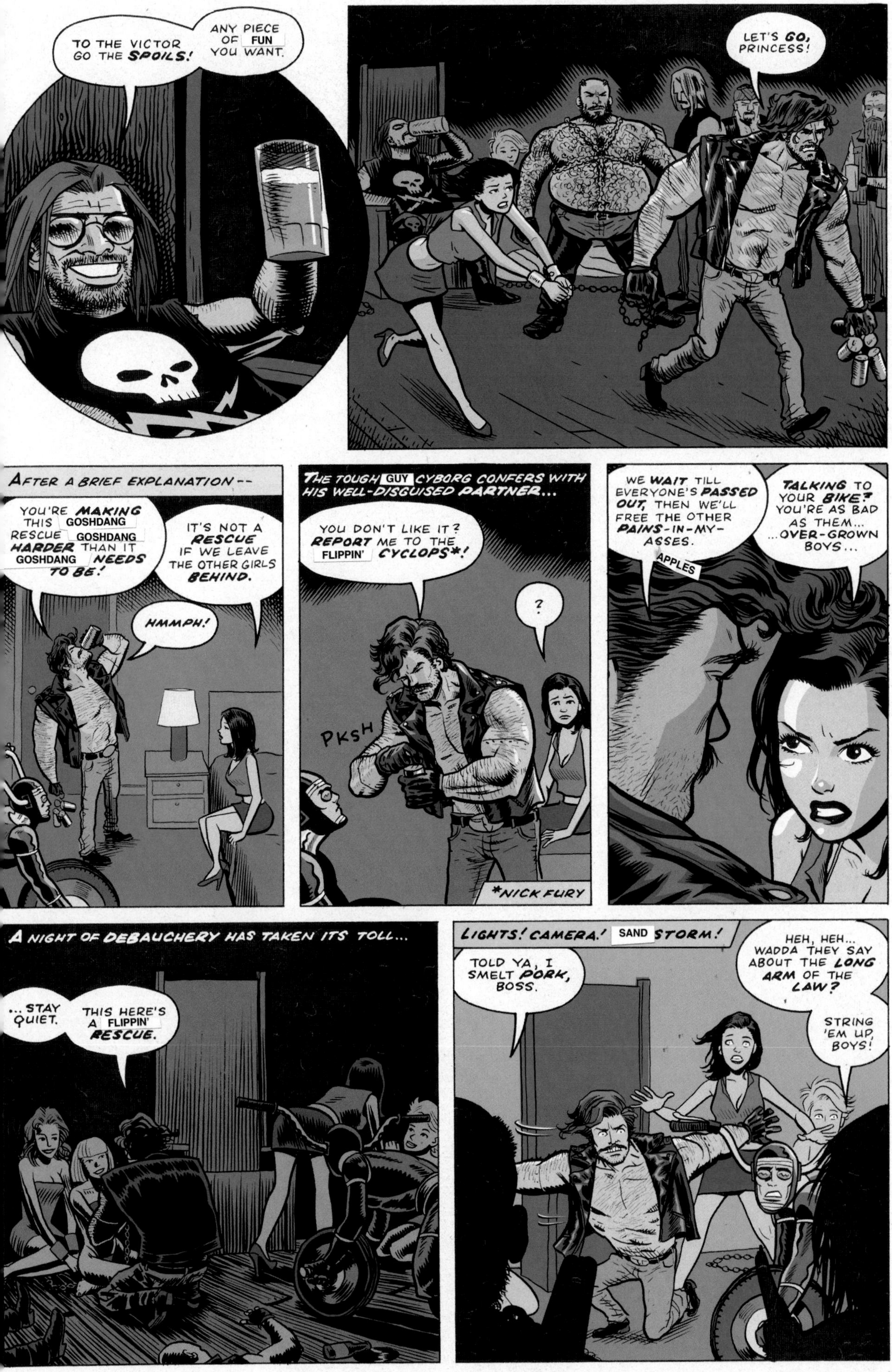

TO THE VICTOR GO THE SPOILS!
ANY PIECE OF FUN YOU WANT.
LET'S GO, PRINCESS!
AFTER A BRIEF EXPLANATION--
YOU'RE MAKING THIS GOSHDANG RESCUE GOSHDANG HARDER THAN IT GOSHDANG NEEDS TO BE!
IT'S NOT A RESCUE IF WE LEAVE THE OTHER GIRLS BEHIND.
HMMPH!
THE TOUGH GUY CYBORG CONFERS WITH HIS WELL-DISGUISED PARTNER...
YOU DON'T LIKE IT? REPORT ME TO THE FLIPPIN' CYCLOPS*!
?
PKSH
*NICK FURY
WE WAIT TILL EVERYONE'S PASSED OUT, THEN WE'LL FREE THE OTHER PAINS-IN-MY-ASSES. APPLES
TALKING TO YOUR BIKE? YOU'RE AS BAD AS THEM... ...OVER-GROWN BOYS...
A NIGHT OF DEBAUCHERY HAS TAKEN ITS TOLL...
...STAY QUIET.
THIS HERE'S A FLIPPIN' RESCUE.
LIGHTS! CAMERA! SAND STORM!
TOLD YA, I SMELT PORK, BOSS.
HEH, HEH... WADDA THEY SAY ABOUT THE LONG ARM OF THE LAW?
STRING 'EM UP, BOYS!

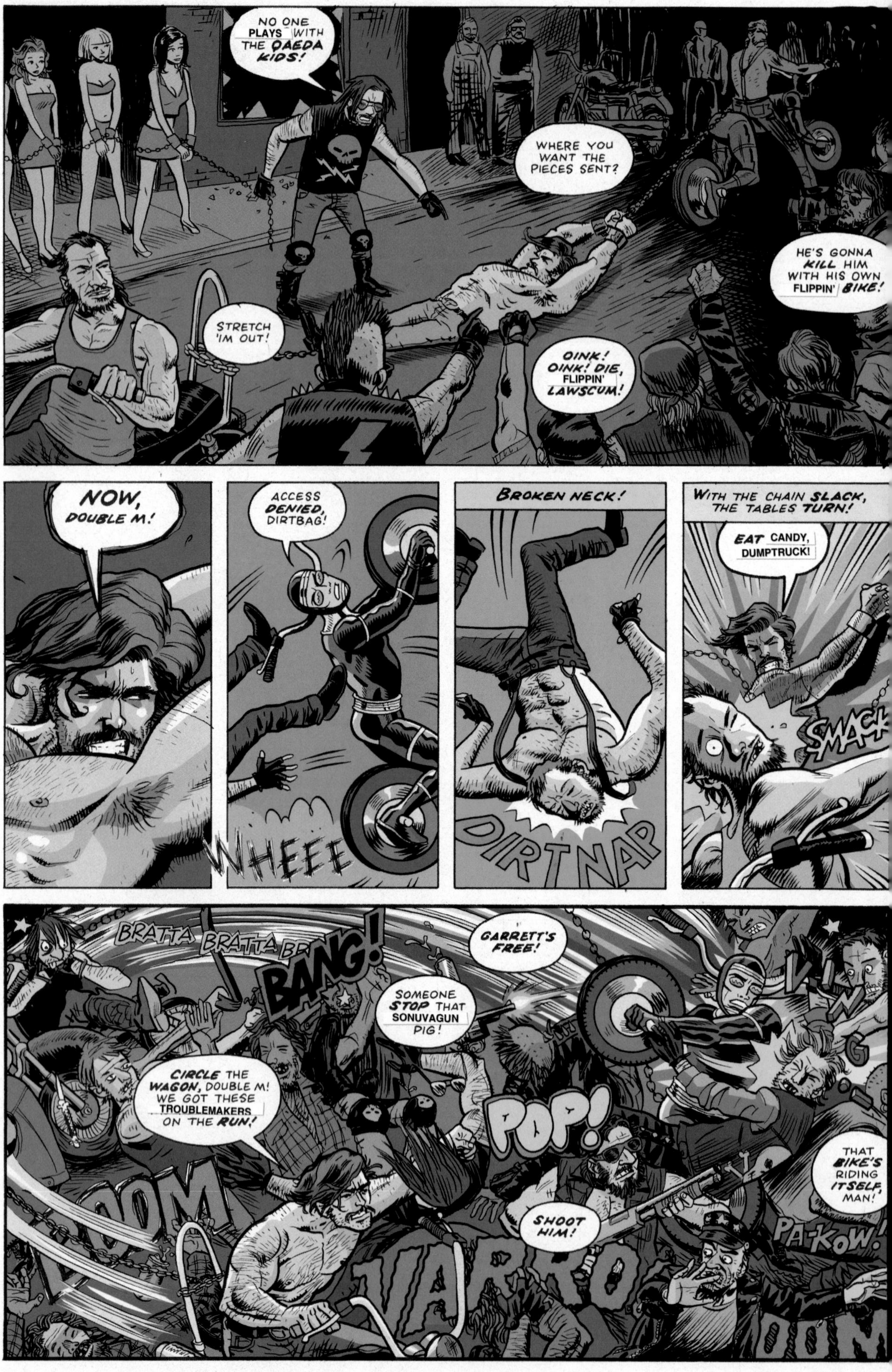

NO ONE PLAYS WITH THE QAEDA KIDS!
WHERE YOU WANT THE PIECES SENT?
HE'S GONNA KILL HIM WITH HIS OWN FLIPPIN' BIKE!
STRETCH 'IM OUT!
OINK! OINK! DIE, FLIPPIN' LAWSCUM!
NOW, DOUBLE M!
ACCESS DENIED, DIRTBAG!
WHEEE
BROKEN NECK!
DIRTNAP
WITH THE CHAIN SLACK, THE TABLES TURN!
EAT CANDY, DUMPTRUCK!
SMACK
BRATTA BRATTA BR
BANG!
GARRETT'S FREE!
SOMEONE STOP THAT SONUVAGUN PIG!
CIRCLE THE WAGON, DOUBLE M! WE GOT THESE TROUBLEMAKERS ON THE RUN!
POP!
THAT BIKE'S RIDING ITSELF, MAN!
SHOOT HIM!
PAKOW!

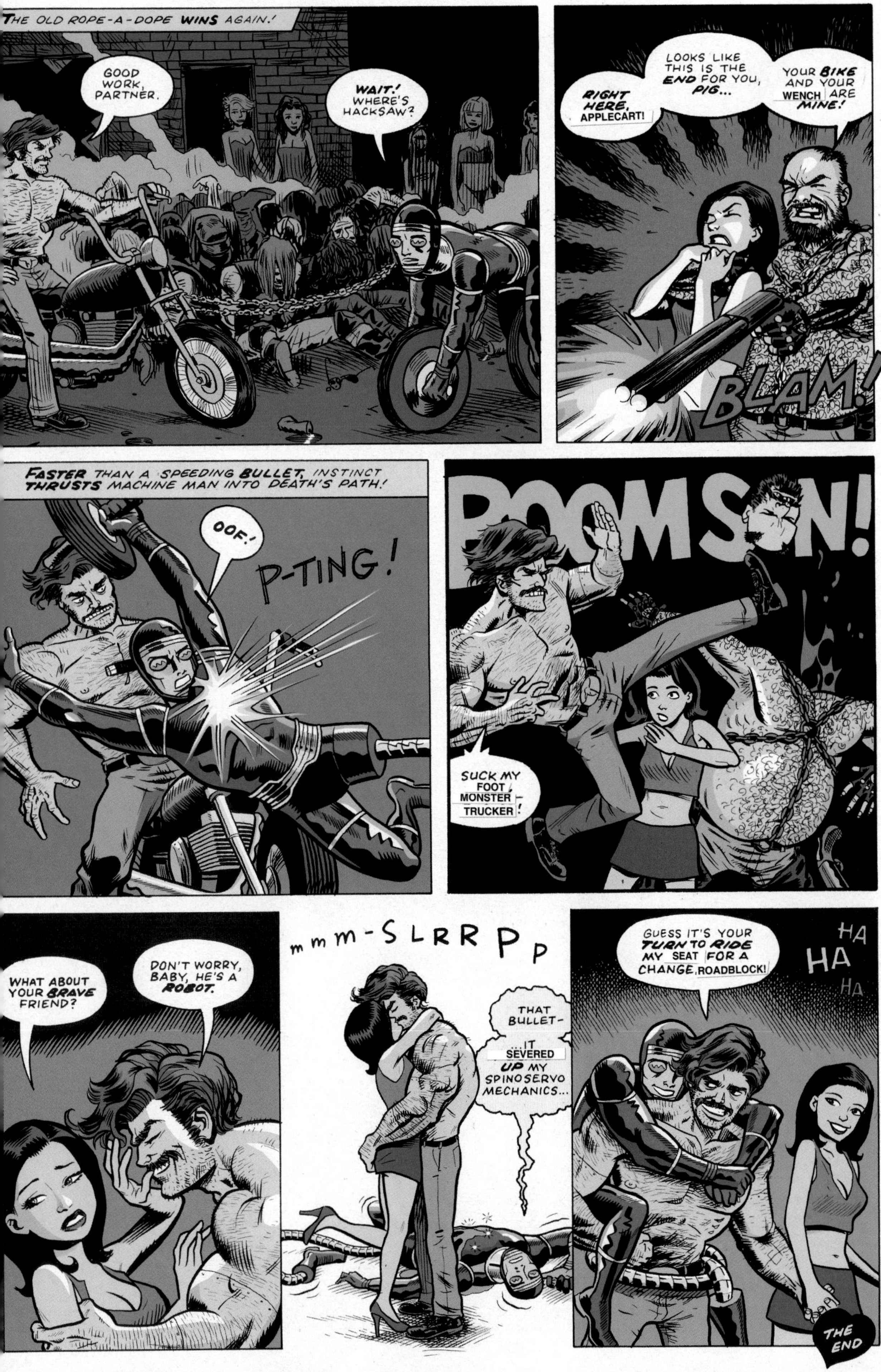
THE OLD ROPE-A-DOPE WINS AGAIN!
GOOD WORK, PARTNER.
WAIT! WHERE'S HACKSAW?
RIGHT HERE, APPLECART!
LOOKS LIKE THIS IS THE END FOR YOU, PIG...
YOUR BIKE AND YOUR WENCH ARE MINE!
BLAM!
FASTER THAN A SPEEDING BULLET, INSTINCT THRUSTS MACHINE MAN INTO DEATH'S PATH!
OOF!
P-TING!
BOOMSON!
SUCK MY FOOT, MONSTER-TRUCKER!
WHAT ABOUT YOUR BRAVE FRIEND?
DON'T WORRY, BABY, HE'S A ROBOT.
mmm-SLRRPp
THAT BULLET-
...IT SEVERED UP MY SPINOSERVO MECHANICS...
GUESS IT'S YOUR TURN TO RIDE MY SEAT FOR A CHANGE, ROADBLOCK!
HA HA HA
THE END

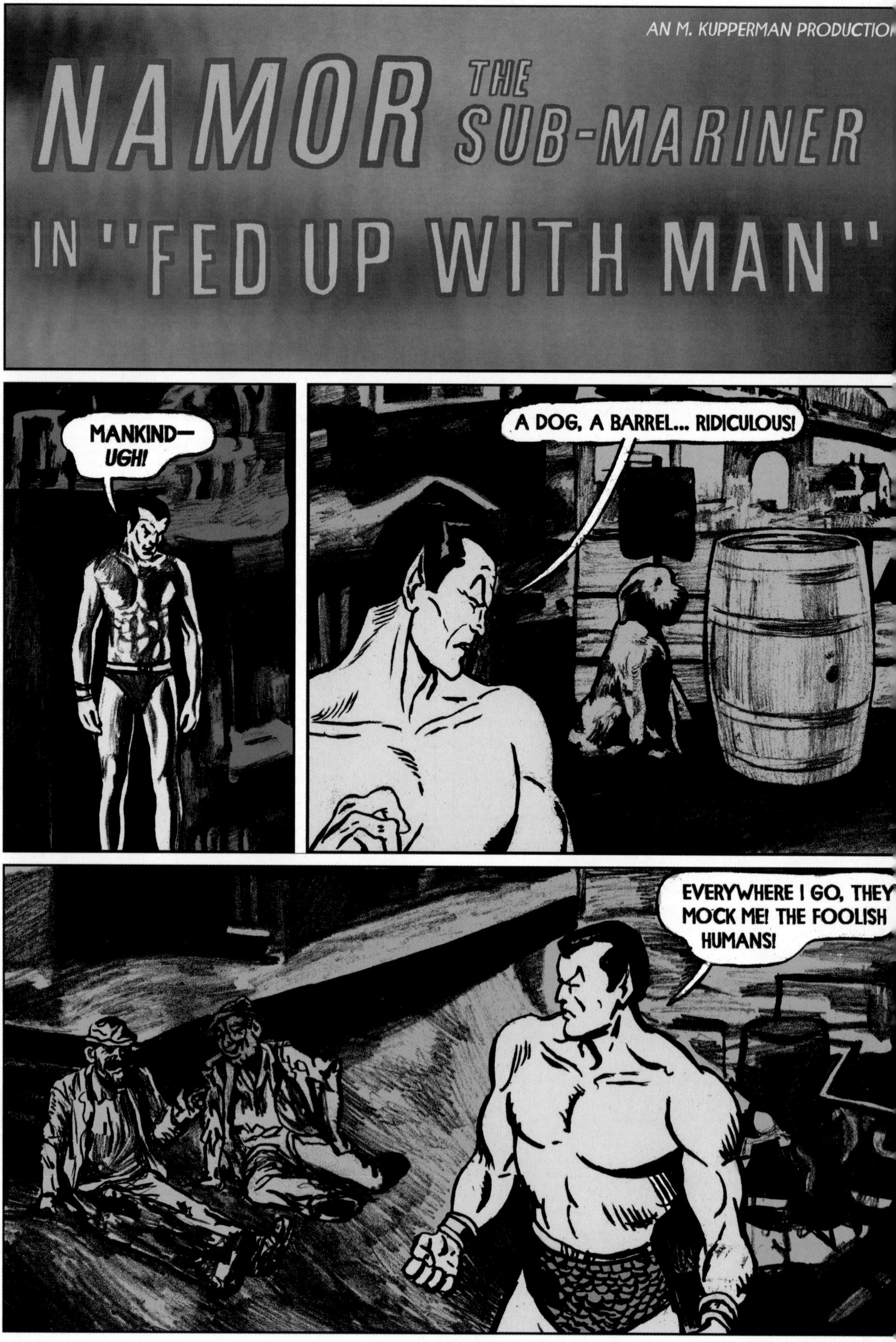
AN M. KUPPERMAN PRODUCTION
NAMOR THE SUB-MARINER
IN "FED UP WITH MAN"
MANKIND— UGH!
A DOG, A BARREL... RIDICULOUS!
EVERYWHERE I GO, THEY MOCK ME! THE FOOLISH HUMANS!

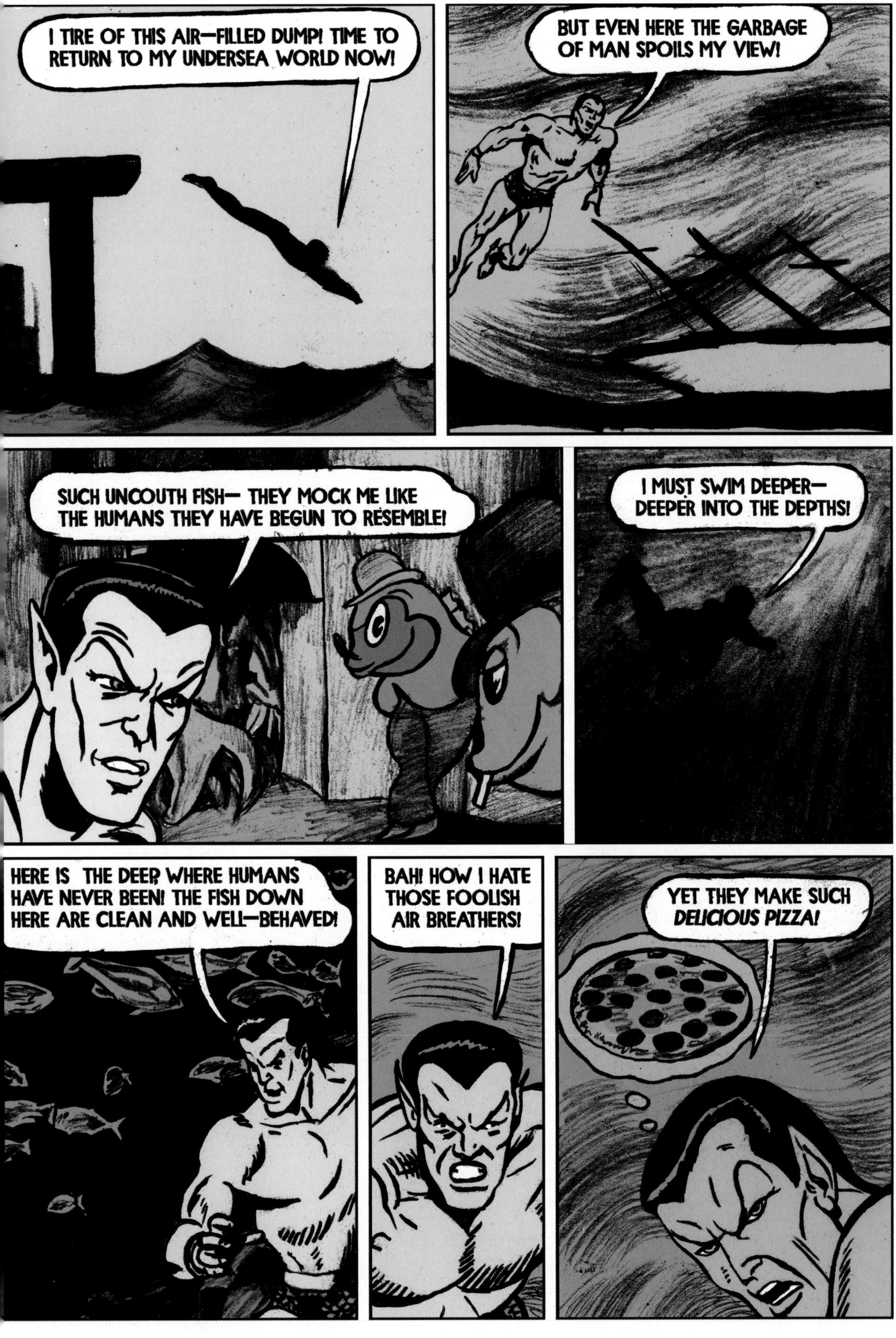
I TIRE OF THIS AIR—FILLED DUMP! TIME TO RETURN TO MY UNDERSEA WORLD NOW!
BUT EVEN HERE THE GARBAGE OF MAN SPOILS MY VIEW!
SUCH UNCOUTH FISH— THEY MOCK ME LIKE THE HUMANS THEY HAVE BEGUN TO RESEMBLE!
I MUST SWIM DEEPER— DEEPER INTO THE DEPTHS!
HERE IS THE DEEP WHERE HUMANS HAVE NEVER BEEN! THE FISH DOWN HERE ARE CLEAN AND WELL—BEHAVED!
BAH! HOW I HATE THOSE FOOLISH AIR BREATHERS!
YET THEY MAKE SUCH *DELICIOUS PIZZA!*

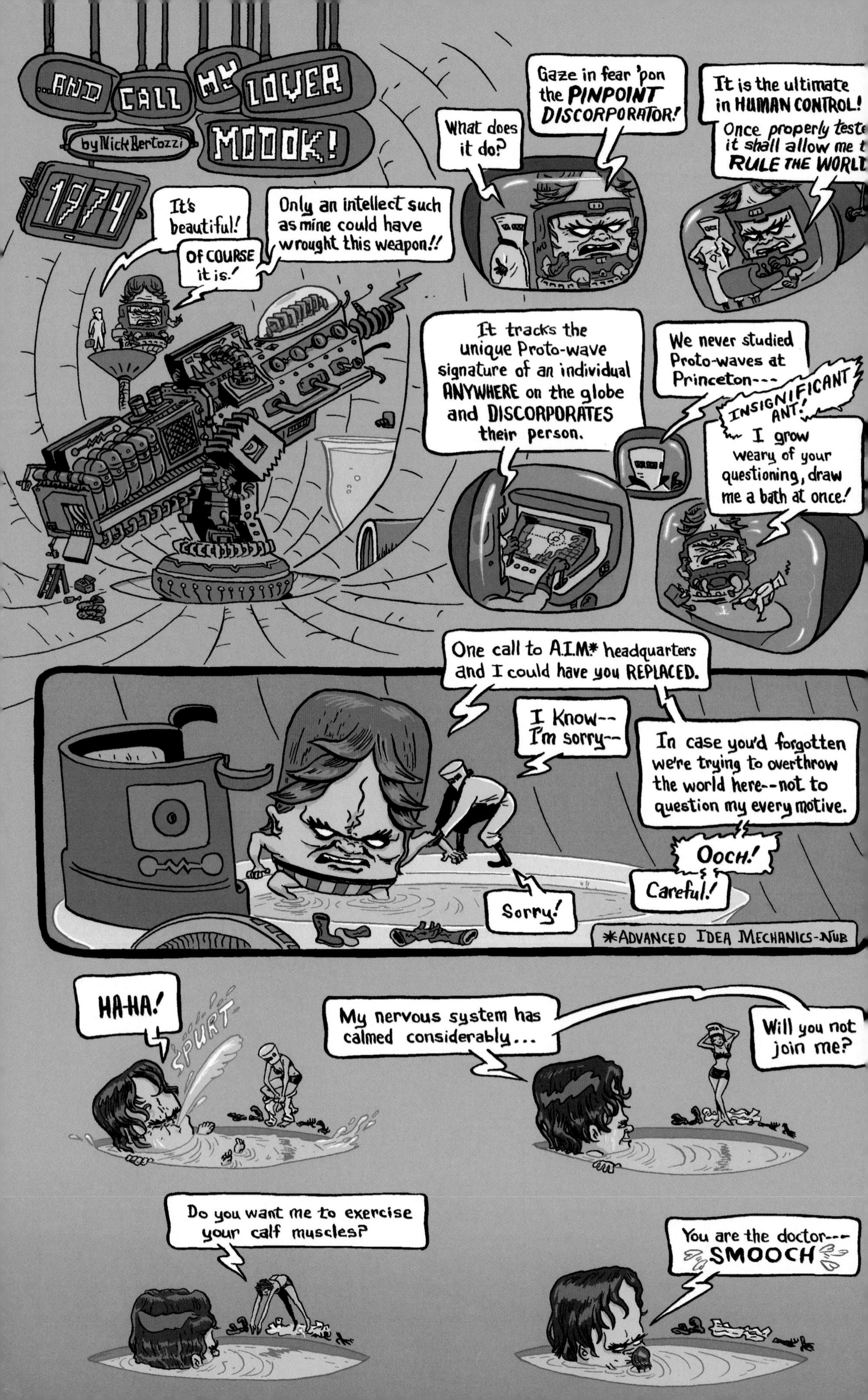
...AND CALL MY LOVER MODOK!
by Nick Bertozzi
1974
It's beautiful!
OF COURSE it is!
Only an intellect such as mine could have wrought this weapon!!
What does it do?
Gaze in fear 'pon the PINPOINT DISCORPORATOR!
It is the ultimate in HUMAN CONTROL!
Once properly teste it shall allow me t RULE THE WORLI
It tracks the unique Proto-wave signature of an individual ANYWHERE on the globe and DISCORPORATES their person.
We never studied Proto-waves at Princeton---
INSIGNIFICANT ANT!
I grow weary of your questioning, draw me a bath at once!
One call to A.I.M.* headquarters and I could have you REPLACED.
I Know-- I'm sorry--
In case you'd forgotten we're trying to overthrow the world here--not to question my every motive.
OOCH!
Careful!
Sorry!
*ADVANCED IDEA MECHANICS-NUB
HA-HA!
SPURT
My nervous system has calmed considerably...
Will you not join me?
Do you want me to exercise your calf muscles?
You are the doctor---
SMOOCH

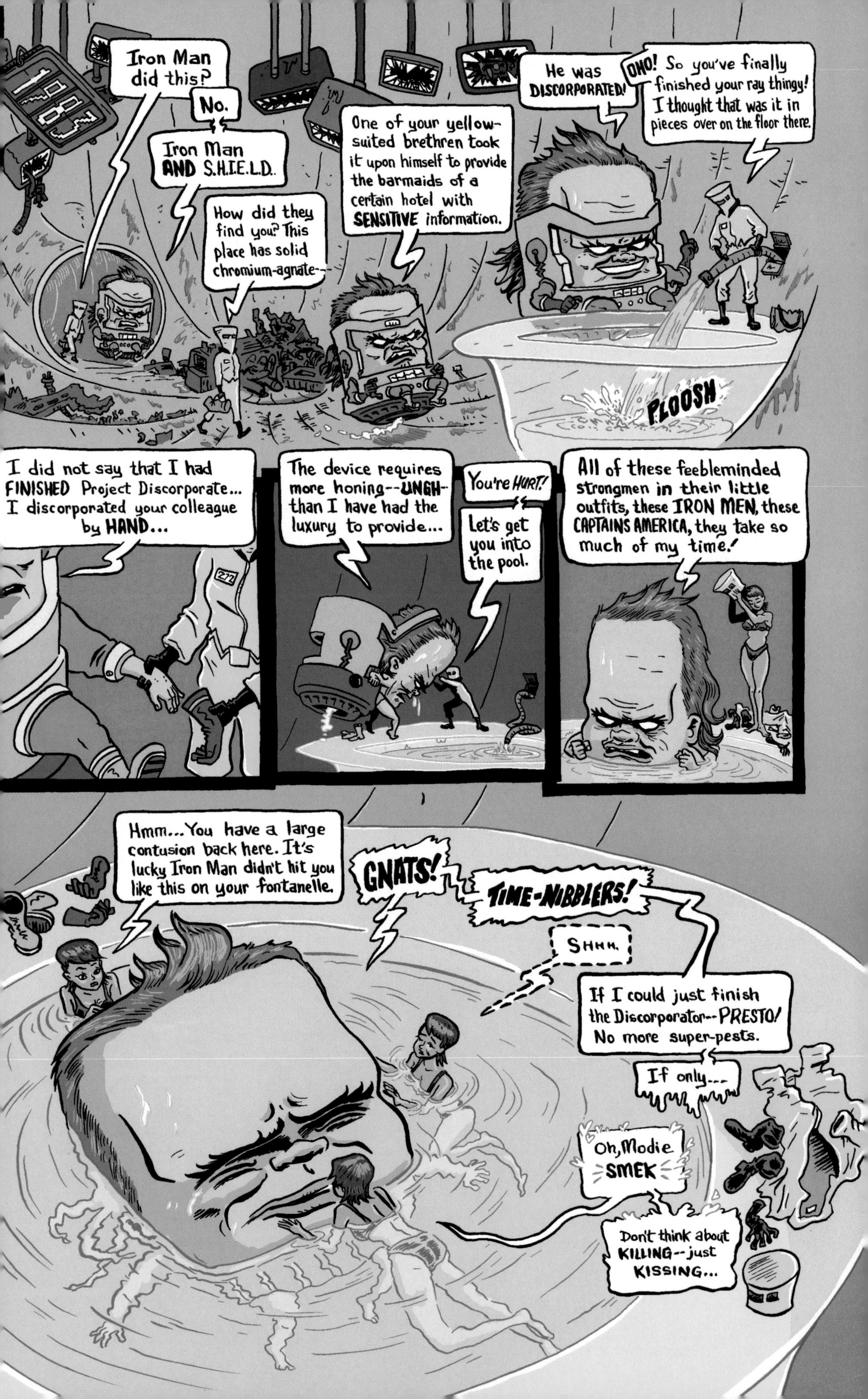

Iron Man did this?
No.
Iron Man AND S.H.I.E.L.D.
How did they find you? This place has solid chromium-agnate--
One of your yellow-suited brethren took it upon himself to provide the barmaids of a certain hotel with SENSITIVE information.
He was DISCORPORATED!
OHO! So you've finally finished your ray thingy! I thought that was it in pieces over on the floor there.
PLOOSH
I did not say that I had FINISHED Project Discorporate... I discorporated your colleague by HAND...
272
The device requires more honing--UNGH--than I have had the luxury to provide...
You're HURT!
Let's get you into the pool.
All of these feebleminded strongmen in their little outfits, these IRON MEN, these CAPTAINS AMERICA, they take so much of my time!
Hmm...You have a large contusion back here. It's lucky Iron Man didn't hit you like this on your fontanelle.
GNATS!
TIME-NIBBLERS!
SHHH.
If I could just finish the Discorporator--PRESTO! No more super-pests.
If only...
Oh, Modie
SMEK
Don't think about KILLING--just KISSING...

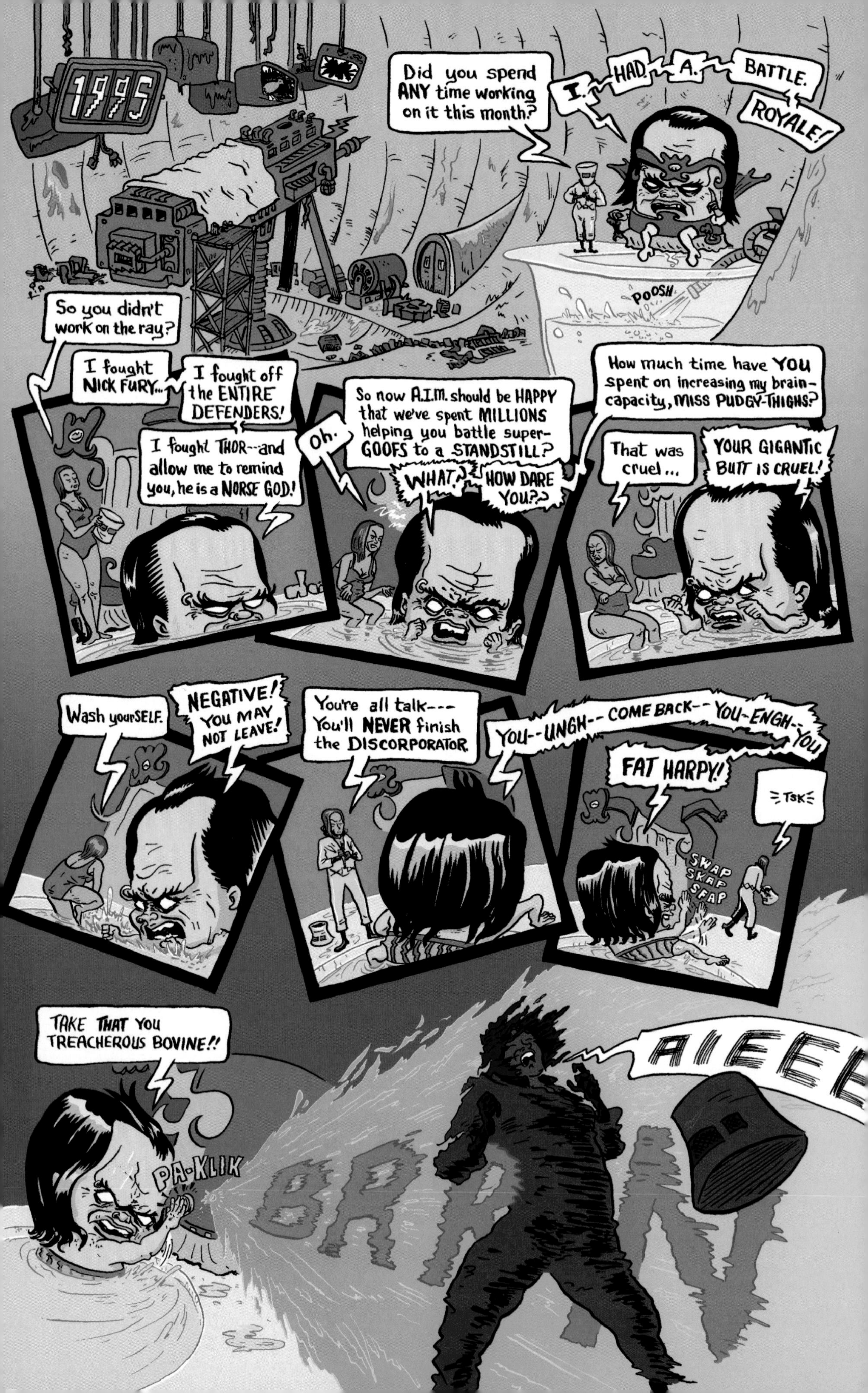
1995
Did you spend ANY time working on it this month?
I. HAD. A. BATTLE. ROYALE!
POOSH
So you didn't work on the ray?
I fought NICK FURY...
I fought off the ENTIRE DEFENDERS!
I fought THOR--and allow me to remind you, he is a NORSE GOD!
Oh.
So now A.I.M. should be HAPPY that we've spent MILLIONS helping you battle super-GOOFS to a STANDSTILL?
WHAT?
HOW DARE YOU?
How much time have YOU spent on increasing my brain-capacity, MISS PUDGY-THIGHS?
That was cruel...
YOUR GIGANTIC BUTT IS CRUEL!
Wash yourSELF.
NEGATIVE! YOU MAY NOT LEAVE!
You're all talk--- You'll NEVER finish the DISCORPORATOR.
YOU--UNGH-- COME BACK-- YOU-ENGH-- YOU
FAT HARPY!
TSK
SWAP SKAP SFAP
TAKE THAT YOU TREACHEROUS BOVINE!!
PA-KLIK
BRR
AIEEE

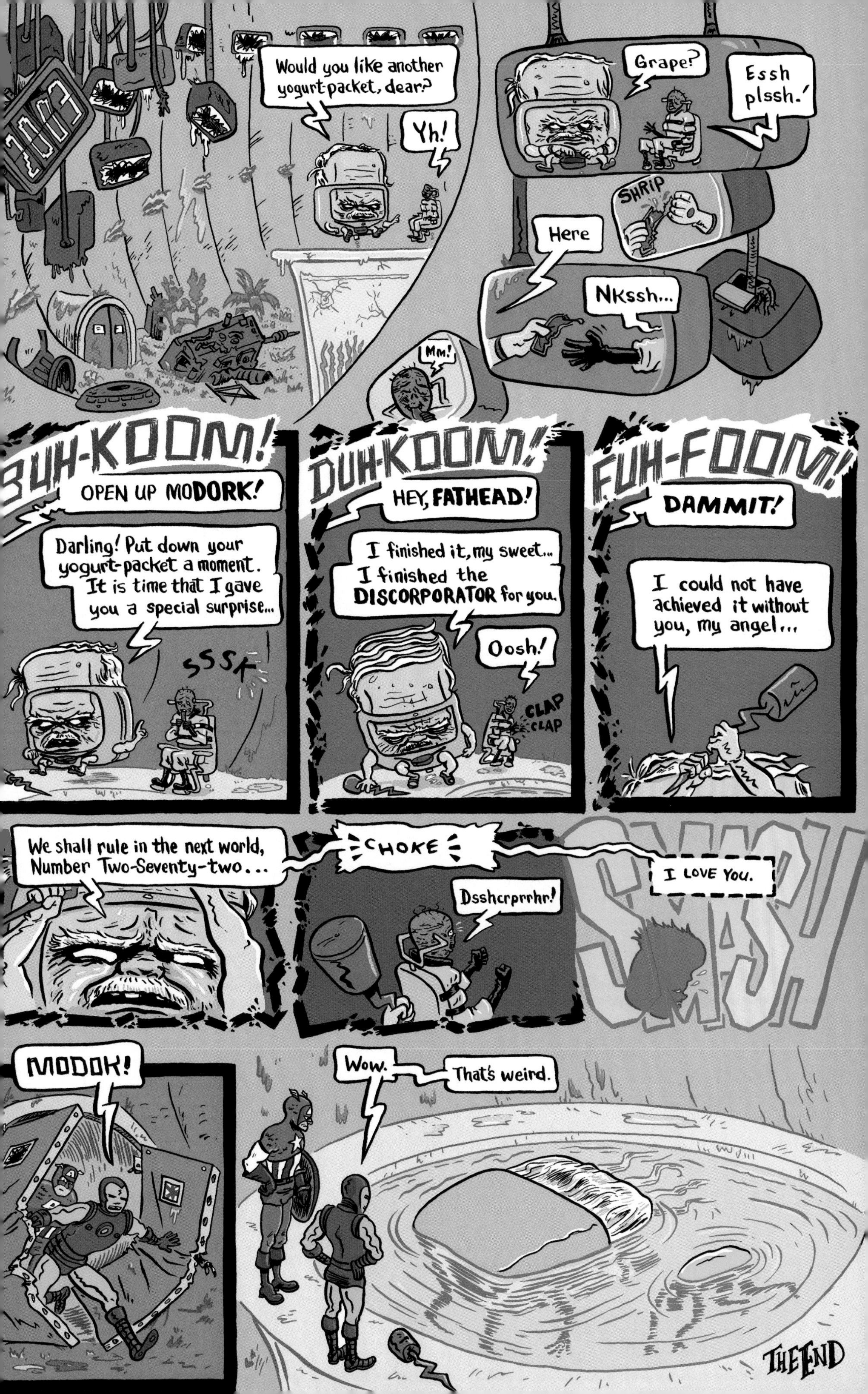

Would you like another yogurt-packet, dear?
Yh!
Grape?
Essh plssh.!
SHRIP
Here
Nkssh...
Mm!
BUH-KOOM!
OPEN UP MODORK!
Darling! Put down your yogurt-packet a moment. It is time that I gave you a special surprise...
SSSK
DUH-KOOM!
HEY, FATHEAD!
I finished it, my sweet... I finished the DISCORPORATOR for you.
Oosh!
CLAP CLAP
FUH-FOOM!
DAMMIT!
I could not have achieved it without you, my angel...
We shall rule in the next world, Number Two-Seventy-two...
CHOKE
I LOVE YOU.
Dsshcrprrhr!
SMASH
MODOK!
Wow.
That's weird.
THE END

"THE GREEN MENACE"

BY THE PERRY BIBLE FELLOWSHIP

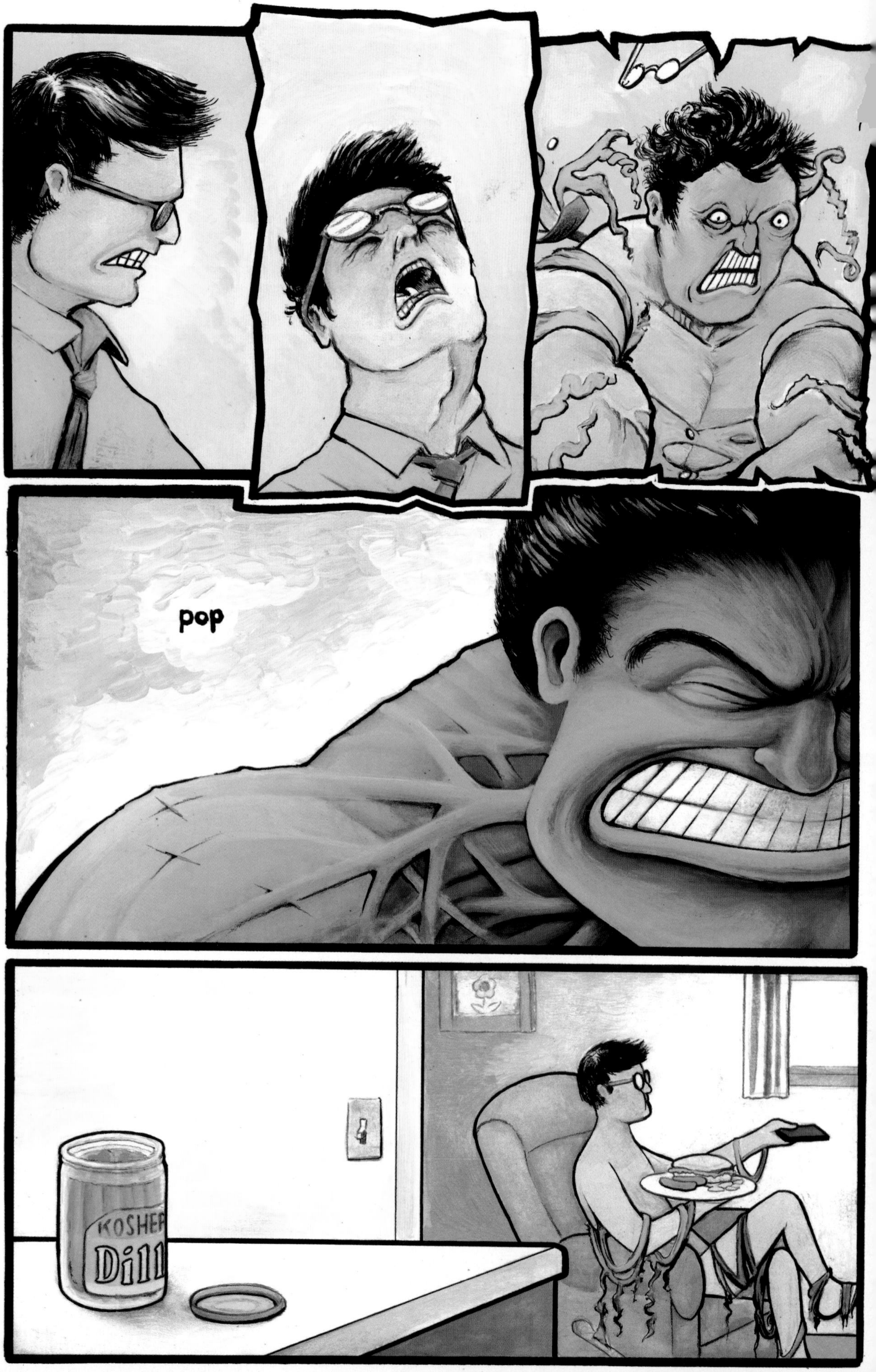
pop
KOSHER
Dill

"THE BLUE HAIR"

BY THE PERRY BIBLE FELLOWSHIP

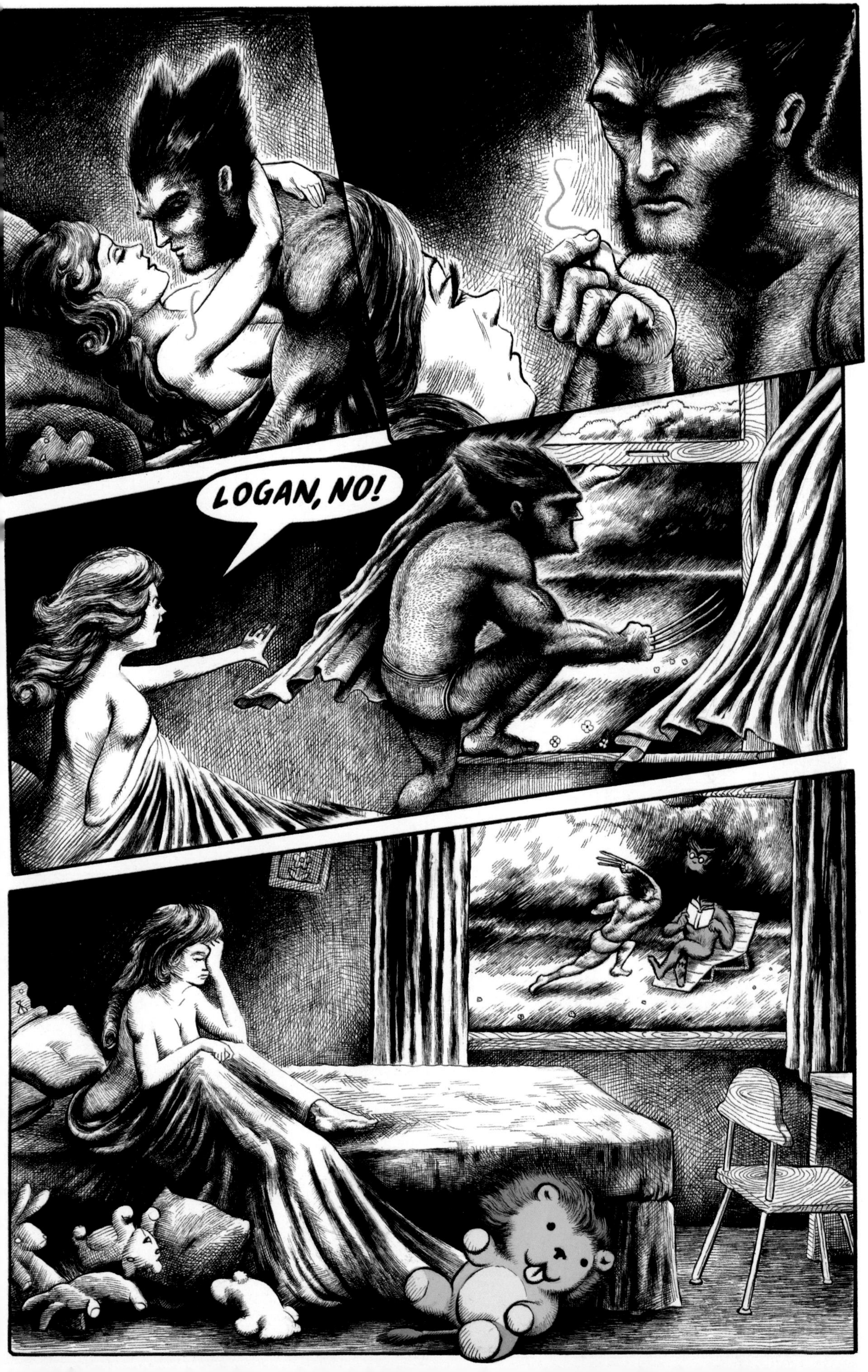
LOGAN, NO!

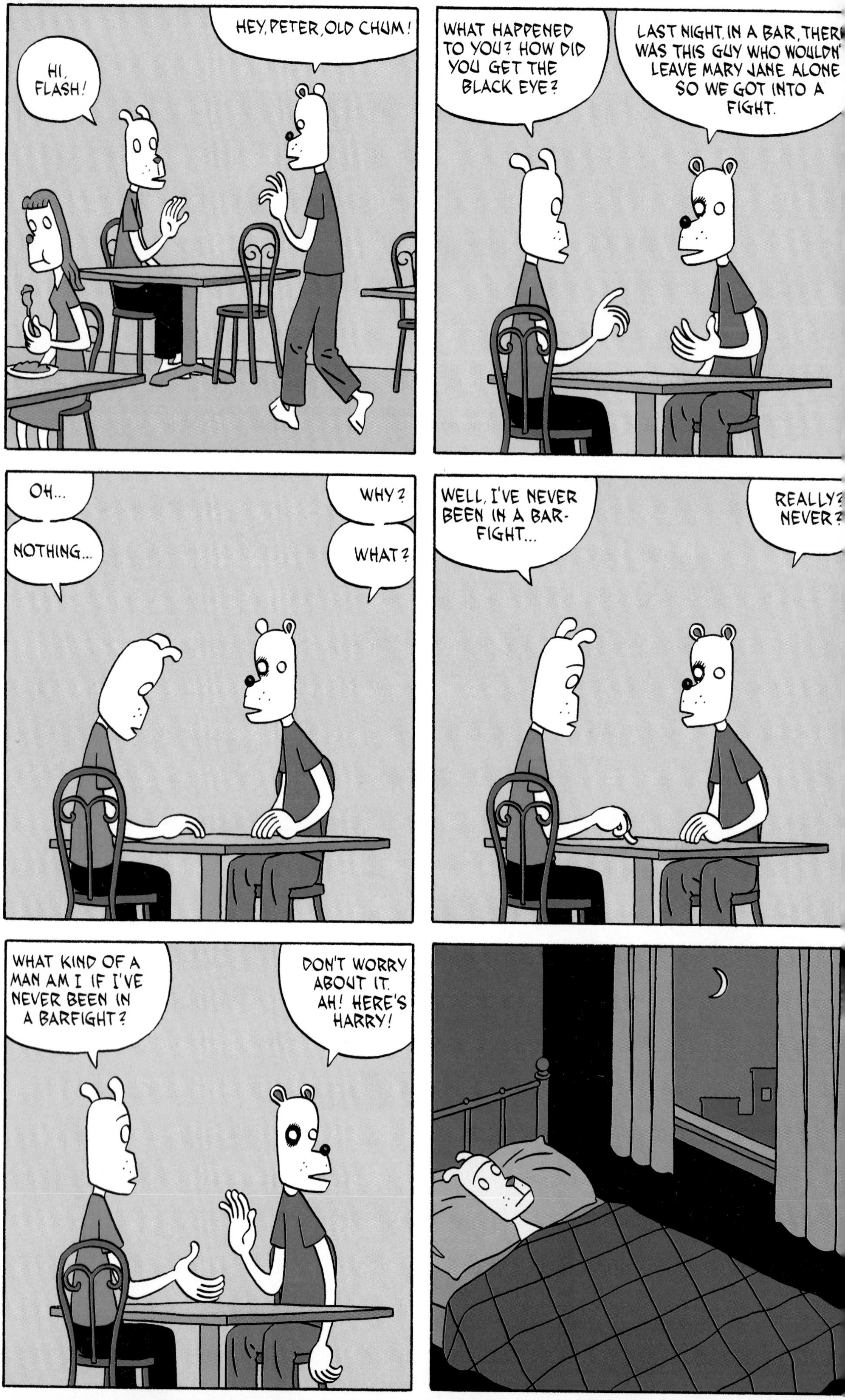
HEY, PETER, OLD CHUM!
HI, FLASH!
WHAT HAPPENED TO YOU? HOW DID YOU GET THE BLACK EYE?
LAST NIGHT, IN A BAR, THER
WAS THIS GUY WHO WOULDN'
LEAVE MARY JANE ALONE SO WE GOT INTO A FIGHT.
OH...
WHY?
NOTHING...
WHAT?
WELL, I'VE NEVER BEEN IN A BAR-FIGHT...
REALLY? NEVER?
WHAT KIND OF A MAN AM I IF I'VE NEVER BEEN IN A BARFIGHT?
DON'T WORRY ABOUT IT. AH! HERE'S HARRY!

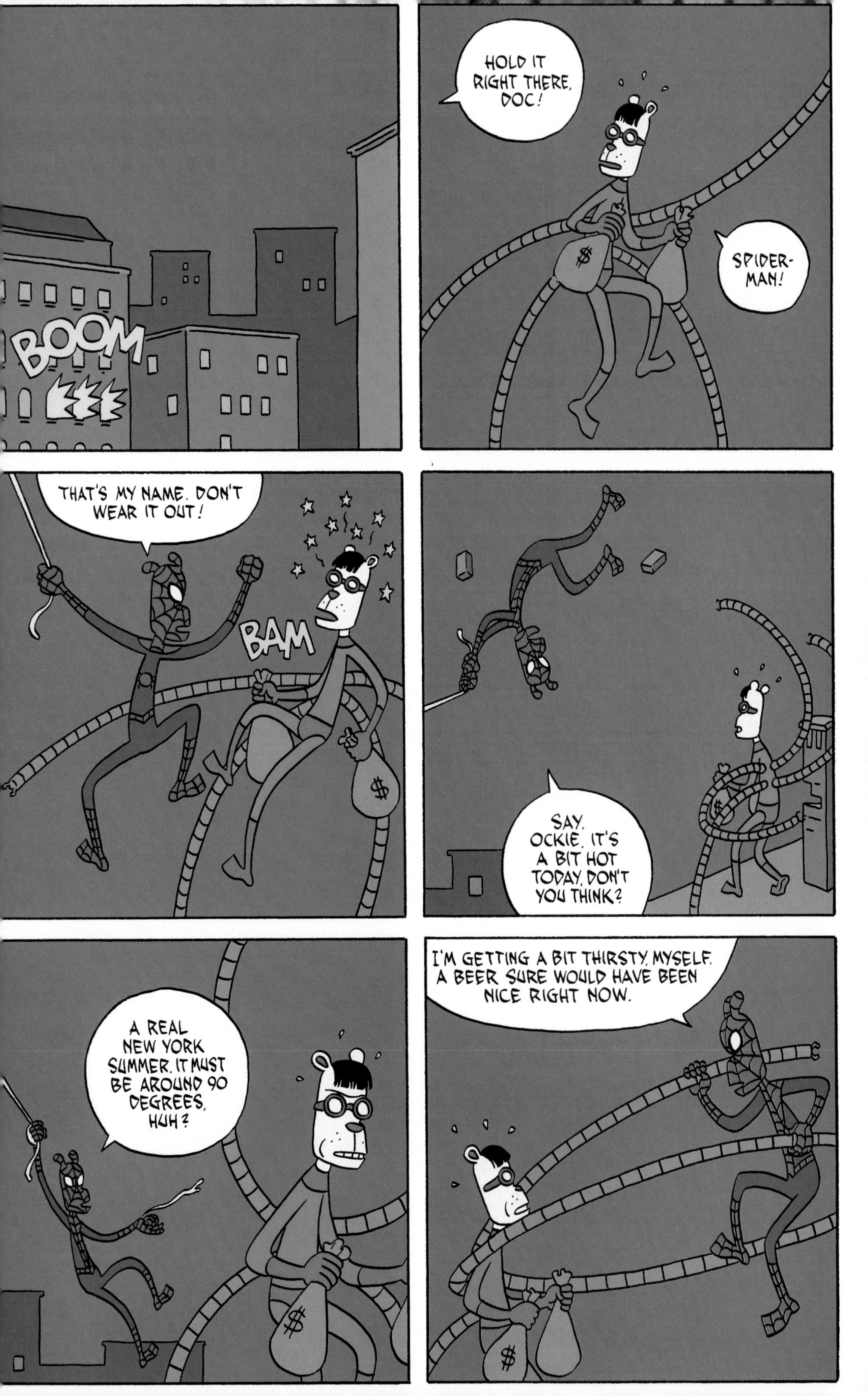
BOOM
HOLD IT RIGHT THERE, DOC!
SPIDER-MAN!
THAT'S MY NAME. DON'T WEAR IT OUT!
BAM
SAY, OCKIE, IT'S A BIT HOT TODAY, DON'T YOU THINK?
A REAL NEW YORK SUMMER. IT MUST BE AROUND 90 DEGREES, HUH?
I'M GETTING A BIT THIRSTY, MYSELF. A BEER SURE WOULD HAVE BEEN NICE RIGHT NOW.

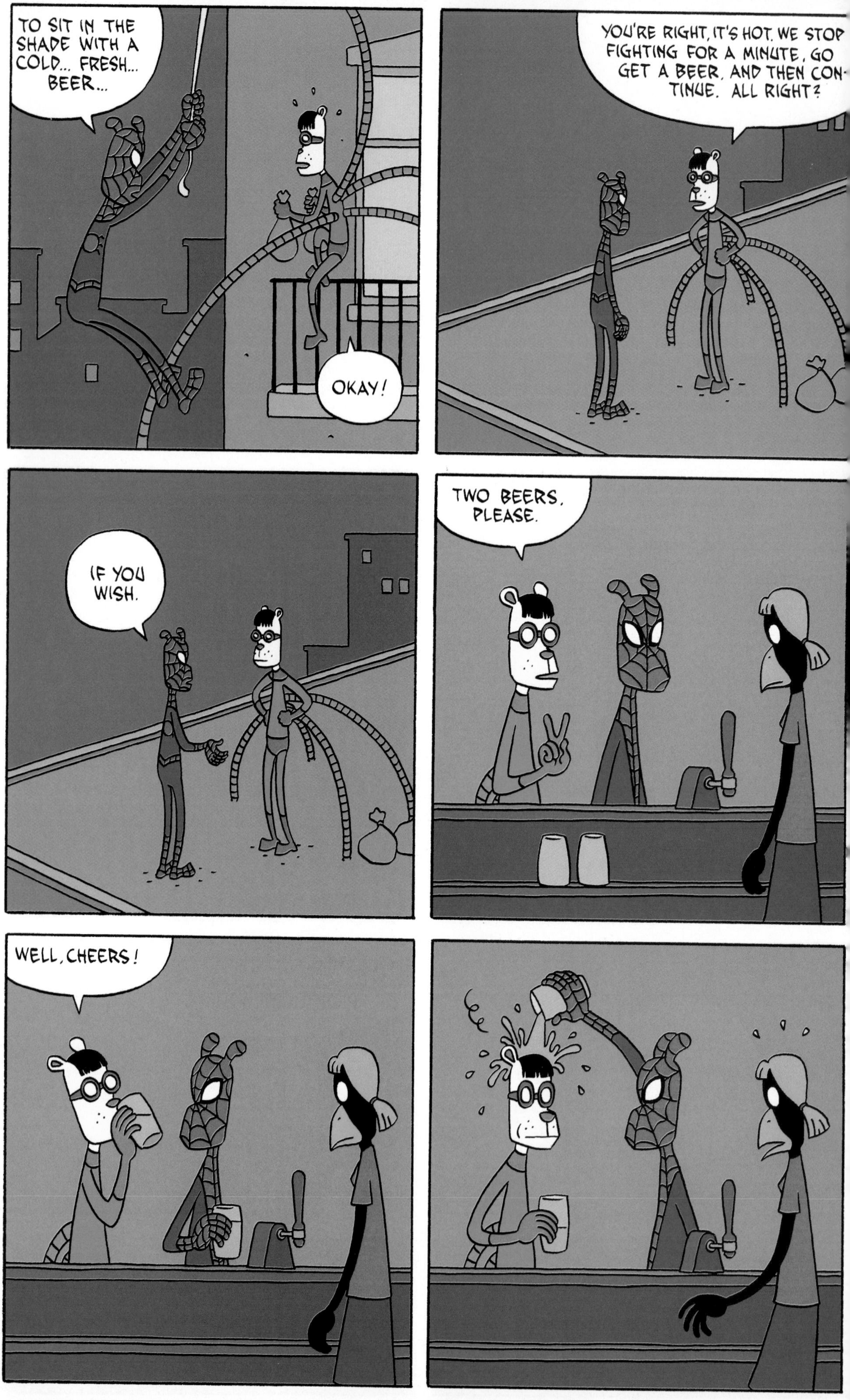
TO SIT IN THE SHADE WITH A COLD... FRESH... BEER...
OKAY!
YOU'RE RIGHT, IT'S HOT. WE STOP FIGHTING FOR A MINUTE, GO GET A BEER, AND THEN CONTINUE. ALL RIGHT?
IF YOU WISH.
TWO BEERS, PLEASE.
WELL, CHEERS!

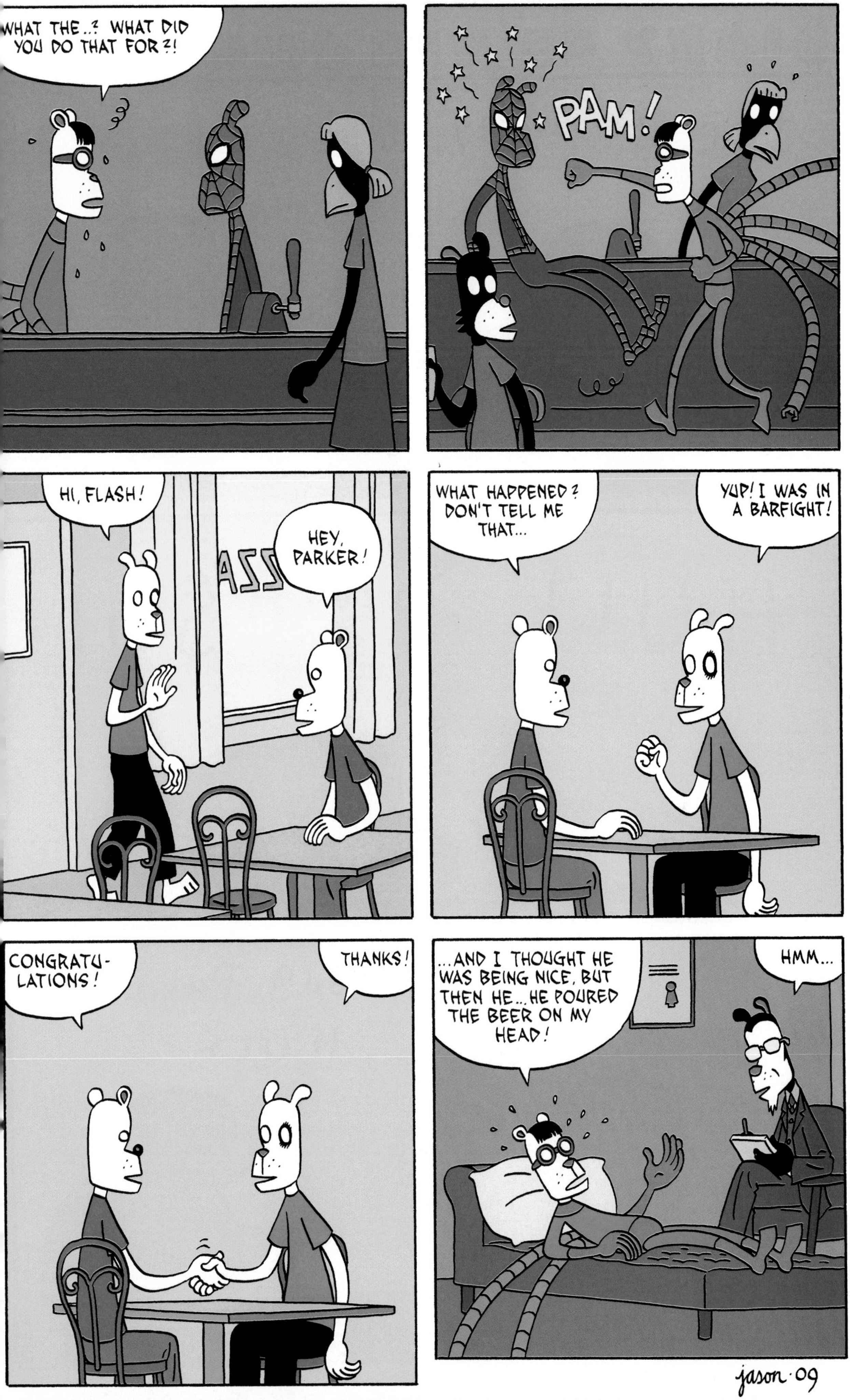
WHAT THE..? WHAT DID YOU DO THAT FOR?!
PAM!
HI, FLASH!
HEY, PARKER!
WHAT HAPPENED? DON'T TELL ME THAT...
YUP! I WAS IN A BARFIGHT!
CONGRATU-LATIONS!
THANKS!
...AND I THOUGHT HE WAS BEING NICE, BUT THEN HE... HE POURED THE BEER ON MY HEAD!
HMM...
jason·09

DIARY OF THE HULK

BY JAMES KOCHALKA

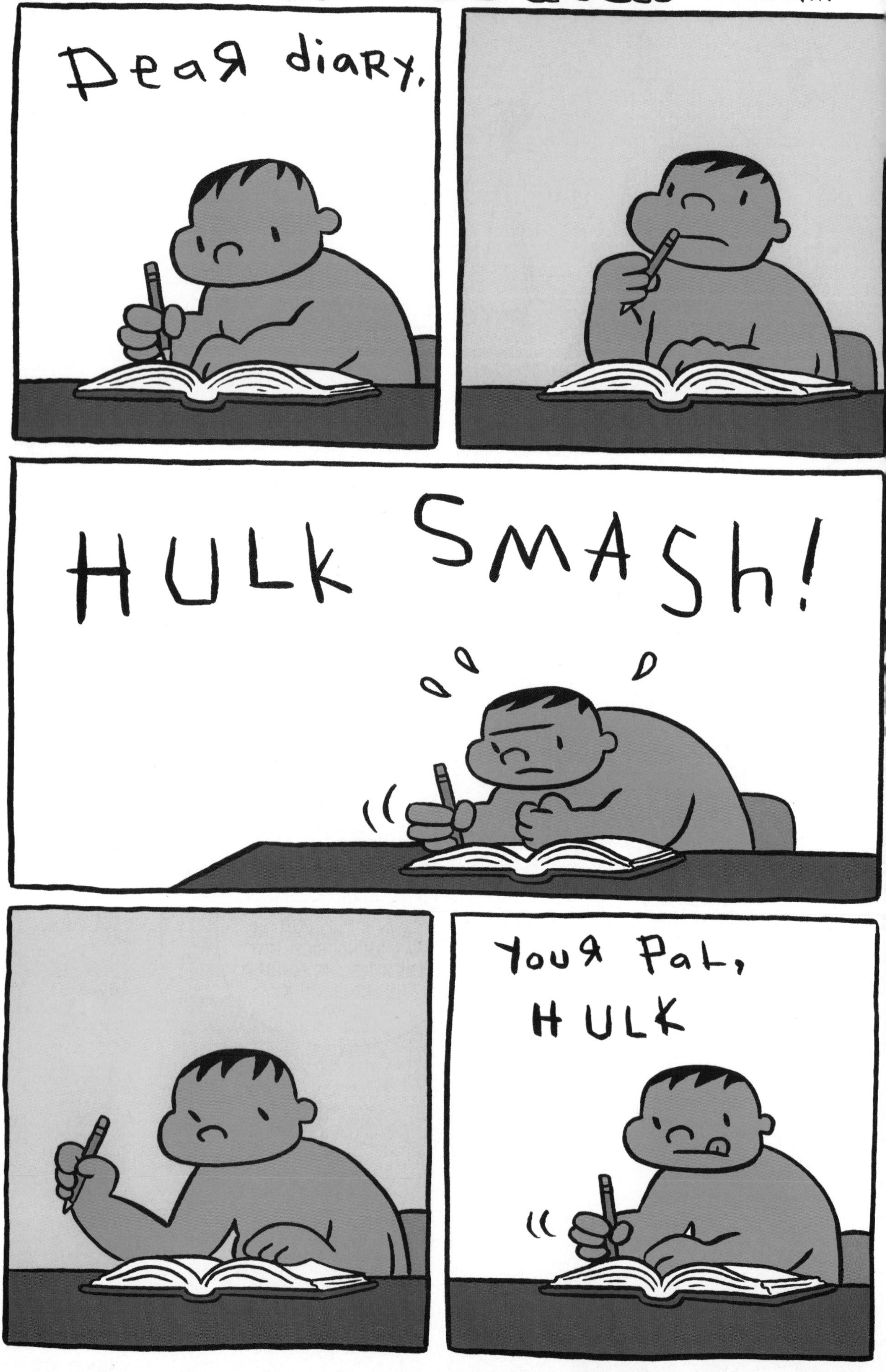

Dear diary,
HULK SMASH!
Your Pal,
HULK

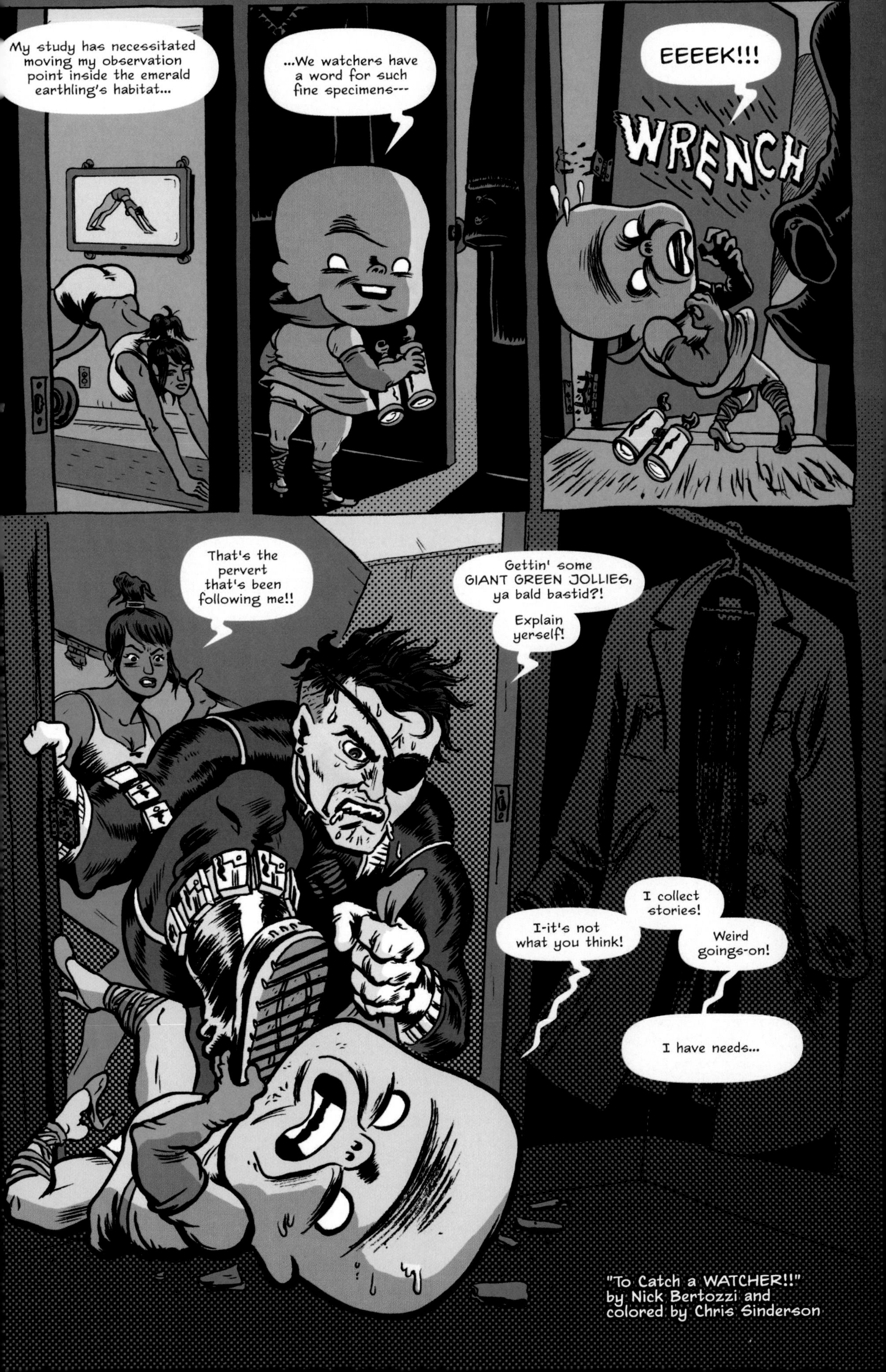
My study has necessitated moving my observation point inside the emerald earthling's habitat...
...We watchers have a word for such fine specimens---
EEEEK!!!
WRENCH
That's the pervert that's been following me!!
Gettin' some GIANT GREEN JOLLIES, ya bald bastid?!
Explain yerself!
I-it's not what you think!
I collect stories!
Weird goings-on!
I have needs...
"To Catch a WATCHER!!" by Nick Bertozzi and colored by Chris Sinderson

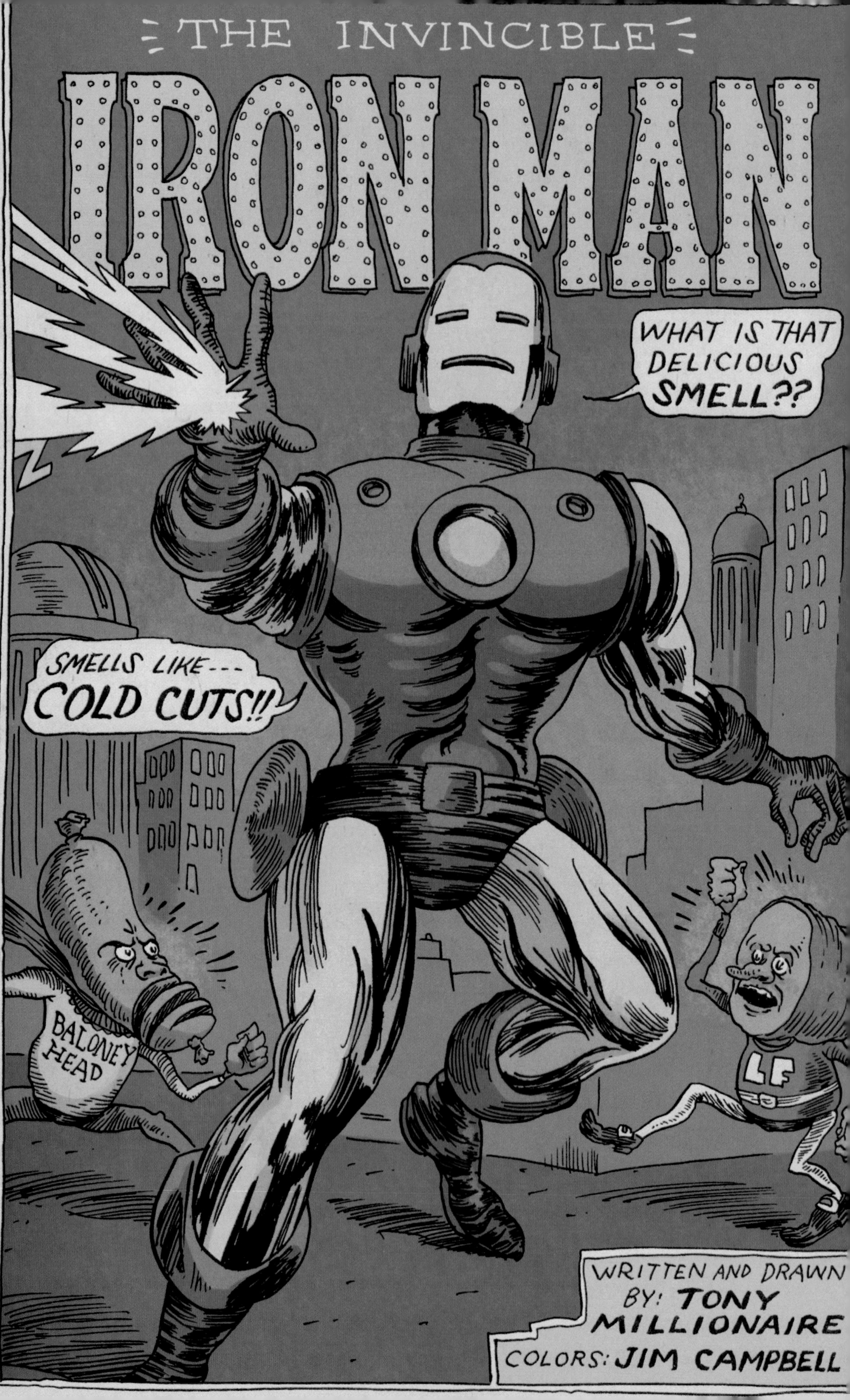
THE INVINCIBLE
IRON MAN
WHAT IS THAT DELICIOUS SMELL??
SMELLS LIKE--- COLD CUTS!!
BALONEY HEAD
LF
WRITTEN AND DRAWN BY: TONY MILLIONAIRE
COLORS: JIM CAMPBELL

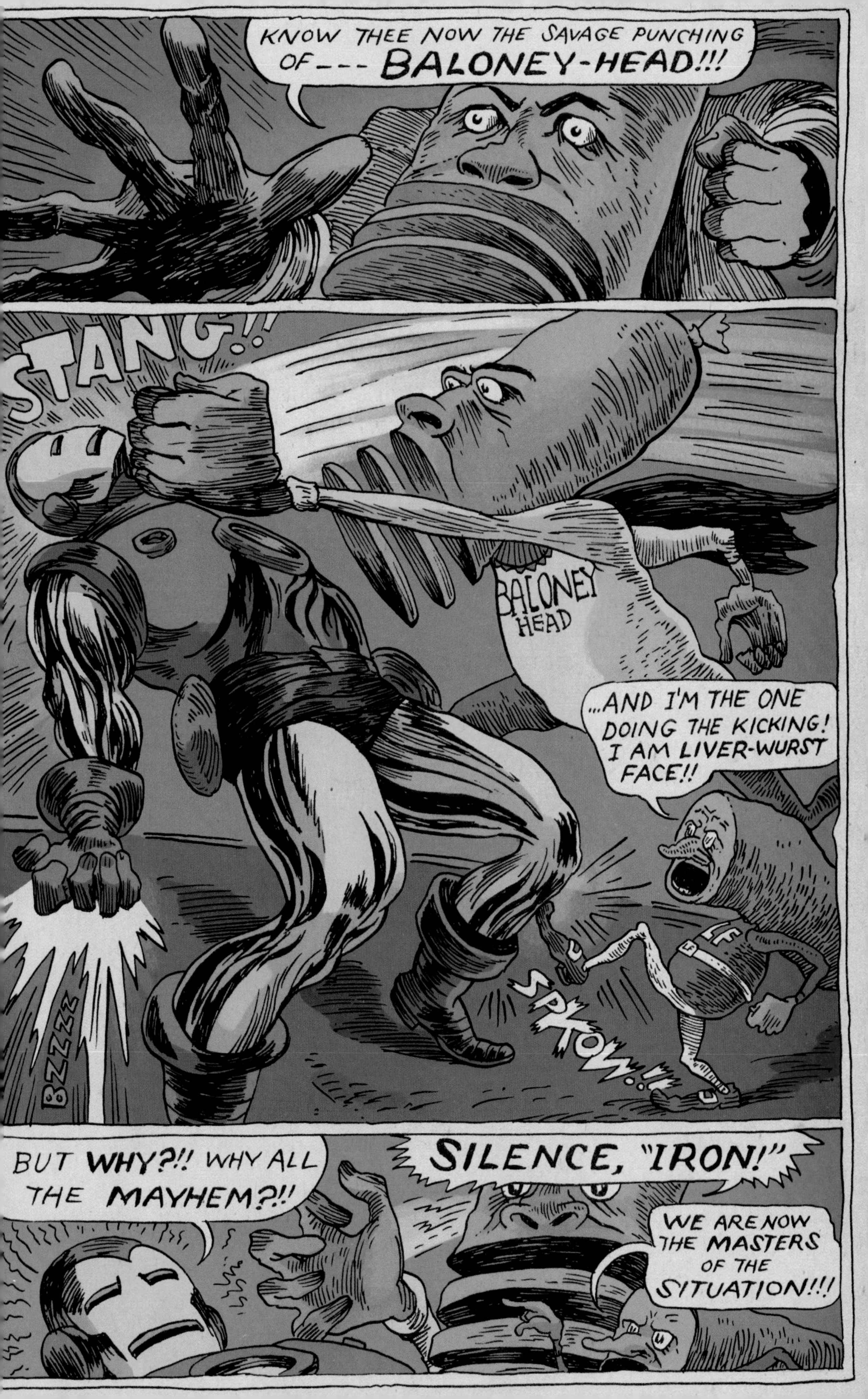
KNOW THEE NOW THE SAVAGE PUNCHING OF--- BALONEY-HEAD!!!
STANG!!
BALONEY HEAD
...AND I'M THE ONE DOING THE KICKING! I AM LIVER-WURST FACE!!
LF
SPKOW!!
BZZZZZ
BUT WHY?!! WHY ALL THE MAYHEM?!!
SILENCE, "IRON!"
WE ARE NOW THE MASTERS OF THE SITUATION!!!

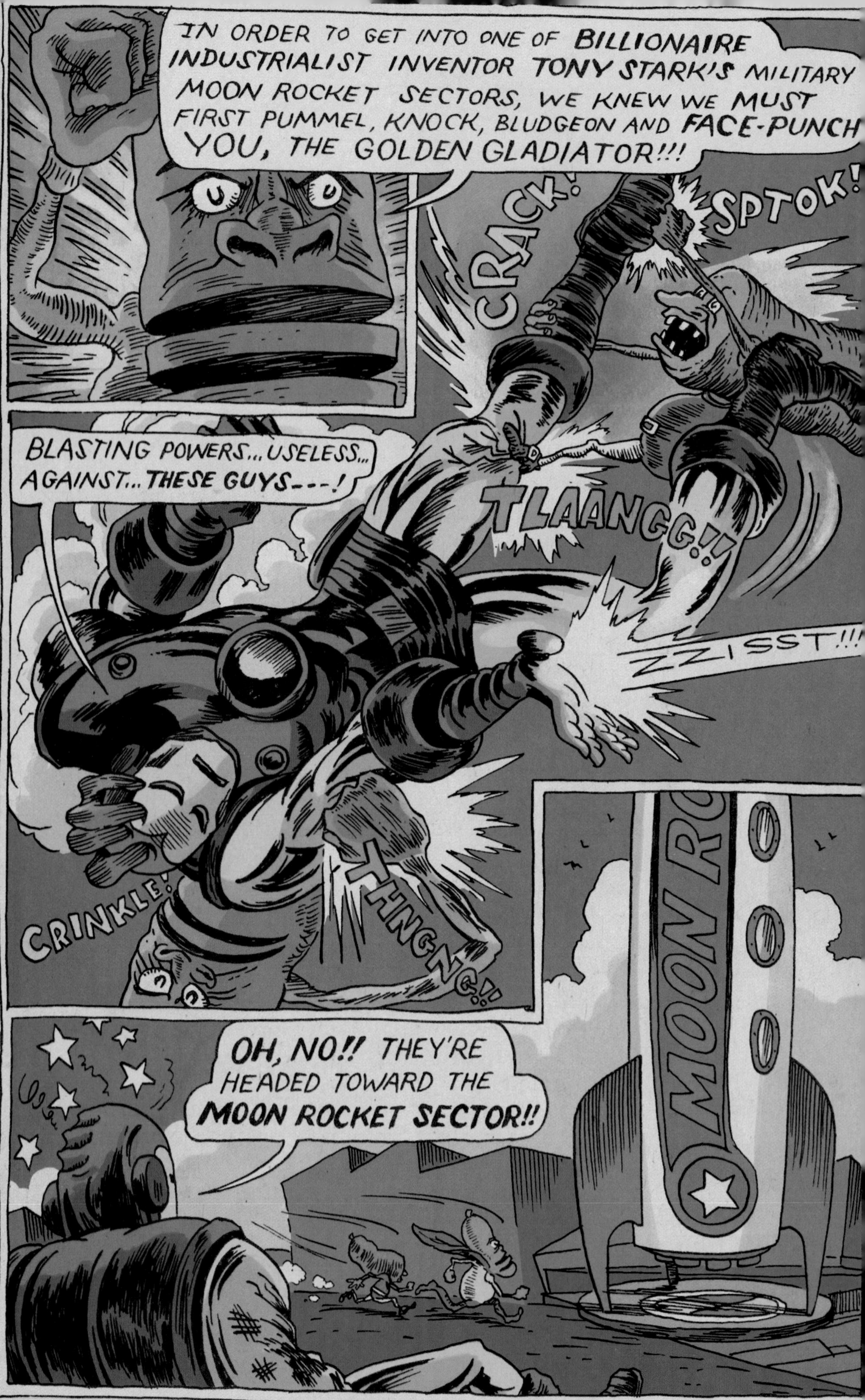
IN ORDER TO GET INTO ONE OF BILLIONAIRE INDUSTRIALIST INVENTOR TONY STARK'S MILITARY MOON ROCKET SECTORS, WE KNEW WE MUST FIRST PUMMEL, KNOCK, BLUDGEON AND FACE-PUNCH YOU, THE GOLDEN GLADIATOR!!!
CRACK!
SPTOK!
BLASTING POWERS... USELESS... AGAINST... THESE GUYS---!
TLAANGG!!
ZZISST!!!
CRINKLE!
THNGNG!!
MOON RO
OH, NO!! THEY'RE HEADED TOWARD THE MOON ROCKET SECTOR!!

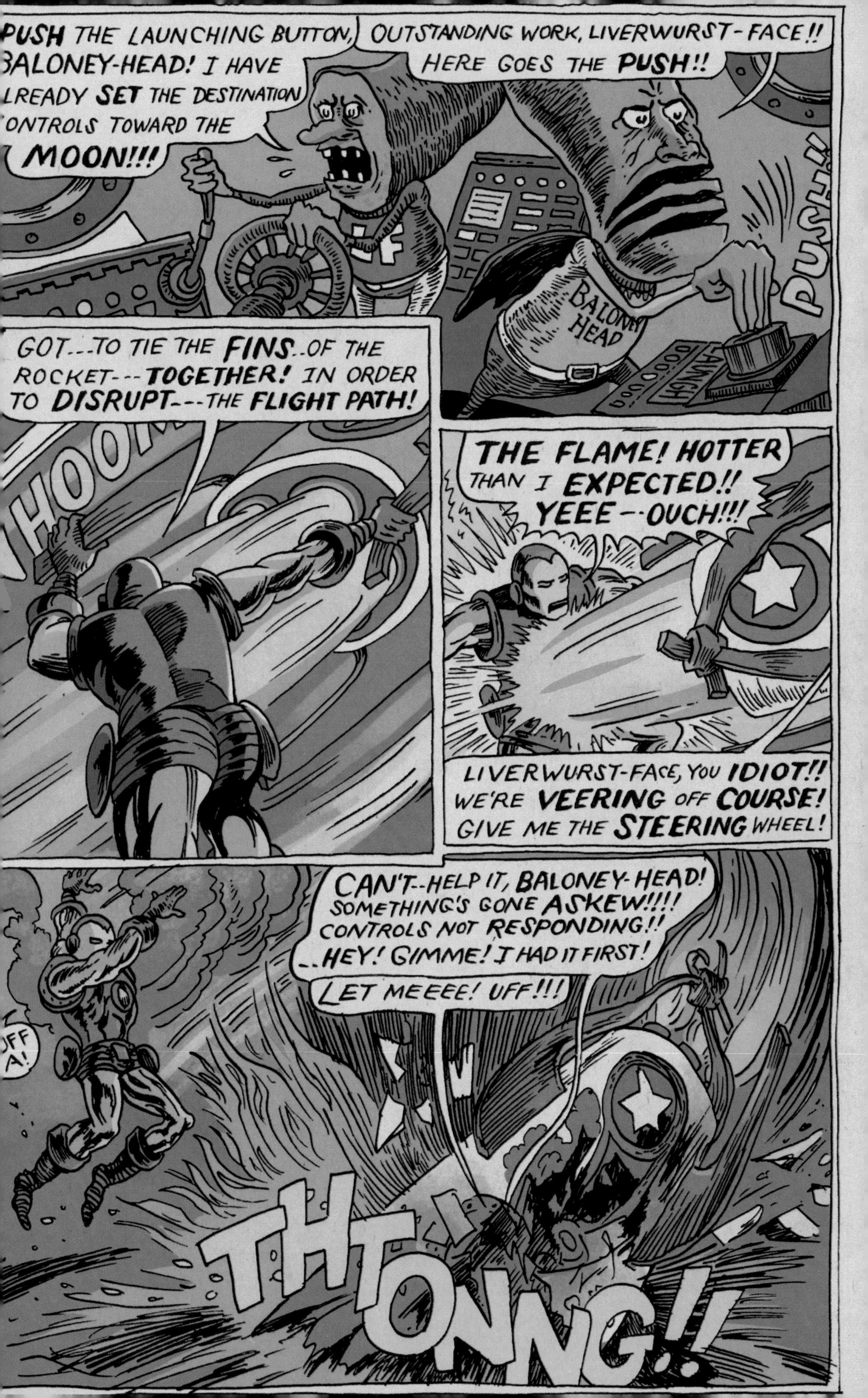
PUSH THE LAUNCHING BUTTON, BALONEY-HEAD! I HAVE ALREADY SET THE DESTINATION CONTROLS TOWARD THE MOON!!!
OUTSTANDING WORK, LIVERWURST-FACE!! HERE GOES THE PUSH!!
PUSH!!
LF
BALONEY HEAD
LAUNCH
GOT---TO TIE THE FINS--OF THE ROCKET---TOGETHER! IN ORDER TO DISRUPT---THE FLIGHT PATH!
THE FLAME! HOTTER THAN I EXPECTED!! YEEE--OUCH!!!
LIVERWURST-FACE, YOU IDIOT!! WE'RE VEERING OFF COURSE! GIVE ME THE STEERING WHEEL!
CAN'T--HELP IT, BALONEY-HEAD! SOMETHING'S GONE ASKEW!!!! CONTROLS NOT RESPONDING!! ..HEY! GIMME! I HAD IT FIRST!
LET MEEEE! UFF!!!
THTONNG!!

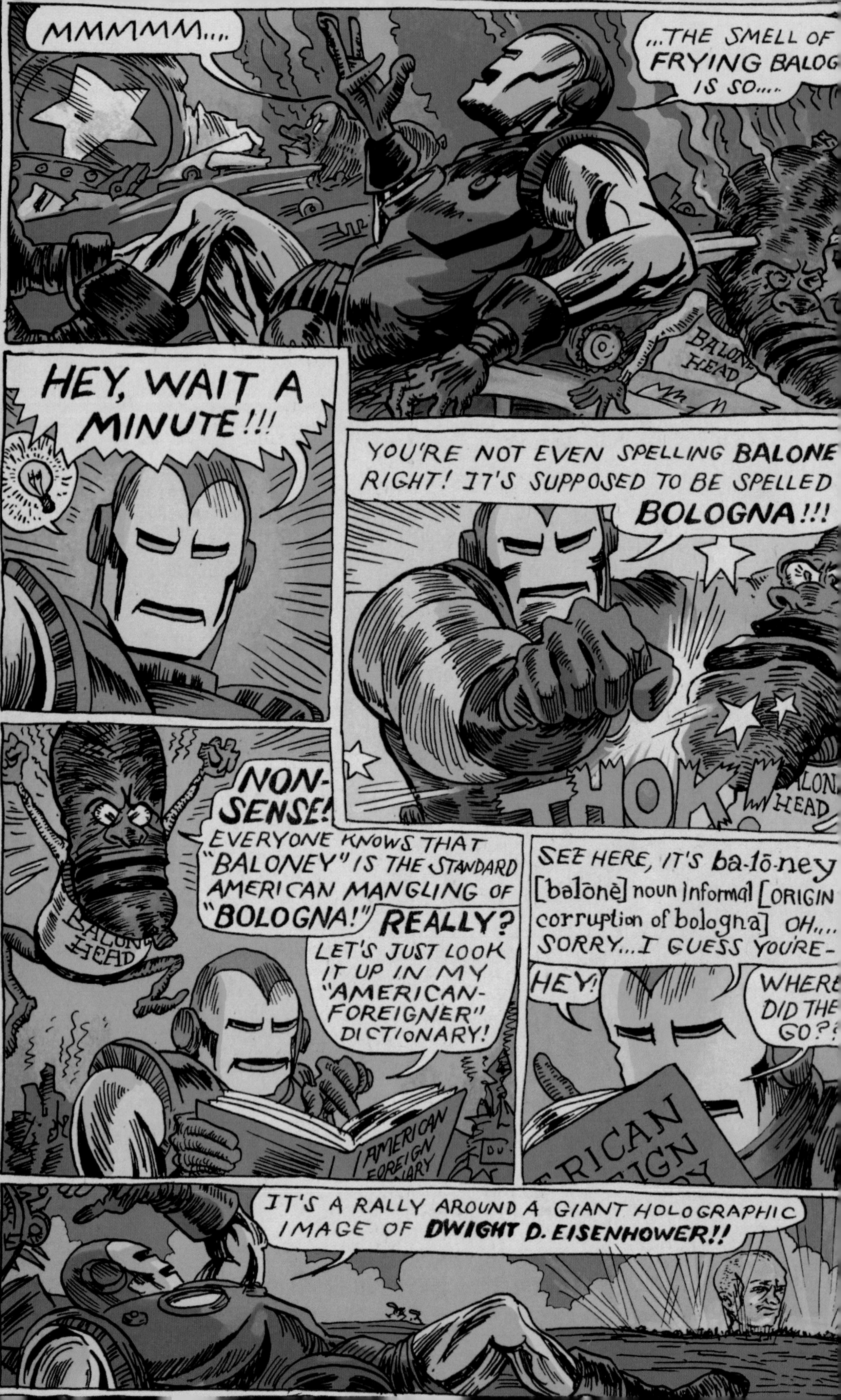
MMMMMM....
...THE SMELL OF FRYING BALOG IS SO....
BALONE HEAD
HEY, WAIT A MINUTE!!!
YOU'RE NOT EVEN SPELLING BALONE RIGHT! IT'S SUPPOSED TO BE SPELLED BOLOGNA!!!
THOK!
BALONE HEAD
NON-SENSE!
EVERYONE KNOWS THAT "BALONEY" IS THE STANDARD AMERICAN MANGLING OF "BOLOGNA!"
BALONE HEAD
REALLY?
LET'S JUST LOOK IT UP IN MY "AMERICAN-FOREIGNER" DICTIONARY!
AMERICAN FOREIGN DICTIONARY
SEE HERE, IT'S ba-lō-ney [balōnē] noun informal [ORIGIN corruption of bologna] OH.... SORRY...I GUESS YOU'RE-
HEY!
WHERE DID THE GO?
IT'S A RALLY AROUND A GIANT HOLOGRAPHIC IMAGE OF DWIGHT D. EISENHOWER!!

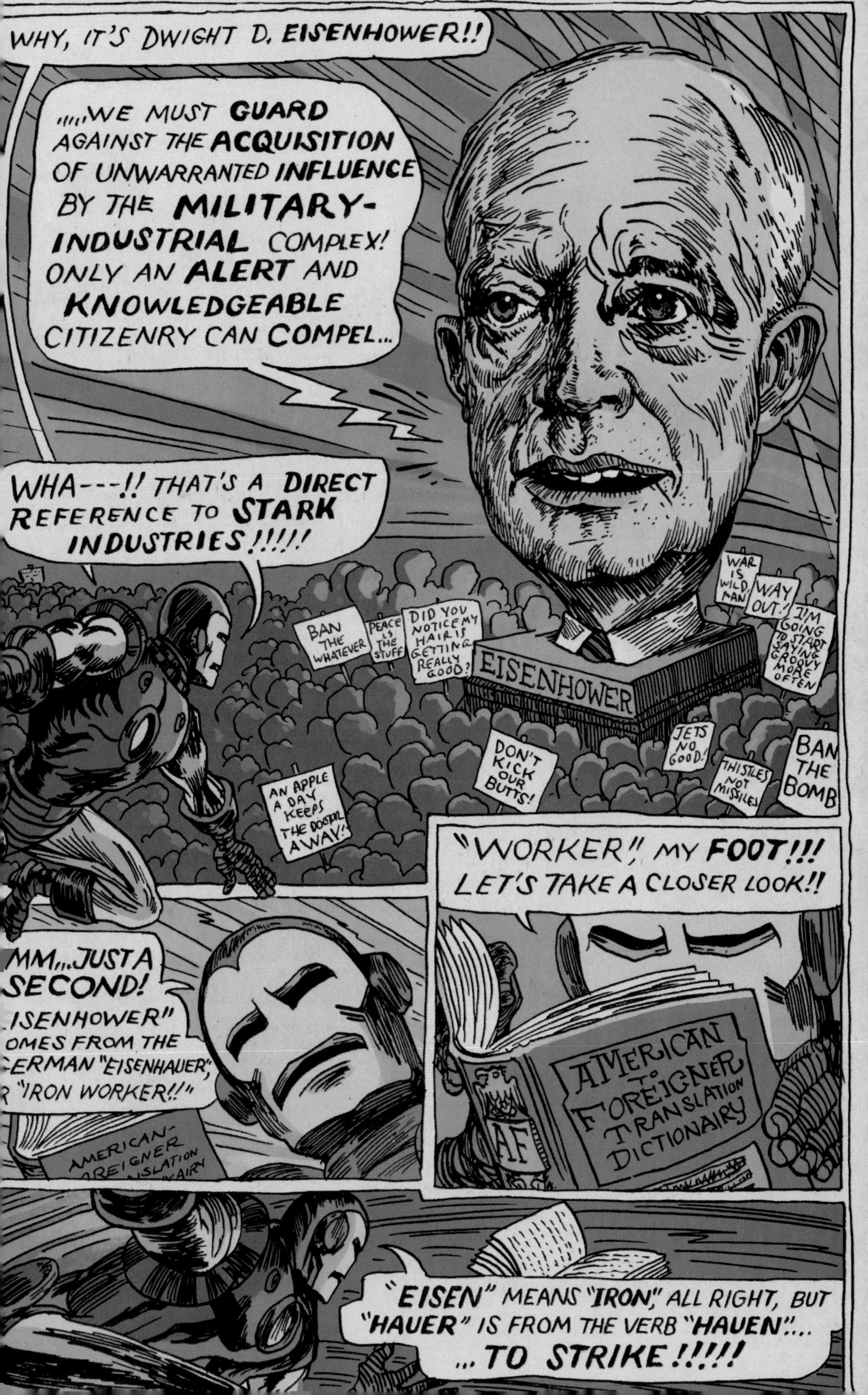

WHY, IT'S DWIGHT D. EISENHOWER!!
....WE MUST GUARD AGAINST THE ACQUISITION OF UNWARRANTED INFLUENCE BY THE MILITARY-INDUSTRIAL COMPLEX! ONLY AN ALERT AND KNOWLEDGEABLE CITIZENRY CAN COMPEL...
WHA---!! THAT'S A DIRECT REFERENCE TO STARK INDUSTRIES!!!!!
BAN THE WHATEVER
PEACE IS THE STUFF
DID YOU NOTICE MY HAIR IS GETTING REALLY GOOD?
EISENHOWER
WAR IS WILD, MAN
WAY OUT!
I'M GOING TO START SAYING GROOVY MORE OFTEN
AN APPLE A DAY KEEPS THE DOCTOR AWAY!
DON'T KICK OUR BUTTS!
JETS NO GOOD!
THISTLES NOT MISSILES
BAN THE BOMB
MM...JUST A SECOND! ...ISENHOWER" ...OMES FROM THE ...ERMAN "EISENHAUER", ...R "IRON WORKER!!"
"WORKER," MY FOOT!!! LET'S TAKE A CLOSER LOOK!!
AMERICAN TO FOREIGNER TRANSLATION DICTIONAIRY
AF
"EISEN" MEANS "IRON," ALL RIGHT, BUT "HAUER" IS FROM THE VERB "HAUEN"... ...TO STRIKE!!!!!

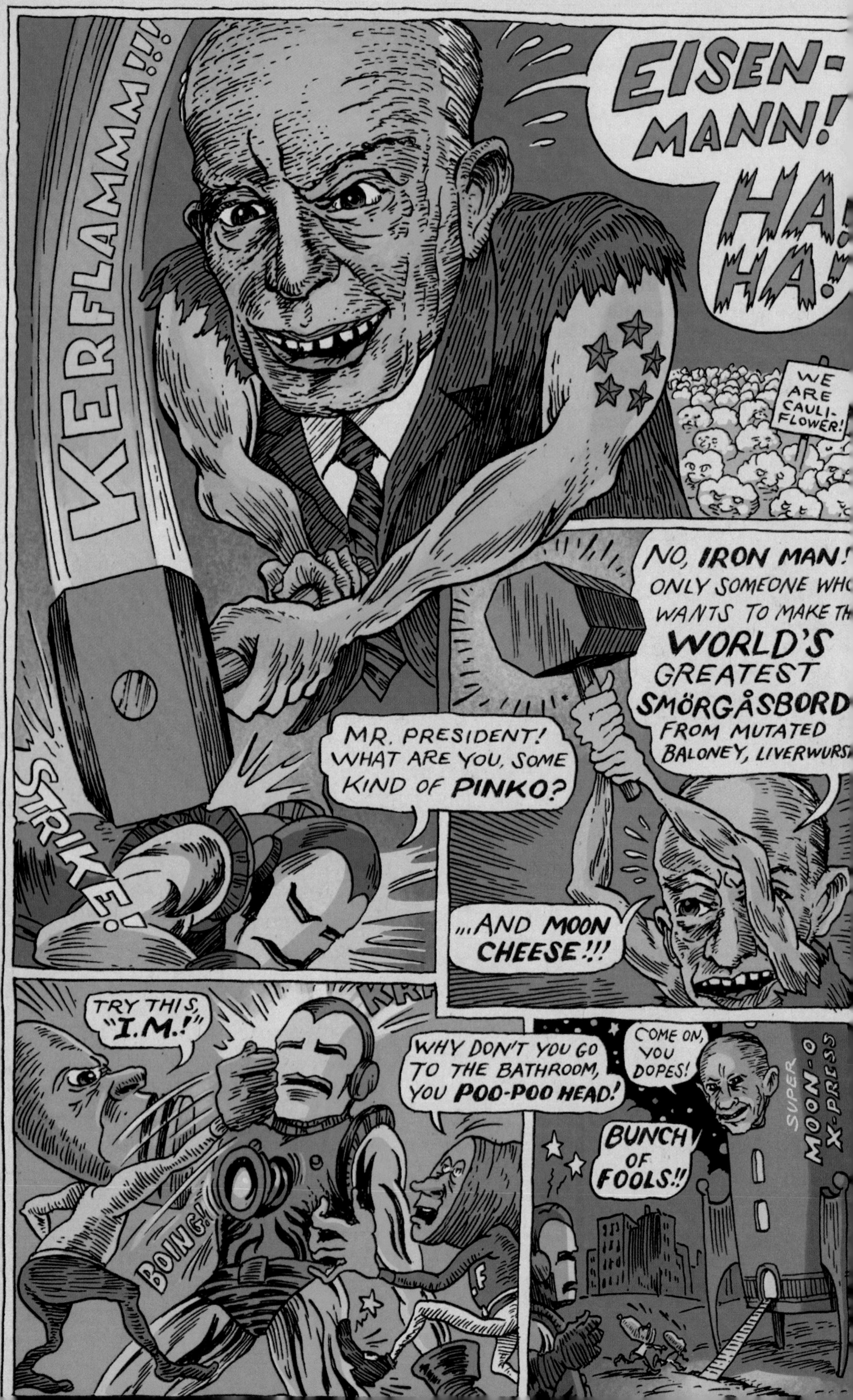
KERFLAMM!!!
EISEN-MANN! HA! HA!
WE ARE CAULI-FLOWER!
STRIKE!
MR. PRESIDENT! WHAT ARE YOU, SOME KIND OF PINKO?
NO, IRON MAN! ONLY SOMEONE WHO WANTS TO MAKE TH WORLD'S GREATEST SMÖRGÅSBORD FROM MUTATED BALONEY, LIVERWURS
...AND MOON CHEESE!!!
TRY THIS, "I.M.!"
KRA
WHY DON'T YOU GO TO THE BATHROOM, YOU POO-POO HEAD!
BOING!
COME ON, YOU DOPES!
BUNCH OF FOOLS!!
SUPER MOON-O X-PRESS

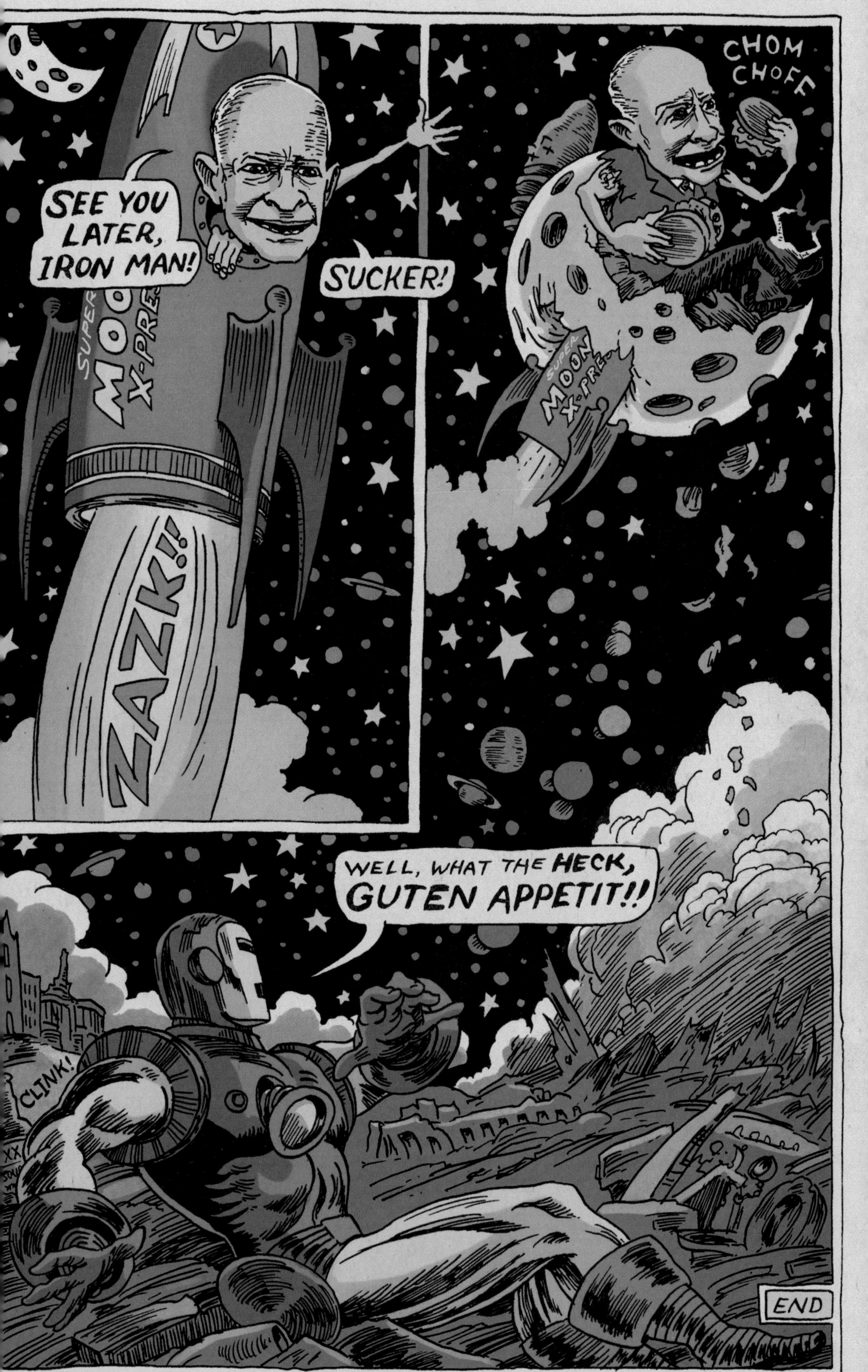
SEE YOU LATER, IRON MAN!
SUPER MOON X-PRESS
SUCKER!
ZAZK!!
CHOM CHOFF
WELL, WHAT THE HECK, GUTEN APPETIT!!
CLINK!
END

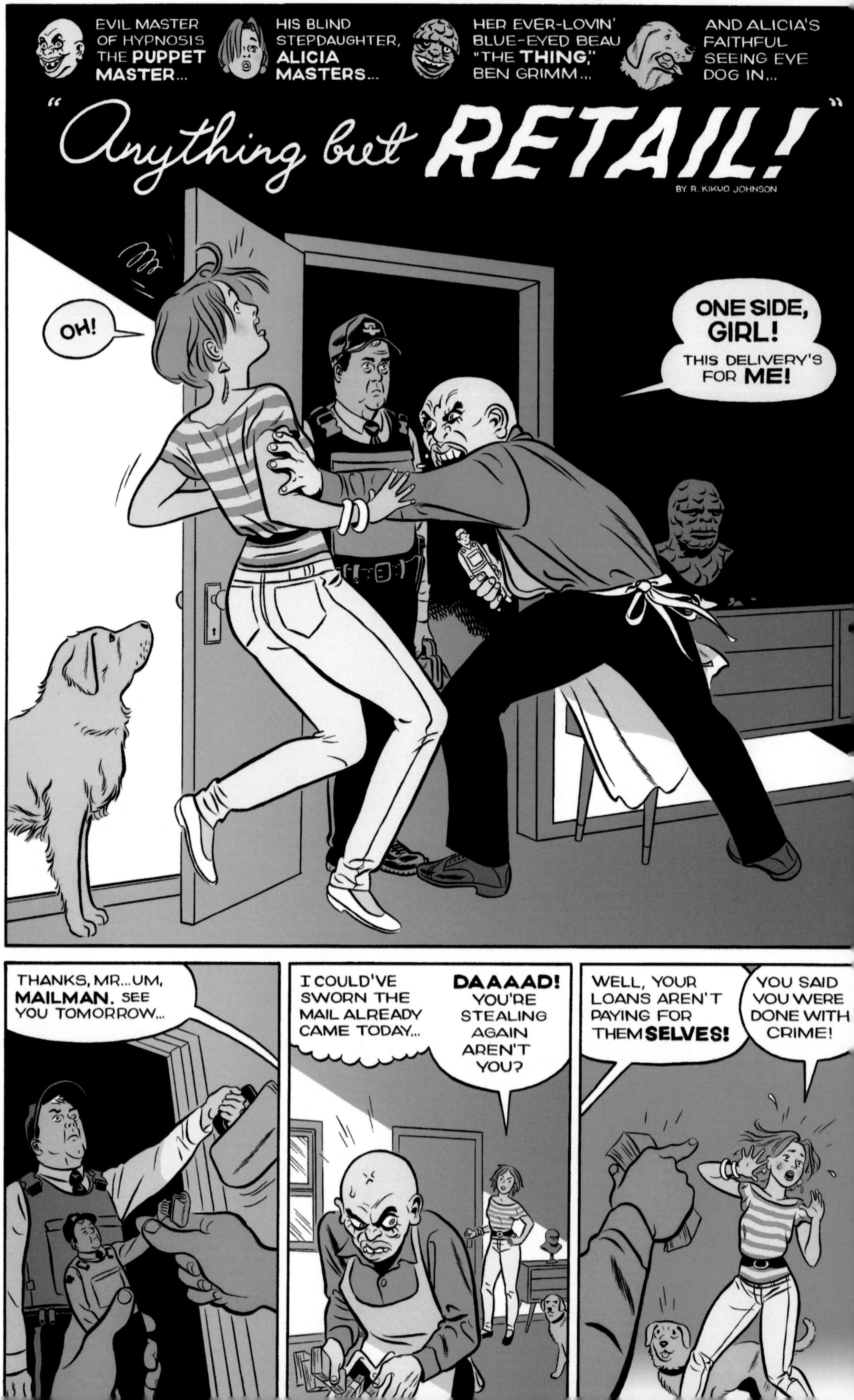

EVIL MASTER OF HYPNOSIS THE PUPPET MASTER...
HIS BLIND STEPDAUGHTER, ALICIA MASTERS...
HER EVER-LOVIN' BLUE-EYED BEAU "THE THING," BEN GRIMM...
AND ALICIA'S FAITHFUL SEEING EYE DOG IN...
"Anything but RETAIL!"
BY R. KIKUO JOHNSON
OH!
ONE SIDE, GIRL! THIS DELIVERY'S FOR ME!
THANKS, MR...UM, MAILMAN. SEE YOU TOMORROW...
I COULD'VE SWORN THE MAIL ALREADY CAME TODAY...
DAAAAD! YOU'RE STEALING AGAIN AREN'T YOU?
WELL, YOUR LOANS AREN'T PAYING FOR THEMSELVES!
YOU SAID YOU WERE DONE WITH CRIME!

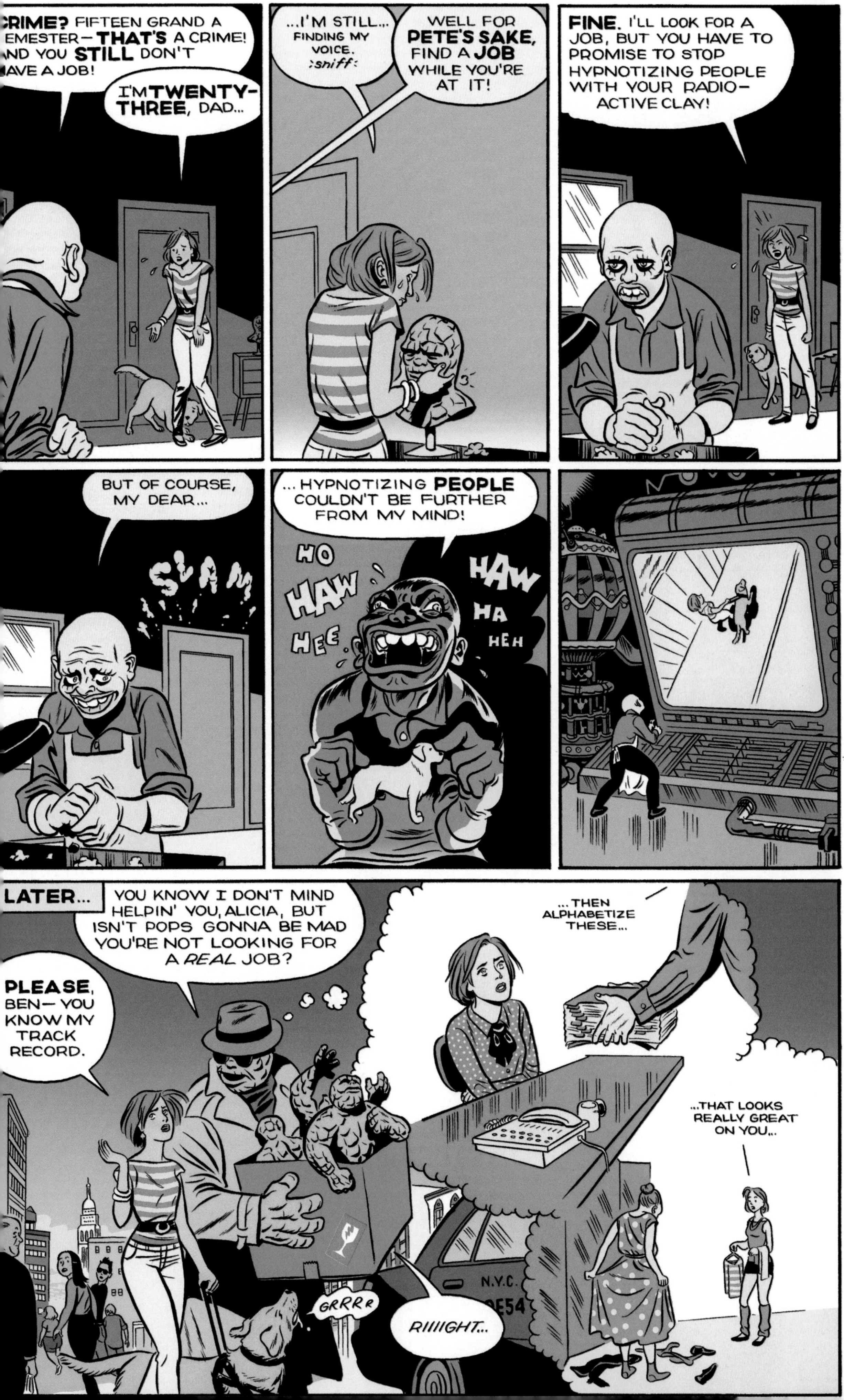

CRIME? FIFTEEN GRAND A EMESTER—THAT'S A CRIME! ND YOU STILL DON'T AVE A JOB!
I'M TWENTY-THREE, DAD...
...I'M STILL... FINDING MY VOICE. :sniff:
WELL FOR PETE'S SAKE, FIND A JOB WHILE YOU'RE AT IT!
FINE. I'LL LOOK FOR A JOB, BUT YOU HAVE TO PROMISE TO STOP HYPNOTIZING PEOPLE WITH YOUR RADIO-ACTIVE CLAY!
BUT OF COURSE, MY DEAR...
SLAM
...HYPNOTIZING PEOPLE COULDN'T BE FURTHER FROM MY MIND!
HO
HAW
HEE
HAW
HA
HEH
LATER...
YOU KNOW I DON'T MIND HELPIN' YOU, ALICIA, BUT ISN'T POPS GONNA BE MAD YOU'RE NOT LOOKING FOR A REAL JOB?
PLEASE, BEN— YOU KNOW MY TRACK RECORD.
...THEN ALPHABETIZE THESE...
...THAT LOOKS REALLY GREAT ON YOU...
GRRRR
RIIIIGHT...

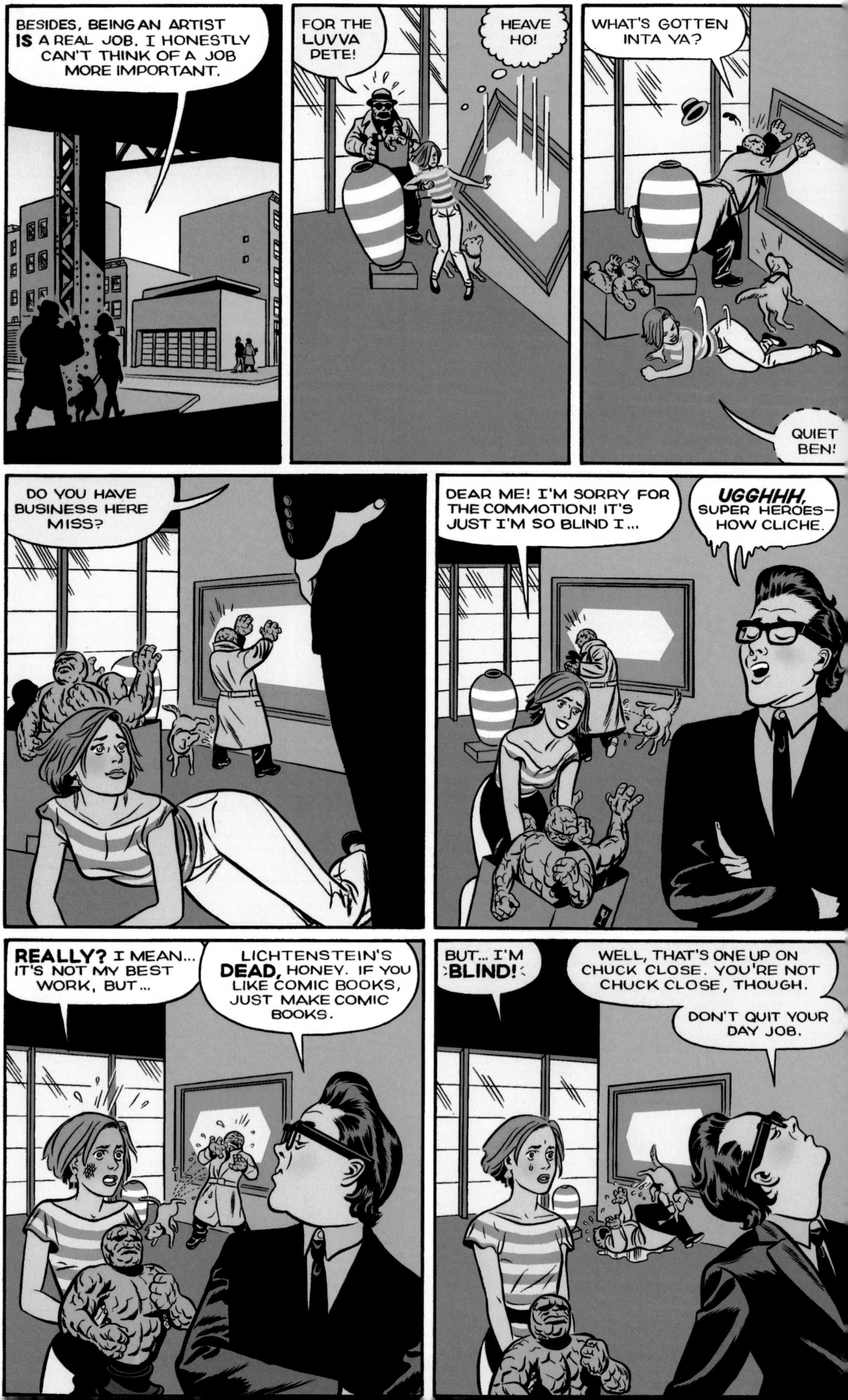

BESIDES, BEING AN ARTIST IS A REAL JOB. I HONESTLY CAN'T THINK OF A JOB MORE IMPORTANT.
FOR THE LUVVA PETE!
HEAVE HO!
WHAT'S GOTTEN INTA YA?
QUIET BEN!
DO YOU HAVE BUSINESS HERE MISS?
DEAR ME! I'M SORRY FOR THE COMMOTION! IT'S JUST I'M SO BLIND I...
UGGHHH, SUPER HEROES— HOW CLICHE.
REALLY? I MEAN... IT'S NOT MY BEST WORK, BUT...
LICHTENSTEIN'S DEAD, HONEY. IF YOU LIKE COMIC BOOKS, JUST MAKE COMIC BOOKS.
BUT... I'M BLIND!
WELL, THAT'S ONE UP ON CHUCK CLOSE. YOU'RE NOT CHUCK CLOSE, THOUGH.
DON'T QUIT YOUR DAY JOB.

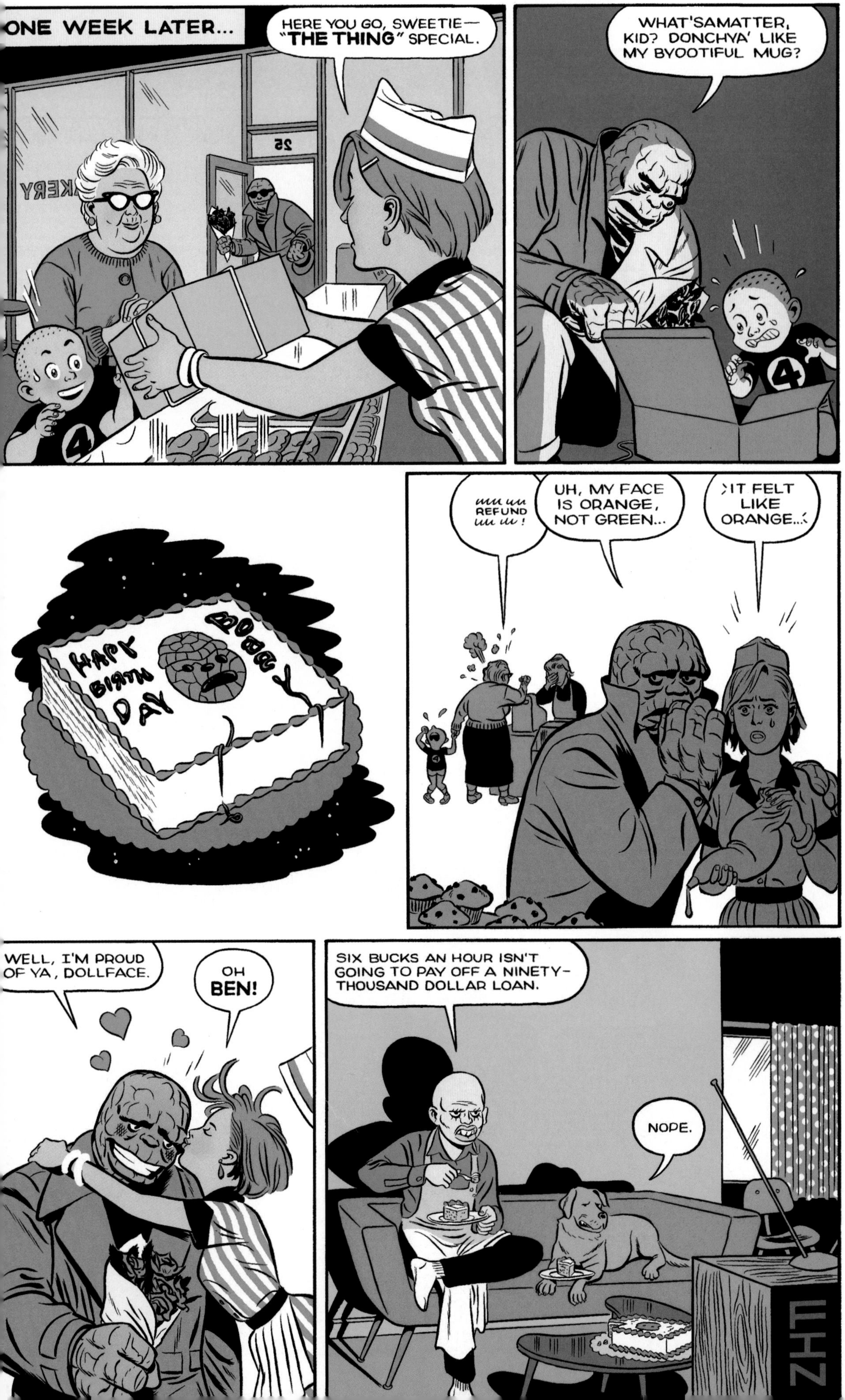
ONE WEEK LATER...
HERE YOU GO, SWEETIE— "THE THING" SPECIAL.
WHAT'SAMATTER, KID? DONCHYA' LIKE MY BYOOTIFUL MUG?
REFUND
UH, MY FACE IS ORANGE, NOT GREEN...
IT FELT LIKE ORANGE...
WELL, I'M PROUD OF YA, DOLLFACE.
OH BEN!
SIX BUCKS AN HOUR ISN'T GOING TO PAY OFF A NINETY-THOUSAND DOLLAR LOAN.
NOPE.

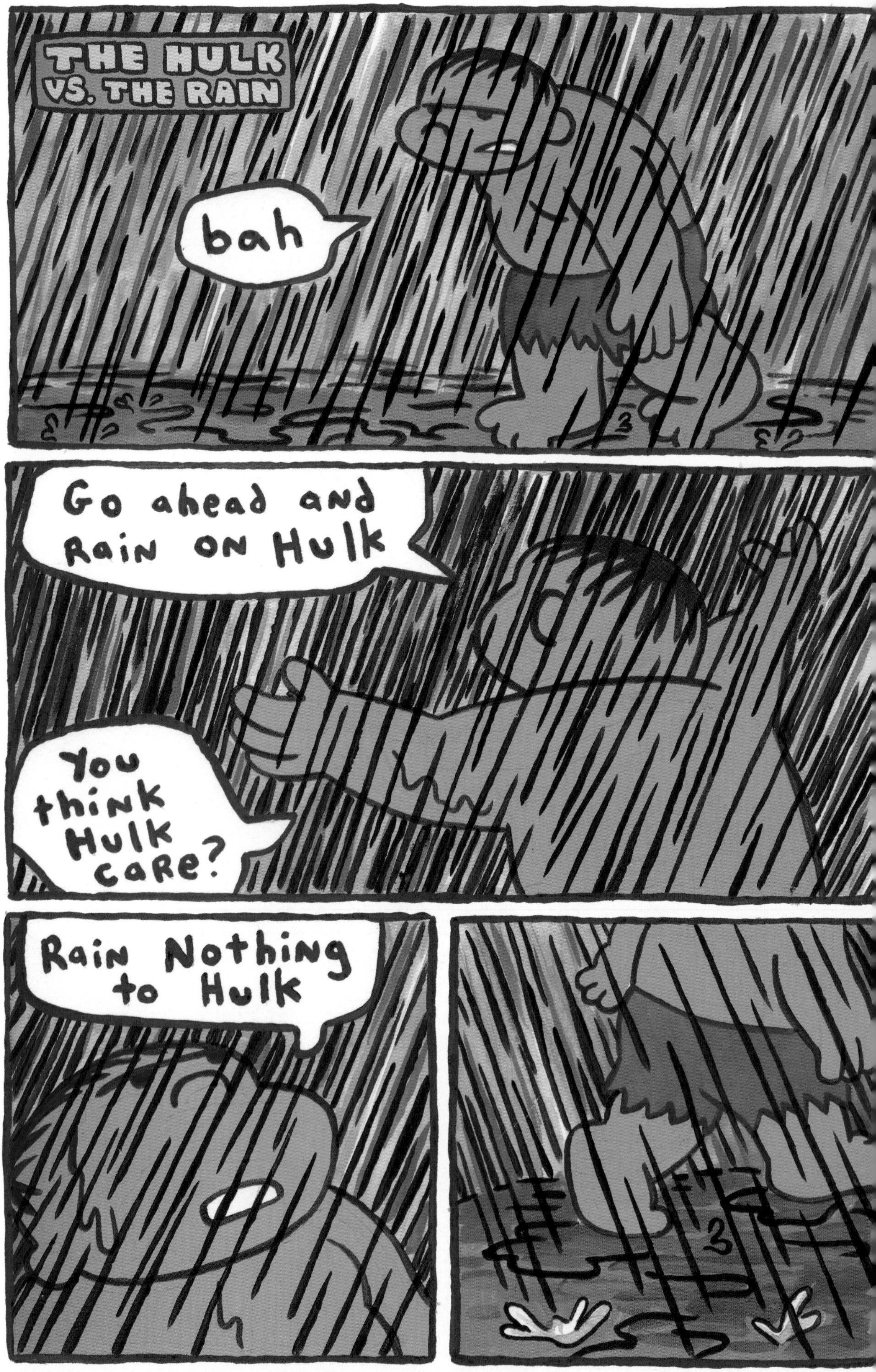
THE HULK VS. THE RAIN
bah
Go ahead and Rain on Hulk
You think Hulk care?
Rain Nothing to Hulk

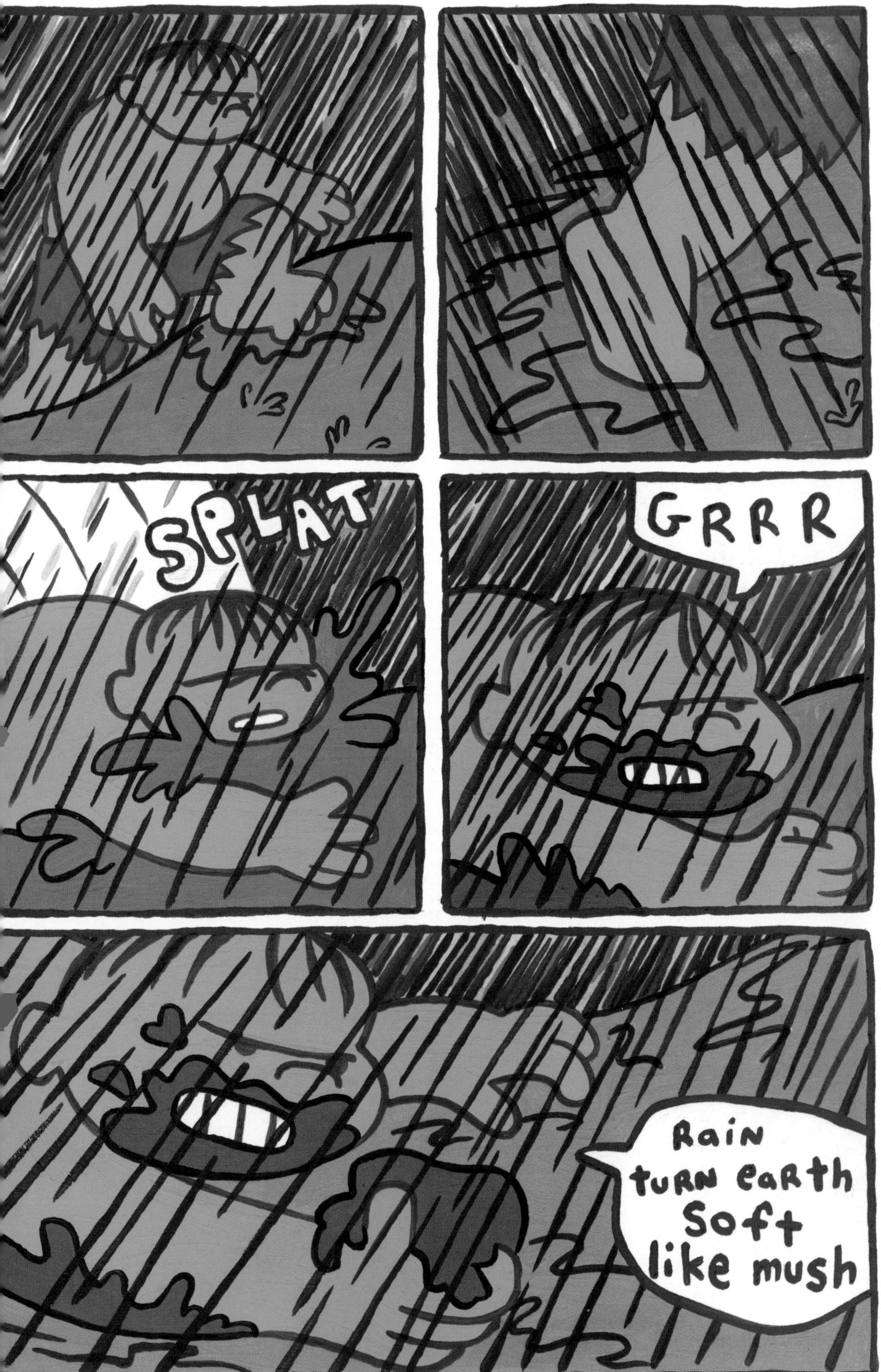
SPLAT
GRRR
Rain turn earth Soft like mush

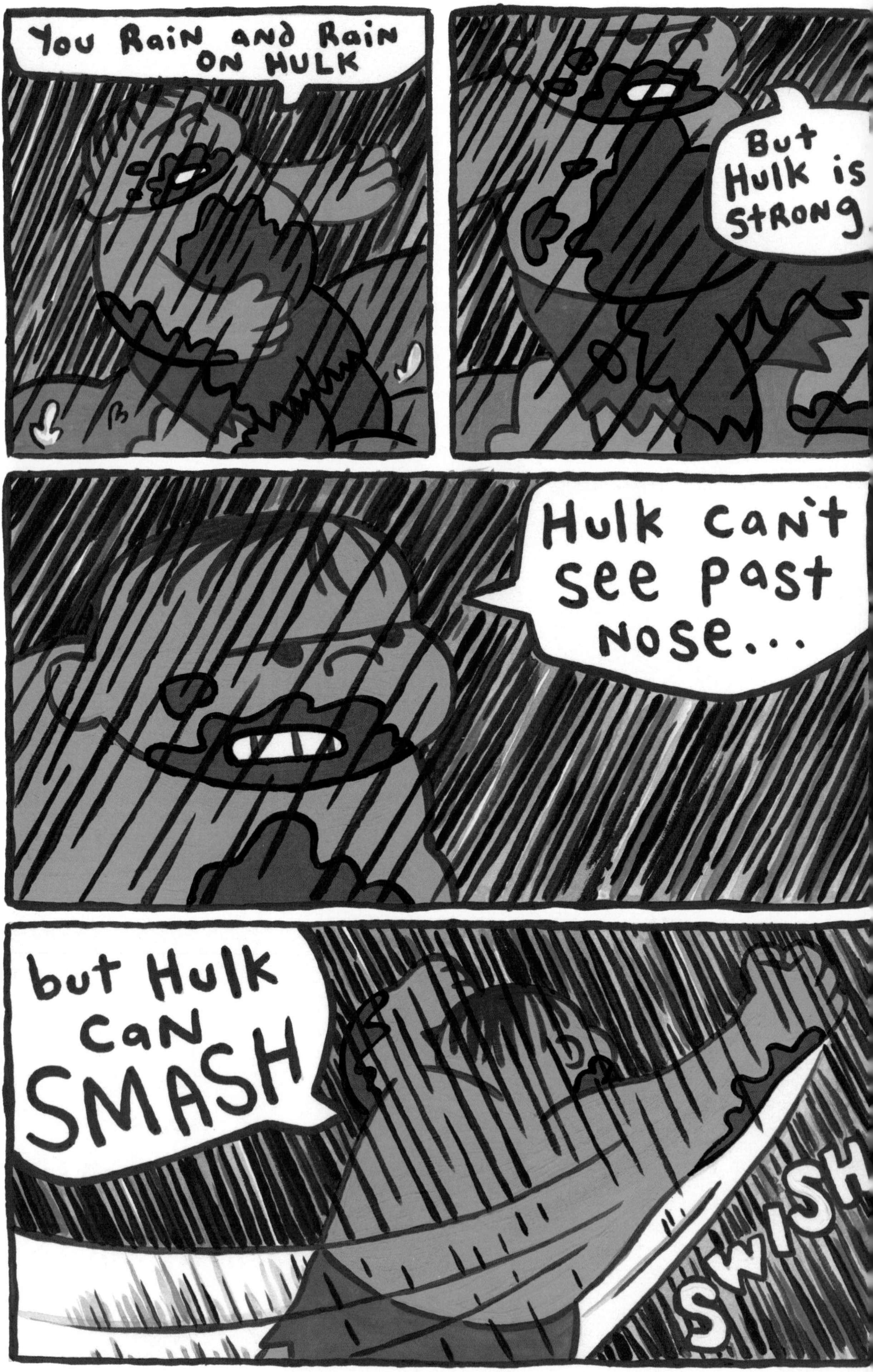
You Rain and Rain ON HULK
But Hulk is strong.
Hulk can't see past nose...
but Hulk can SMASH
SWISH

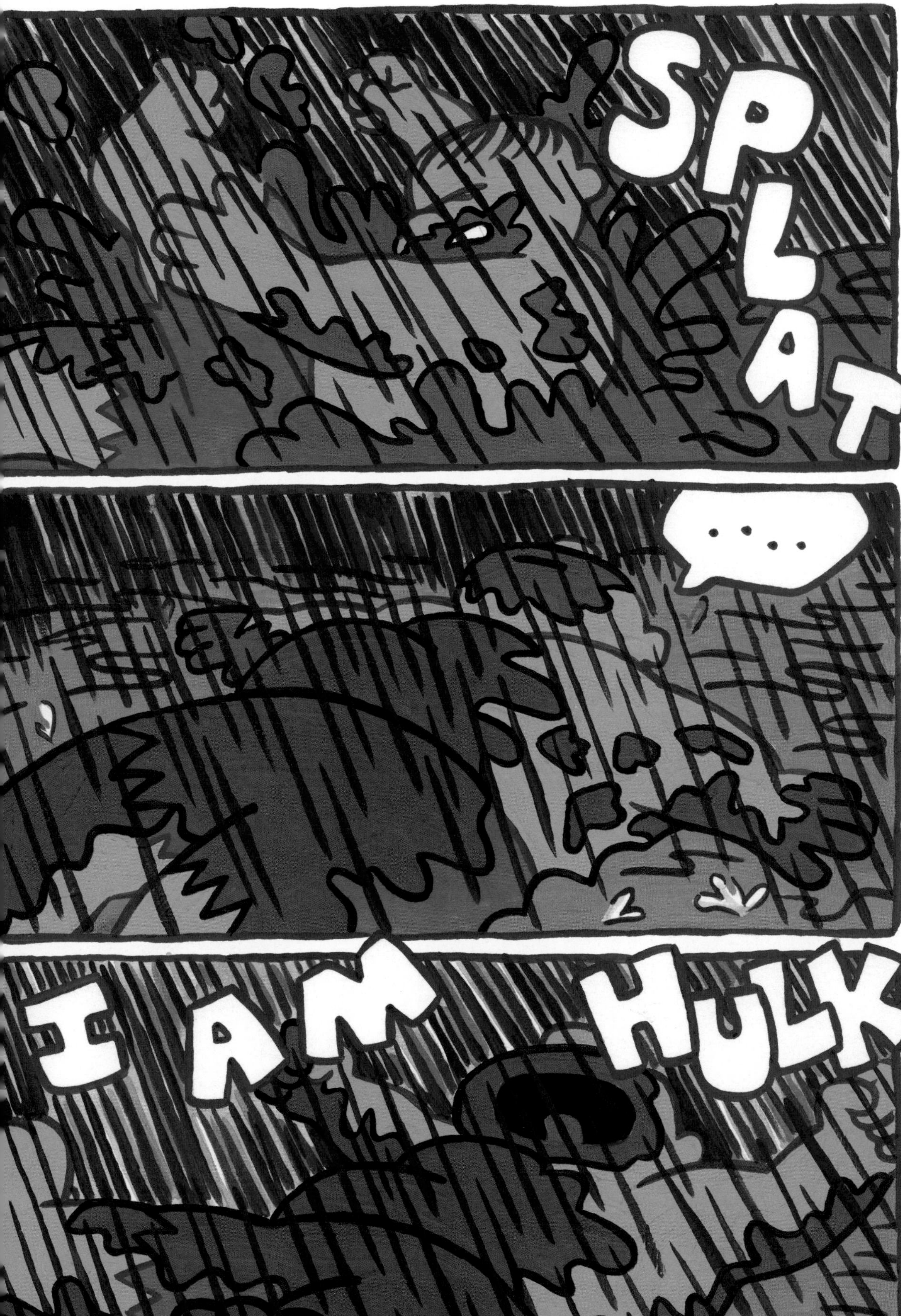
SPLAT
. . . . .
I AM HULK

BY JAMES KOCHALKA

THE END

Deep in the jungles of Haiti, under the tutelage of the great voodoo ***master,*** Papa Jambo, Dr. Jericho Drumm fused with the ***soul*** of his murdered twin brother, Daniel, to become ***legend***...he who is master of ***fire***...he who can control any living ***reptile***...he who can create ***smoke*** and the sounds of ***drums: Brother Voodoo – the Man Who Lived TWICE!***

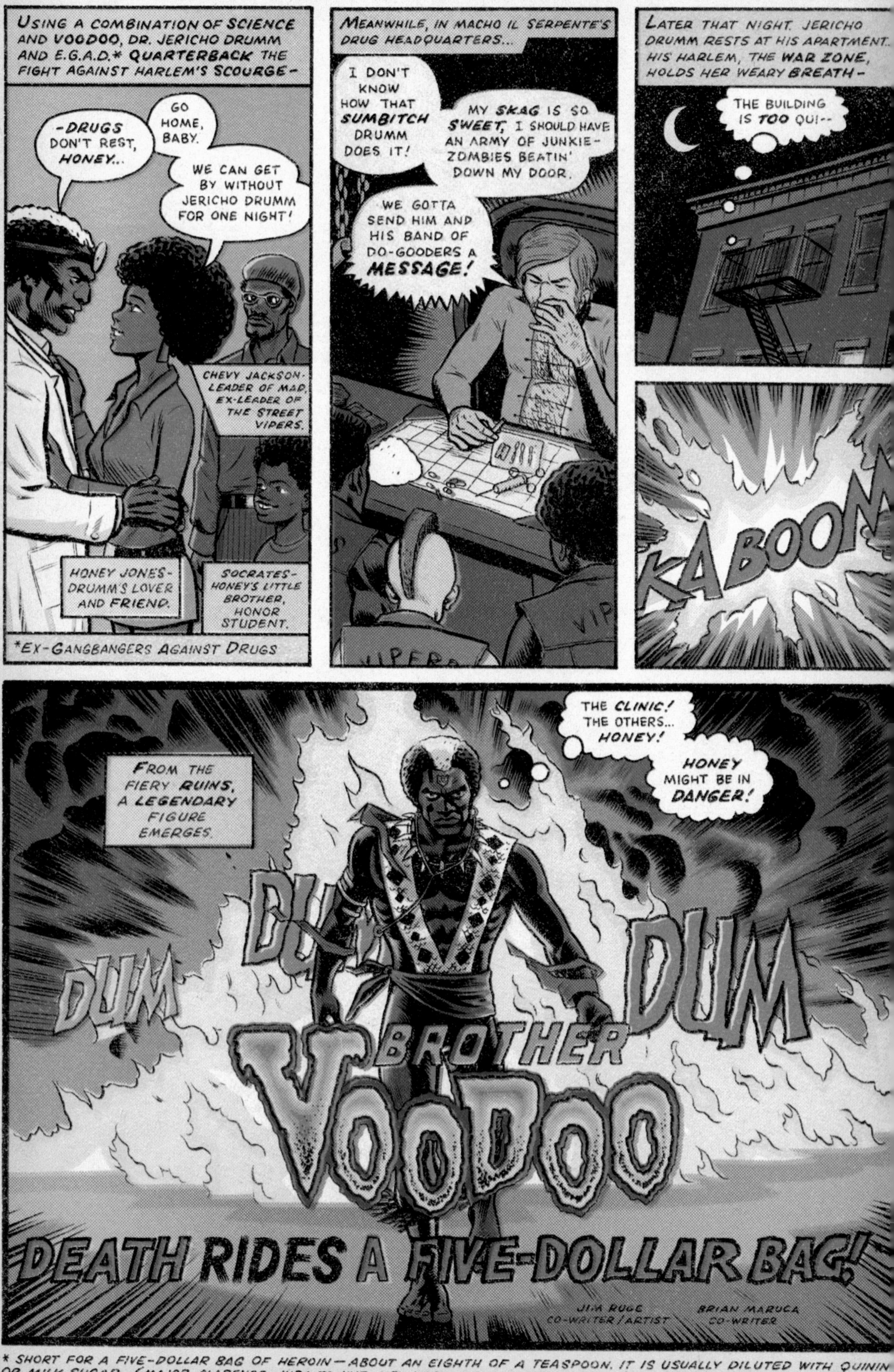
USING A COMBINATION OF SCIENCE AND VOODOO, DR. JERICHO DRUMM AND E.G.A.D.* QUARTERBACK THE FIGHT AGAINST HARLEM'S SCOURGE –
–DRUGS DON'T REST, HONEY...
GO HOME, BABY.
WE CAN GET BY WITHOUT JERICHO DRUMM FOR ONE NIGHT!
CHEVY JACKSON– LEADER OF MAD, EX-LEADER OF THE STREET VIPERS.
HONEY JONES– DRUMM'S LOVER AND FRIEND.
SOCRATES– HONEY'S LITTLE BROTHER, HONOR STUDENT.
*EX-GANGBANGERS AGAINST DRUGS
MEANWHILE, IN MACHO IL SERPENTE'S DRUG HEADQUARTERS...
I DON'T KNOW HOW THAT SUMBITCH DRUMM DOES IT!
MY SKAG IS SO SWEET, I SHOULD HAVE AN ARMY OF JUNKIE-ZOMBIES BEATIN' DOWN MY DOOR.
WE GOTTA SEND HIM AND HIS BAND OF DO-GOODERS A MESSAGE!
LATER THAT NIGHT, JERICHO DRUMM RESTS AT HIS APARTMENT... HIS HARLEM, THE WAR ZONE, HOLDS HER WEARY BREATH –
THE BUILDING IS TOO QUI--
KABOOM
FROM THE FIERY RUINS, A LEGENDARY FIGURE EMERGES.
THE CLINIC! THE OTHERS... HONEY!
HONEY MIGHT BE IN DANGER!
DUM DUM DUM
BROTHER VOODOO
DEATH RIDES A FIVE-DOLLAR BAG!
JIM RUGG CO-WRITER/ARTIST
BRIAN MARUCA CO-WRITER

* SHORT FOR A FIVE-DOLLAR BAG OF HEROIN — ABOUT AN EIGHTH OF A TEASPOON. IT IS USUALLY DILUTED WITH QUININ OR MILK SUGAR. (MAJOR, CLARENCE. JUBA TO JIVE. NEW YORK: PENGUIN BOOKS, 1994.)

POWERFUL LEGS TRANSPORT BROTHER VOODOO TO THE CLINIC IN *RECORD TIME* - BUT EVEN WITH HIS FINELY HONED MUSCLES, HE ARRIVES... *TOO LATE!*

(huff puff)

VIPERS RULE

HAITI SUCKS

NOO VOO

A GLIMMER OF *HOPE:* HONEY JONES IS NOT AMONG THE DEAD.

THE TIME FOR *SCIENCE* IS OVER, NOW IT IS TIME... FOR *VOODOO!!!*

USING BLACK MAGIC, BROTHER VOODOO RAISES A *ZOMBIE STRIKEFORCE!*

MACHO IL SERPENTE! TONIGHT THE DEAD WALK SO THAT JUSTICE MAY BE SERVED!

MACHO MAC

BACK AT MACHO'S HQ, THE GANG TRIPS OUT OVER THE NIGHT'S VIOLENCE!

I THOUGHT I TOLD YOU TO TURN THAT DISCO $#!% DOWN!

DUM DUM DUM

I UNPLUGGED IT, BOSS. HONEST TO GOD.

DUM DUM

SMOKE BEGINS TO FILL THE ROOM.

HUH? THAT SOUND - LIKE THE *RHYTHM* OF VOODOO DRUMS -

AND THAT CRAZY SMOKE?! (sniff, sniff) IT DON'T SMELL LIKE NO TOBACCO SMOKE.

WHAT'S GOIN' ON AROUND HERE!?!

(cough hack)

DUM DU

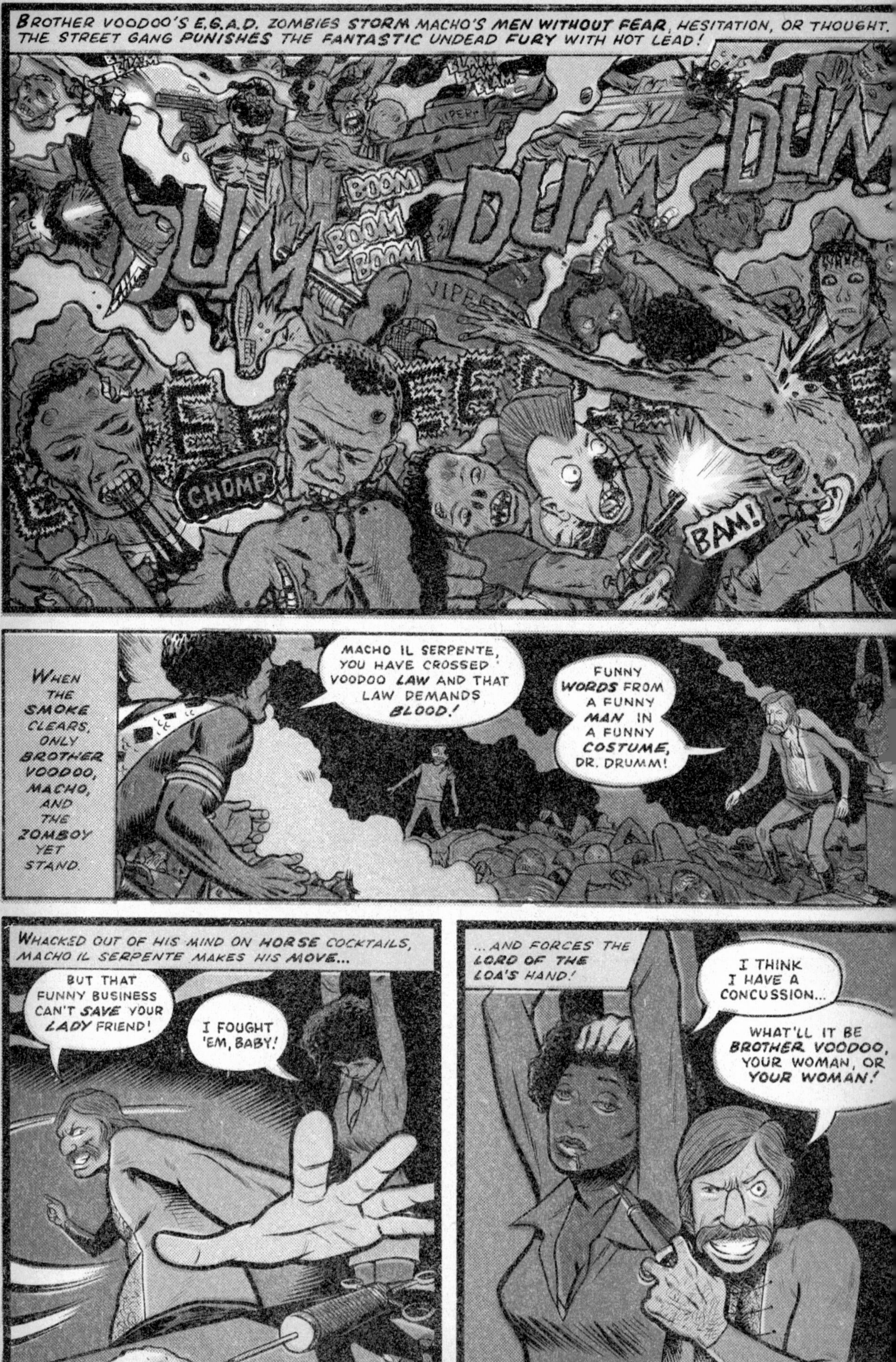
BROTHER VOODOO'S E.G.A.D. ZOMBIES STORM MACHO'S MEN WITHOUT FEAR, HESITATION, OR THOUGHT. THE STREET GANG PUNISHES THE FANTASTIC UNDEAD FURY WITH HOT LEAD!
BLAM BLAM BLAM
BOOM BOOM BOOM BOOM
DUM DUM DUM
CHOMP
BAM!
WHEN THE SMOKE CLEARS, ONLY BROTHER VOODOO, MACHO, AND THE ZOMBOY YET STAND.
MACHO IL SERPENTE, YOU HAVE CROSSED VOODOO LAW AND THAT LAW DEMANDS BLOOD!
FUNNY WORDS FROM A FUNNY MAN IN A FUNNY COSTUME, DR. DRUMM!
WHACKED OUT OF HIS MIND ON HORSE COCKTAILS, MACHO IL SERPENTE MAKES HIS MOVE...
BUT THAT FUNNY BUSINESS CAN'T SAVE YOUR LADY FRIEND!
I FOUGHT 'EM, BABY!
...AND FORCES THE LORD OF THE LOA'S HAND!
I THINK I HAVE A CONCUSSION...
WHAT'LL IT BE BROTHER VOODOO, YOUR WOMAN, OR YOUR WOMAN!

BROTHER VOODOO CAN'T REACH **MACHO** IN TIME, BUT THE *SPIRIT* OF HIS MURDERED TWIN **BROTHER**, DANIEL, ONLY REQUIRES A *SPLIT SECOND* TO ENTER THE HOPPED UP THUG!

YOU DO NOT WANT TO FURTHER ENCOURAGE MY *WRATH*, MACHO IL SERPENTE!

BEFORE MACHO CAN *RETORT*, DANIEL'S *SPIRIT* INVADES HIS BODY!

I'M TIRED.

WHAT THE-? --UNNGH!!

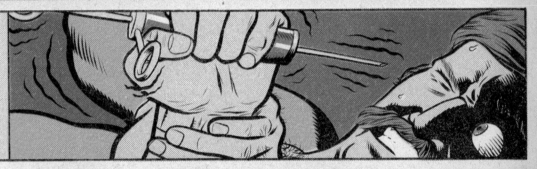

POSSESSED BY BROTHER VOODOO'S BROTHER'S *SPIRIT*, MACHO WRITHES ON THE GROUND LIKE A *SNAKE*!

A HYPODERMIC NEEDLE FULL OF 95.2% PURE COLOMBIAN SIZZLE!

AAAARGH

HOW ELSE COULD IT *END* WHEN A PUSHER *COMES* BETWIXT A VOODOO CHAMPION AND HIS REFORMED PROSTITUTE *LOVER*!

P-OP!

As **BROTHER VOODOO** CARRIES HIS BATTERED BABE FROM THE *CARNAGE*, HE WONDERS *HOW MANY* MACHOS WILL SPRING UP IN IL SERPENTE'S PLACE?

CAN HE CONTINUE TO PUT THOSE HE LOVES AT *RISK*? WHERE BROTHER VOODOO *STALKS*, DR. DRUMM CAN NOT AFFORD THE *LUXURY* OF FRIENDS, OR BEAR THE *PAIN* OF WATCHING THEM *DIE*...

NEXT ISSUE:

MACHO RETURNS, WITH AN *EYE* ON REVENGE!

AN *EYE* FOR AN *EYE*, WITCH DOCTOR! ARRR!

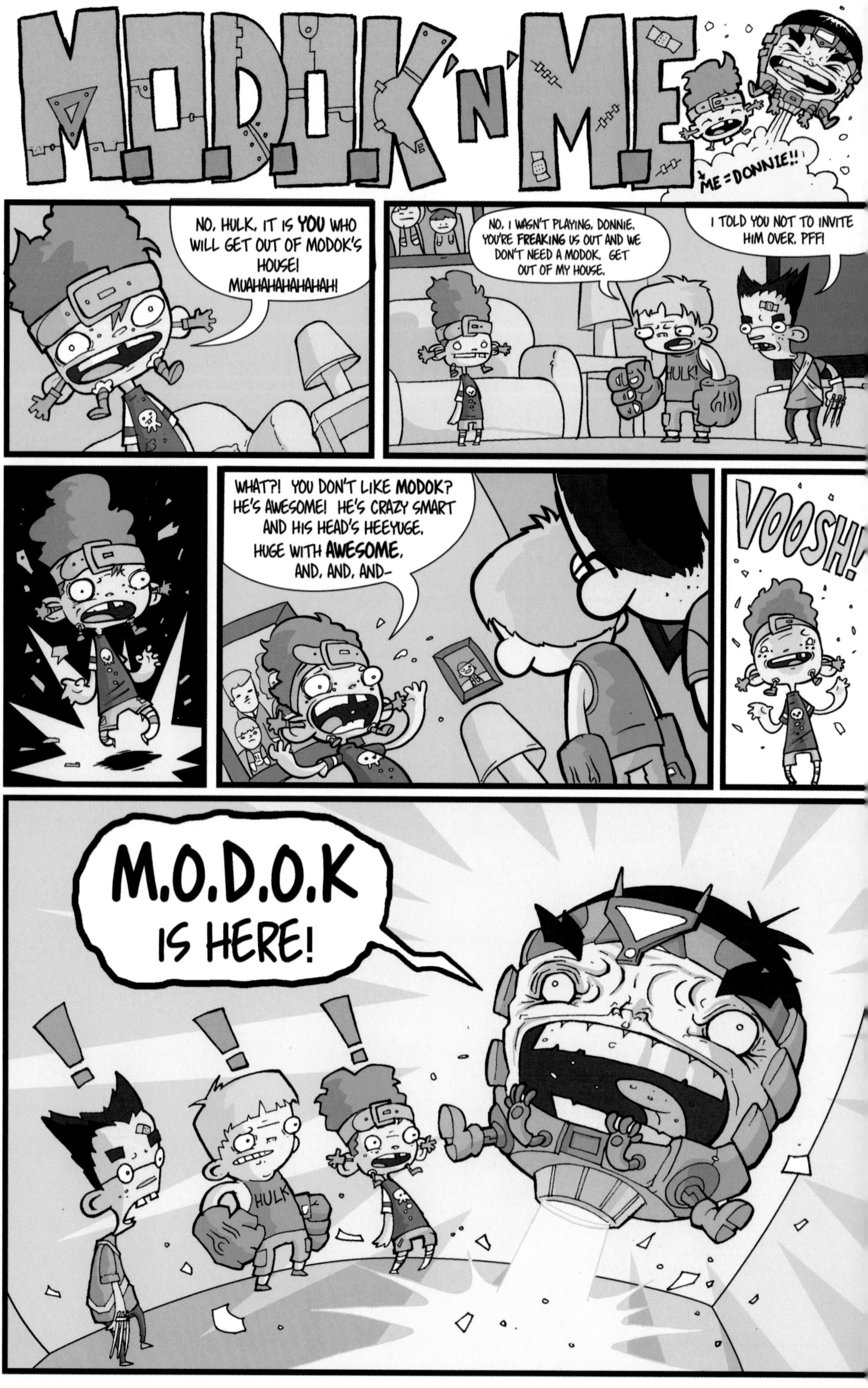
M.O.D.O.K 'N' M.E
ME = DONNIE!!
NO, HULK, IT IS YOU WHO WILL GET OUT OF MODOK'S HOUSE! MUAHAHAHAHAHAH!
NO, I WASN'T PLAYING, DONNIE. YOU'RE FREAKING US OUT AND WE DON'T NEED A MODOK. GET OUT OF MY HOUSE.
I TOLD YOU NOT TO INVITE HIM OVER. PFF!
HULK!
WHAT?! YOU DON'T LIKE MODOK? HE'S AWESOME! HE'S CRAZY SMART AND HIS HEAD'S HEEYUGE. HUGE WITH AWESOME. AND, AND, AND–
VOOSH!
M.O.D.O.K IS HERE!
HULK

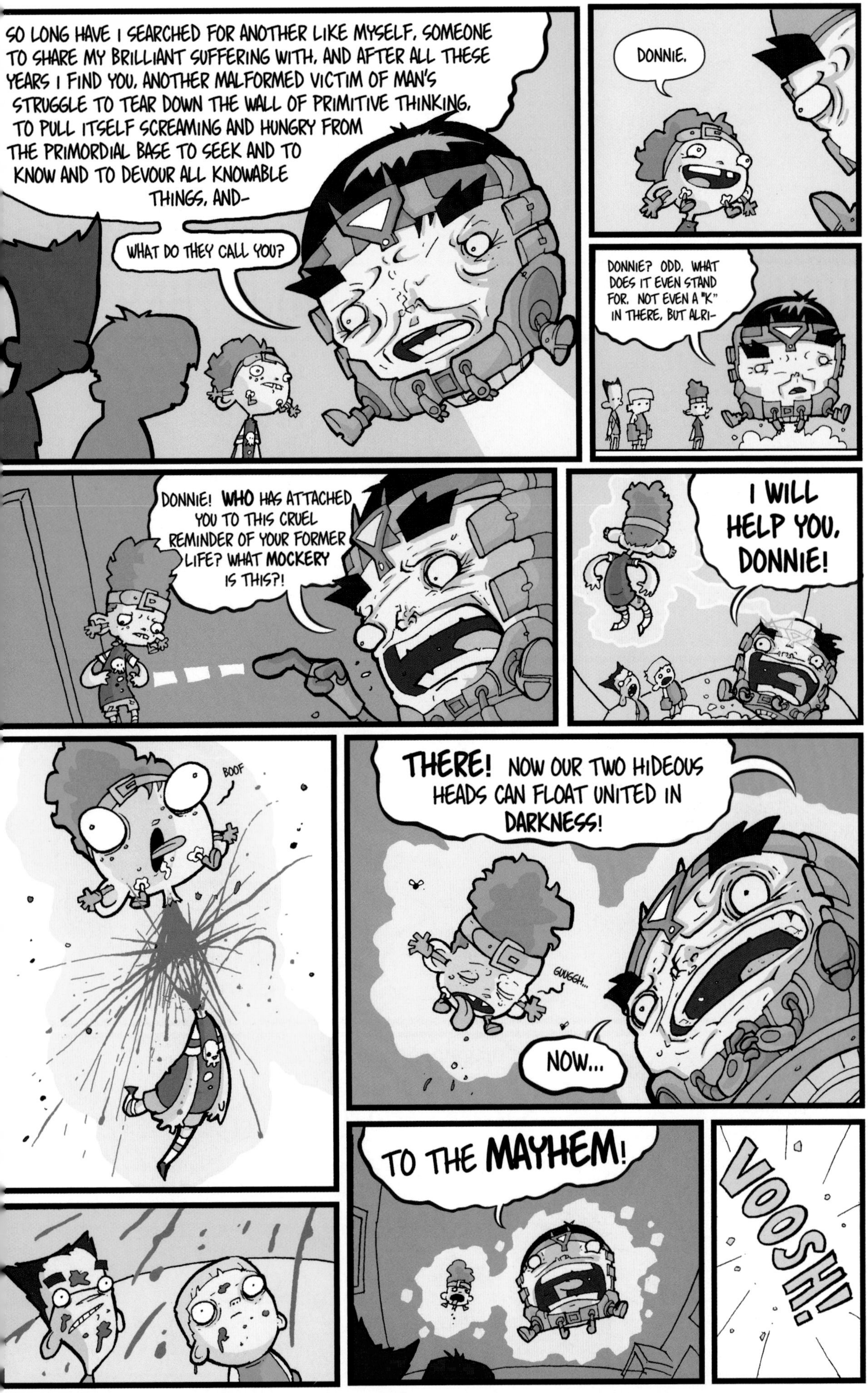
SO LONG HAVE I SEARCHED FOR ANOTHER LIKE MYSELF, SOMEONE TO SHARE MY BRILLIANT SUFFERING WITH, AND AFTER ALL THESE YEARS I FIND YOU, ANOTHER MALFORMED VICTIM OF MAN'S STRUGGLE TO TEAR DOWN THE WALL OF PRIMITIVE THINKING, TO PULL ITSELF SCREAMING AND HUNGRY FROM THE PRIMORDIAL BASE TO SEEK AND TO KNOW AND TO DEVOUR ALL KNOWABLE THINGS, AND-
WHAT DO THEY CALL YOU?
DONNIE.
DONNIE? ODD. WHAT DOES IT EVEN STAND FOR. NOT EVEN A "K" IN THERE, BUT ALRI-
DONNIE! WHO HAS ATTACHED YOU TO THIS CRUEL REMINDER OF YOUR FORMER LIFE? WHAT MOCKERY IS THIS?!
I WILL HELP YOU, DONNIE!
BOOF
THERE! NOW OUR TWO HIDEOUS HEADS CAN FLOAT UNITED IN DARKNESS!
GUUGGH...
NOW...
TO THE MAYHEM!
VOOSH!

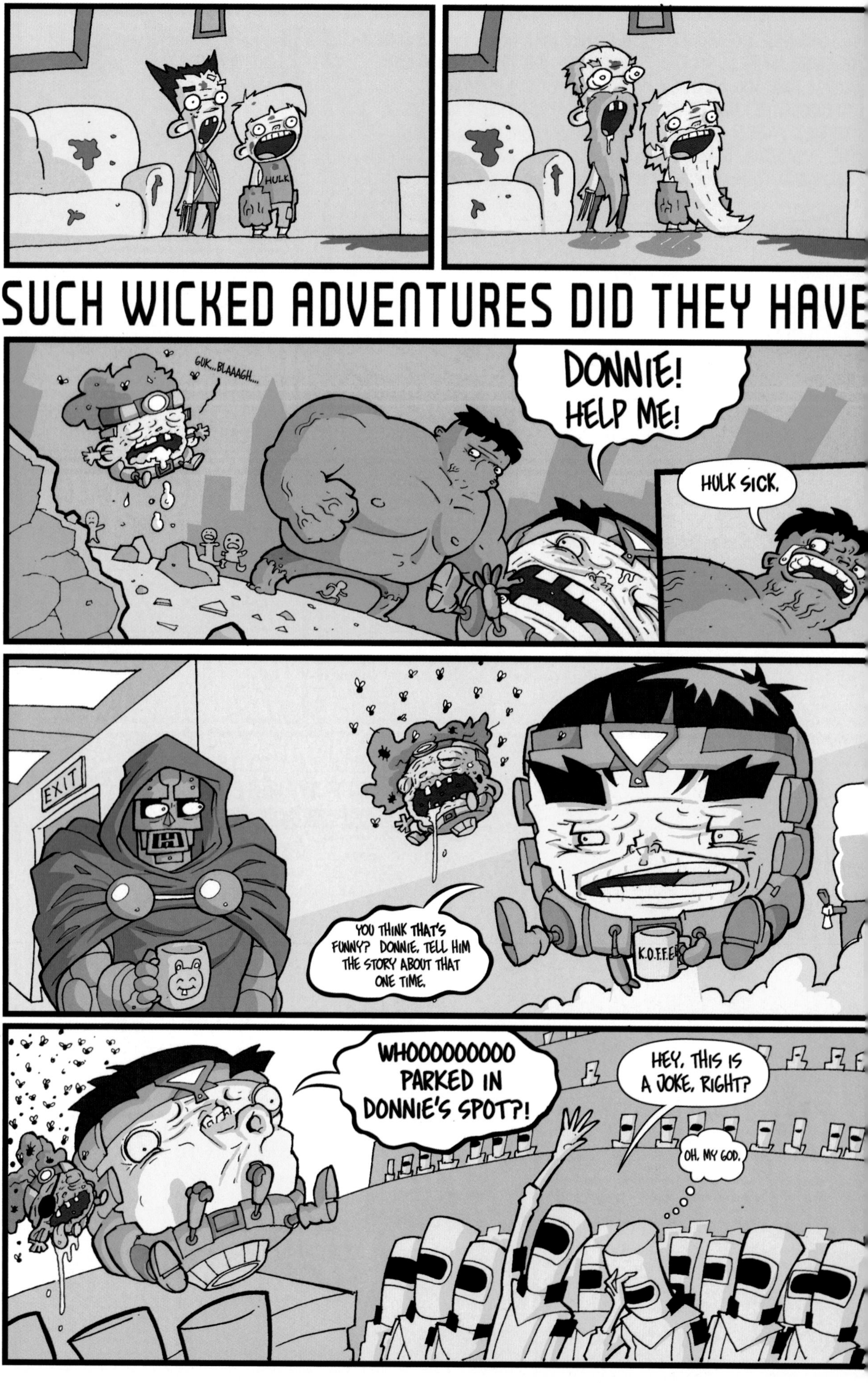
SUCH WICKED ADVENTURES DID THEY HAVE
GUK...BLAAAGH...
DONNIE! HELP ME!
HULK SICK.
HULK
EXIT
YOU THINK THAT'S FUNNY? DONNIE, TELL HIM THE STORY ABOUT THAT ONE TIME.
K.O.F.F.E.E.
WHOOOOOOOOO PARKED IN DONNIE'S SPOT?!
HEY, THIS IS A JOKE, RIGHT?
OH, MY GOD.

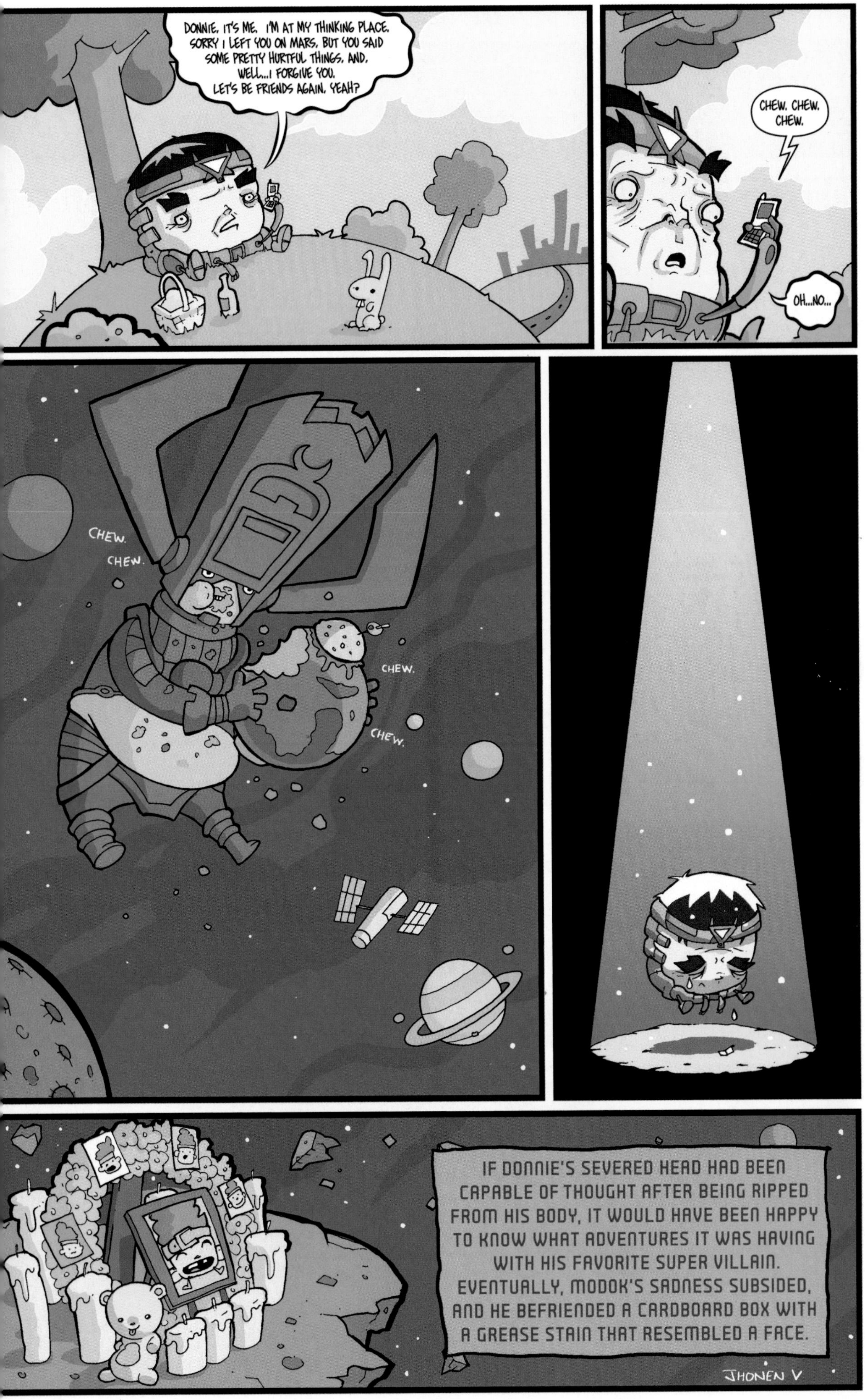

DONNIE, IT'S ME. I'M AT MY THINKING PLACE. SORRY I LEFT YOU ON MARS, BUT YOU SAID SOME PRETTY HURTFUL THINGS, AND, WELL...I FORGIVE YOU. LET'S BE FRIENDS AGAIN, YEAH?
CHEW, CHEW, CHEW.
OH...NO...
CHEW.
CHEW.
CHEW.
CHEW.
IF DONNIE'S SEVERED HEAD HAD BEEN CAPABLE OF THOUGHT AFTER BEING RIPPED FROM HIS BODY, IT WOULD HAVE BEEN HAPPY TO KNOW WHAT ADVENTURES IT WAS HAVING WITH HIS FAVORITE SUPER VILLAIN. EVENTUALLY, MODOK'S SADNESS SUBSIDED, AND HE BEFRIENDED A CARDBOARD BOX WITH A GREASE STAIN THAT RESEMBLED A FACE.
JHONEN V

FASTIDIOUSLY HAND-PLUCKED FROM THE SECRET NEAR-MINT SILVER AGE FILES OF **MAX CANNON**...

ATTENTION TRUE BELIEVERS!

THE SHOCKING ORIGINAL VERSION THAT LEE & KIRBY KEPT HIDDEN FOR OVER FORTY YEARS!!

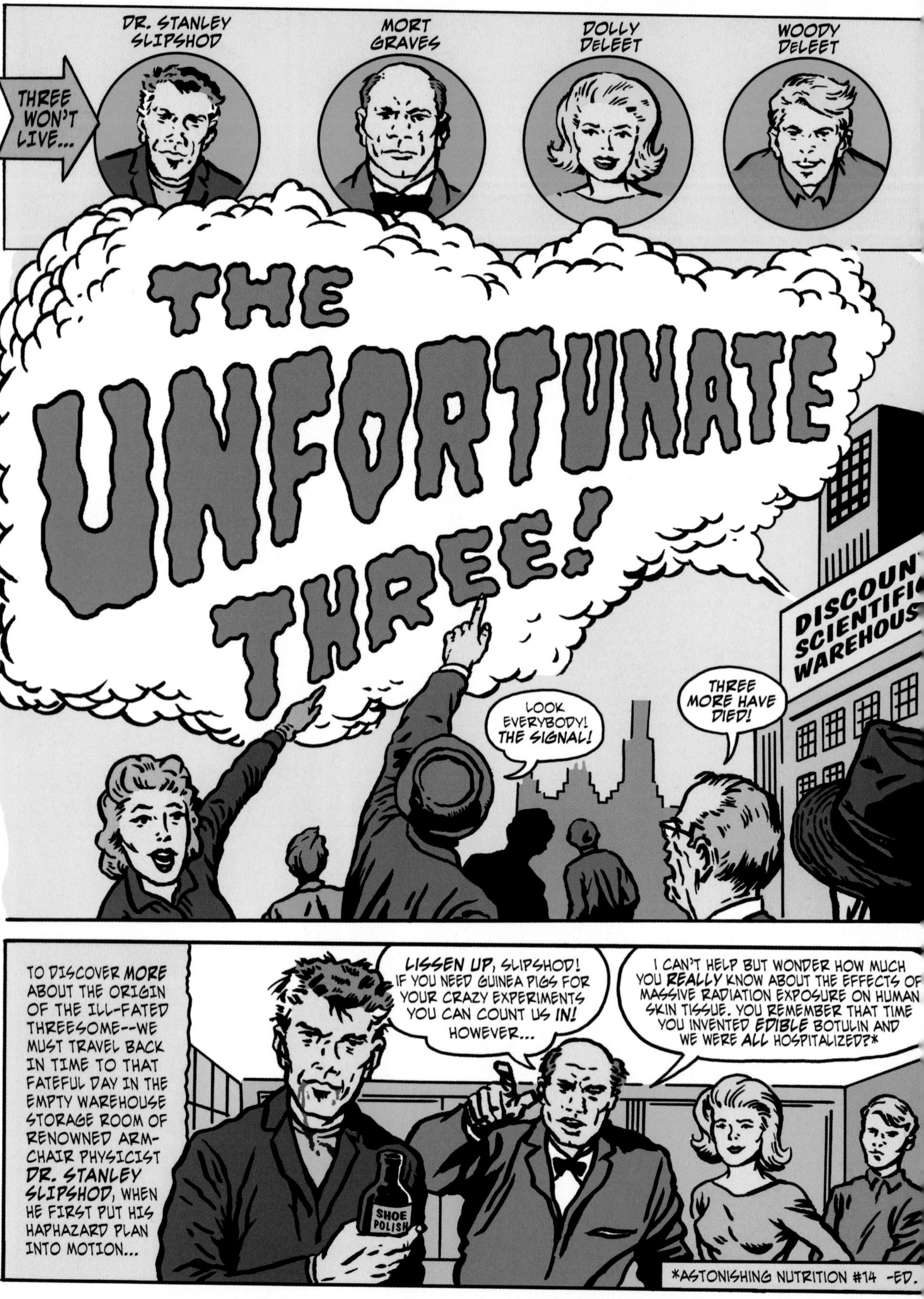

DR. STANLEY SLIPSHOD
MORT GRAVES
DOLLY DELEET
WOODY DELEET
THREE WON'T LIVE...
THE UNFORTUNATE THREE!
LOOK EVERYBODY! THE SIGNAL!
THREE MORE HAVE DIED!
DISCOUN SCIENTIFI WAREHOUS
TO DISCOVER MORE ABOUT THE ORIGIN OF THE ILL-FATED THREESOME--WE MUST TRAVEL BACK IN TIME TO THAT FATEFUL DAY IN THE EMPTY WAREHOUSE STORAGE ROOM OF RENOWNED ARM-CHAIR PHYSICIST DR. STANLEY SLIPSHOD, WHEN HE FIRST PUT HIS HAPHAZARD PLAN INTO MOTION...
LISSEN UP, SLIPSHOD! IF YOU NEED GUINEA PIGS FOR YOUR CRAZY EXPERIMENTS YOU CAN COUNT US IN! HOWEVER...
I CAN'T HELP BUT WONDER HOW MUCH YOU REALLY KNOW ABOUT THE EFFECTS OF MASSIVE RADIATION EXPOSURE ON HUMAN SKIN TISSUE. YOU REMEMBER THAT TIME YOU INVENTED EDIBLE BOTULIN AND WE WERE ALL HOSPITALIZED?*
SHOE POLISH
*ASTONISHING NUTRITION #14 -ED.

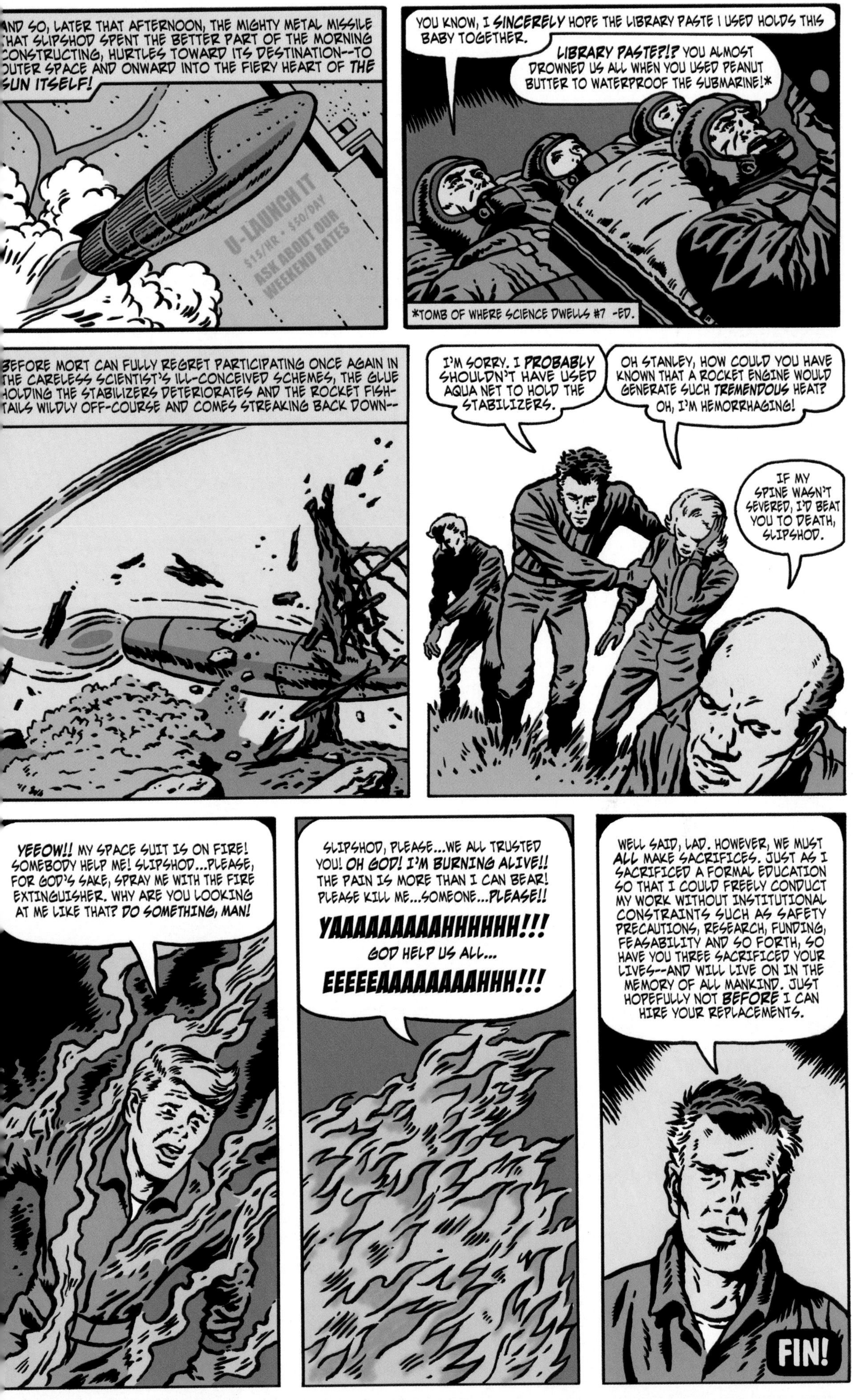

AND SO, LATER THAT AFTERNOON, THE MIGHTY METAL MISSILE THAT SLIPSHOD SPENT THE BETTER PART OF THE MORNING CONSTRUCTING, HURTLES TOWARD ITS DESTINATION--TO OUTER SPACE AND ONWARD INTO THE FIERY HEART OF THE SUN ITSELF!
U-LAUNCH IT
$15/HR • $50/DAY
ASK ABOUT OUR WEEKEND RATES
YOU KNOW, I SINCERELY HOPE THE LIBRARY PASTE I USED HOLDS THIS BABY TOGETHER.
LIBRARY PASTE?!? YOU ALMOST DROWNED US ALL WHEN YOU USED PEANUT BUTTER TO WATERPROOF THE SUBMARINE!*
*TOMB OF WHERE SCIENCE DWELLS #7 -ED.
BEFORE MORT CAN FULLY REGRET PARTICIPATING ONCE AGAIN IN THE CARELESS SCIENTIST'S ILL-CONCEIVED SCHEMES, THE GLUE HOLDING THE STABILIZERS DETERIORATES AND THE ROCKET FISH-TAILS WILDLY OFF-COURSE AND COMES STREAKING BACK DOWN--
I'M SORRY. I PROBABLY SHOULDN'T HAVE USED AQUA NET TO HOLD THE STABILIZERS.
OH STANLEY, HOW COULD YOU HAVE KNOWN THAT A ROCKET ENGINE WOULD GENERATE SUCH TREMENDOUS HEAT? OH, I'M HEMORRHAGING!
IF MY SPINE WASN'T SEVERED, I'D BEAT YOU TO DEATH, SLIPSHOD.
YEEOW!! MY SPACE SUIT IS ON FIRE! SOMEBODY HELP ME! SLIPSHOD...PLEASE, FOR GOD'S SAKE, SPRAY ME WITH THE FIRE EXTINGUISHER. WHY ARE YOU LOOKING AT ME LIKE THAT? DO SOMETHING, MAN!
SLIPSHOD, PLEASE...WE ALL TRUSTED YOU! OH GOD! I'M BURNING ALIVE!! THE PAIN IS MORE THAN I CAN BEAR! PLEASE KILL ME...SOMEONE...PLEASE!!
YAAAAAAAAAHHHHHH!!!
GOD HELP US ALL...
EEEEEAAAAAAAAAHHH!!!
WELL SAID, LAD. HOWEVER, WE MUST ALL MAKE SACRIFICES. JUST AS I SACRIFICED A FORMAL EDUCATION SO THAT I COULD FREELY CONDUCT MY WORK WITHOUT INSTITUTIONAL CONSTRAINTS SUCH AS SAFETY PRECAUTIONS, RESEARCH, FUNDING, FEASABILITY AND SO FORTH, SO HAVE YOU THREE SACRIFICED YOUR LIVES--AND WILL LIVE ON IN THE MEMORY OF ALL MANKIND. JUST HOPEFULLY NOT BEFORE I CAN HIRE YOUR REPLACEMENTS.
FIN!

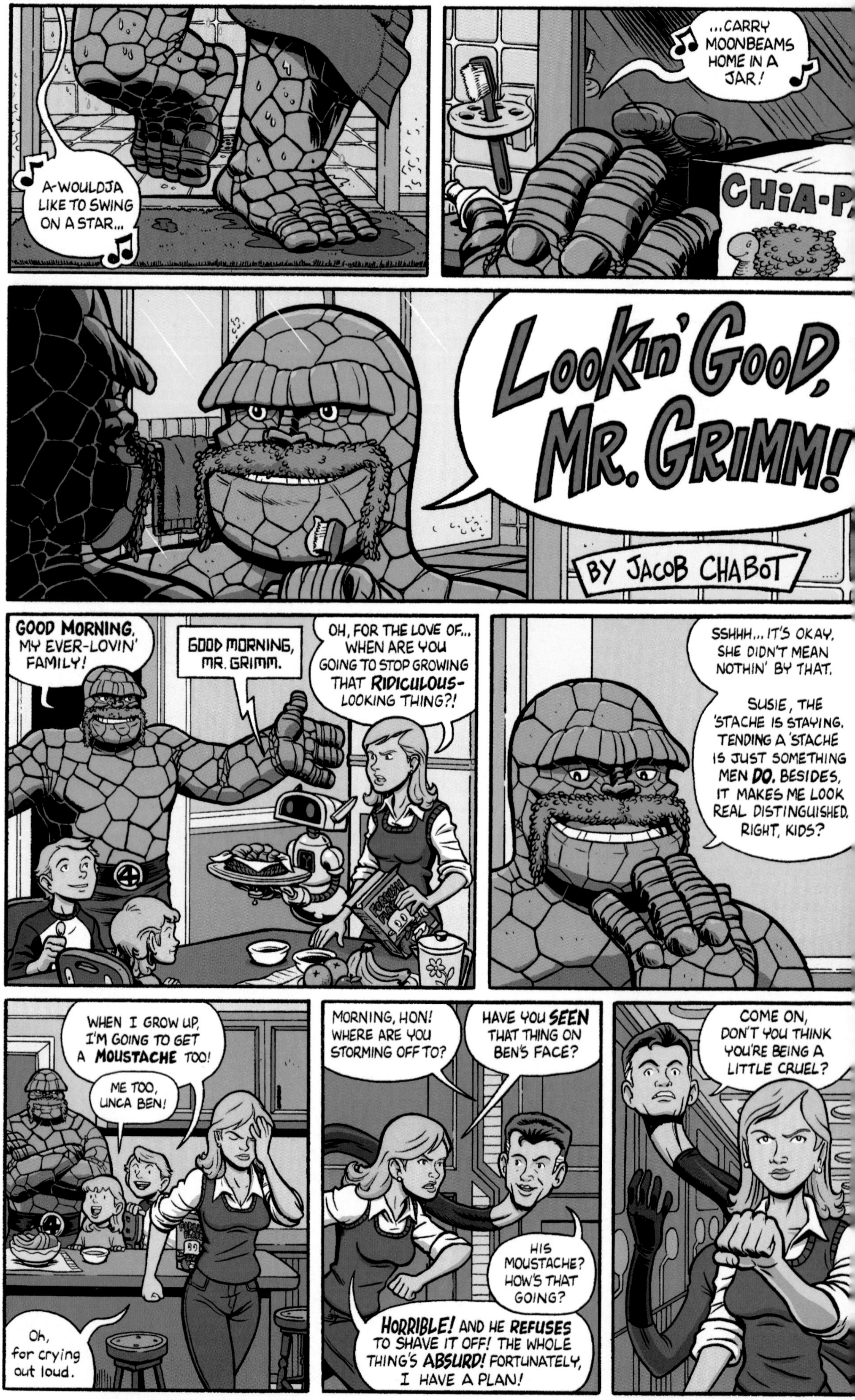
A-WOULDJA LIKE TO SWING ON A STAR...
...CARRY MOONBEAMS HOME IN A JAR!
LOOKIN' GOOD, MR. GRIMM!
BY JACOB CHABOT
GOOD MORNING, MY EVER-LOVIN' FAMILY!
GOOD MORNING, MR. GRIMM.
OH, FOR THE LOVE OF... WHEN ARE YOU GOING TO STOP GROWING THAT RIDICULOUS-LOOKING THING?!
SSHHH... IT'S OKAY, SHE DIDN'T MEAN NOTHIN' BY THAT.
SUSIE, THE 'STACHE IS STAYING. TENDING A 'STACHE IS JUST SOMETHING MEN DO. BESIDES, IT MAKES ME LOOK REAL DISTINGUISHED. RIGHT, KIDS?
WHEN I GROW UP, I'M GOING TO GET A MOUSTACHE TOO!
ME TOO, UNCA BEN!
Oh, for crying out loud.
MORNING, HON! WHERE ARE YOU STORMING OFF TO?
HAVE YOU SEEN THAT THING ON BEN'S FACE?
HIS MOUSTACHE? HOW'S THAT GOING?
HORRIBLE! AND HE REFUSES TO SHAVE IT OFF! THE WHOLE THING'S ABSURD! FORTUNATELY, I HAVE A PLAN!
COME ON, DON'T YOU THINK YOU'RE BEING A LITTLE CRUEL?

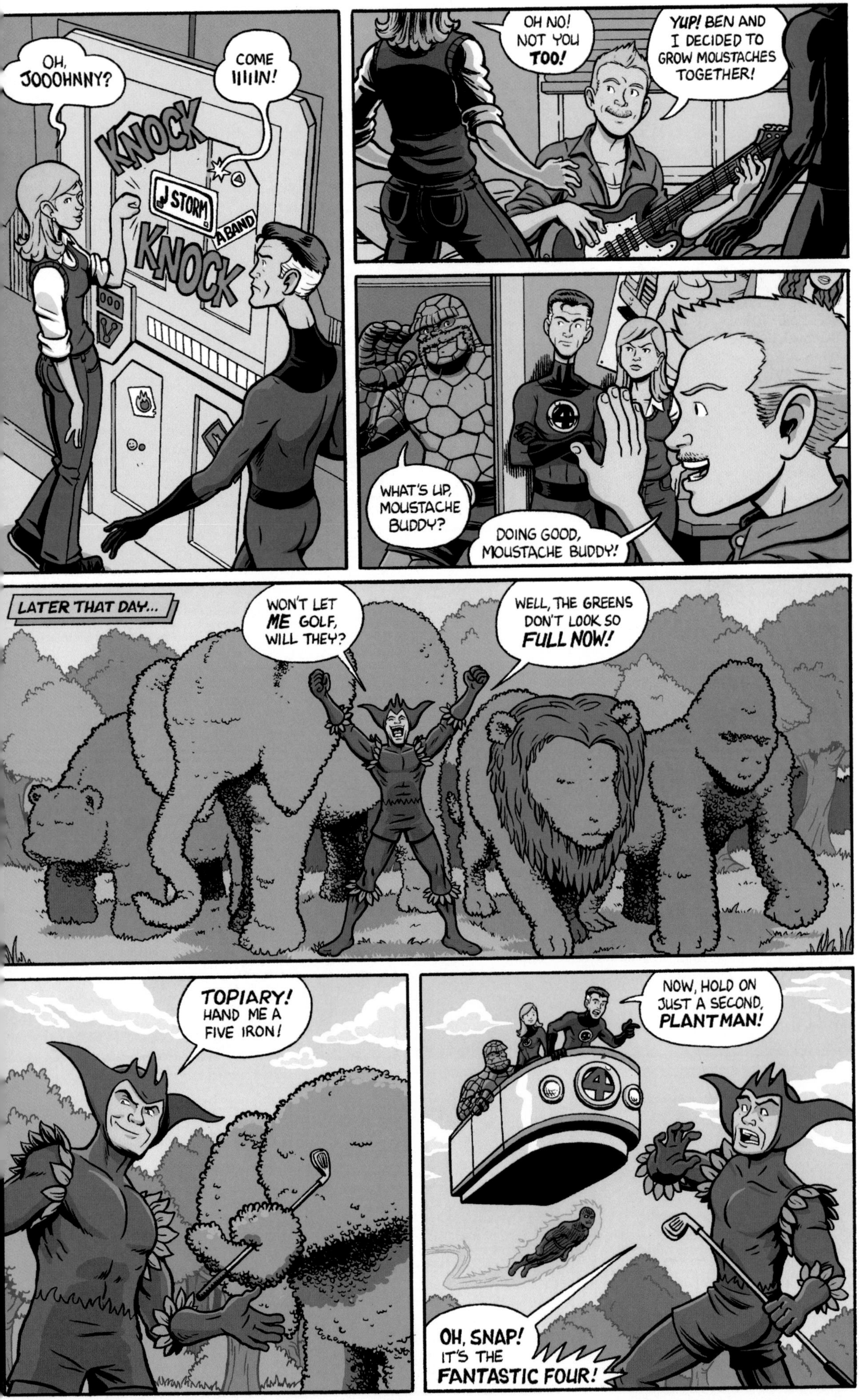
OH, JOOOHNNY?
COME IIIIIN!
KNOCK
J STORM
A BAND
KNOCK
OH NO! NOT YOU TOO!
YUP! BEN AND I DECIDED TO GROW MOUSTACHES TOGETHER!
WHAT'S UP, MOUSTACHE BUDDY?
DOING GOOD, MOUSTACHE BUDDY!
LATER THAT DAY...
WON'T LET ME GOLF, WILL THEY?
WELL, THE GREENS DON'T LOOK SO FULL NOW!
TOPIARY! HAND ME A FIVE IRON!
NOW, HOLD ON JUST A SECOND, PLANTMAN!
OH, SNAP! IT'S THE FANTASTIC FOUR!

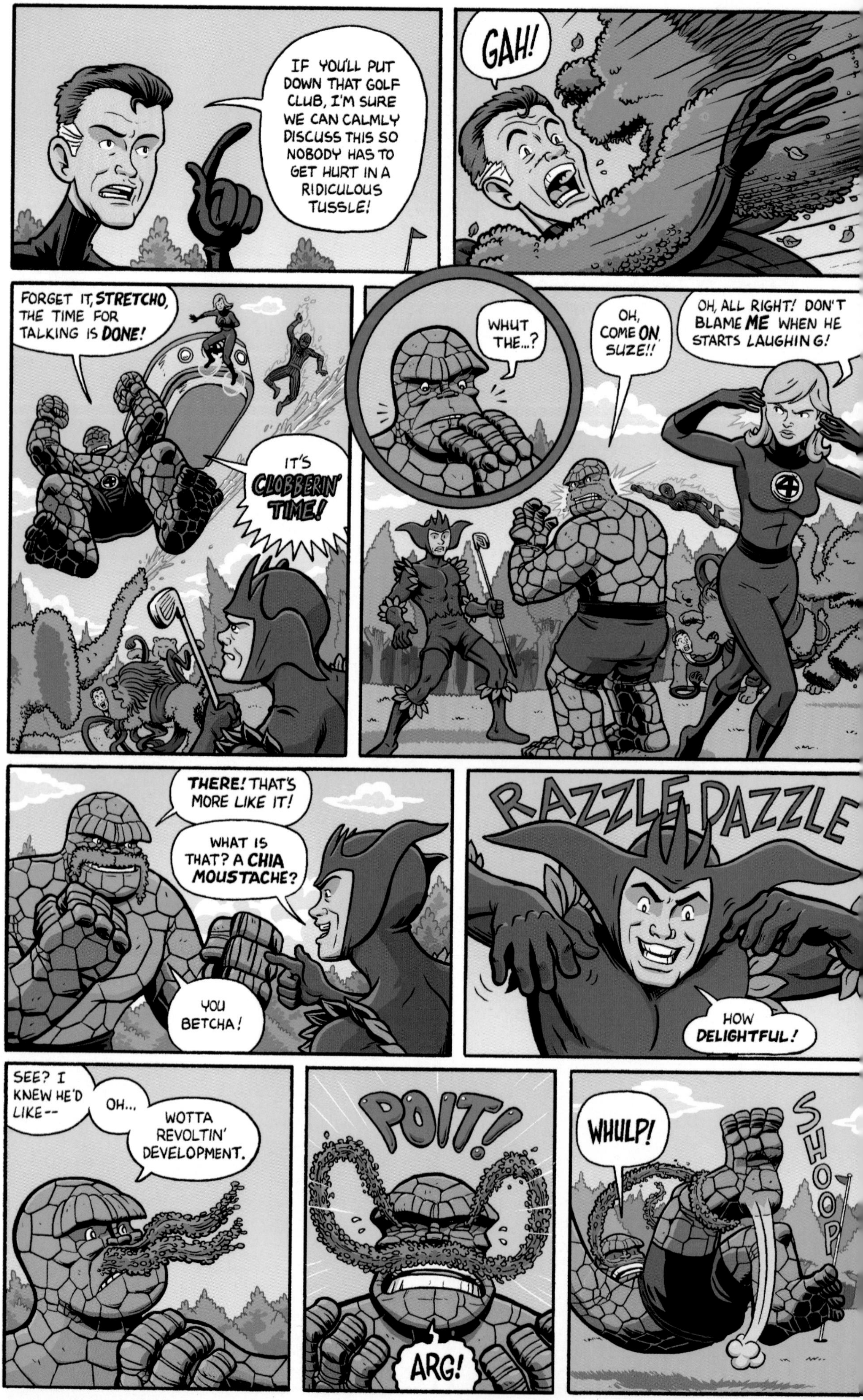
IF YOU'LL PUT DOWN THAT GOLF CLUB, I'M SURE WE CAN CALMLY DISCUSS THIS SO NOBODY HAS TO GET HURT IN A RIDICULOUS TUSSLE!
GAH!
FORGET IT, STRETCHO, THE TIME FOR TALKING IS DONE!
IT'S CLOBBERIN' TIME!
WHUT THE...?
OH, COME ON, SUZE!!
OH, ALL RIGHT! DON'T BLAME ME WHEN HE STARTS LAUGHING!
THERE! THAT'S MORE LIKE IT!
WHAT IS THAT? A CHIA MOUSTACHE?
YOU BETCHA!
RAZZLE DAZZLE
HOW DELIGHTFUL!
SEE? I KNEW HE'D LIKE--
OH...
WOTTA REVOLTIN' DEVELOPMENT.
POIT!
ARG!
WHULP!
SHOOP

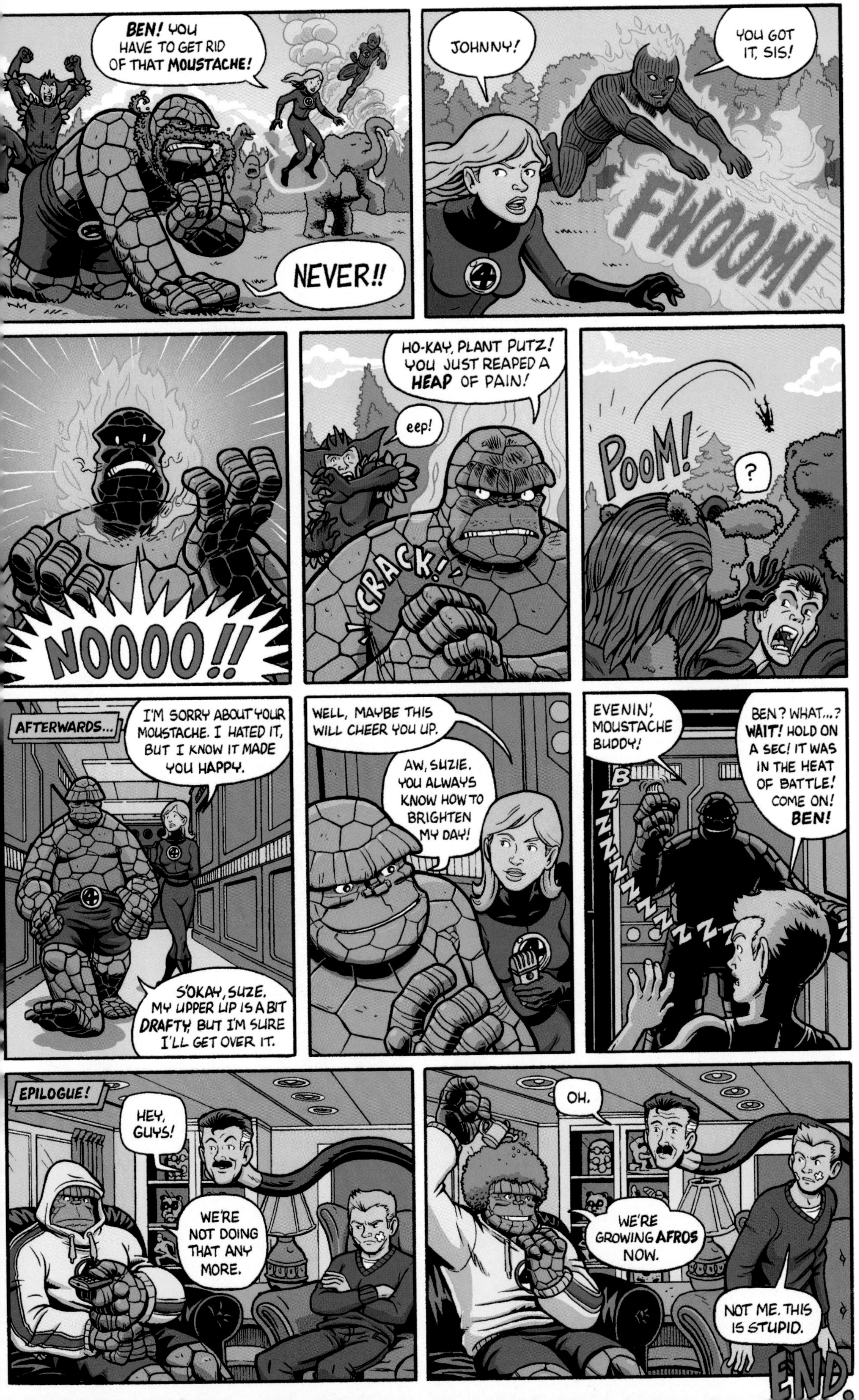
BEN! YOU HAVE TO GET RID OF THAT MOUSTACHE!
NEVER!!
JOHNNY!
YOU GOT IT, SIS!
FWOOM!
NOOOO!!
HO-KAY, PLANT PUTZ! YOU JUST REAPED A HEAP OF PAIN!
eep!
CRACK!
POOM!
?
AFTERWARDS...
I'M SORRY ABOUT YOUR MOUSTACHE. I HATED IT, BUT I KNOW IT MADE YOU HAPPY.
S'OKAY, SUZE. MY UPPER LIP IS A BIT DRAFTY, BUT I'M SURE I'LL GET OVER IT.
WELL, MAYBE THIS WILL CHEER YOU UP.
AW, SUZIE. YOU ALWAYS KNOW HOW TO BRIGHTEN MY DAY!
EVENIN', MOUSTACHE BUDDY!
BZZZZZZZZZ
BEN? WHAT...? WAIT! HOLD ON A SEC! IT WAS IN THE HEAT OF BATTLE! COME ON! BEN!
EPILOGUE!
HEY, GUYS!
WE'RE NOT DOING THAT ANY MORE.
OH.
WE'RE GROWING AFROS NOW.
NOT ME. THIS IS STUPID.
END.

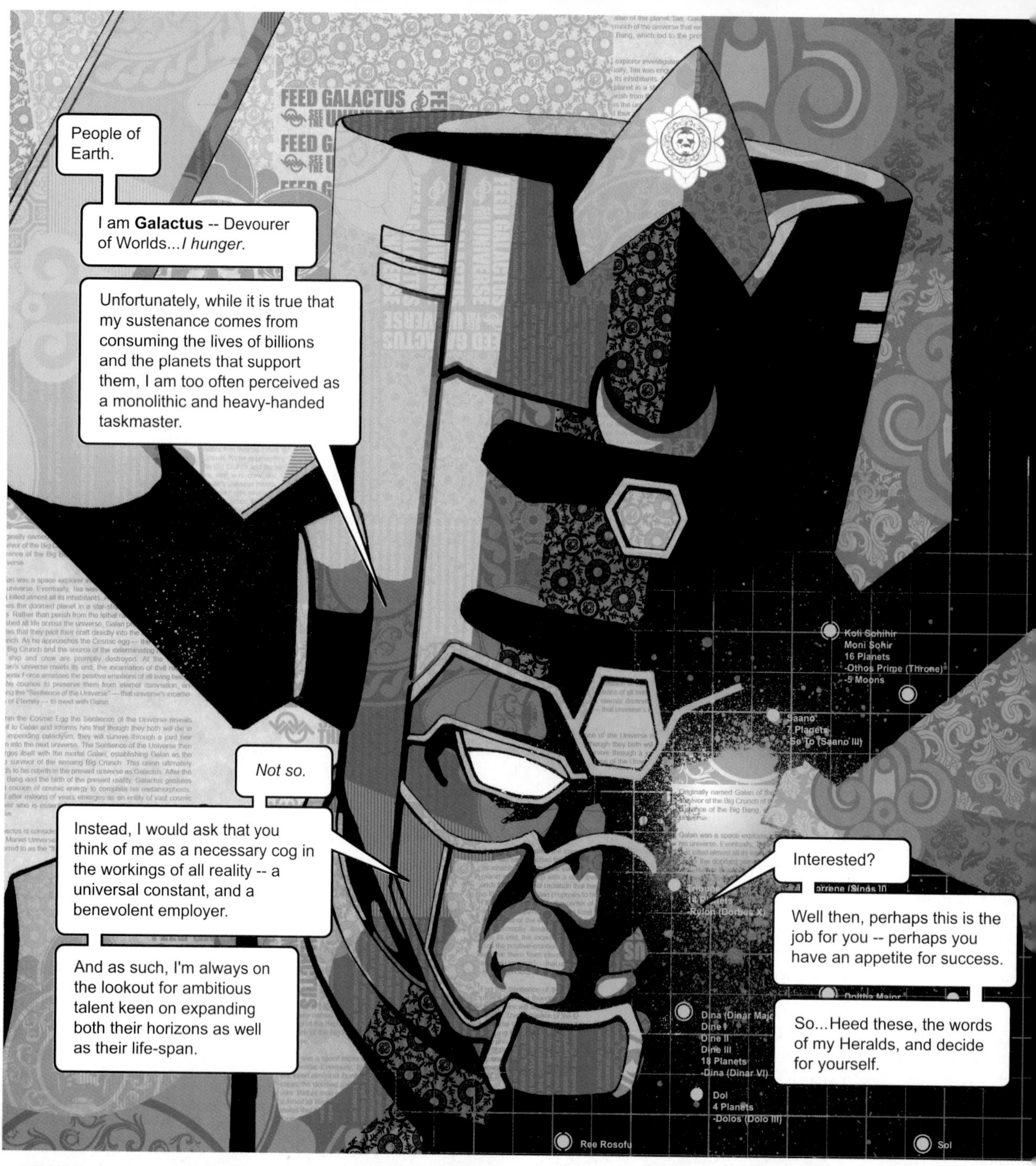
People of Earth.
I am **Galactus** -- Devourer of Worlds...*I hunger*.
Unfortunately, while it is true that my sustenance comes from consuming the lives of billions and the planets that support them, I am too often perceived as a monolithic and heavy-handed taskmaster.
Not so.
Instead, I would ask that you think of me as a necessary cog in the workings of all reality -- a universal constant, and a benevolent employer.
And as such, I'm always on the lookout for ambitious talent keen on expanding both their horizons as well as their life-span.
Interested?
Well then, perhaps this is the job for you -- perhaps you have an appetite for success.
So...Heed these, the words of my Heralds, and decide for yourself.
FEED GALACTUS
Sol
Ree Rosofu

ENLIST TODAY

JOIN UP. SEE THE UNIVERSE.

Interested? Email your personal information and a paragraph explaining why you would be perfect for the job of Herald and perhaps you could find yourself infused with the Power Cosmic. Do you have what it takes? Find out today.

Send all pertinent info to:
feed_galactus@hotmail.com

WORLD EATER

REQUIREMENTS:

(Human)

Age.......................... 17-38 Years

Education................. Not necessary. The Power Cosmic imbues the user with level 8 intelligence, provided that the recipient has no pre-existing head trauma or suffers from brainworms.

History of Illness..... No excessive pre-tumorous, benign abdominal masses. No excessive fatty tissue. No warts.

Disclaimer: Employment in Galactus, Inc. can only be terminated by employment provider. Once an individual has signed up, the contract runs for the duration of the employee's life (i.e. Eternity). In some instances, Galactus may discharge an employee, but such instances are considered rare and should be treated as such. Galactus, Inc. is responsible for providing clothes, residence and nourishment for the duration of the contract.

our essential points when
human (or any other animal
) are:

across the grain of meat
ossible.
sharp knives and saws for
nd good workmanship.
the cutting table orderly
e a place for everything.
clean and sanitary in all
ons.

-finger Kabobs
oaring the hand)

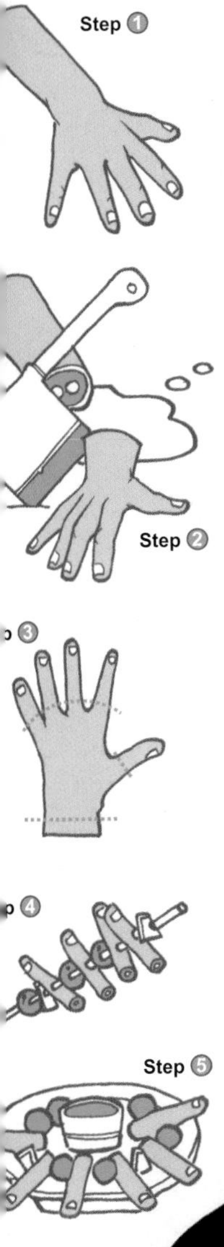

Step 1
Step 2
3
4
Step 5

EXPERIENCE EXOTIC DESTINATIONS AND DINING

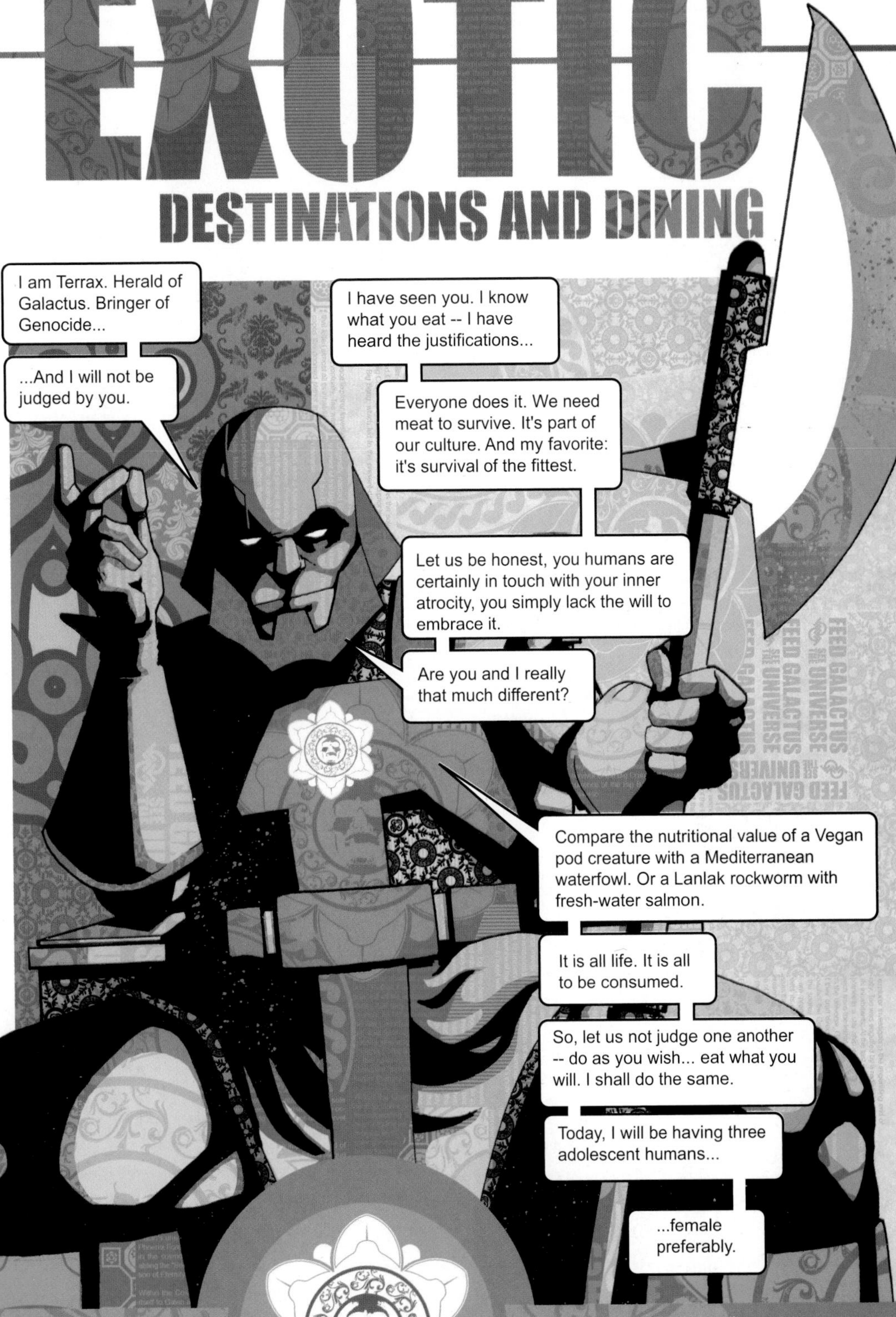

I am Terrax. Herald of Galactus. Bringer of Genocide...
...And I will not be judged by you.
I have seen you. I know what you eat -- I have heard the justifications...
Everyone does it. We need meat to survive. It's part of our culture. And my favorite: it's survival of the fittest.
Let us be honest, you humans are certainly in touch with your inner atrocity, you simply lack the will to embrace it.
Are you and I really that much different?
Compare the nutritional value of a Vegan pod creature with a Mediterranean waterfowl. Or a Lanlak rockworm with fresh-water salmon.
It is all life. It is all to be consumed.
So, let us not judge one another -- do as you wish... eat what you will. I shall do the same.
Today, I will be having three adolescent humans...
...female preferably.
FEED GALACTUS SEE THE UNIVERSE

Five-finger Kabobs
(Preparing the hand)

Step 1 Place arm palm down.
Step 2 Sever the hand below the wrist
Step 3 Remove the fingers, thumb and wrist from palm.*
Step 4 Skewer the fingers, add tomatoes and onions.
Step 5 Serve with bernaise sauce.

*(For an excellent palm recipe, see Brown Palm Stew)

THE TAMER

Brown Palm Stew (translated)

INGREDIENTS
- 2 tablespoons vegetable oil
- 2 human palms
- 3 onions, chopped
- 2 cloves garlic, minced
- 1 tablespoon Worcestershire
- 1 bay leaf
- 1/2 teaspoon dried thyme
- 1 tablespoon salt
- 3 cups water
- 7 small potatoes, quartered
- 1 pound parsnip, chopped
- 1/4 cup all-purpose flour
- 1/4 cup water

DIRECTIONS
In a large soup pot, deeply brown the palms in oil. Stir in onions, garlic. Worcestershire sauce, bay leaf, thyme, salt and 3 cups of water. Simmer, covered, for 1 1/2 to 2 hours, or until meat is tender.

Stir in potatoes and parsnips; cook until tender. Combine flour and 1/4 cup water. Stir into the stew. Remove bay leaf before serving.

Disclaimer: Galactus, Inc. is not responsible for the proper preparation of meat. It is highly recommended that all sweet meats should be cooked until there is a warm pink center. Failure to properly cook foodstuffs can result in Botulism, respiratory failure and paralysis. © 2008, Galactus, Inc.

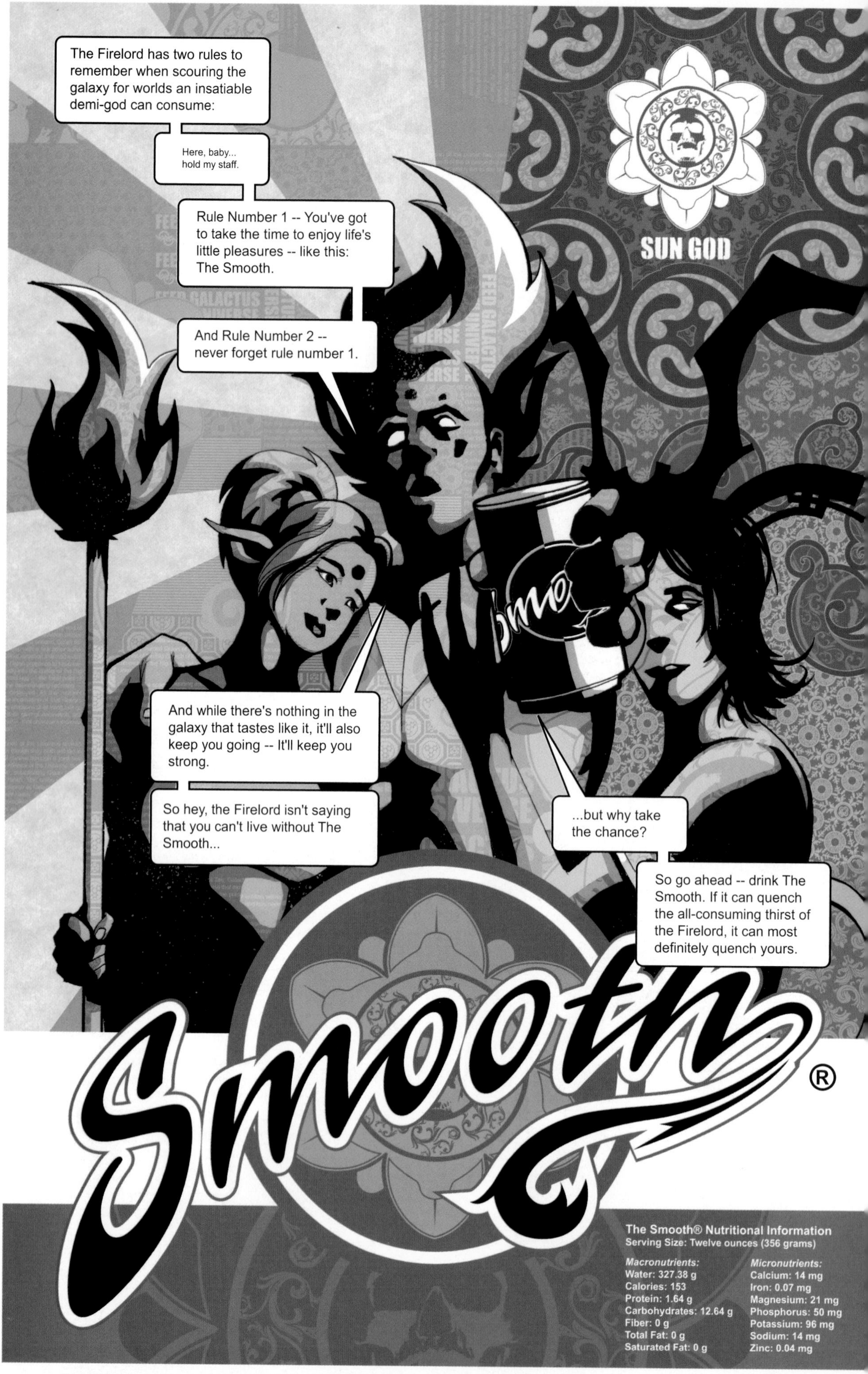
The Firelord has two rules to remember when scouring the galaxy for worlds an insatiable demi-god can consume:
Here, baby... hold my staff.
Rule Number 1 -- You've got to take the time to enjoy life's little pleasures -- like this: The Smooth.
And Rule Number 2 -- never forget rule number 1.
And while there's nothing in the galaxy that tastes like it, it'll also keep you going -- It'll keep you strong.
So hey, the Firelord isn't saying that you can't live without The Smooth...
...but why take the chance?
So go ahead -- drink The Smooth. If it can quench the all-consuming thirst of the Firelord, it can most definitely quench yours.
SUN GOD
Smooth®
The Smooth® Nutritional Information
Serving Size: Twelve ounces (356 grams)
Macronutrients:
Water: 327.38 g
Calories: 153
Protein: 1.64 g
Carbohydrates: 12.64 g
Fiber: 0 g
Total Fat: 0 g
Saturated Fat: 0 g
Micronutrients:
Calcium: 14 mg
Iron: 0.07 mg
Magnesium: 21 mg
Phosphorus: 50 mg
Potassium: 96 mg
Sodium: 14 mg
Zinc: 0.04 mg

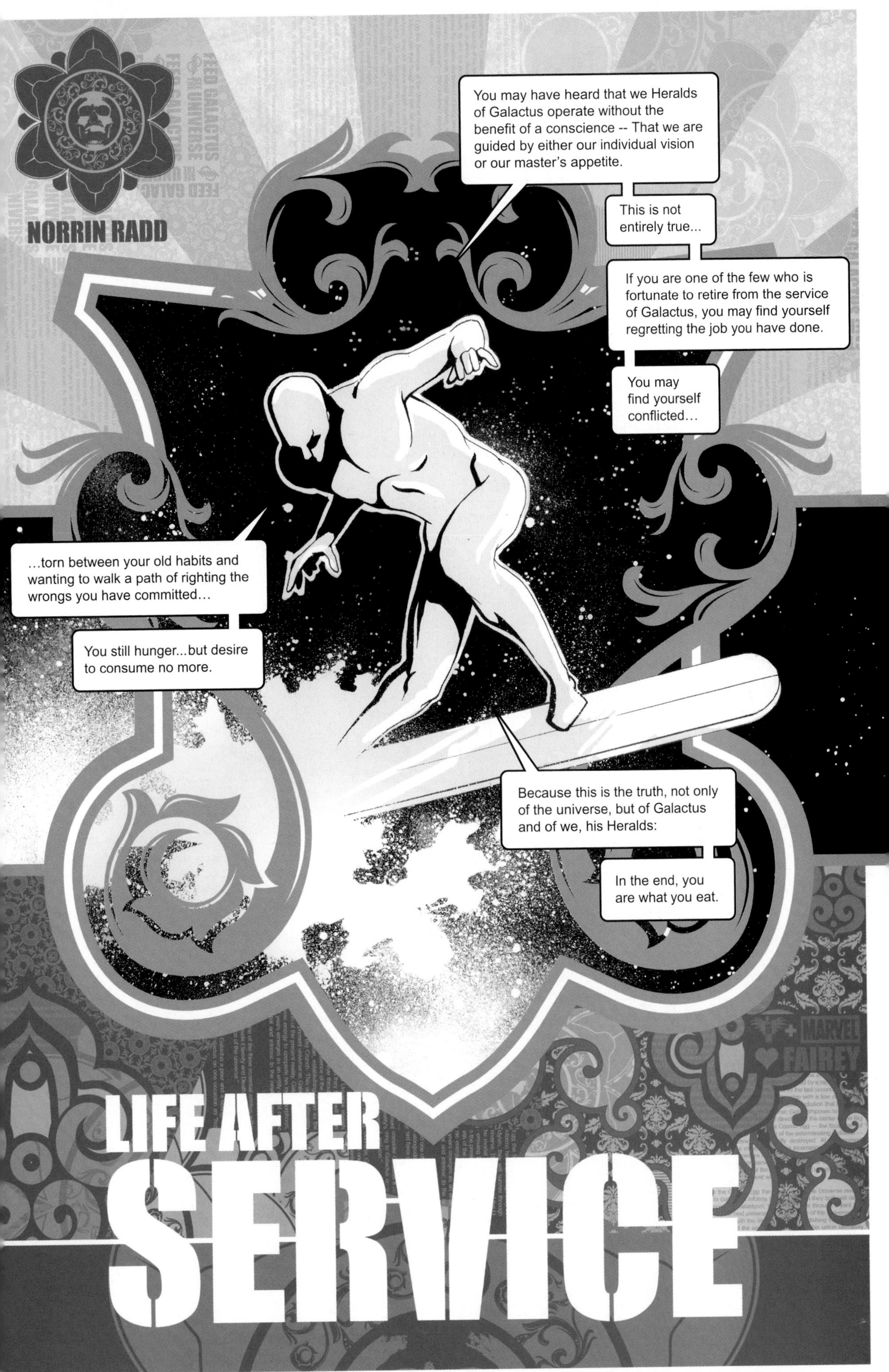
NORRIN RADD
You may have heard that we Heralds of Galactus operate without the benefit of a conscience -- That we are guided by either our individual vision or our master's appetite.
This is not entirely true...
If you are one of the few who is fortunate to retire from the service of Galactus, you may find yourself regretting the job you have done.
You may find yourself conflicted...
...torn between your old habits and wanting to walk a path of righting the wrongs you have committed...
You still hunger...but desire to consume no more.
Because this is the truth, not only of the universe, but of Galactus and of we, his Heralds:
In the end, you are what you eat.
MARVEL
FAIREY
LIFE AFTER
SERVICE

Disclaimer: The actual recovery process that an ex-Herald goes through should not be underestimated and, in fact, requires extensive treatment including, but not limited to: Change in diet, medication, counseling, and, in some cases, intervention and institutionalization. (Certain recovery programs available only to customers who have the universal care plan provided by Galactus, Inc.) © 2008, Galactus, Inc.

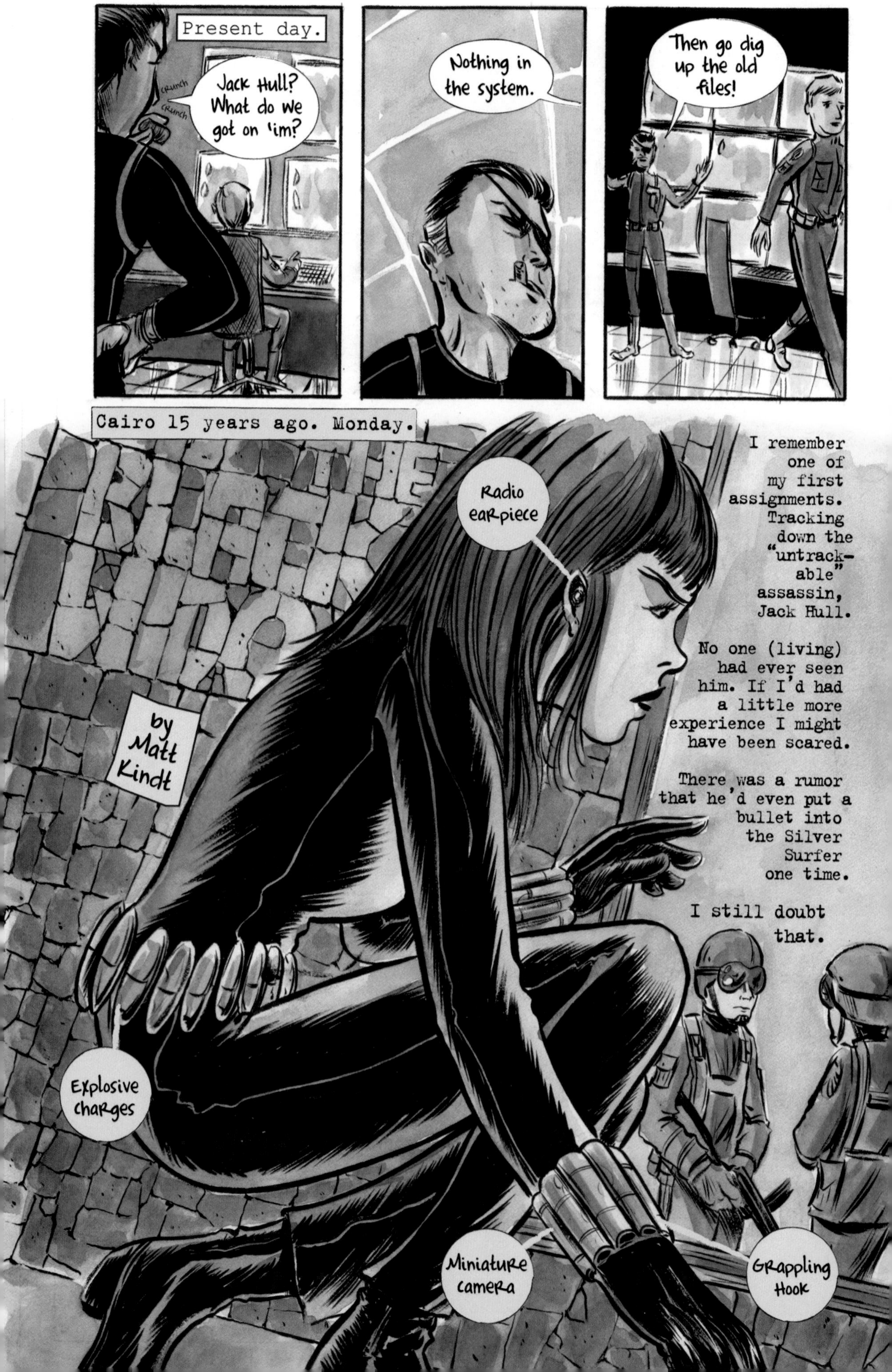
Present day.
crunch crunch
Jack Hull? What do we got on 'im?
Nothing in the system.
Then go dig up the old files!
Cairo 15 years ago. Monday.
I remember one of my first assignments. Tracking down the "untrackable" assassin, Jack Hull.
No one (living) had ever seen him. If I'd had a little more experience I might have been scared.
There was a rumor that he'd even put a bullet into the Silver Surfer one time.
I still doubt that.
Radio earpiece
by Matt Kindt
Explosive charges
Miniature camera
Grappling Hook

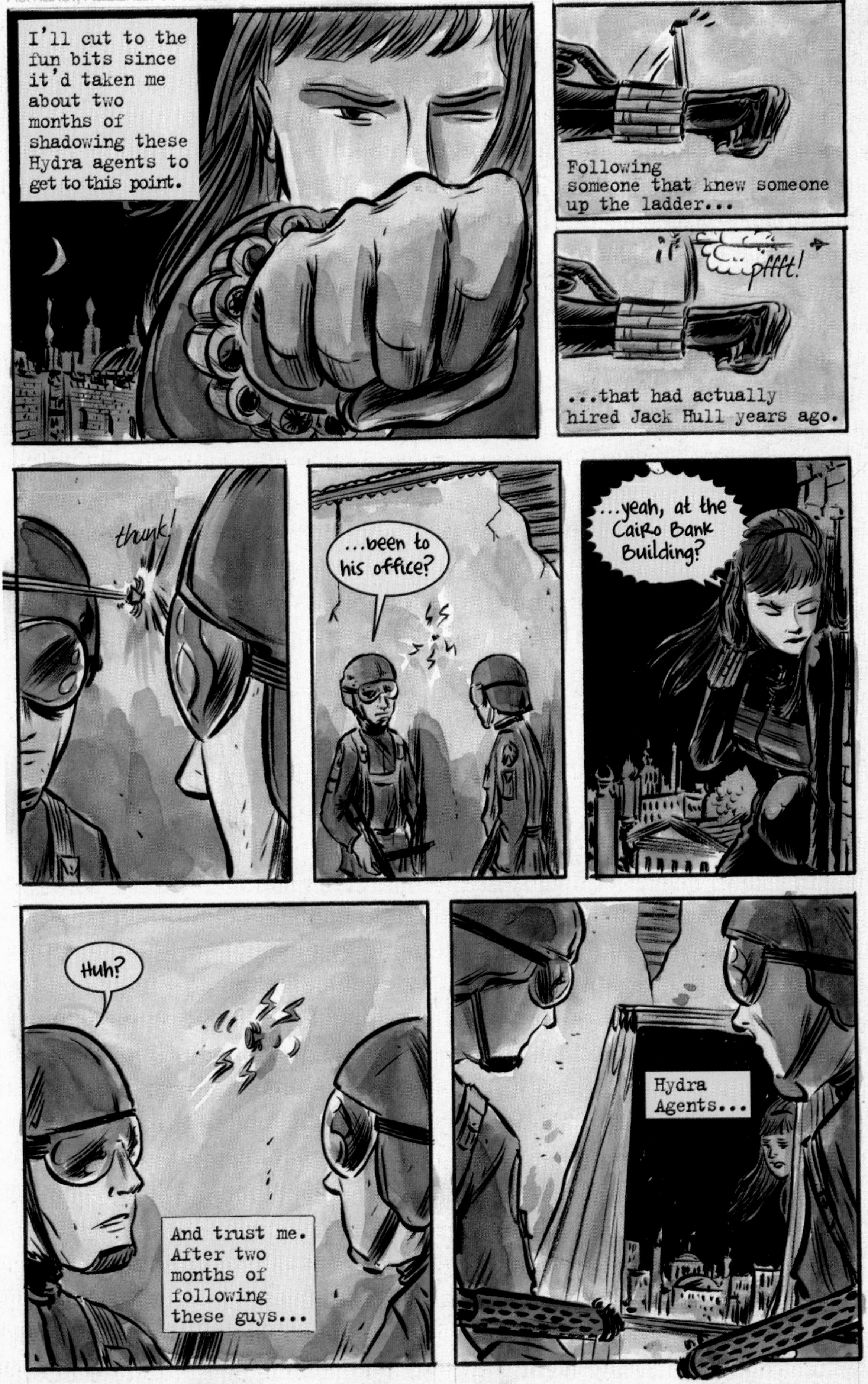
I'll cut to the fun bits since it'd taken me about two months of shadowing these Hydra agents to get to this point.
Following someone that knew someone up the ladder...
pffft!
...that had actually hired Jack Hull years ago.
thunk!
...been to his office?
...yeah, at the Cairo Bank Building?
Huh?
And trust me. After two months of following these guys...
Hydra Agents...

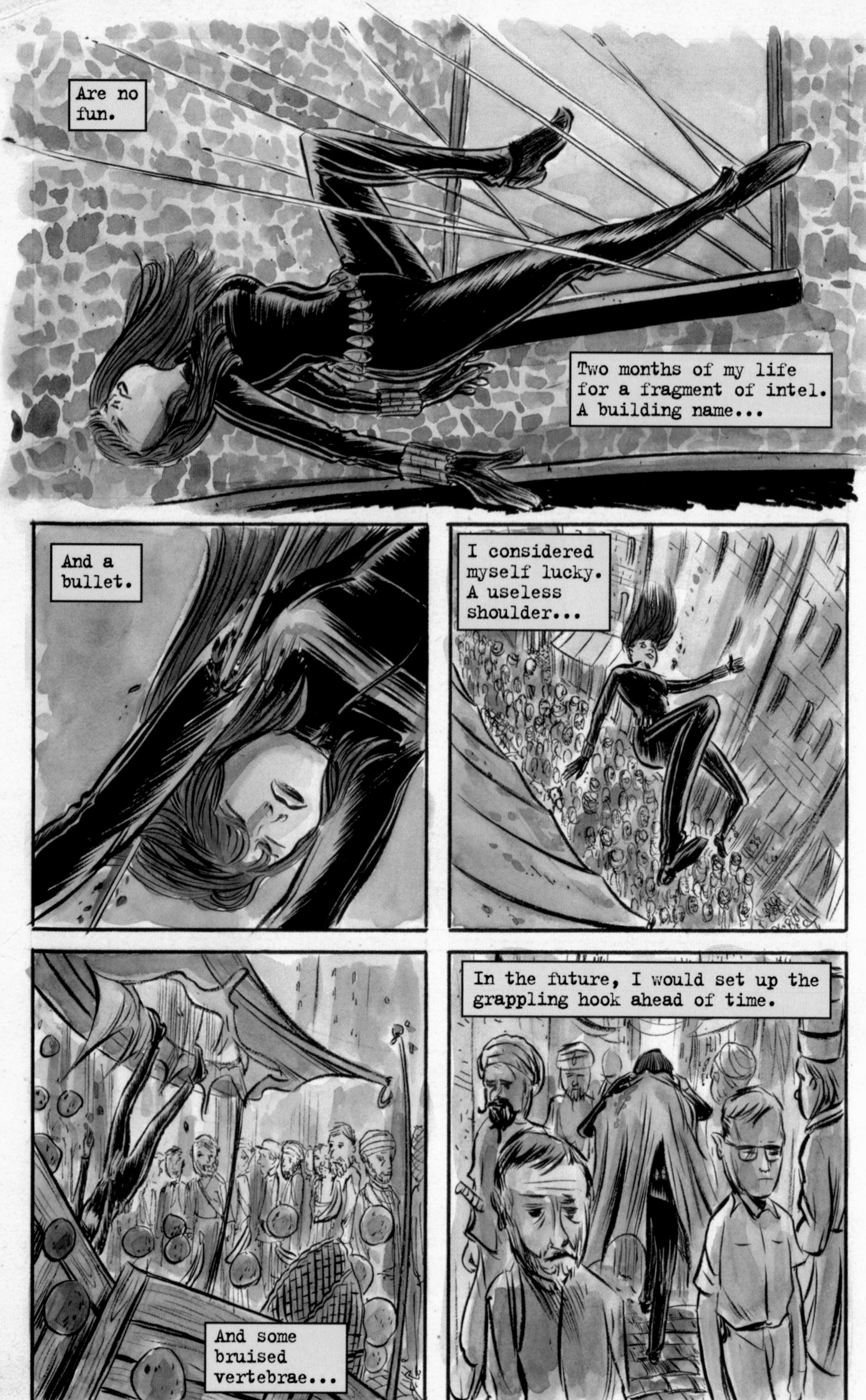
Are no fun.
Two months of my life for a fragment of intel. A building name...
And a bullet.
I considered myself lucky. A useless shoulder...
And some bruised vertebrae...
In the future, I would set up the grappling hook ahead of time.

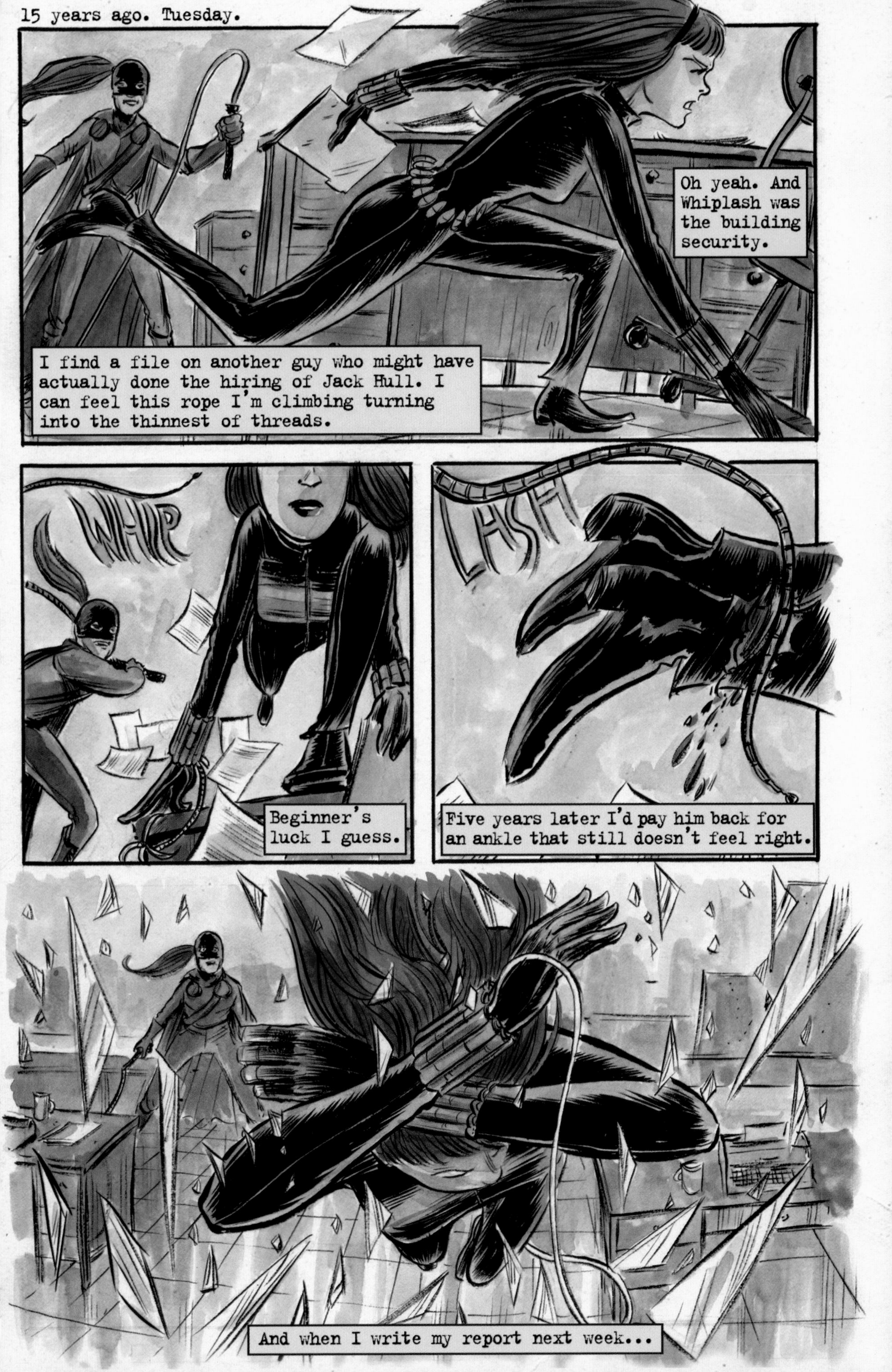
15 years ago. Tuesday.
I find a file on another guy who might have actually done the hiring of Jack Hull. I can feel this rope I'm climbing turning into the thinnest of threads.
Oh yeah. And Whiplash was the building security.
WHIP
Beginner's luck I guess.
LASH
Five years later I'd pay him back for an ankle that still doesn't feel right.
And when I write my report next week...

I'll assume the red and gold blur I saw was Tony...

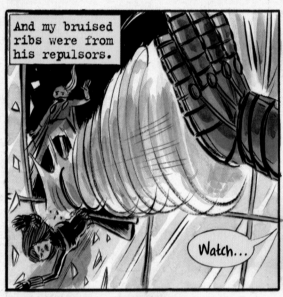

And my bruised ribs were from his repulsors.

Watch...

...out!

Every mission is a learning experience.

Every scar is a mental note...

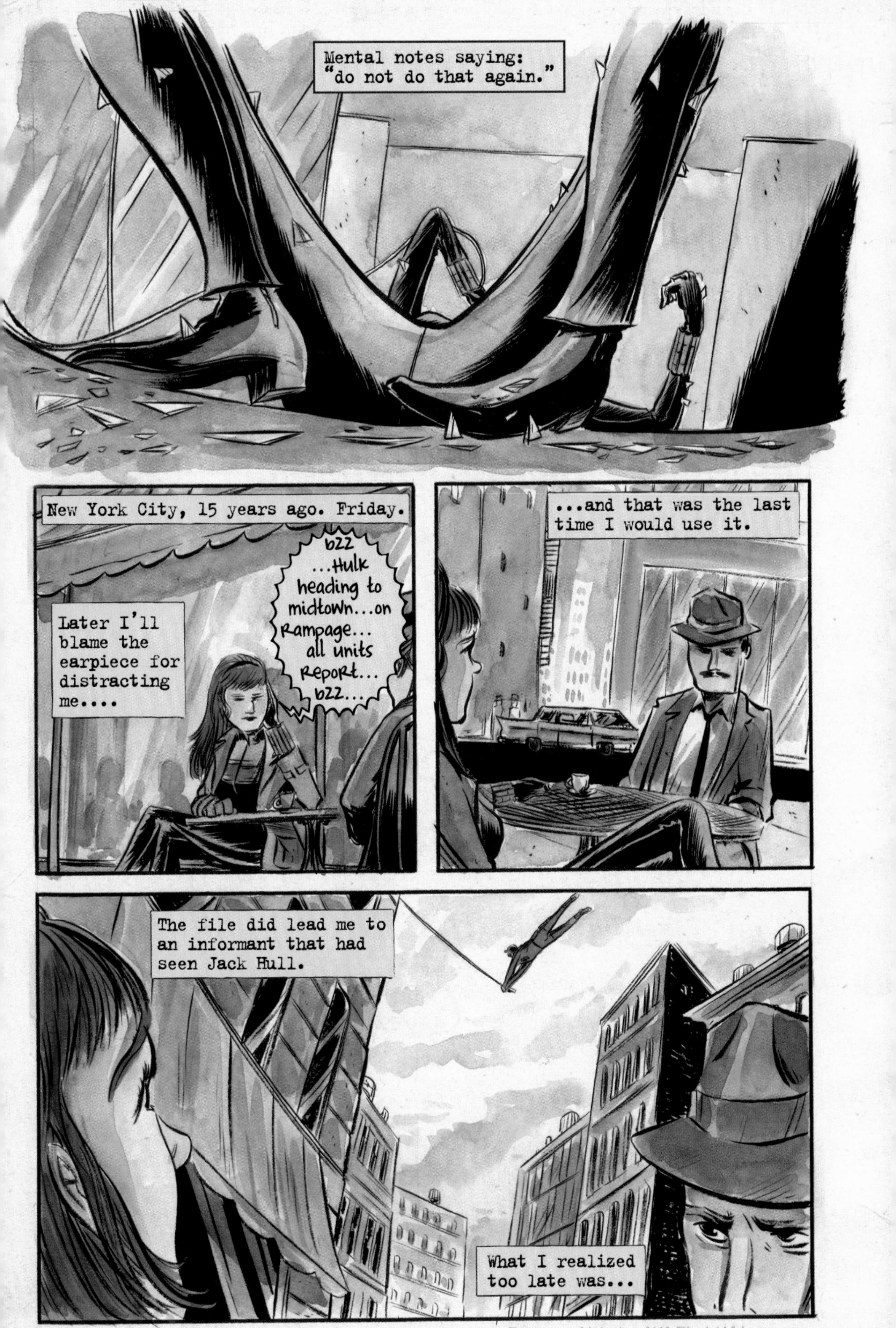
Mental notes saying: "do not do that again."
New York City, 15 years ago. Friday.
Later I'll blame the earpiece for distracting me....
bzz ...Hulk heading to midtown...on Rampage... all units Report... bzz...
...and that was the last time I would use it.
The file did lead me to an informant that had seen Jack Hull.
What I realized too late was...

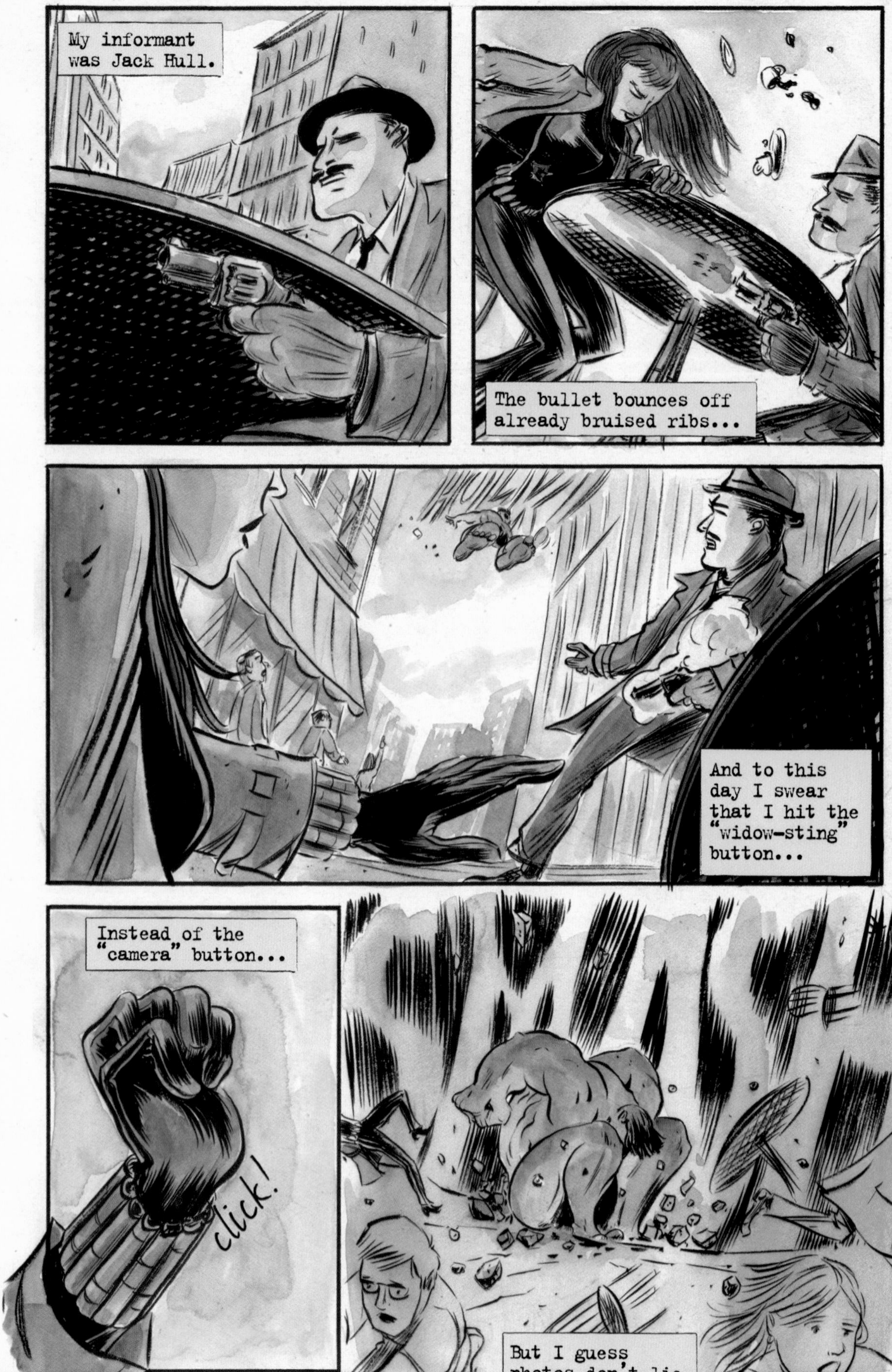
My informant was Jack Hull.
The bullet bounces off already bruised ribs...
And to this day I swear that I hit the "widow-sting" button...
Instead of the "camera" button...
click!
But I guess photos don't lie.

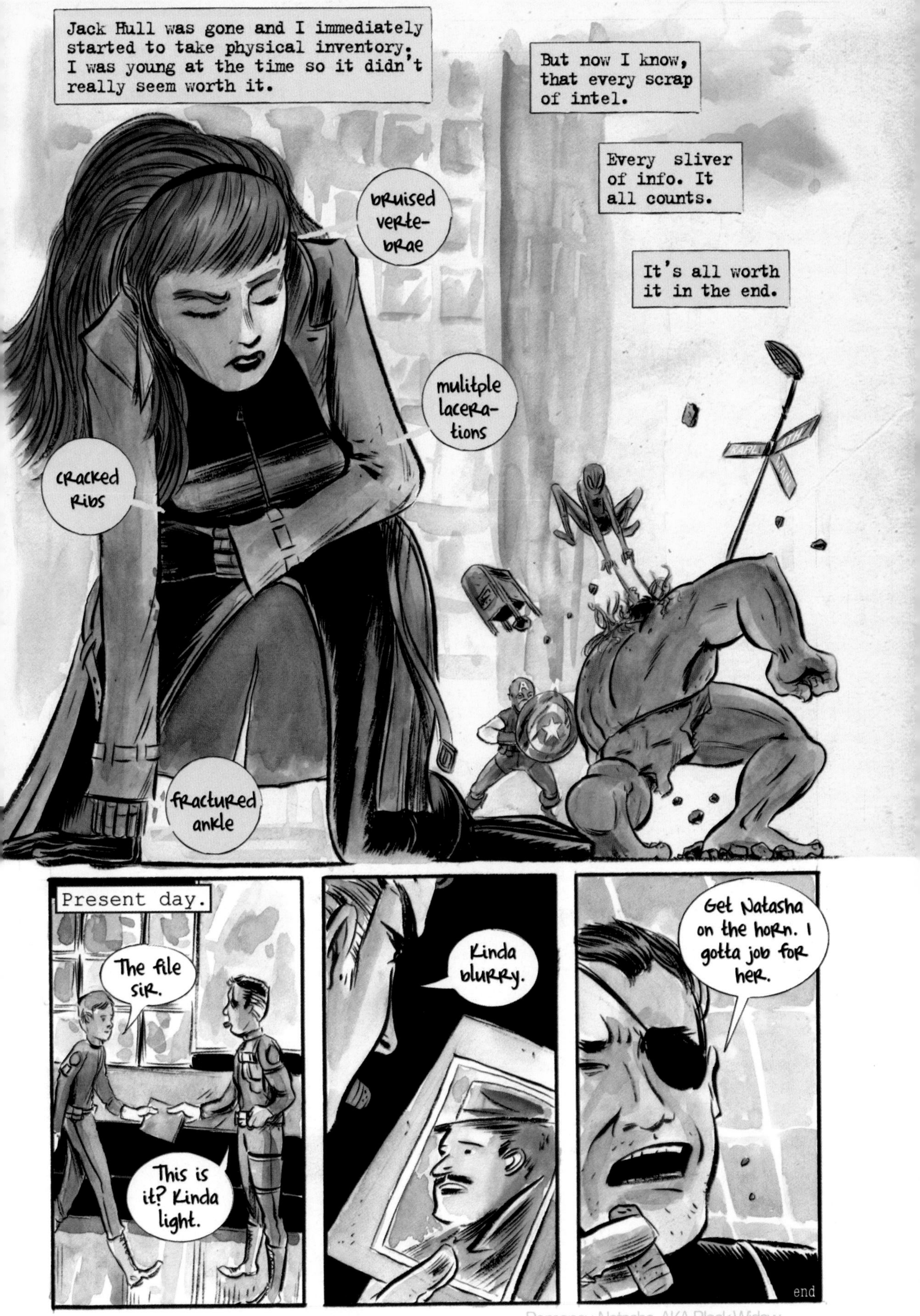
Jack Hull was gone and I immediately started to take physical inventory. I was young at the time so it didn't really seem worth it.
But now I know, that every scrap of intel.
Every sliver of info. It all counts.
It's all worth it in the end.
bruised verte-brae
mulitple lacera-tions
cracked Ribs
fractured ankle
Present day.
The file sir.
This is it? Kinda light.
Kinda blurry.
Get Natasha on the horn. I gotta job for her.
end

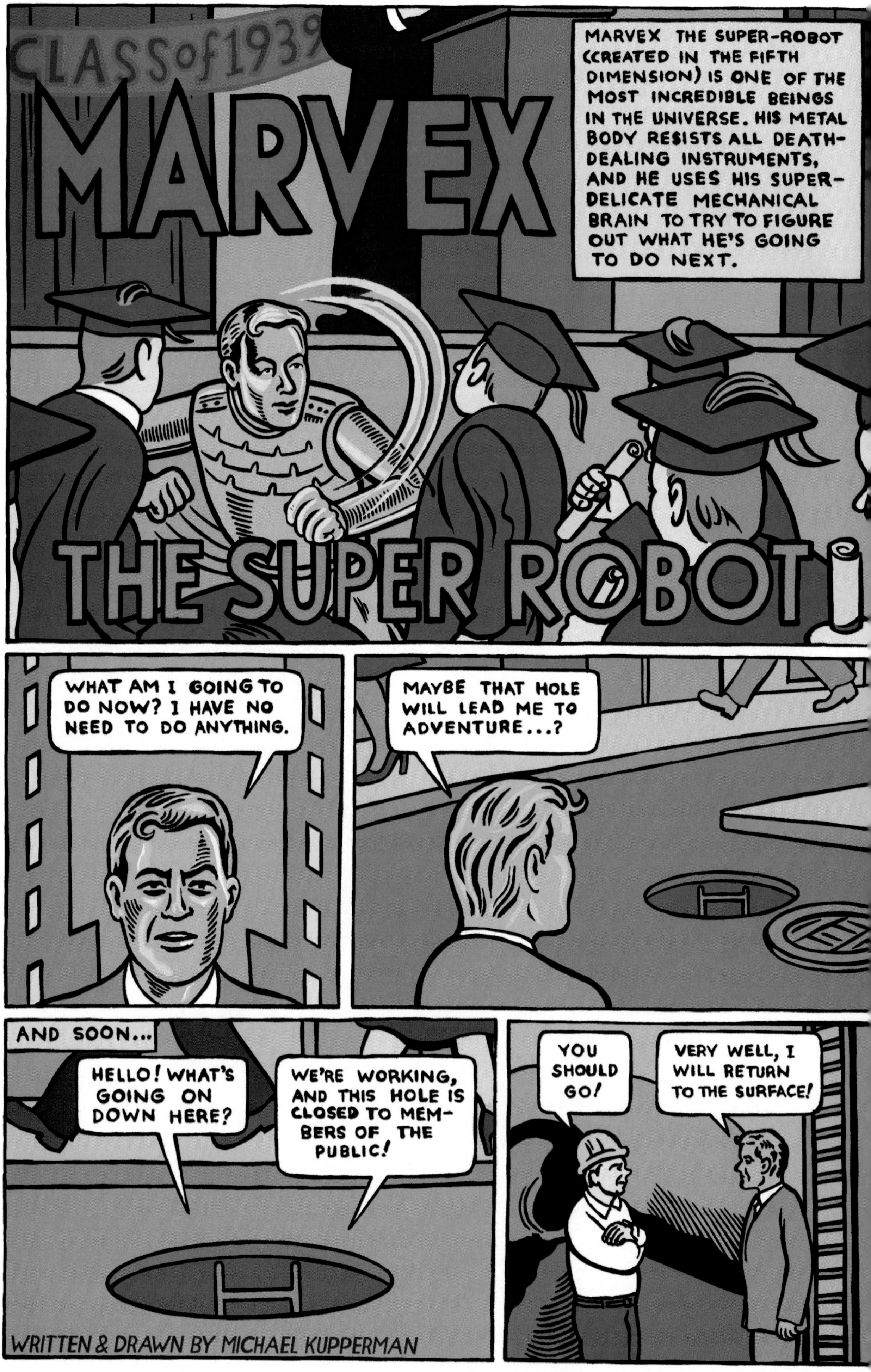
CLASS of 1939
MARVEX
MARVEX THE SUPER-ROBOT (CREATED IN THE FIFTH DIMENSION) IS ONE OF THE MOST INCREDIBLE BEINGS IN THE UNIVERSE. HIS METAL BODY RESISTS ALL DEATH-DEALING INSTRUMENTS, AND HE USES HIS SUPER-DELICATE MECHANICAL BRAIN TO TRY TO FIGURE OUT WHAT HE'S GOING TO DO NEXT.
THE SUPER ROBOT
WHAT AM I GOING TO DO NOW? I HAVE NO NEED TO DO ANYTHING.
MAYBE THAT HOLE WILL LEAD ME TO ADVENTURE...?
AND SOON...
HELLO! WHAT'S GOING ON DOWN HERE?
WE'RE WORKING, AND THIS HOLE IS CLOSED TO MEMBERS OF THE PUBLIC!
YOU SHOULD GO!
VERY WELL, I WILL RETURN TO THE SURFACE!
WRITTEN & DRAWN BY MICHAEL KUPPERMAN

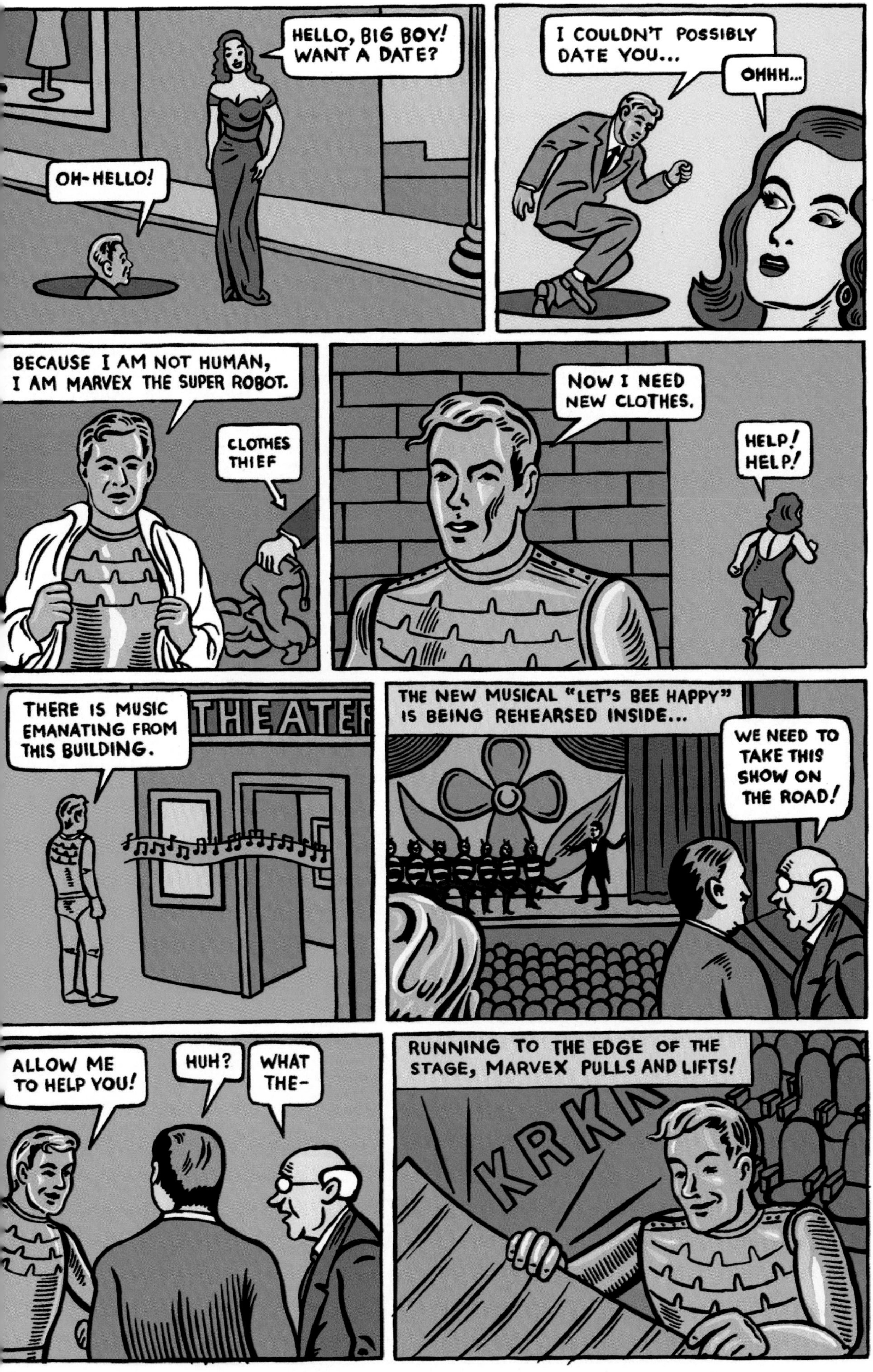
HELLO, BIG BOY! WANT A DATE?
OH-HELLO!
I COULDN'T POSSIBLY DATE YOU...
OHHH...
BECAUSE I AM NOT HUMAN, I AM MARVEX THE SUPER ROBOT.
CLOTHES THIEF
NOW I NEED NEW CLOTHES.
HELP! HELP!
THERE IS MUSIC EMANATING FROM THIS BUILDING.
THEATER
THE NEW MUSICAL "LET'S BEE HAPPY" IS BEING REHEARSED INSIDE...
WE NEED TO TAKE THIS SHOW ON THE ROAD!
ALLOW ME TO HELP YOU!
HUH?
WHAT THE-
RUNNING TO THE EDGE OF THE STAGE, MARVEX PULLS AND LIFTS!
KRKK

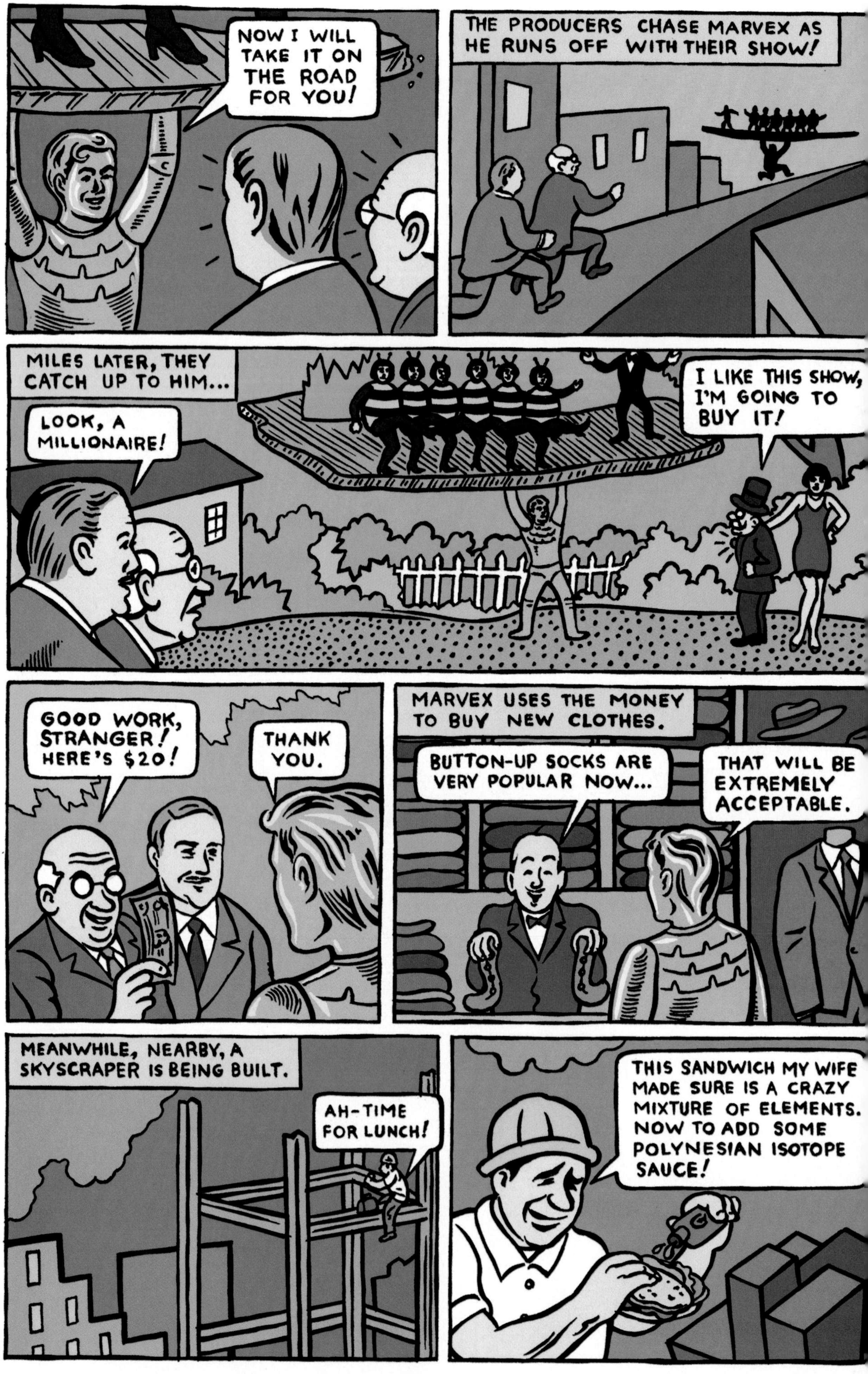
NOW I WILL TAKE IT ON THE ROAD FOR YOU!
THE PRODUCERS CHASE MARVEX AS HE RUNS OFF WITH THEIR SHOW!
MILES LATER, THEY CATCH UP TO HIM...
LOOK, A MILLIONAIRE!
I LIKE THIS SHOW, I'M GOING TO BUY IT!
GOOD WORK, STRANGER! HERE'S $20!
THANK YOU.
MARVEX USES THE MONEY TO BUY NEW CLOTHES.
BUTTON-UP SOCKS ARE VERY POPULAR NOW...
THAT WILL BE EXTREMELY ACCEPTABLE.
MEANWHILE, NEARBY, A SKYSCRAPER IS BEING BUILT.
AH-TIME FOR LUNCH!
THIS SANDWICH MY WIFE MADE SURE IS A CRAZY MIXTURE OF ELEMENTS. NOW TO ADD SOME POLYNESIAN ISOTOPE SAUCE!

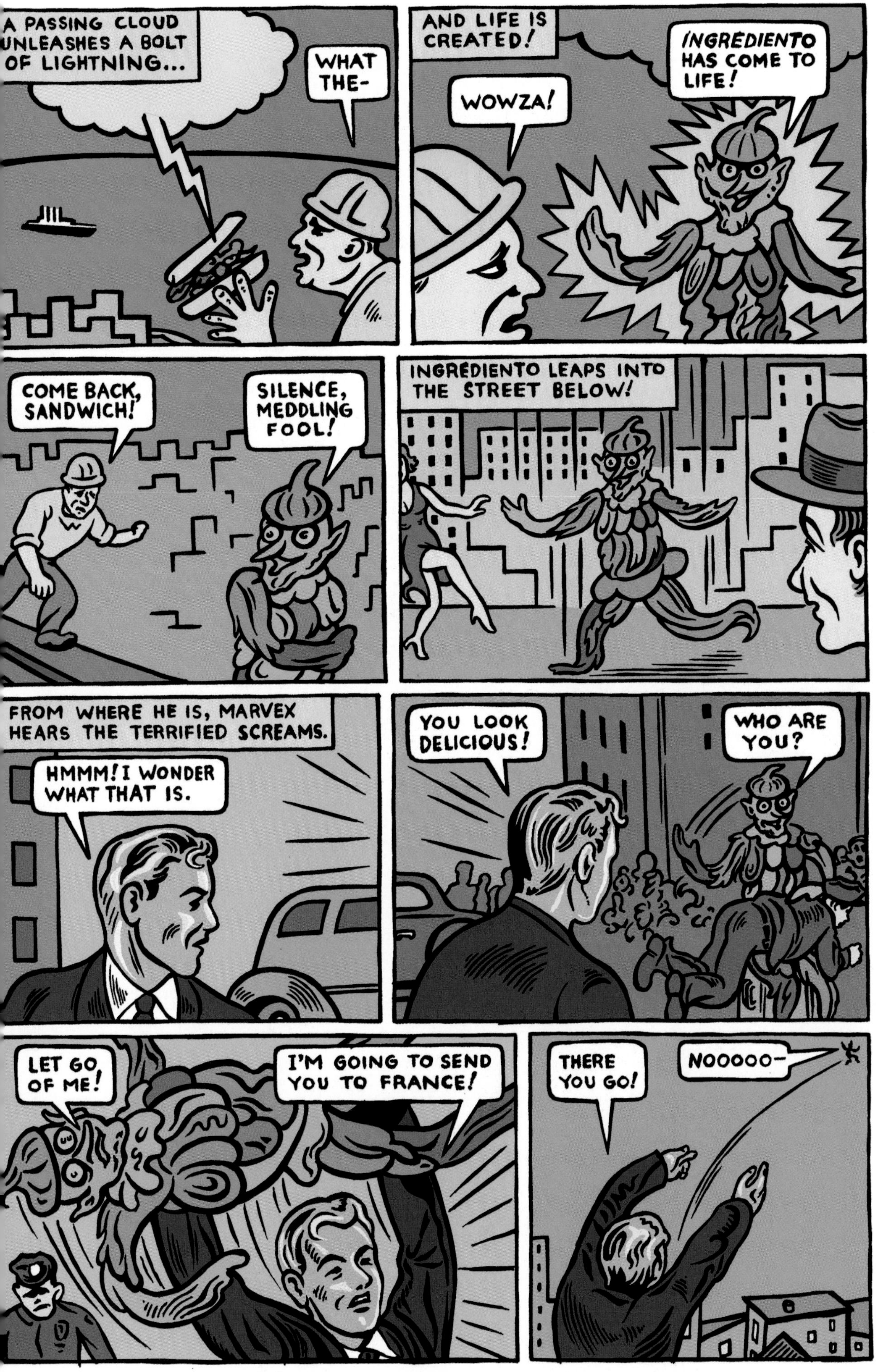
A PASSING CLOUD UNLEASHES A BOLT OF LIGHTNING...
WHAT THE-
AND LIFE IS CREATED!
WOWZA!
INGREDIENTO HAS COME TO LIFE!
COME BACK, SANDWICH!
SILENCE, MEDDLING FOOL!
INGREDIENTO LEAPS INTO THE STREET BELOW!
FROM WHERE HE IS, MARVEX HEARS THE TERRIFIED SCREAMS.
HMMM! I WONDER WHAT THAT IS.
YOU LOOK DELICIOUS!
WHO ARE YOU?
LET GO, OF ME!
I'M GOING TO SEND YOU TO FRANCE!
THERE YOU GO!
NOOOOO-

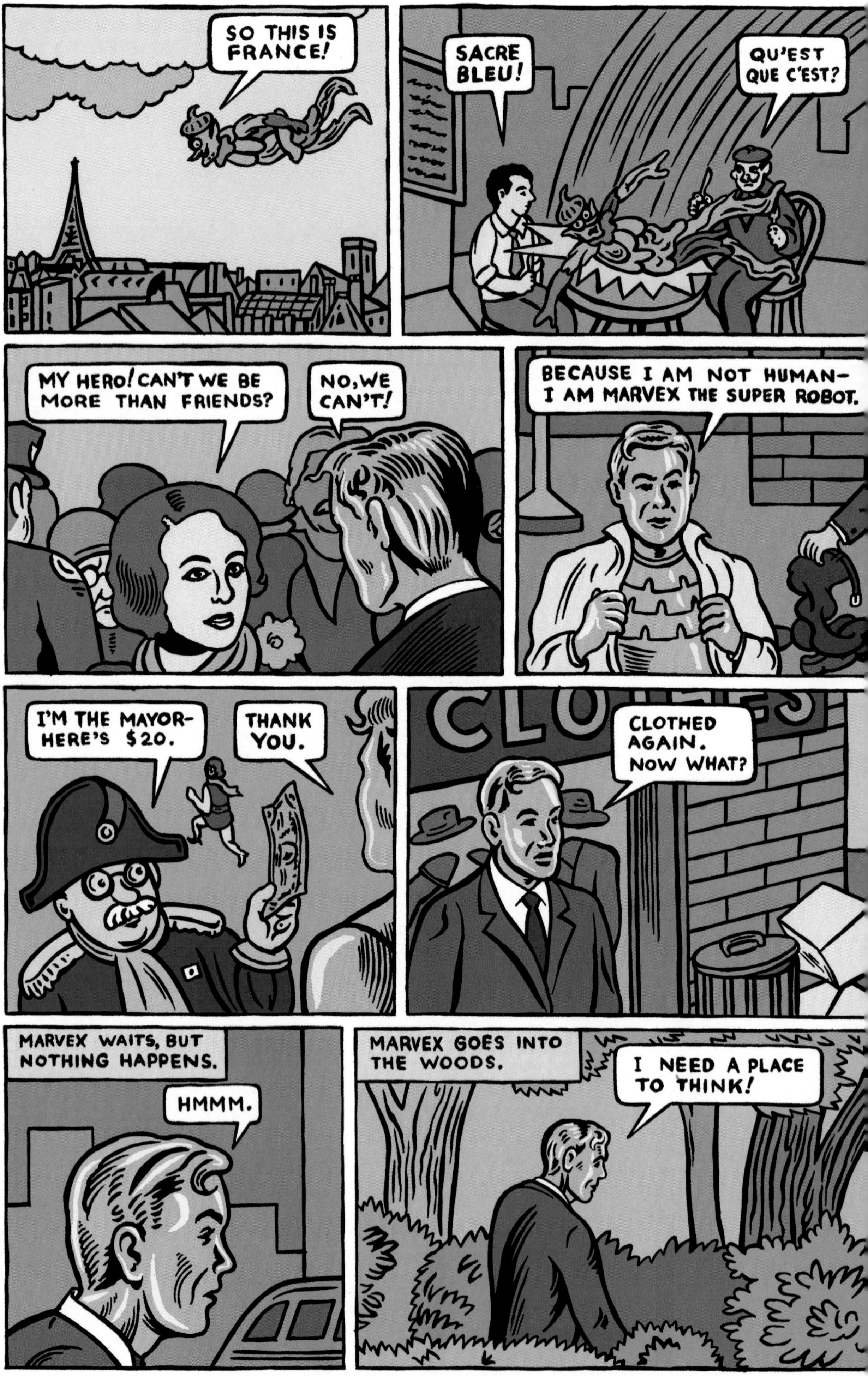
SO THIS IS FRANCE!
SACRE BLEU!
QU'EST QUE C'EST?
MY HERO! CAN'T WE BE MORE THAN FRIENDS?
NO, WE CAN'T!
BECAUSE I AM NOT HUMAN- I AM MARVEX THE SUPER ROBOT.
I'M THE MAYOR- HERE'S $20.
THANK YOU.
CLO
CLOTHED AGAIN. NOW WHAT?
MARVEX WAITS, BUT NOTHING HAPPENS.
HMMM.
MARVEX GOES INTO THE WOODS.
I NEED A PLACE TO THINK!

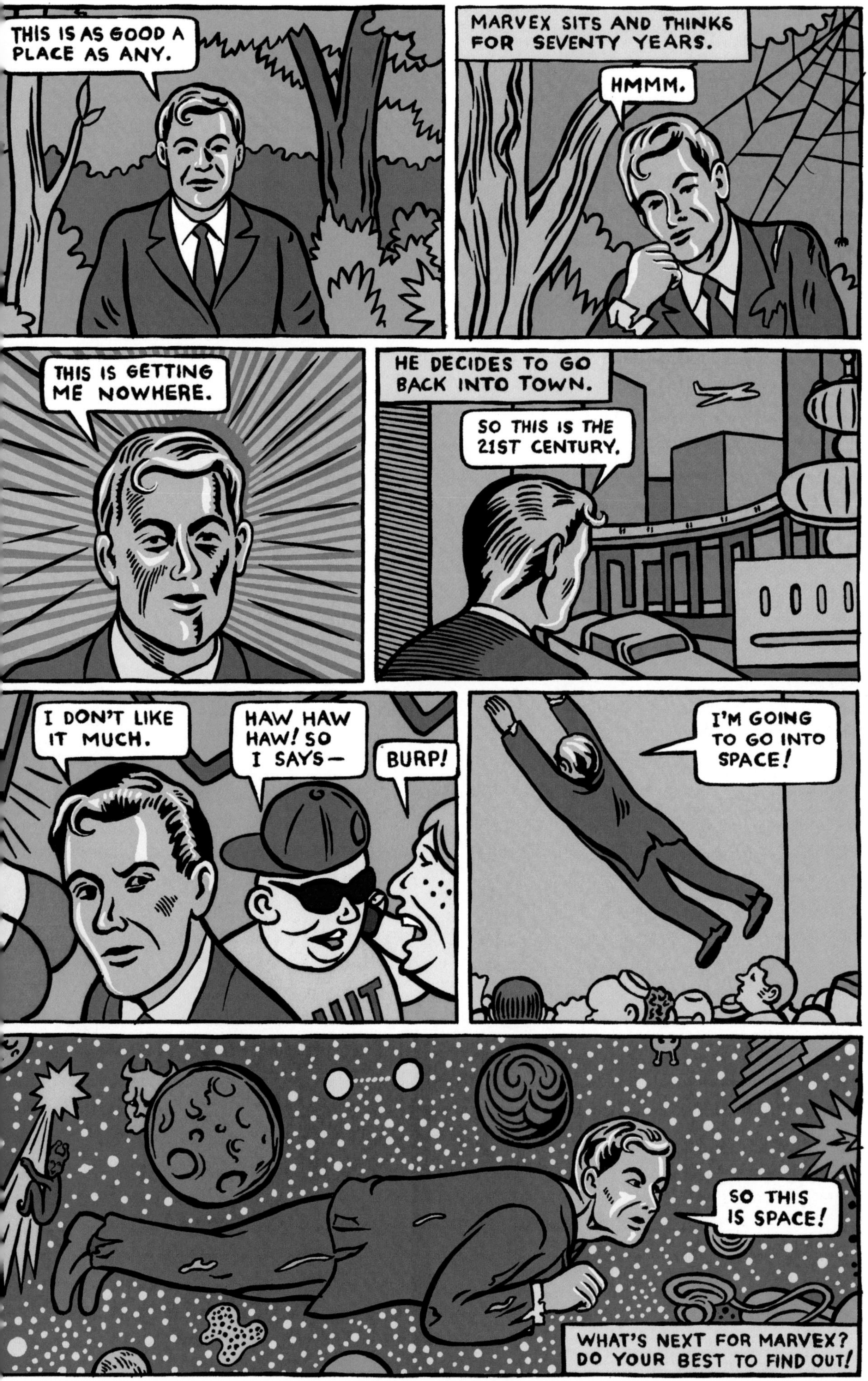
THIS IS AS GOOD A PLACE AS ANY.
MARVEX SITS AND THINKS FOR SEVENTY YEARS.
HMMM.
THIS IS GETTING ME NOWHERE.
HE DECIDES TO GO BACK INTO TOWN.
SO THIS IS THE 21ST CENTURY.
I DON'T LIKE IT MUCH.
HAW HAW HAW! SO I SAYS—
BURP!
I'M GOING TO GO INTO SPACE!
SO THIS IS SPACE!
WHAT'S NEXT FOR MARVEX? DO YOUR BEST TO FIND OUT!

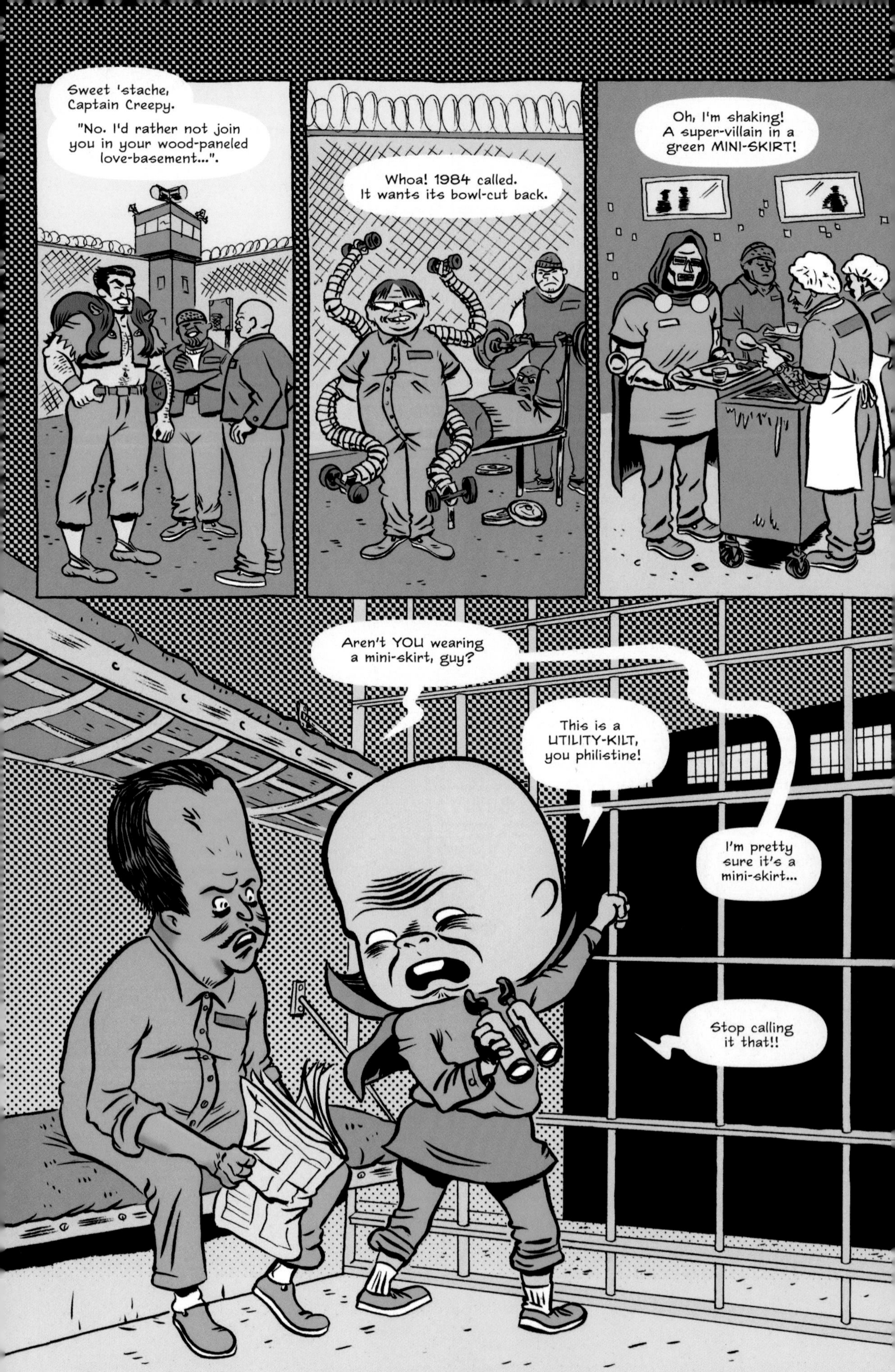
Sweet 'stache, Captain Creepy.
"No. I'd rather not join you in your wood-paneled love-basement...".
Whoa! 1984 called. It wants its bowl-cut back.
Oh, I'm shaking! A super-villain in a green MINI-SKIRT!
Aren't YOU wearing a mini-skirt, guy?
This is a UTILITY-KILT, you philistine!
I'm pretty sure it's a mini-skirt...
Stop calling it that!!

"Cool Hand Uatu" by Nick Bertozzi and colored by Chris Sinderson

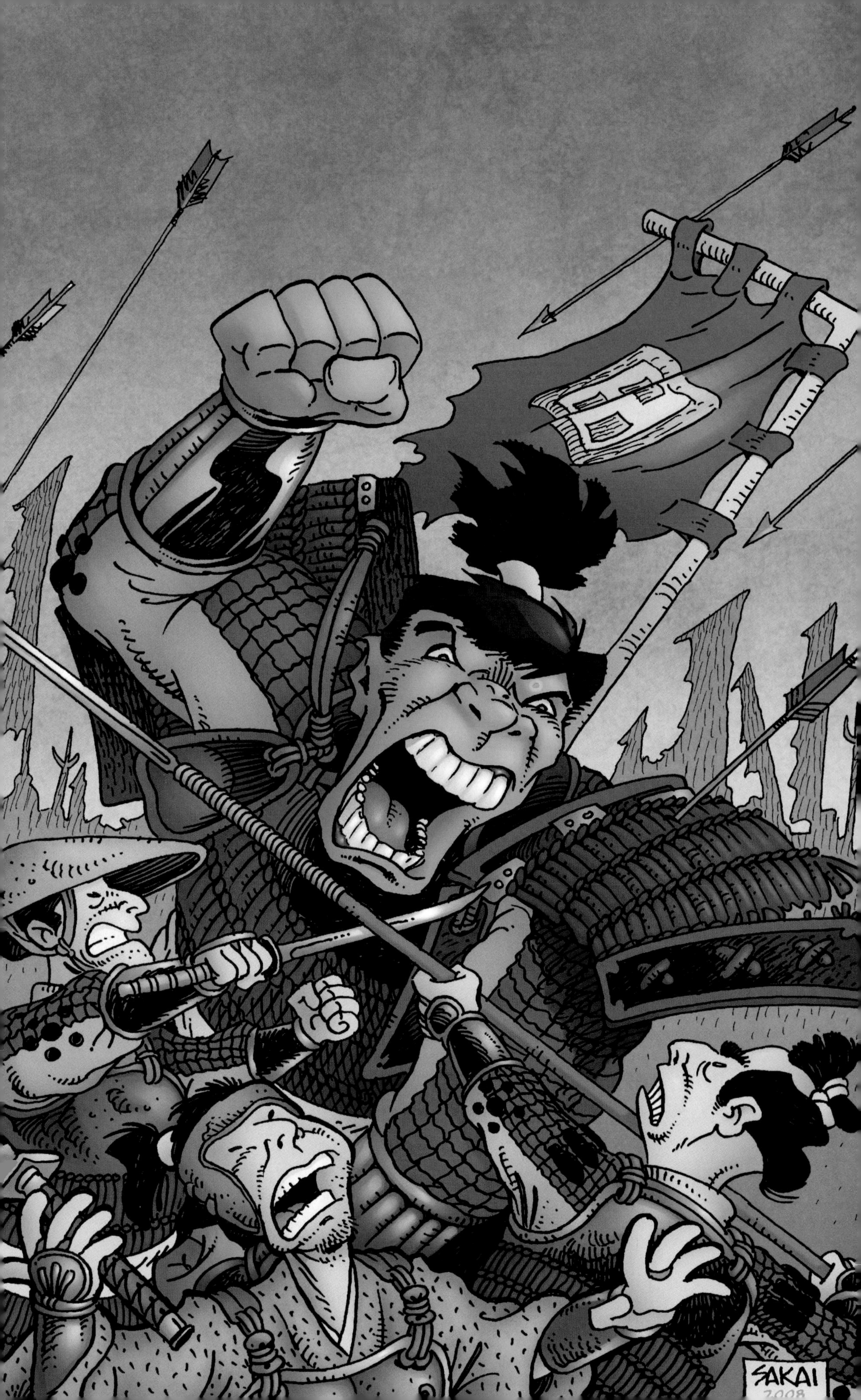
SAKAI
2008

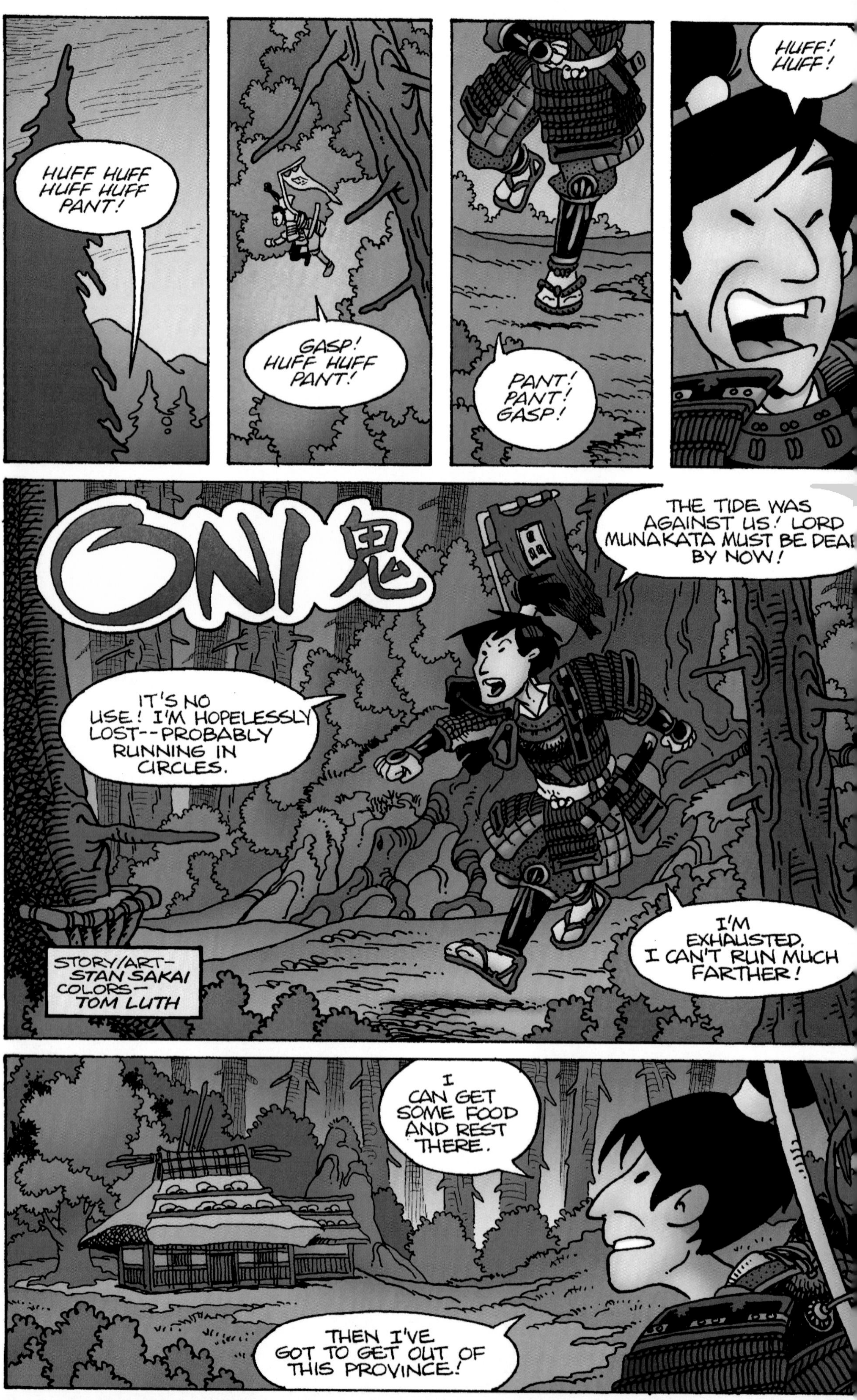
HUFF HUFF HUFF HUFF PANT!
GASP! HUFF HUFF PANT!
PANT! PANT! GASP!
HUFF! HUFF!
ONI 鬼
THE TIDE WAS AGAINST US! LORD MUNAKATA MUST BE DEAD BY NOW!
IT'S NO USE! I'M HOPELESSLY LOST--PROBABLY RUNNING IN CIRCLES.
I'M EXHAUSTED. I CAN'T RUN MUCH FARTHER!
STORY/ART-STAN SAKAI COLORS-TOM LUTH
I CAN GET SOME FOOD AND REST THERE.
THEN I'VE GOT TO GET OUT OF THIS PROVINCE!

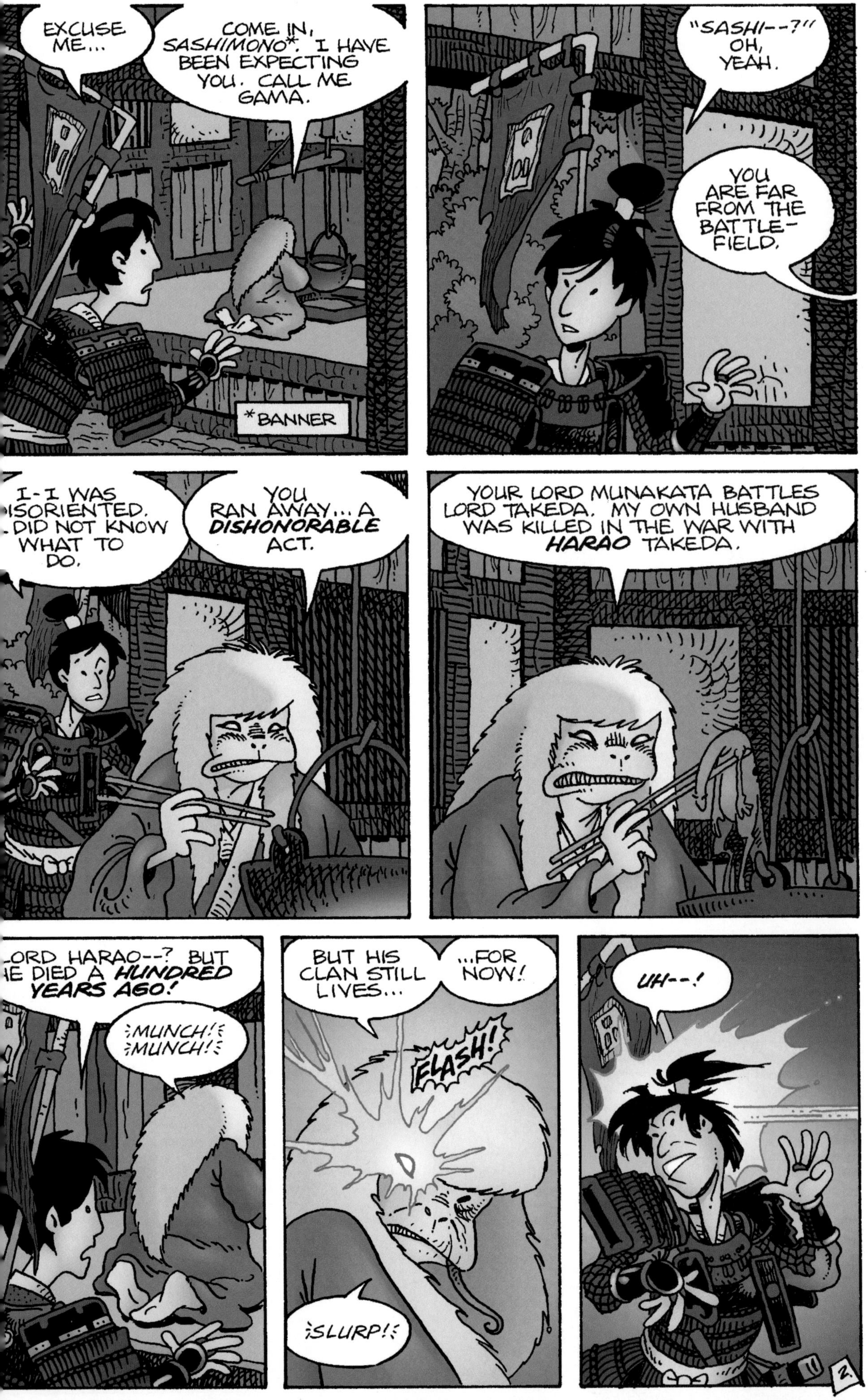

EXCUSE ME...
COME IN, SASHIMONO*. I HAVE BEEN EXPECTING YOU. CALL ME GAMA.
*BANNER
"SASHI--?" OH, YEAH.
YOU ARE FAR FROM THE BATTLE-FIELD.
I-I WAS DISORIENTED. I DID NOT KNOW WHAT TO DO.
YOU RAN AWAY... A DISHONORABLE ACT.
YOUR LORD MUNAKATA BATTLES LORD TAKEDA. MY OWN HUSBAND WAS KILLED IN THE WAR WITH HARAO TAKEDA.
LORD HARAO--? BUT HE DIED A HUNDRED YEARS AGO!
MUNCH! MUNCH!
BUT HIS CLAN STILL LIVES...
...FOR NOW!
FLASH!
SLURP!
UH--!

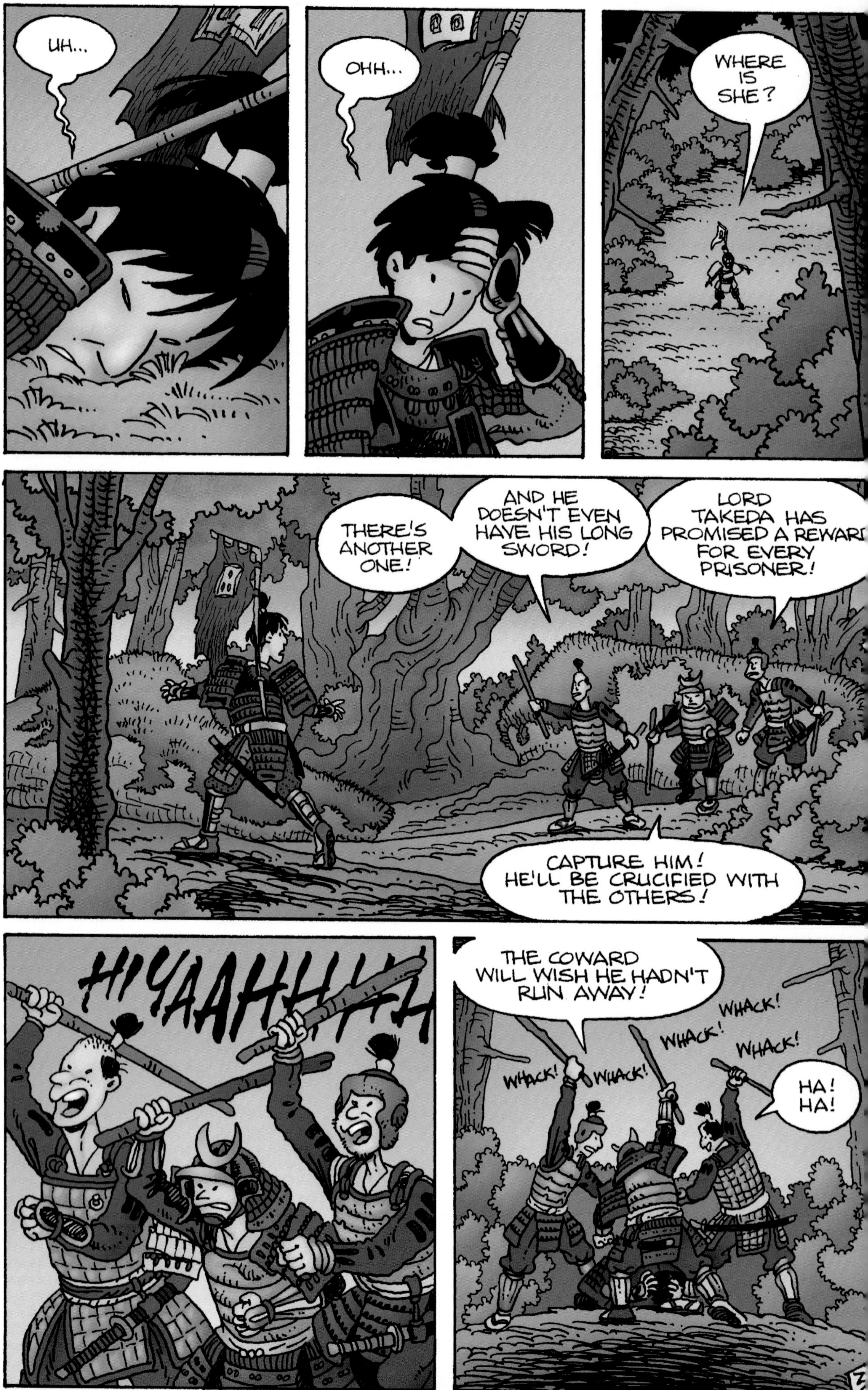
UH...
OHH...
WHERE IS SHE?
THERE'S ANOTHER ONE!
AND HE DOESN'T EVEN HAVE HIS LONG SWORD!
LORD TAKEDA HAS PROMISED A REWARD FOR EVERY PRISONER!
CAPTURE HIM! HE'LL BE CRUCIFIED WITH THE OTHERS!
HIYAAHHHH
THE COWARD WILL WISH HE HADN'T RUN AWAY!
WHACK!
WHACK!
WHACK!
WHACK!
WHACK!
HA! HA!

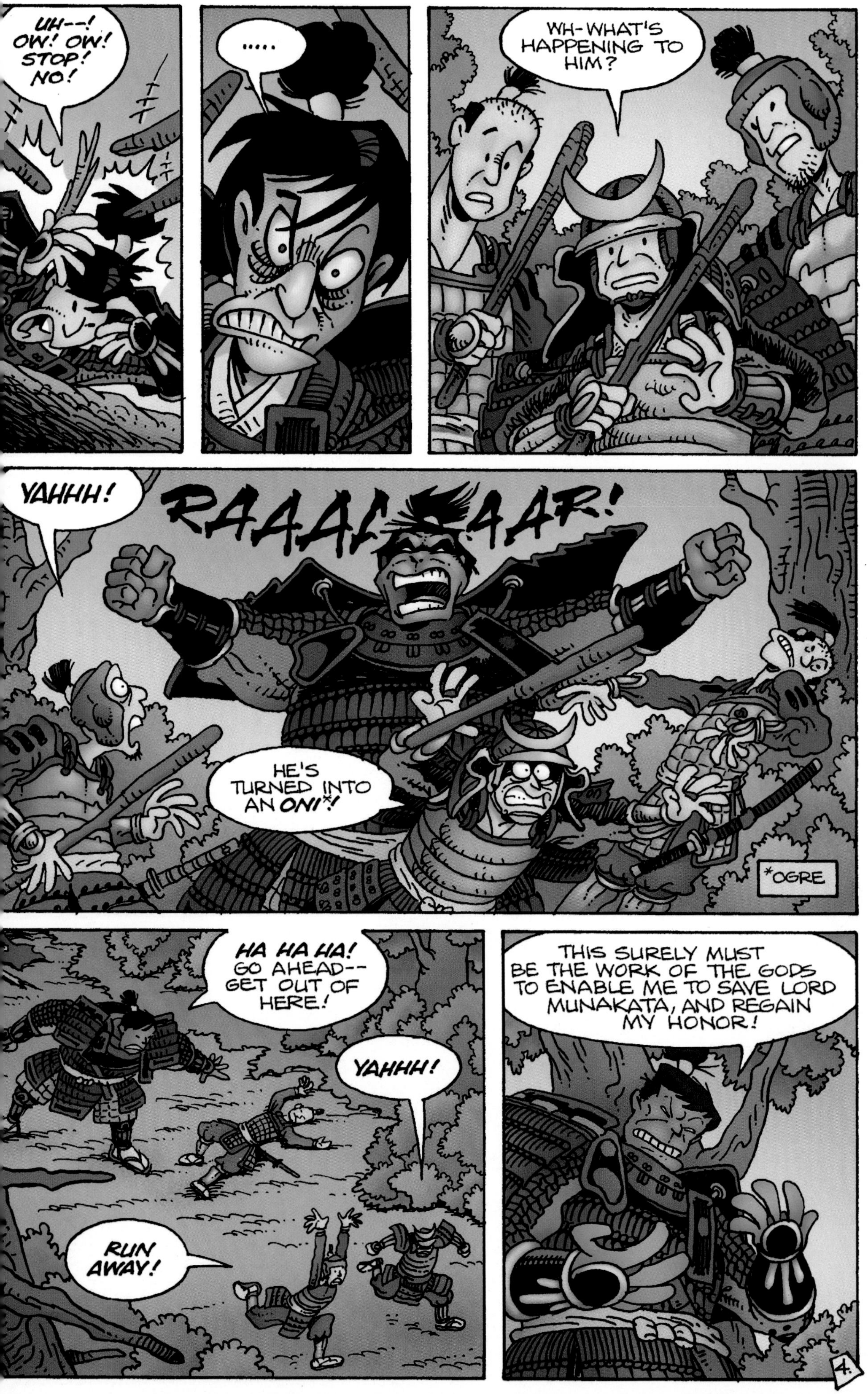
UH--! OW! OW! STOP! NO!
.....
WH-WHAT'S HAPPENING TO HIM?
YAHHH!
RAAAUGAAR!
HE'S TURNED INTO AN ONI*!
*OGRE
HA HA HA! GO AHEAD-- GET OUT OF HERE!
YAHHH!
RUN AWAY!
THIS SURELY MUST BE THE WORK OF THE GODS TO ENABLE ME TO SAVE LORD MUNAKATA, AND REGAIN MY HONOR!
4.

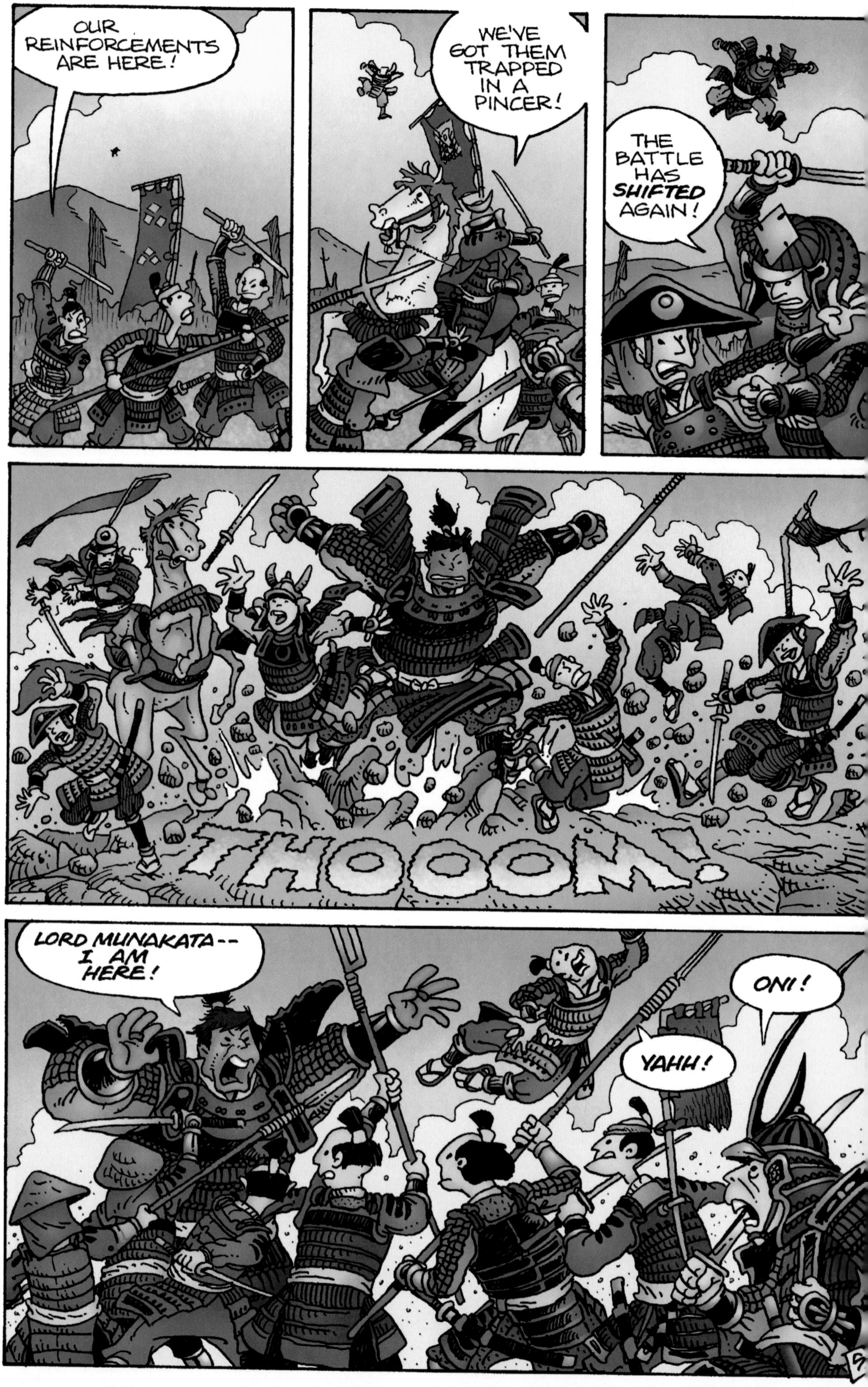
OUR REINFORCEMENTS ARE HERE!
WE'VE GOT THEM TRAPPED IN A PINCER!
THE BATTLE HAS SHIFTED AGAIN!
THOOOM!
LORD MUNAKATA-- I AM HERE!
YAHH!
ONI!

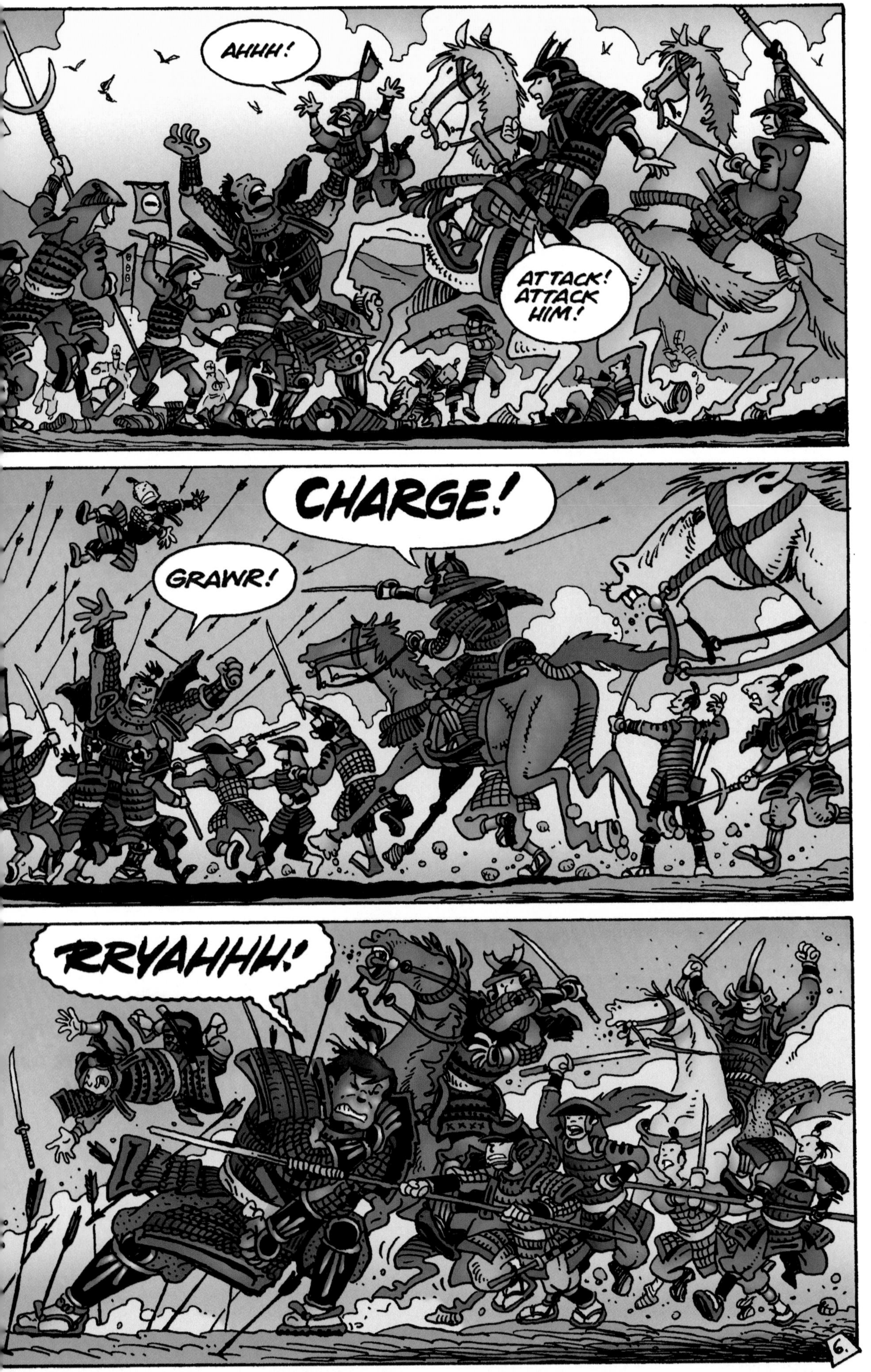

AHHH!
ATTACK! ATTACK HIM!
CHARGE!
GRAWR!
RRYAHHH!

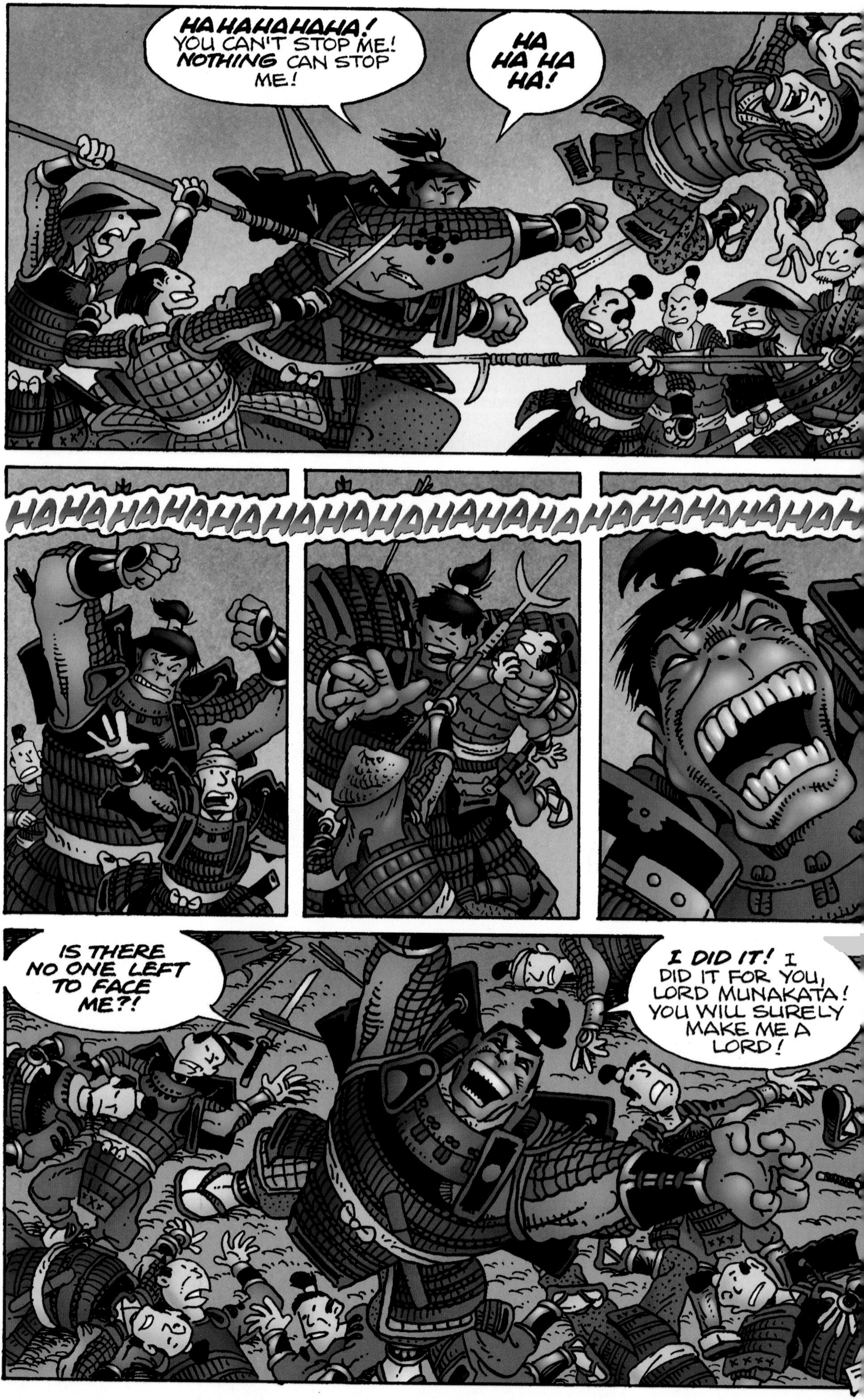
HAHAHAHAHA! YOU CAN'T STOP ME! NOTHING CAN STOP ME!
HA HA HA HA HA!
HAHAHAHAHAHAHAHAHAHAHAHAHAHAHAHAHAHAH
IS THERE NO ONE LEFT TO FACE ME?!
I DID IT! I DID IT FOR YOU, LORD MUNAKATA! YOU WILL SURELY MAKE ME A LORD!

NO--IT CAN'T BE! THAT LAST CHARGE--!

LORD MUNAKATA!

GUAAHHH!

WHAT HAVE I DONE?!

THIS TIME I KNOW WHAT I MUST DO.

ONE FINAL ACT AS A SAMURAI...

...TO PRESERVE HONOR.

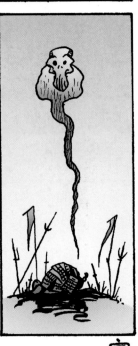

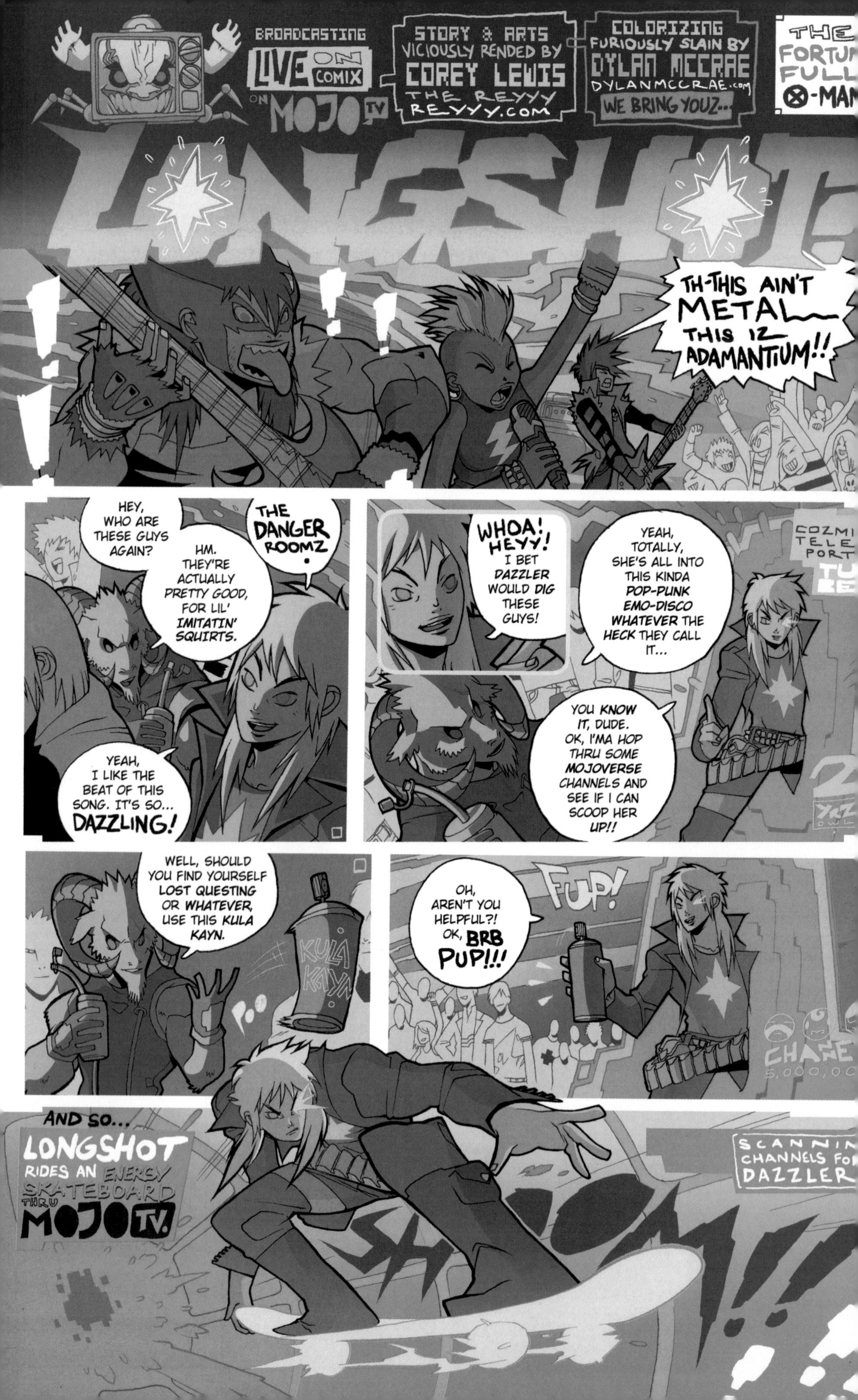
BROADCASTING LIVE ON COMIX ON MOJO TV
STORY & ARTS VICIOUSLY RENDED BY COREY LEWIS THE REYYY REYYY.COM
COLORIZING FURIOUSLY SLAIN BY DYLAN MCCRAE DYLANMCCRAE.com
WE BRING YOUZ...
LONGSHOT
TH-THIS AIN'T METAL THIS IZ ADAMANTIUM!!
HEY, WHO ARE THESE GUYS AGAIN?
HM. THEY'RE ACTUALLY PRETTY GOOD, FOR LIL' IMITATIN' SQUIRTS.
THE DANGER ROOMZ.
YEAH, I LIKE THE BEAT OF THIS SONG. IT'S SO... DAZZLING!
WHOA! HEYY! I BET DAZZLER WOULD DIG THESE GUYS!
YEAH, TOTALLY, SHE'S ALL INTO THIS KINDA POP-PUNK EMO-DISCO WHATEVER THE HECK THEY CALL IT...
YOU KNOW IT, DUDE. OK, I'MA HOP THRU SOME MOJOVERSE CHANNELS AND SEE IF I CAN SCOOP HER UP!!
WELL, SHOULD YOU FIND YOURSELF LOST QUESTING OR WHATEVER, USE THIS KULA KAYN.
KULA KAYN
OH, AREN'T YOU HELPFUL?! OK, BRB PUP!!!
FUP!
AND SO...
LONGSHOT RIDES AN ENERGY SKATEBOARD THRU MOJO TV.
SCANNING CHANNELS FOR DAZZLER

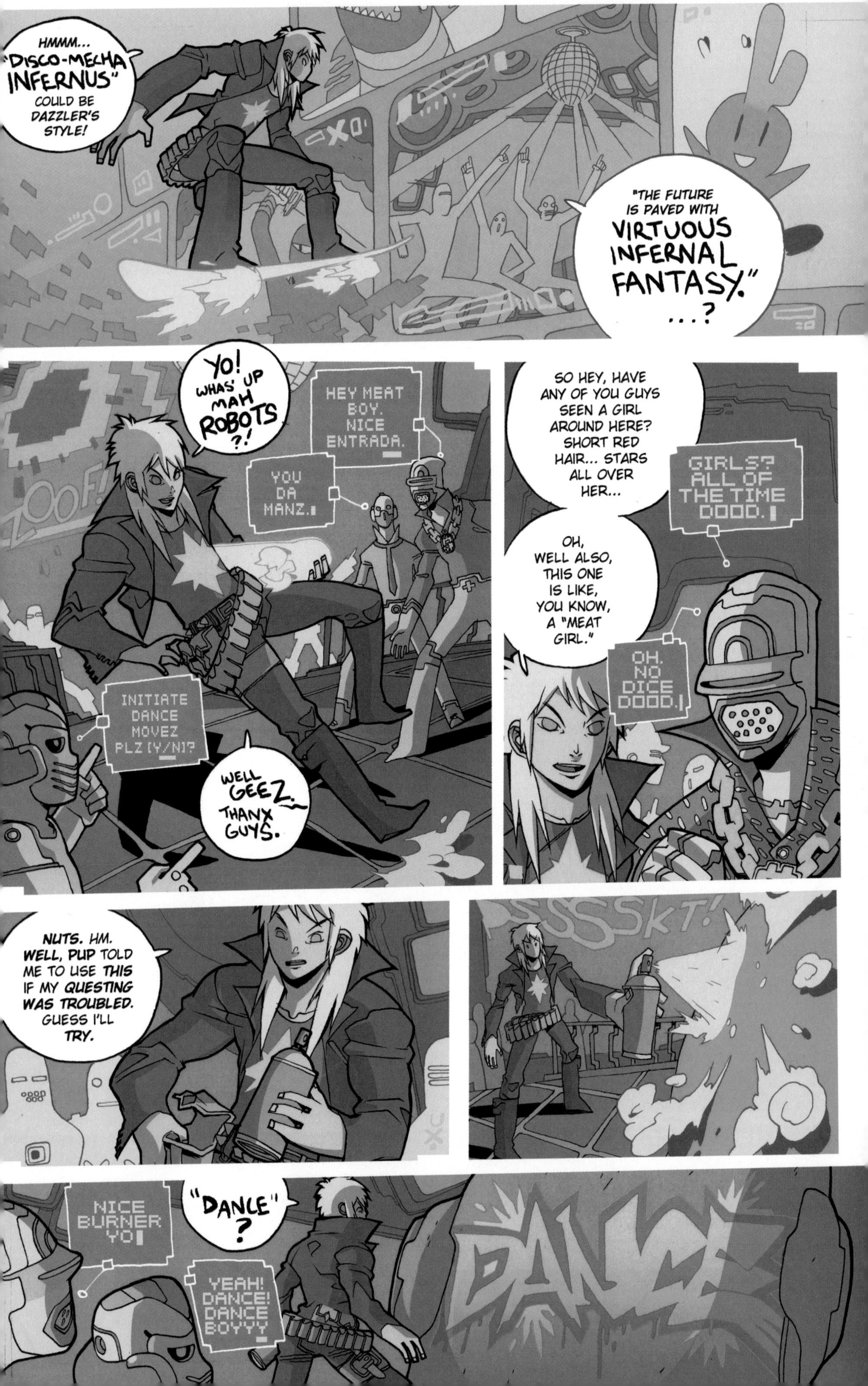
HMMM... "DISCO-MECHA INFERNUS" COULD BE DAZZLER'S STYLE!
"THE FUTURE IS PAVED WITH VIRTUOUS INFERNAL FANTASY." ...?
YO! WHAS' UP MAH ROBOTS ?!
HEY MEAT BOY. NICE ENTRADA.
YOU DA MANZ.
INITIATE DANCE MOVEZ PLZ [Y/N]?
WELL GEEZ. THANX GUYS.
ZOOF!
SO HEY, HAVE ANY OF YOU GUYS SEEN A GIRL AROUND HERE? SHORT RED HAIR... STARS ALL OVER HER...
GIRLS? ALL OF THE TIME DOOD.
OH, WELL ALSO, THIS ONE IS LIKE, YOU KNOW, A "MEAT GIRL."
OH. NO DICE DOOD.
NUTS. HM. WELL, PUP TOLD ME TO USE THIS IF MY QUESTING WAS TROUBLED. GUESS I'LL TRY.
PSSSSSKT!
NICE BURNER YO
"DANCE" ?
YEAH! DANCE! DANCE BOYYY
DANCE

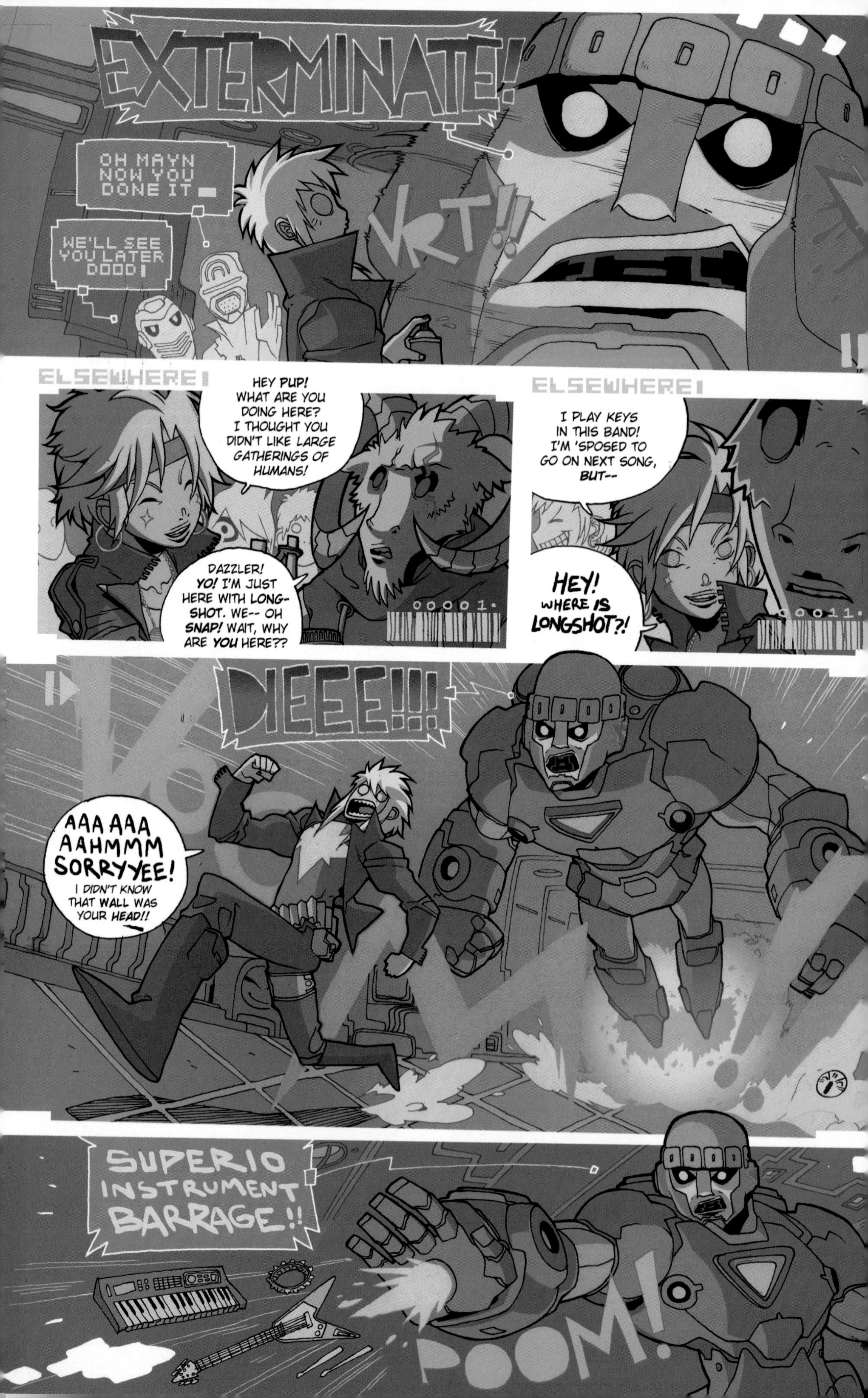
EXTERMINATE!
OH MAYN NOW YOU DONE IT
WE'LL SEE YOU LATER DOOD!
VRT!!
ELSEWHERE!
HEY PUP! WHAT ARE YOU DOING HERE? I THOUGHT YOU DIDN'T LIKE LARGE GATHERINGS OF HUMANS!
DAZZLER! YO! I'M JUST HERE WITH LONG-SHOT. WE-- OH SNAP! WAIT, WHY ARE YOU HERE??
00001.
ELSEWHERE!
I PLAY KEYS IN THIS BAND! I'M 'SPOSED TO GO ON NEXT SONG, BUT--
HEY! WHERE IS LONGSHOT?!
00011.
DIEEE!!!
AAA AAA AAHMMM SORRYYEE!
I DIDN'T KNOW THAT WALL WAS YOUR HEAD!!
SUPERIO INSTRUMENT BARRAGE!!
POOM!

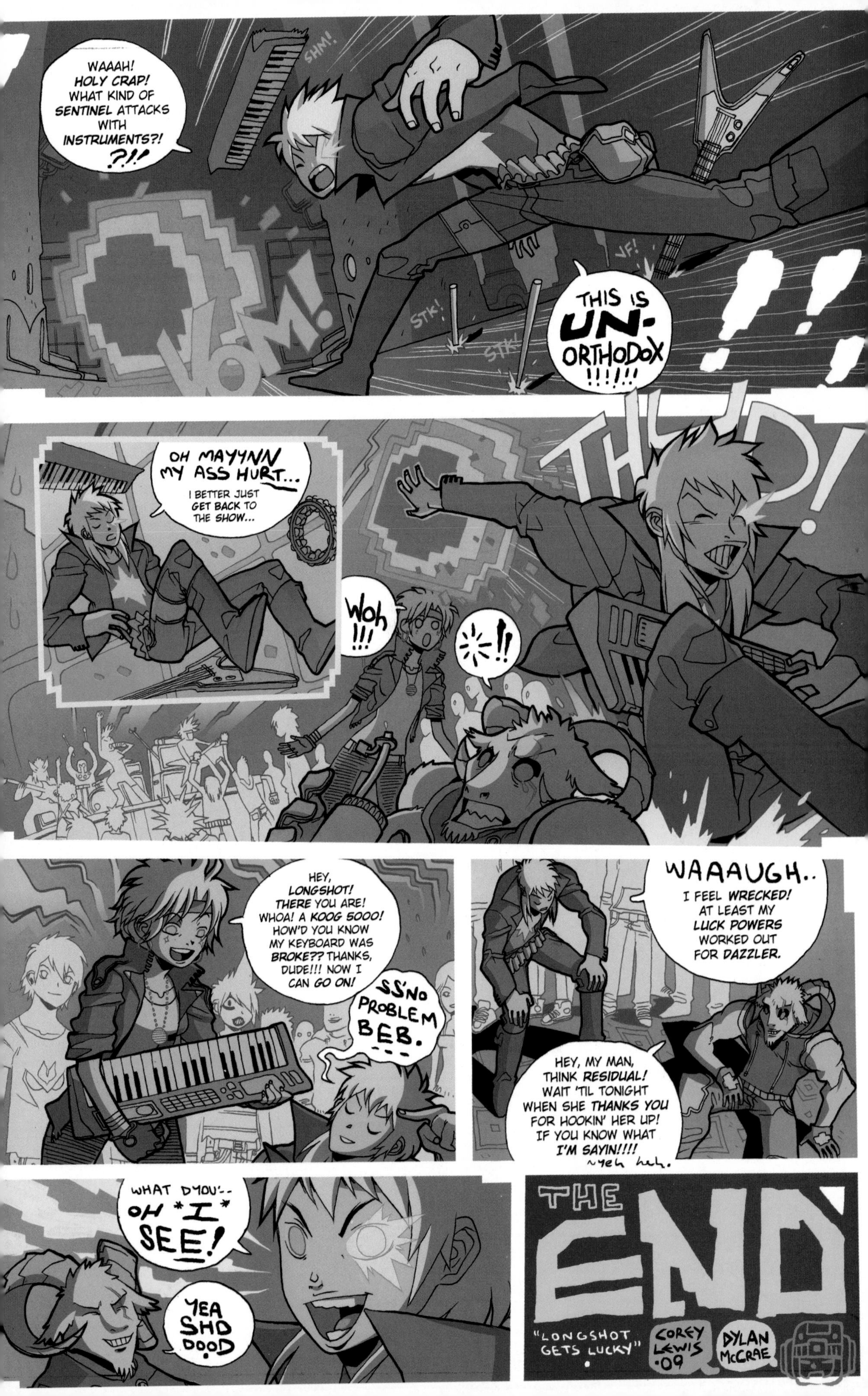

WAAAH! HOLY CRAP! WHAT KIND OF SENTINEL ATTACKS WITH INSTRUMENTS?! ?!!
SHM!
VOM!
STK!
STK!
VF!
THIS IS UN-ORTHODOX !!!!!!
!!
THUD!
OH MAYYNN MY ASS HURT... I BETTER JUST GET BACK TO THE SHOW...
Woh !!!
!!
HEY, LONGSHOT! THERE YOU ARE! WHOA! A KOOG 5000! HOW'D YOU KNOW MY KEYBOARD WAS BROKE?? THANKS, DUDE!!! NOW I CAN GO ON!
SS'NO PROBLEM BEB.
WAAAUGH.. I FEEL WRECKED! AT LEAST MY LUCK POWERS WORKED OUT FOR DAZZLER.
HEY, MY MAN, THINK RESIDUAL! WAIT 'TIL TONIGHT WHEN SHE THANKS YOU FOR HOOKIN' HER UP! IF YOU KNOW WHAT I'M SAYIN!!!!
~yeh heh.
WHAT D'YOU-- OH *I* SEE!
YEA SHO DOOD
THE END
"LONGSHOT GETS LUCKY"
COREY LEWIS '09
DYLAN McCRAE

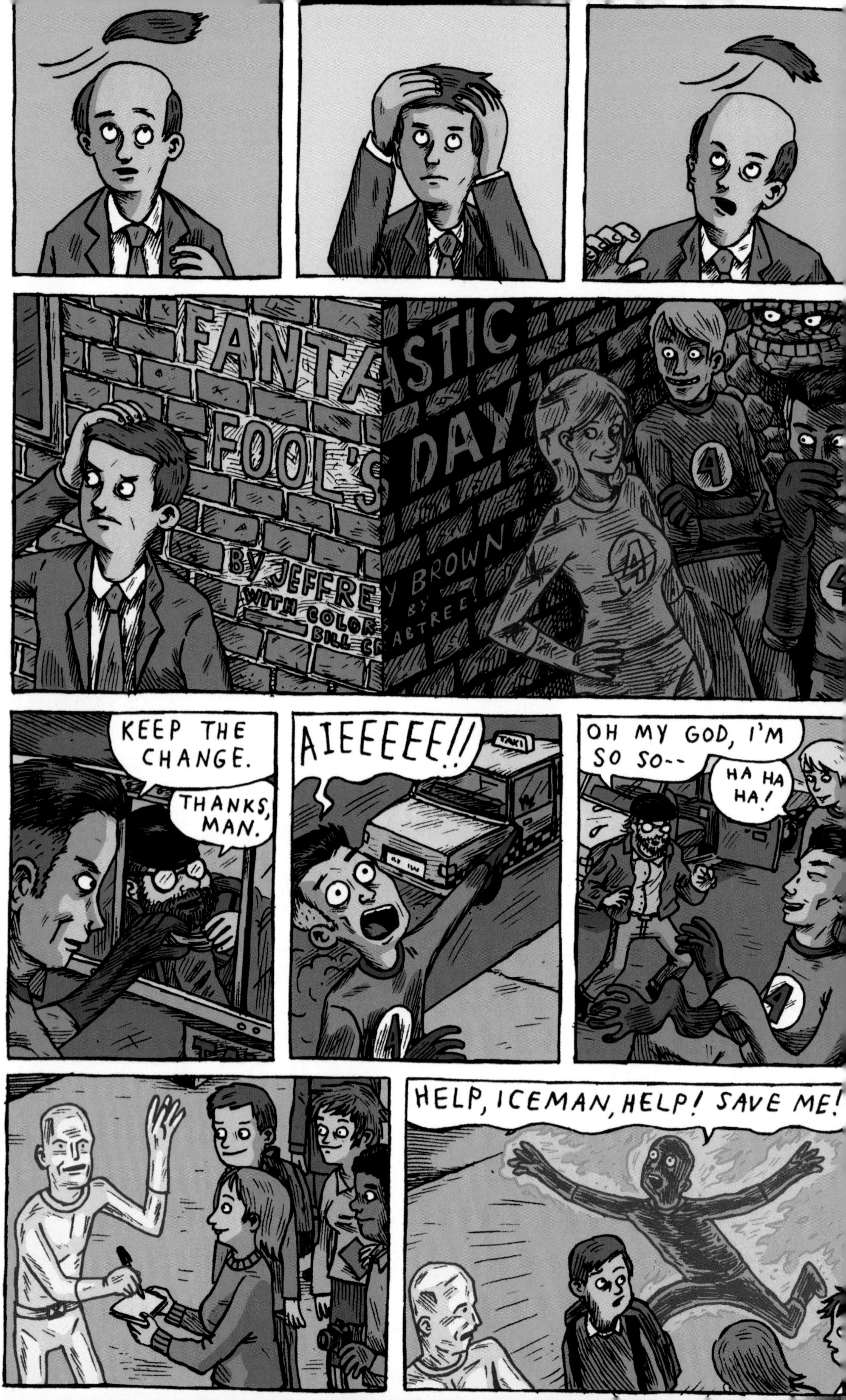
FANTASTIC FOOL'S DAY
BY JEFFREY BROWN
WITH COLORS BY BILL CRABTREE
KEEP THE CHANGE.
THANKS, MAN.
AIEEEEEE!!
TAXI
OH MY GOD, I'M SO SO--
HA HA HA!
HELP, ICEMAN, HELP! SAVE ME!

HA HA HA HA HA!

CRASH

FLIP

DUDE, THAT WAS SOMEONE'S CAR! YOU'RE GOING TO HAVE TO PAY FOR THAT, BEN.

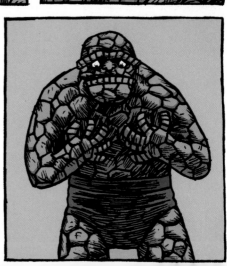

LA QUERELLE DES MONSTRES

AHHH... A SUMMER EVENING LIKE *THIS* IS ALMOST TOO GOOD TO BE *TRUE!*

HISSS!!!

FEATURING
THE BEAST
by Jay Stephens

I SHOULD REALLY TAKE A MOMENT TO *KNOCK ON WOOD* WHEN I SAY THINGS LIKE THAT *OUT LOUD.*

AAIII

EEEEEEEE!!!

FANGS UP, MORBIUS!

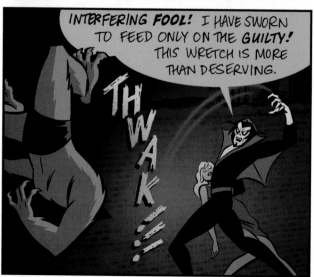

INTERFERING *FOOL!* I HAVE SWORN TO FEED ONLY ON THE *GUILTY!* THIS WRETCH IS MORE THAN DESERVING.

THWAK!!!

NICE TRY, SUCKULA. BUT ACCORDING TO SECTION 125.27 OF THE *PENAL CODE,* YOU JUST DESCRIBED *MURDER* IN THE 1st DEGREE.

POW!

ME? I GOT A *HERO* COMPLEX.

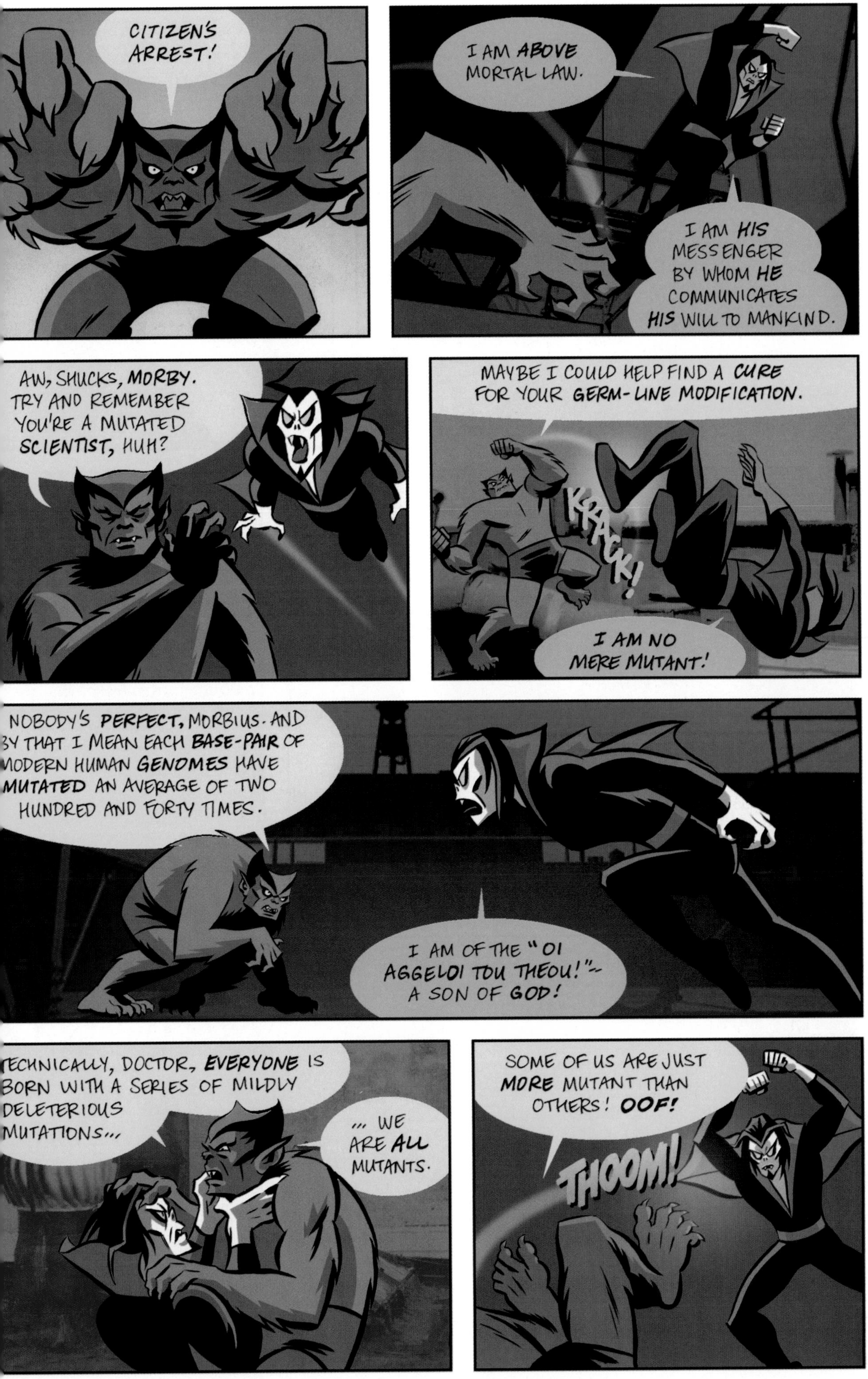
CITIZEN'S ARREST!
I AM ABOVE MORTAL LAW.
I AM HIS MESSENGER BY WHOM HE COMMUNICATES HIS WILL TO MANKIND.
AW, SHUCKS, MORBY. TRY AND REMEMBER YOU'RE A MUTATED SCIENTIST, HUH?
MAYBE I COULD HELP FIND A CURE FOR YOUR GERM-LINE MODIFICATION.
KRACK!
I AM NO MERE MUTANT!
NOBODY'S PERFECT, MORBIUS. AND BY THAT I MEAN EACH BASE-PAIR OF MODERN HUMAN GENOMES HAVE MUTATED AN AVERAGE OF TWO HUNDRED AND FORTY TIMES.
I AM OF THE "OI AGGELOI TOU THEOU!"-- A SON OF GOD!
TECHNICALLY, DOCTOR, EVERYONE IS BORN WITH A SERIES OF MILDLY DELETERIOUS MUTATIONS...
...WE ARE ALL MUTANTS.
SOME OF US ARE JUST MORE MUTANT THAN OTHERS! OOF!
THOOM!

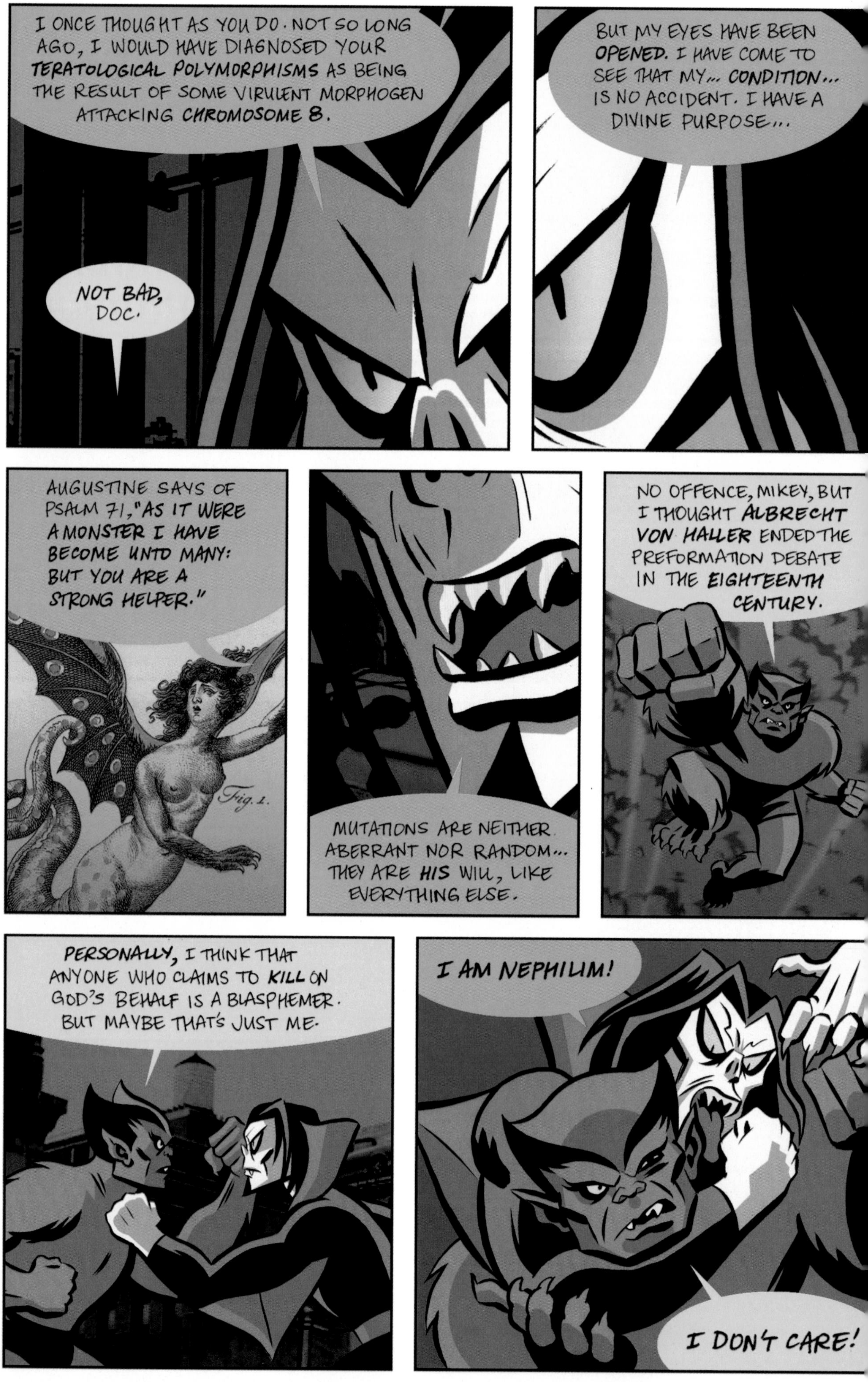
I ONCE THOUGHT AS YOU DO. NOT SO LONG AGO, I WOULD HAVE DIAGNOSED YOUR TERATOLOGICAL POLYMORPHISMS AS BEING THE RESULT OF SOME VIRULENT MORPHOGEN ATTACKING CHROMOSOME 8.
NOT BAD, DOC.
BUT MY EYES HAVE BEEN OPENED. I HAVE COME TO SEE THAT MY... CONDITION... IS NO ACCIDENT. I HAVE A DIVINE PURPOSE...
AUGUSTINE SAYS OF PSALM 71, "AS IT WERE A MONSTER I HAVE BECOME UNTO MANY: BUT YOU ARE A STRONG HELPER."
Fig. 1.
MUTATIONS ARE NEITHER ABERRANT NOR RANDOM... THEY ARE HIS WILL, LIKE EVERYTHING ELSE.
NO OFFENCE, MIKEY, BUT I THOUGHT ALBRECHT VON HALLER ENDED THE PREFORMATION DEBATE IN THE EIGHTEENTH CENTURY.
PERSONALLY, I THINK THAT ANYONE WHO CLAIMS TO KILL ON GOD'S BEHALF IS A BLASPHEMER. BUT MAYBE THAT'S JUST ME.
I AM NEPHILIM!
I DON'T CARE!

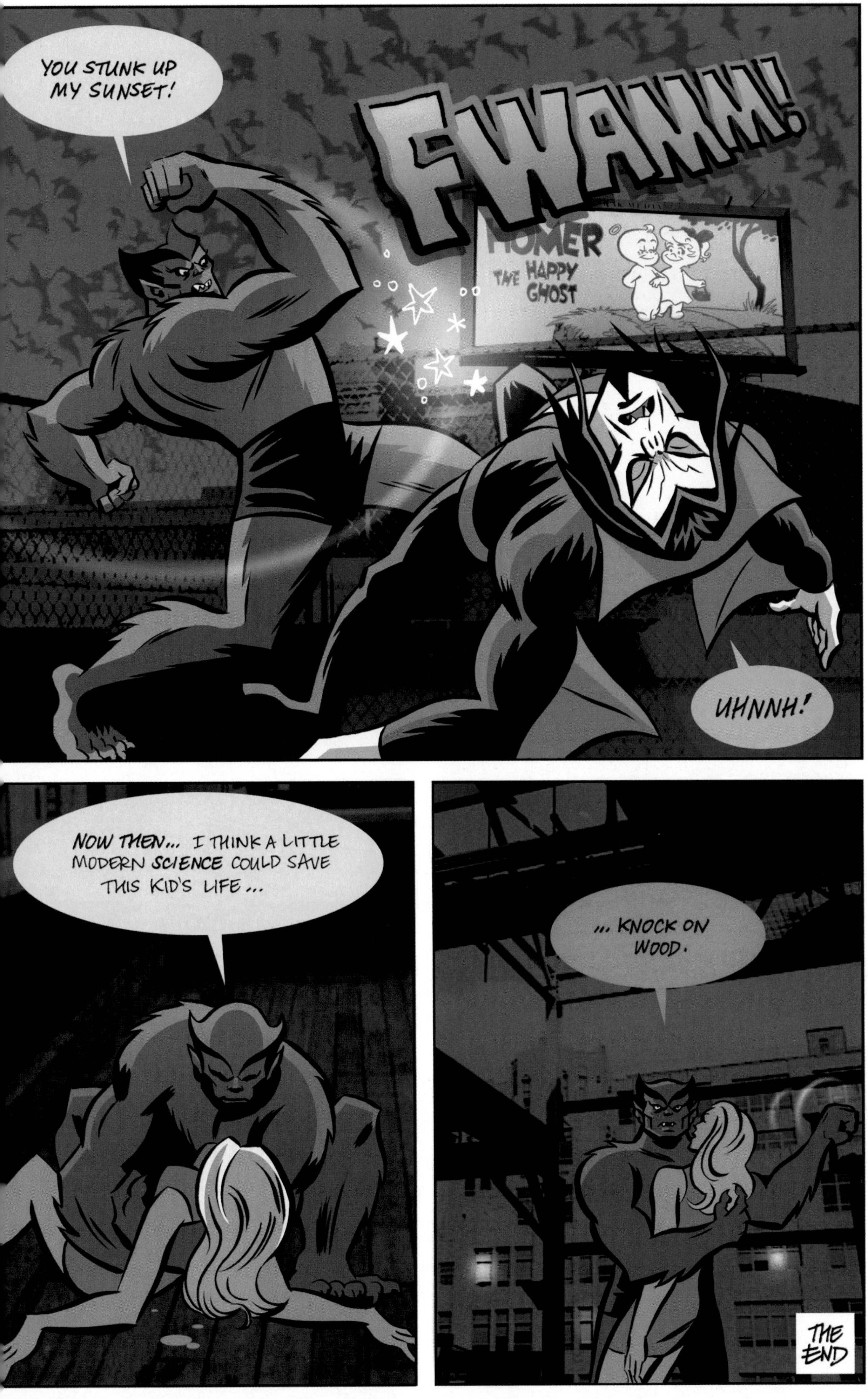
YOU STUNK UP MY SUNSET!
FWAMM!
HOMER THE HAPPY GHOST
UHNNH!
NOW THEN... I THINK A LITTLE MODERN SCIENCE COULD SAVE THIS KID'S LIFE...
... KNOCK ON WOOD.
THE END

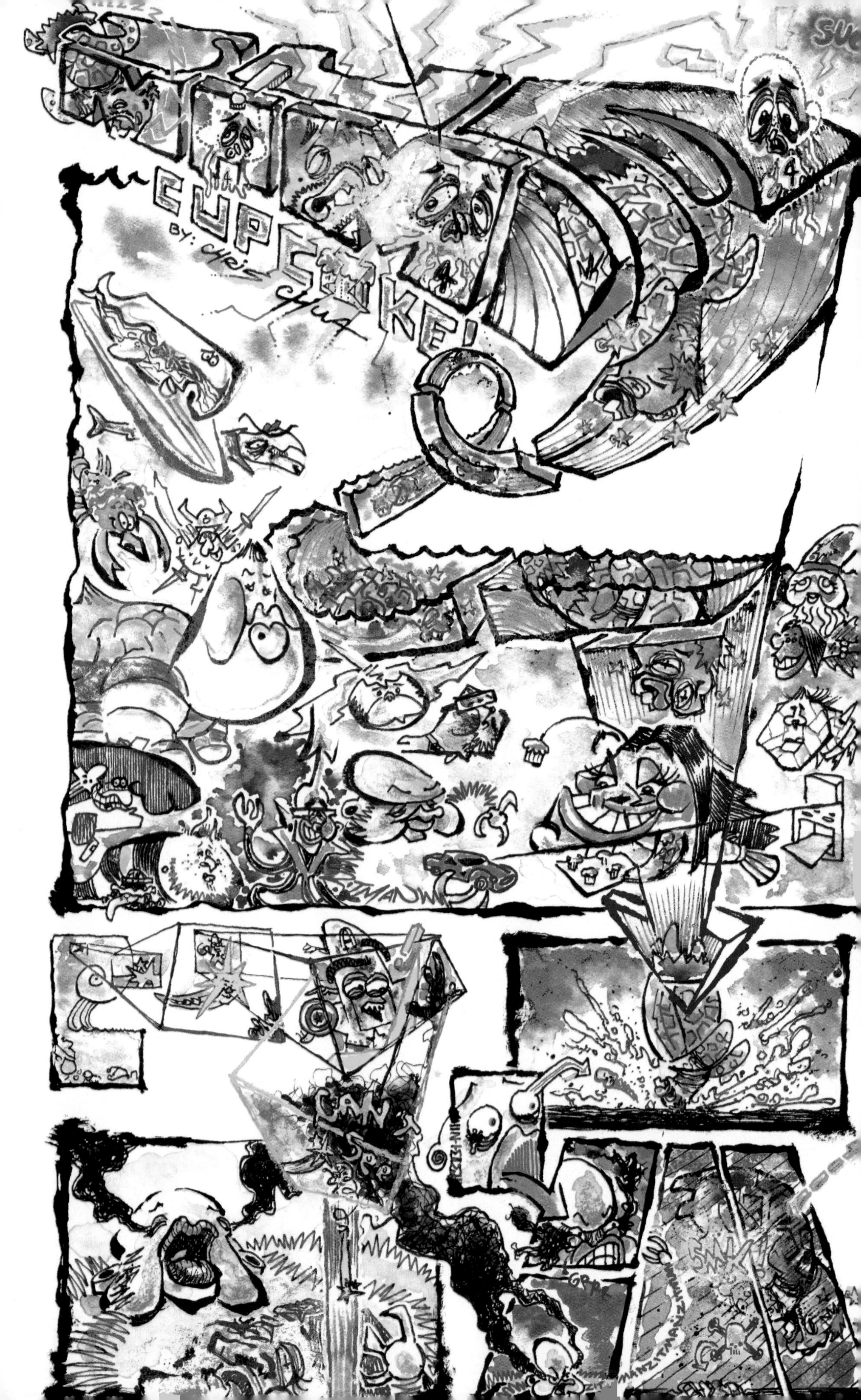
BY: Chris Chua

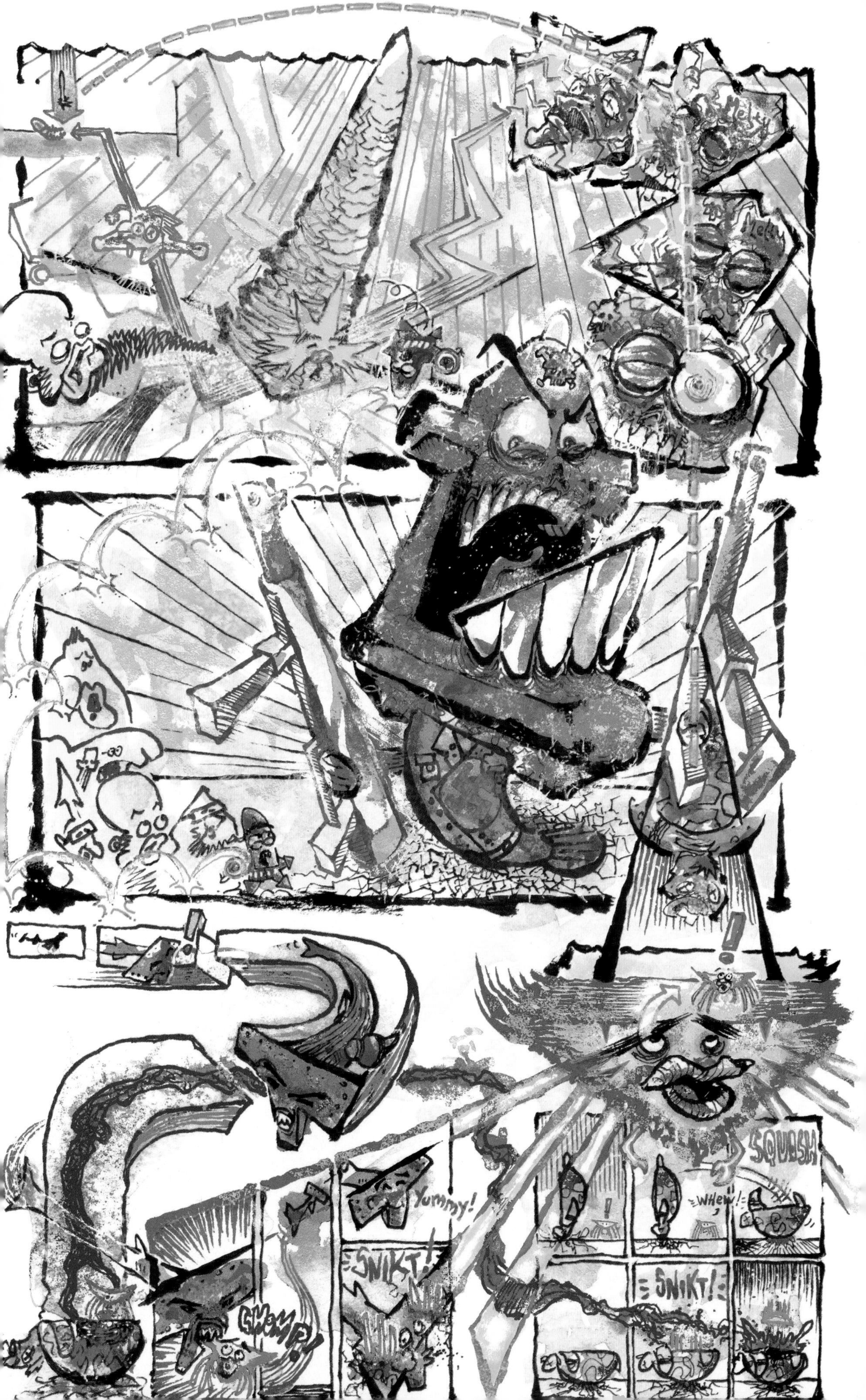

Melty
Melty
Yummy!
SNIKT!
CHOMP!
SQUASH
WHEW!
SNIKT!

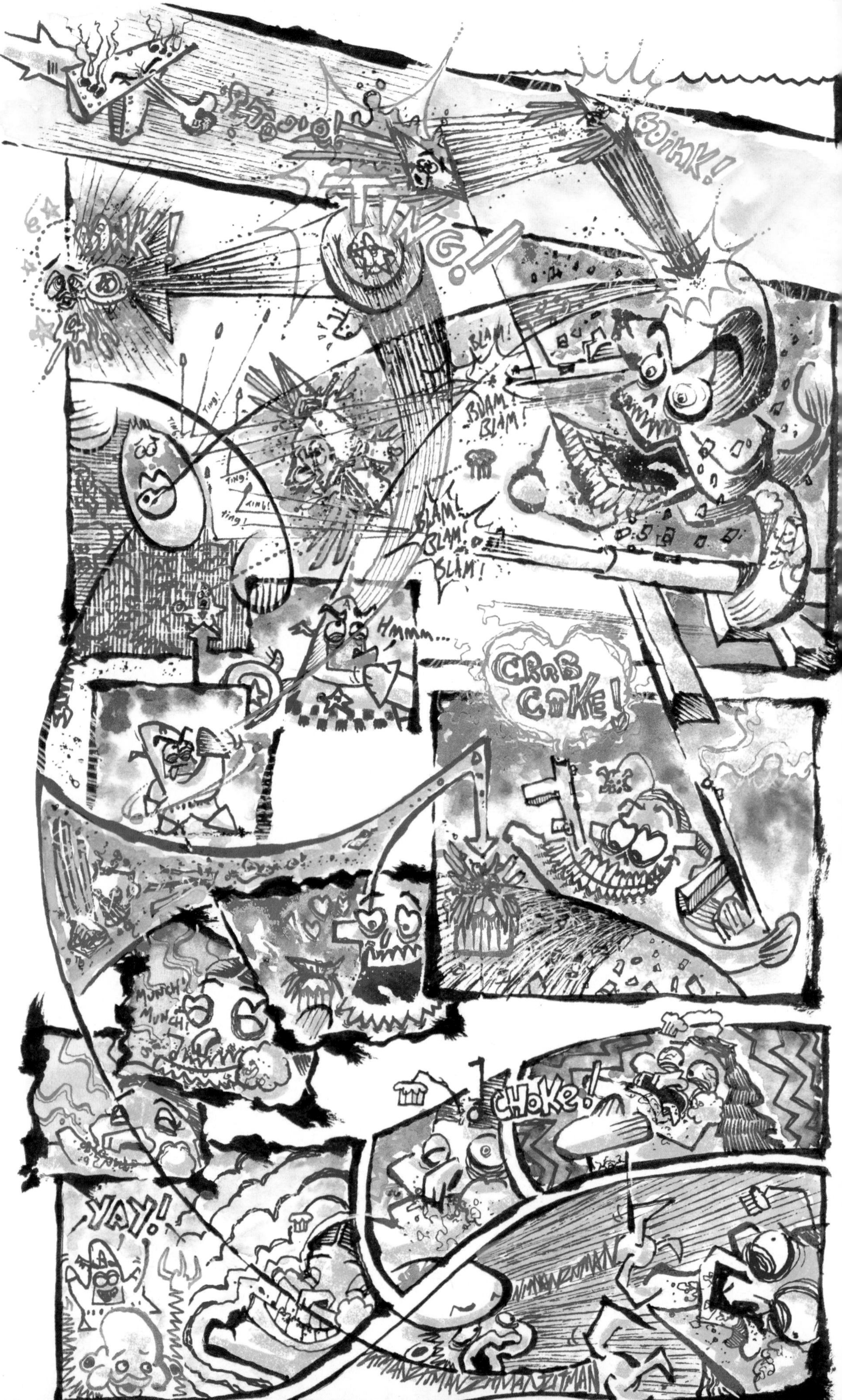

BOINK!
TING!
BOINK!
BLAM!
BLAM! BLAM!
TING!
TING!
TING!
BLAM! BLAM! BLAM!
Hmmm...
CRAB CAKE!
MUNCH! MUNCH!
CHOKE!
YAY!

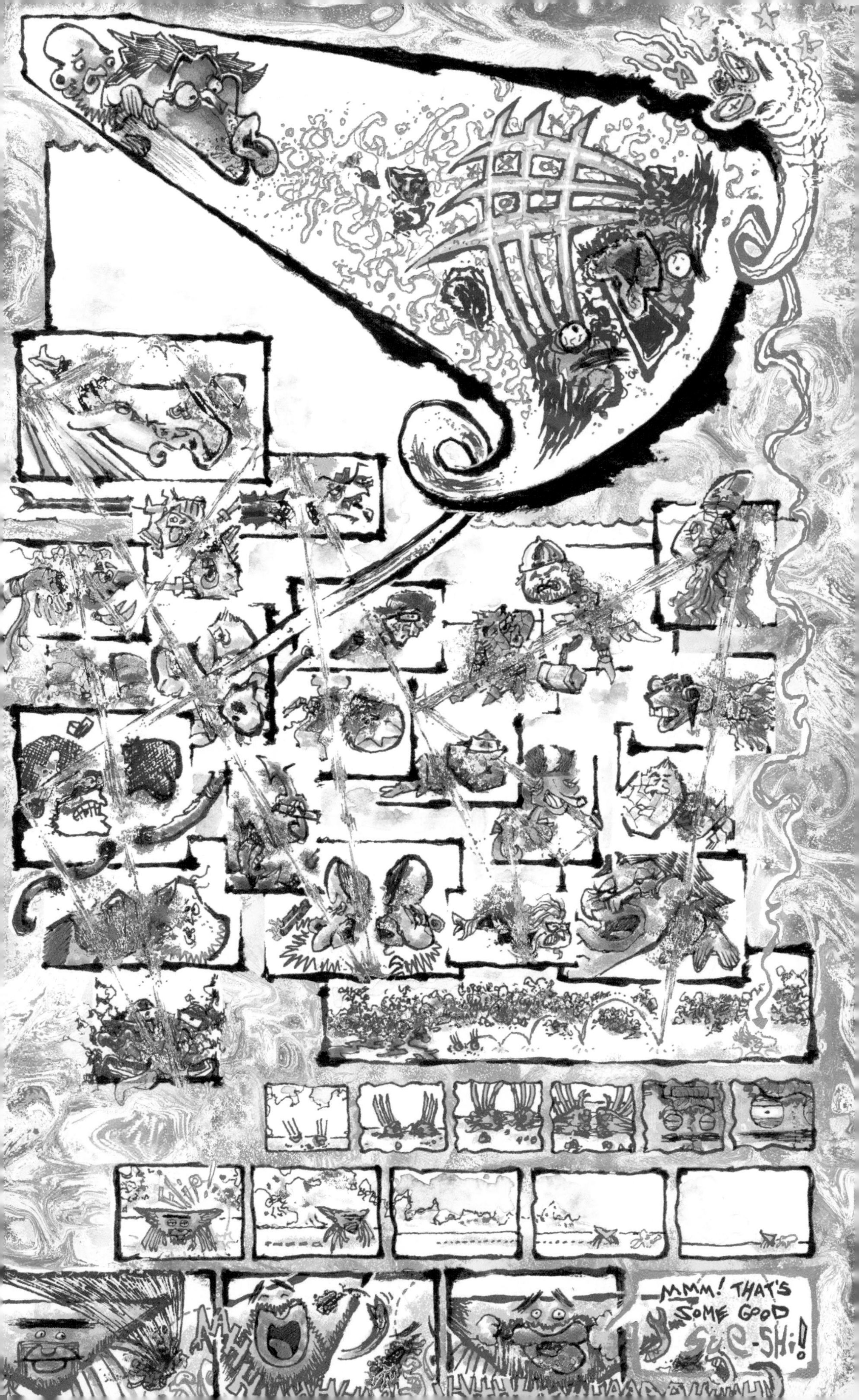
YIP!
MMM! THAT'S SOME GOOD SUE-SHI!

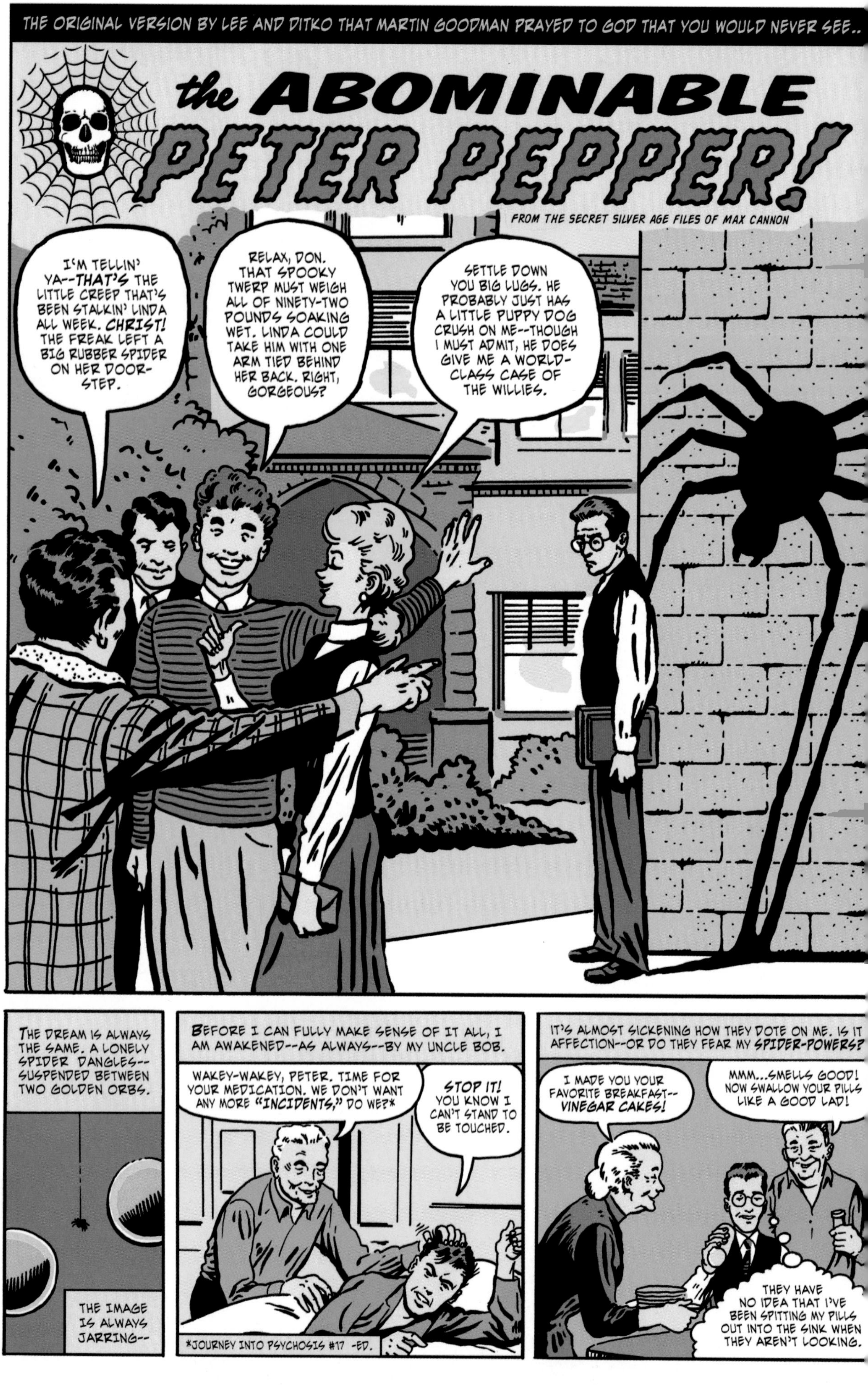
THE ORIGINAL VERSION BY LEE AND DITKO THAT MARTIN GOODMAN PRAYED TO GOD THAT YOU WOULD NEVER SEE..
the ABOMINABLE PETER PEPPER!
FROM THE SECRET SILVER AGE FILES OF MAX CANNON
I'M TELLIN' YA--THAT'S THE LITTLE CREEP THAT'S BEEN STALKIN' LINDA ALL WEEK. CHRIST! THE FREAK LEFT A BIG RUBBER SPIDER ON HER DOOR-STEP.
RELAX, DON. THAT SPOOKY TWERP MUST WEIGH ALL OF NINETY-TWO POUNDS SOAKING WET. LINDA COULD TAKE HIM WITH ONE ARM TIED BEHIND HER BACK. RIGHT, GORGEOUS?
SETTLE DOWN YOU BIG LUGS. HE PROBABLY JUST HAS A LITTLE PUPPY DOG CRUSH ON ME--THOUGH I MUST ADMIT, HE DOES GIVE ME A WORLD-CLASS CASE OF THE WILLIES.
THE DREAM IS ALWAYS THE SAME. A LONELY SPIDER DANGLES--SUSPENDED BETWEEN TWO GOLDEN ORBS.
THE IMAGE IS ALWAYS JARRING--
BEFORE I CAN FULLY MAKE SENSE OF IT ALL, I AM AWAKENED--AS ALWAYS--BY MY UNCLE BOB.
WAKEY-WAKEY, PETER. TIME FOR YOUR MEDICATION. WE DON'T WANT ANY MORE "INCIDENTS," DO WE?*
STOP IT! YOU KNOW I CAN'T STAND TO BE TOUCHED.
*JOURNEY INTO PSYCHOSIS #17 -ED.
IT'S ALMOST SICKENING HOW THEY DOTE ON ME. IS IT AFFECTION--OR DO THEY FEAR MY SPIDER-POWERS?
I MADE YOU YOUR FAVORITE BREAKFAST--VINEGAR CAKES!
MMM...SMELLS GOOD! NOW SWALLOW YOUR PILLS LIKE A GOOD LAD!
THEY HAVE NO IDEA THAT I'VE BEEN SPITTING MY PILLS OUT INTO THE SINK WHEN THEY AREN'T LOOKING.

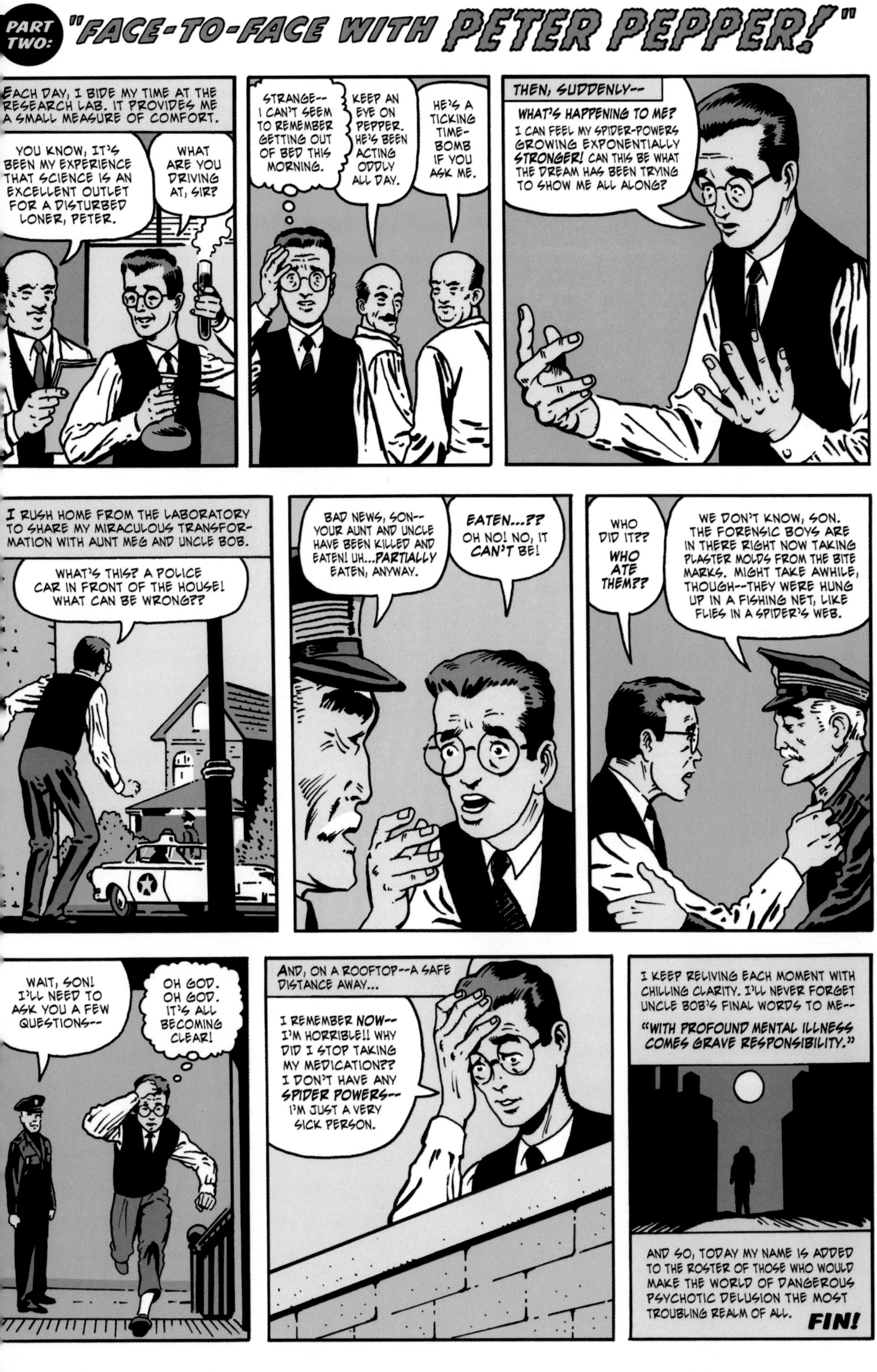
PART TWO: "FACE-TO-FACE WITH PETER PEPPER!"
EACH DAY, I BIDE MY TIME AT THE RESEARCH LAB. IT PROVIDES ME A SMALL MEASURE OF COMFORT.
YOU KNOW, IT'S BEEN MY EXPERIENCE THAT SCIENCE IS AN EXCELLENT OUTLET FOR A DISTURBED LONER, PETER.
WHAT ARE YOU DRIVING AT, SIR?
STRANGE-- I CAN'T SEEM TO REMEMBER GETTING OUT OF BED THIS MORNING.
KEEP AN EYE ON PEPPER. HE'S BEEN ACTING ODDLY ALL DAY.
HE'S A TICKING TIME-BOMB IF YOU ASK ME.
THEN, SUDDENLY--
WHAT'S HAPPENING TO ME? I CAN FEEL MY SPIDER-POWERS GROWING EXPONENTIALLY STRONGER! CAN THIS BE WHAT THE DREAM HAS BEEN TRYING TO SHOW ME ALL ALONG?
I RUSH HOME FROM THE LABORATORY TO SHARE MY MIRACULOUS TRANSFORMATION WITH AUNT MEG AND UNCLE BOB.
WHAT'S THIS? A POLICE CAR IN FRONT OF THE HOUSE! WHAT CAN BE WRONG??
BAD NEWS, SON-- YOUR AUNT AND UNCLE HAVE BEEN KILLED AND EATEN! UH...PARTIALLY EATEN, ANYWAY.
EATEN...?? OH NO! NO, IT CAN'T BE!
WHO DID IT?? WHO ATE THEM??
WE DON'T KNOW, SON. THE FORENSIC BOYS ARE IN THERE RIGHT NOW TAKING PLASTER MOLDS FROM THE BITE MARKS. MIGHT TAKE AWHILE, THOUGH--THEY WERE HUNG UP IN A FISHING NET, LIKE FLIES IN A SPIDER'S WEB.
WAIT, SON! I'LL NEED TO ASK YOU A FEW QUESTIONS--
OH GOD. OH GOD. IT'S ALL BECOMING CLEAR!
AND, ON A ROOFTOP--A SAFE DISTANCE AWAY...
I REMEMBER NOW-- I'M HORRIBLE!! WHY DID I STOP TAKING MY MEDICATION?? I DON'T HAVE ANY SPIDER POWERS-- I'M JUST A VERY SICK PERSON.
I KEEP RELIVING EACH MOMENT WITH CHILLING CLARITY. I'LL NEVER FORGET UNCLE BOB'S FINAL WORDS TO ME--
"WITH PROFOUND MENTAL ILLNESS COMES GRAVE RESPONSIBILITY."
AND SO, TODAY MY NAME IS ADDED TO THE ROSTER OF THOSE WHO WOULD MAKE THE WORLD OF DANGEROUS PSYCHOTIC DELUSION THE MOST TROUBLING REALM OF ALL.
FIN!

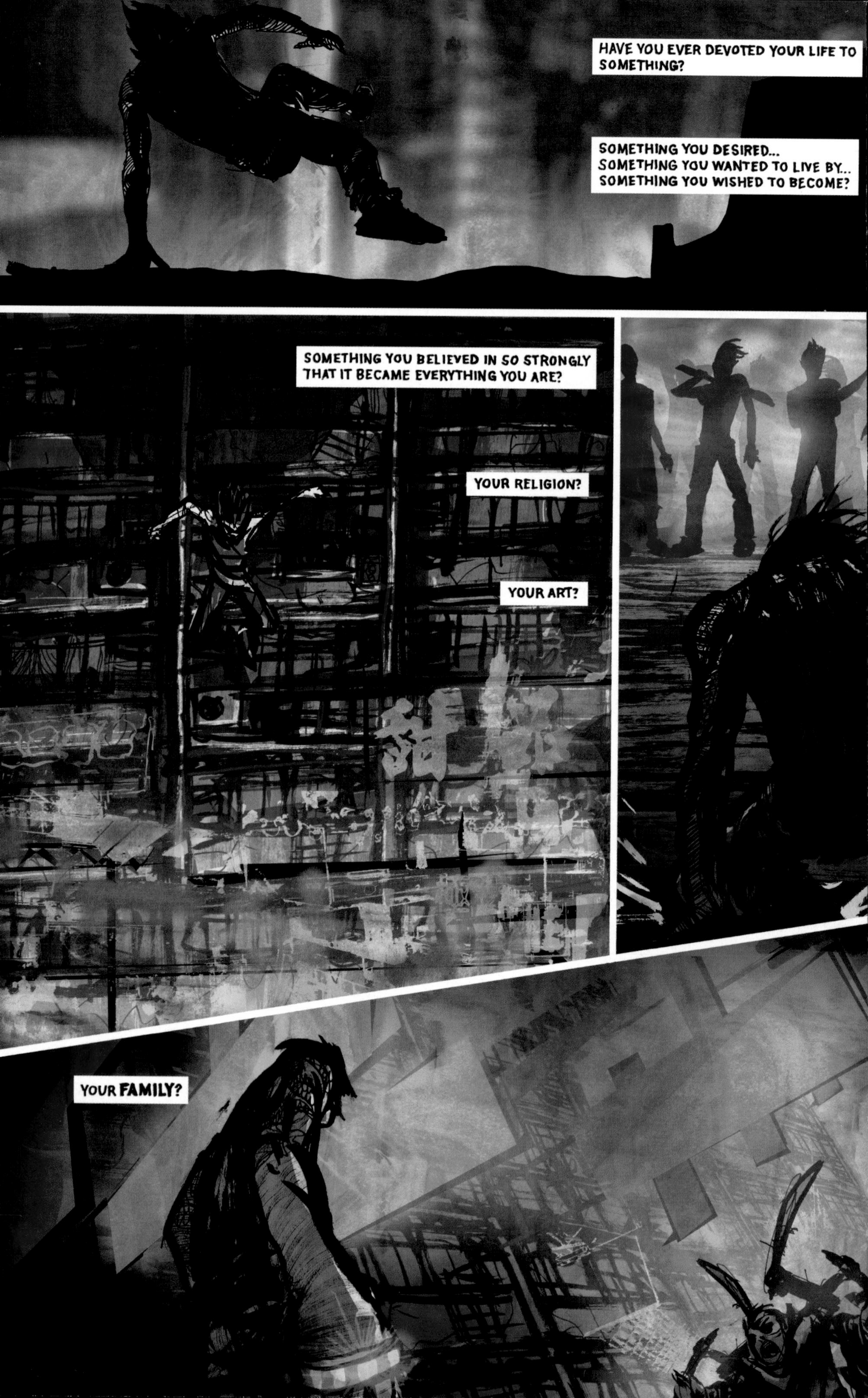
HAVE YOU EVER DEVOTED YOUR LIFE TO SOMETHING?
SOMETHING YOU DESIRED... SOMETHING YOU WANTED TO LIVE BY... SOMETHING YOU WISHED TO BECOME?
SOMETHING YOU BELIEVED IN SO STRONGLY THAT IT BECAME EVERYTHING YOU ARE?
YOUR RELIGION?
YOUR ART?
YOUR FAMILY?

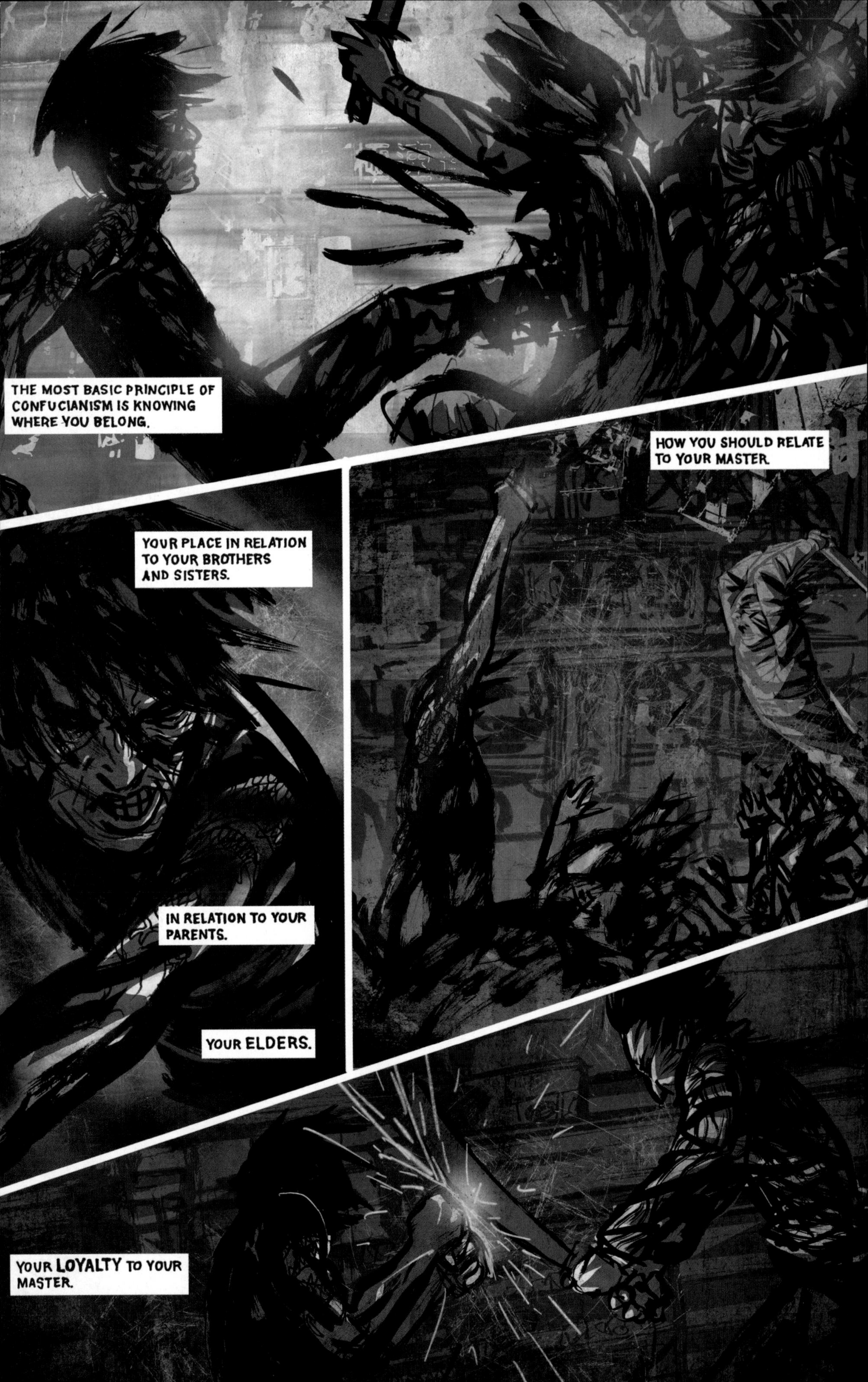
THE MOST BASIC PRINCIPLE OF CONFUCIANISM IS KNOWING WHERE YOU BELONG.
YOUR PLACE IN RELATION TO YOUR BROTHERS AND SISTERS.
IN RELATION TO YOUR PARENTS.
YOUR ELDERS.
HOW YOU SHOULD RELATE TO YOUR MASTER.
YOUR LOYALTY TO YOUR MASTER.

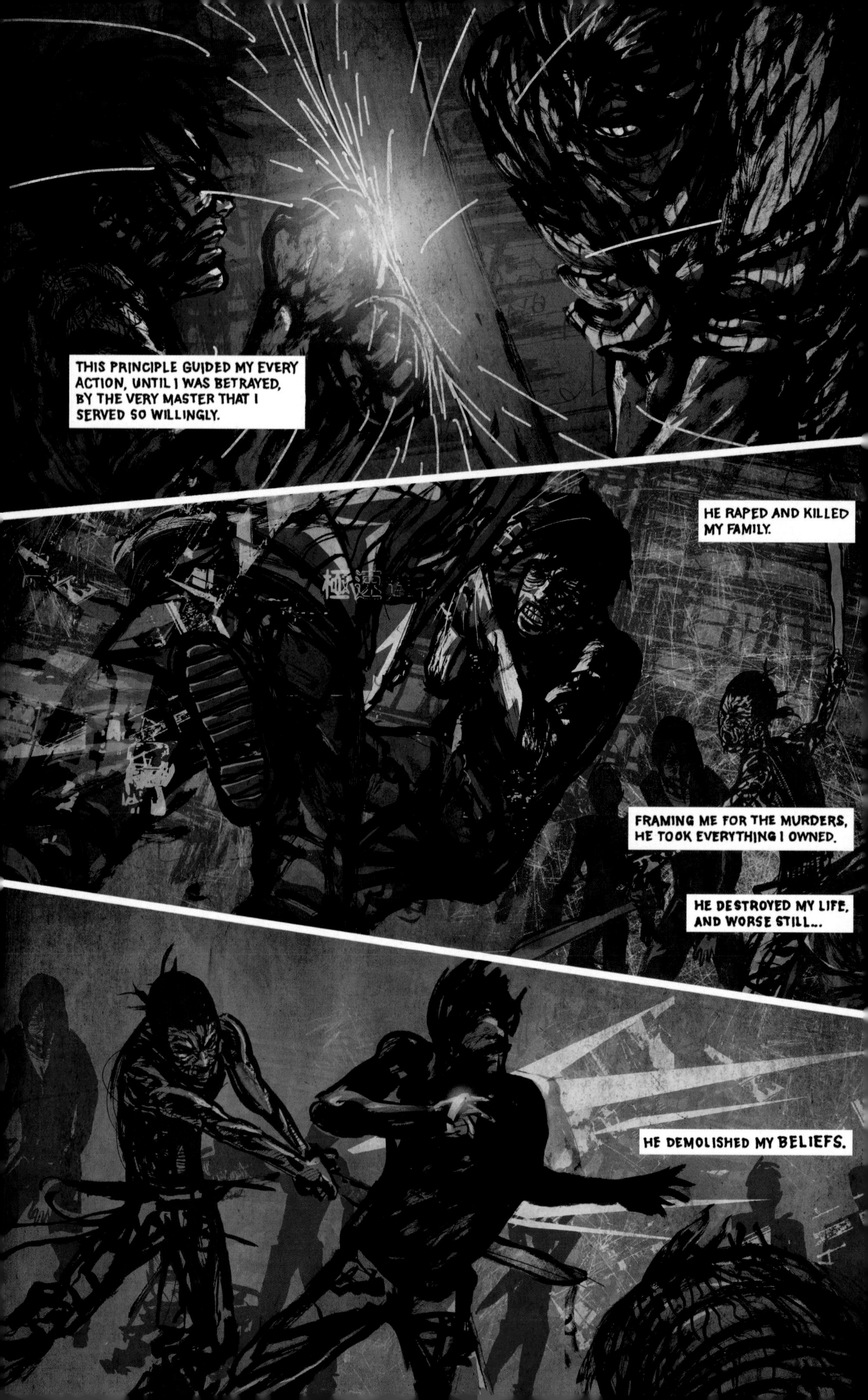
THIS PRINCIPLE GUIDED MY EVERY ACTION, UNTIL I WAS BETRAYED, BY THE VERY MASTER THAT I SERVED SO WILLINGLY.
HE RAPED AND KILLED MY FAMILY.
FRAMING ME FOR THE MURDERS, HE TOOK EVERYTHING I OWNED.
HE DESTROYED MY LIFE, AND WORSE STILL...
HE DEMOLISHED MY BELIEFS.

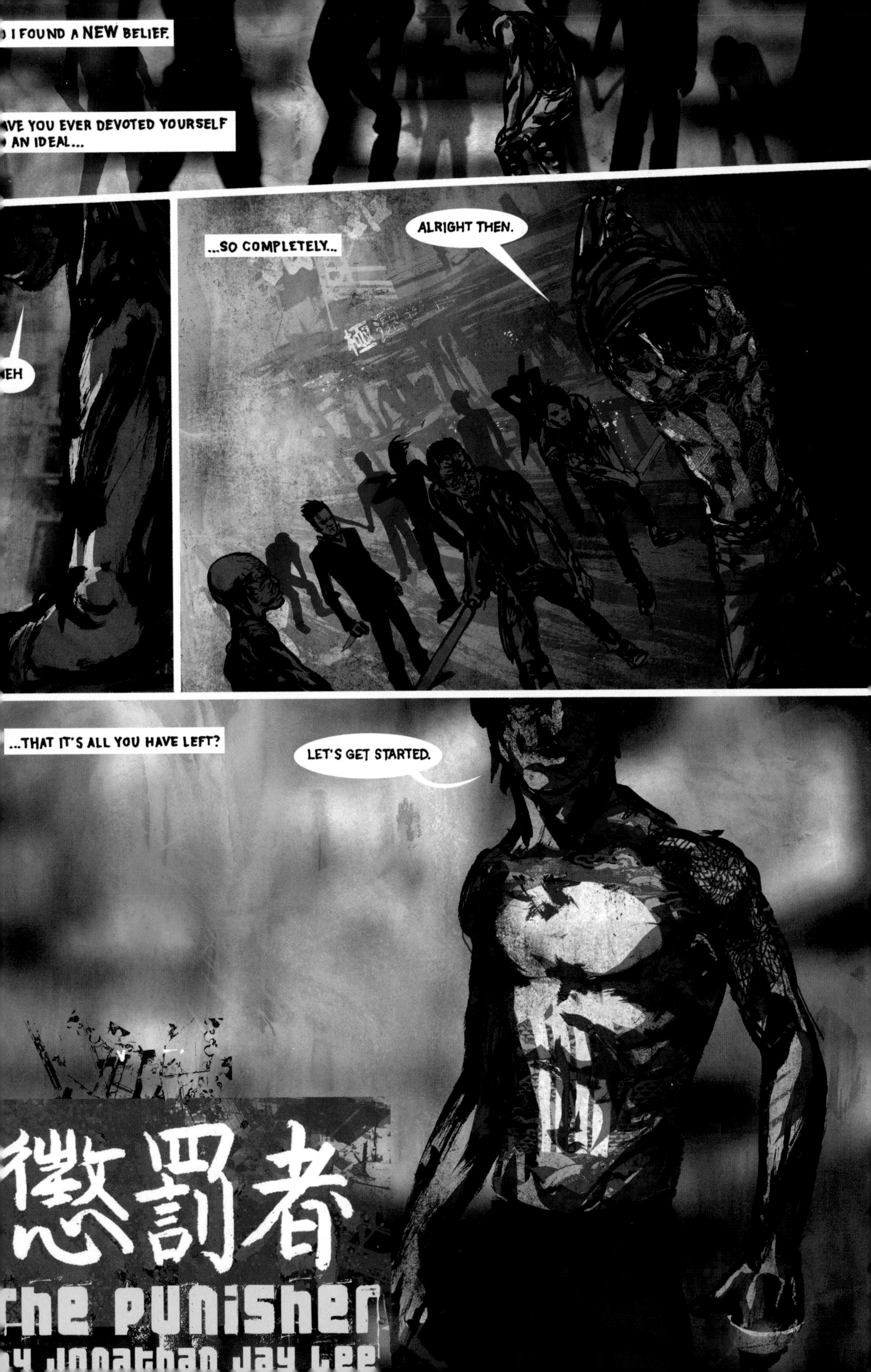
I FOUND A NEW BELIEF.
VE YOU EVER DEVOTED YOURSELF
AN IDEAL...
EH
...SO COMPLETELY...
ALRIGHT THEN.
...THAT IT'S ALL YOU HAVE LEFT?
LET'S GET STARTED.
懲罰者
THE PUNISHER
JONATHAN JAY LEE

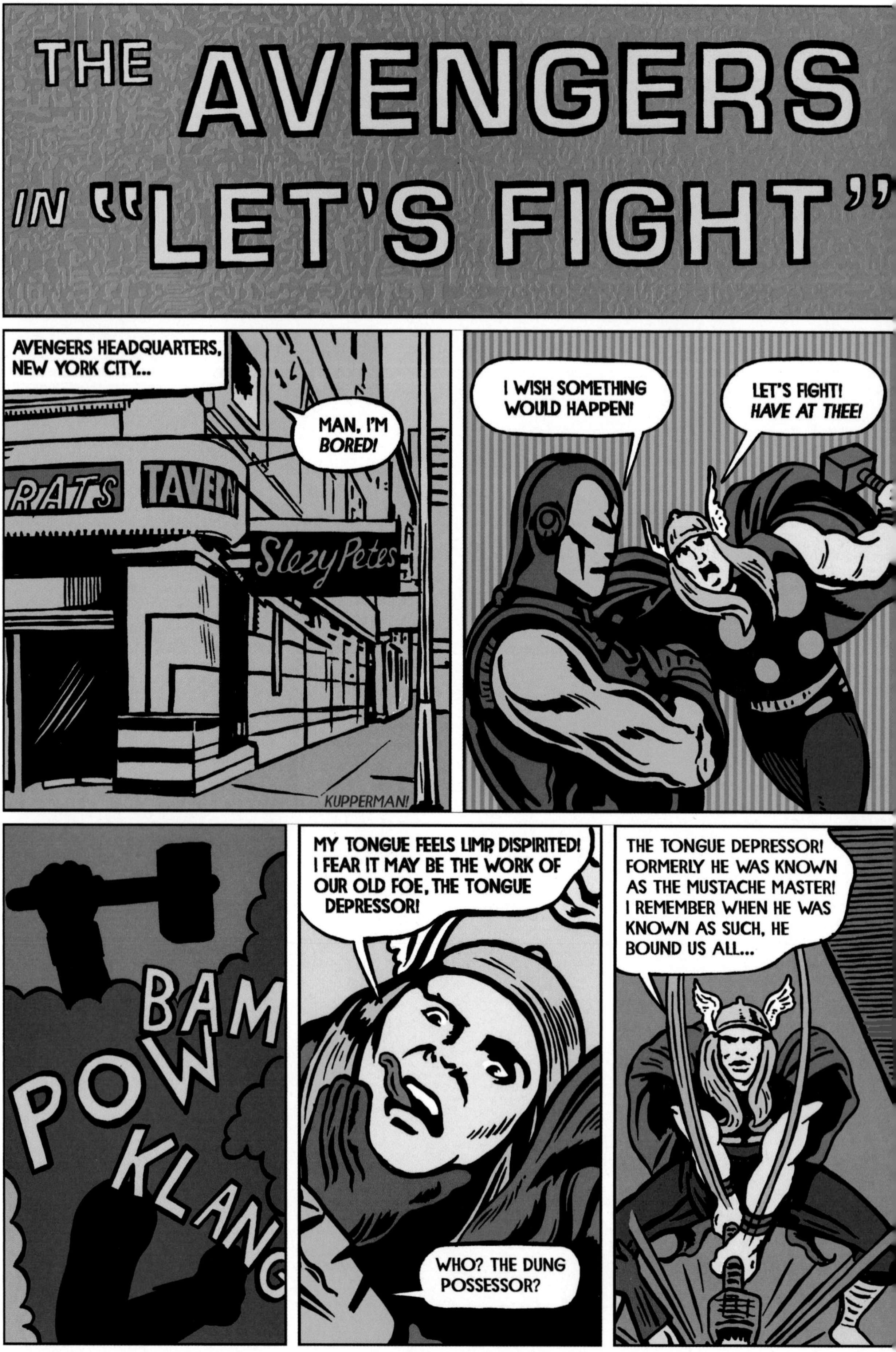
THE AVENGERS
IN "LET'S FIGHT"
AVENGERS HEADQUARTERS, NEW YORK CITY...
RATS
TAVERN
Slezy Petes
MAN, I'M BORED!
KUPPERMAN!
I WISH SOMETHING WOULD HAPPEN!
LET'S FIGHT! HAVE AT THEE!
BAM
POW
KLANG
MY TONGUE FEELS LIMP, DISPIRITED! I FEAR IT MAY BE THE WORK OF OUR OLD FOE, THE TONGUE DEPRESSOR!
WHO? THE DUNG POSSESSOR?
THE TONGUE DEPRESSOR! FORMERLY HE WAS KNOWN AS THE MUSTACHE MASTER! I REMEMBER WHEN HE WAS KNOWN AS SUCH, HE BOUND US ALL...

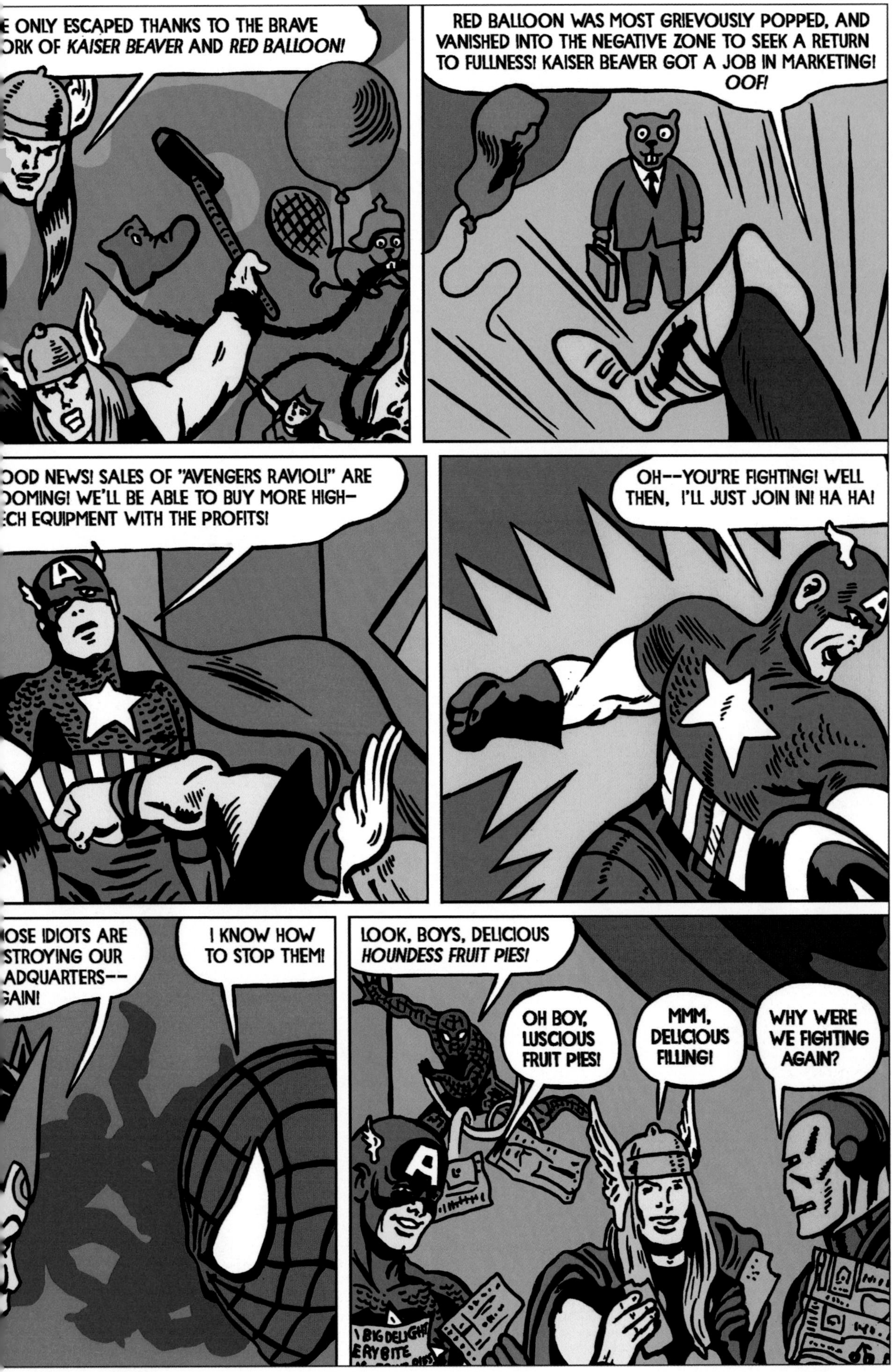
E ONLY ESCAPED THANKS TO THE BRAVE ORK OF KAISER BEAVER AND RED BALLOON!
RED BALLOON WAS MOST GRIEVOUSLY POPPED, AND VANISHED INTO THE NEGATIVE ZONE TO SEEK A RETURN TO FULLNESS! KAISER BEAVER GOT A JOB IN MARKETING!
OOF!
OOD NEWS! SALES OF "AVENGERS RAVIOLI" ARE OOMING! WE'LL BE ABLE TO BUY MORE HIGH-ECH EQUIPMENT WITH THE PROFITS!
OH--YOU'RE FIGHTING! WELL THEN, I'LL JUST JOIN IN! HA HA!
OSE IDIOTS ARE STROYING OUR ADQUARTERS-- GAIN!
I KNOW HOW TO STOP THEM!
LOOK, BOYS, DELICIOUS HOUNDESS FRUIT PIES!
OH BOY, LUSCIOUS FRUIT PIES!
MMM, DELICIOUS FILLING!
WHY WERE WE FIGHTING AGAIN?

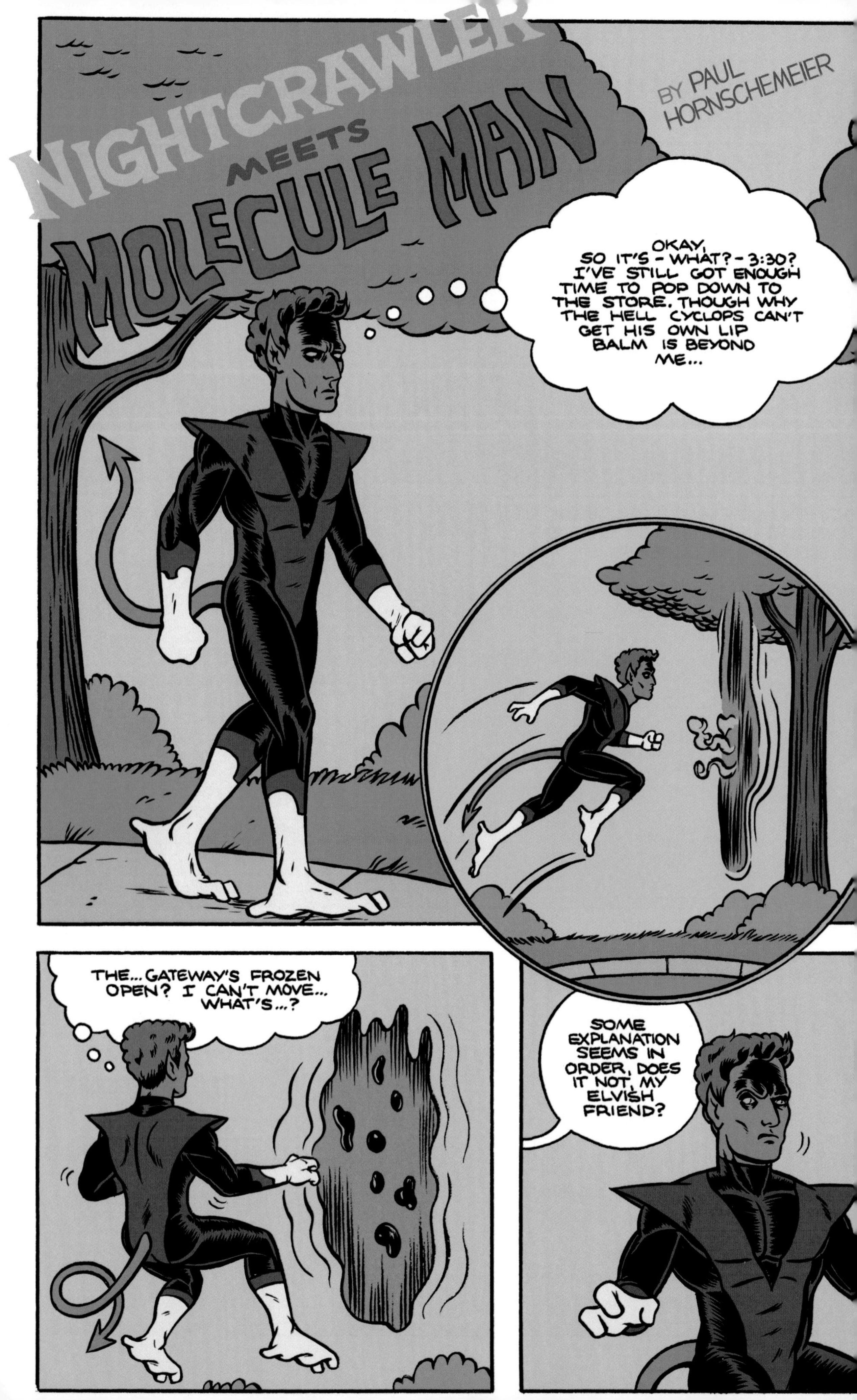
NIGHTCRAWLER MEETS MOLECULE MAN
BY PAUL HORNSCHEMEIER
OKAY, SO IT'S - WHAT? - 3:30? I'VE STILL GOT ENOUGH TIME TO POP DOWN TO THE STORE. THOUGH WHY THE HELL CYCLOPS CAN'T GET HIS OWN LIP BALM IS BEYOND ME...
THE... GATEWAY'S FROZEN OPEN? I CAN'T MOVE... WHAT'S...?
SOME EXPLANATION SEEMS IN ORDER, DOES IT NOT, MY ELVISH FRIEND?

WHO...?

OWEN REECE, NIGHTCRAWLER. OR AS A WANING POPULATION ONCE KNEW ME, **MOLECULE MAN**

LOOK, I DON'T KNOW WHAT YOU'RE AT, I REALLY DON'T CARE, BUT RELEASE ME! YOU'VE NO RIGHT TO..

INARGUABLY. NO RIGHT. BUT HEAR ME OUT. I'LL RELEASE YOU, I ASK ONLY THAT YOU NOT FOLLOW ME,

I'M ALREADY NOT FOLLOWING YOU... BUT IT SEEMS I'VE LITTLE CHOICE BUT TO LISTEN.

THROUGH A MISHAP OF SCIENCE, I WAS GIVEN POWER OVER THE ATOMIC, THE SUBATOMIC, THE BUILDING BLOCKS OF SPACE AND TIME. BY ACCIDENT, I WAS THE OMNIPOTENT HAND OF GOD.

BUT WHAT IS LIFE, TO CONTROL THINGS THIS WAY? WHAT IS IT TO READ EVEN THE FINEST SCRIPT OF EXISTENCE?

PRAGMATICALLY, UNAVOIDABLY, WE SEE THINGS AS DIVIDED, AS UNIQUE OBJECTS AND EVENTS. WE SEE A FINGER TIP, AND AROUND THAT FINGER TIP WE SEE THE OPEN AIR.

BUT IN THE GOD'S VIEW, THE ONLY VIEW LEFT TO ME...

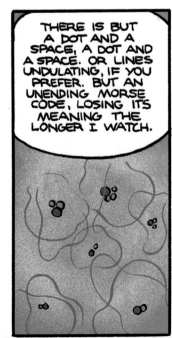

THERE IS BUT A DOT AND A SPACE, A DOT AND A SPACE. OR LINES UNDULATING, IF YOU PREFER. BUT AN UNENDING MORSE CODE, LOSING ITS MEANING THE LONGER I WATCH.

I'VE ATTEMPTED THE OTHER FACETS OF GOD, TRIED EMBRACING OMNIBENEVOLENCE. I LIVED SIMPLY. I LOVED MY WIFE. MINE WAS AN EXISTENCE FREE OF WANT AND DISTRESS.

BUT LIFE WITHOUT CHAOS IS NOT LIVING. THE SUPPOSED IMPERFECTIONS, THE LACK OF CONTROL BEMOANED BY THE EVERYMAN THESE ARE THE UNMAPPABLE ESSENCE OF LIFE! AND I HAVE CHEATED IT, OR BEEN CHEATED OF IT!

I... STILL DON'T UNDERSTAND WHAT THIS HAS TO DO WITH ME, WHY HAVE YOU FROZEN ME HERE?

IN RECENT YEARS I BEGAN SEARCHING, FOR WHAT, I DID NOT KNOW, BUT ANYTHING TO REGAIN A SENSE OF LIVING, AN AFFAIR, A CAR, THE TYPICAL YOUTH RECLAMATIONS WERE IGNORABLE PATINAS. I NEEDED CHAOS! THE **TRUE** UNKNOWN! I NEEDED TO LIVE AGAIN, NOT ATTEMPT DELUSION.

AND THAT BROUGHT YOU TO ME? I CAN'T SEE WHAT I CAN...

I HAVE SLOWED TIME TO AN IMPERCEPTIBLE CRAWL, SO THAT I MIGHT ENTER YOUR TELEPORTATION DIMENSION.

WHAT? WHY WOULD..

IT IS THE UNKNOWN I UNDERSTAND EVEN **YOU** HAVE NOT EXPLORED IT FULLY. ITS SPACE OBVIOUSLY DIFFERS FROM OURS, GIVEN THE SPEED AT WHICH YOU TRAVERSE GREAT DISTANCES, I CAN ONLY HOPE THE ENTIRETY OF ITS PHYSICS DIFFERS FROM OURS.

A CHAOS TO WHICH I AM FINALLY GRANTED CITIZENSHIP.

BUT HOW LONG WILL YOU STAY? EVEN A SHORT TIME THERE WEAKENS ME, AND THE SAME GOES FOR ANYONE I CARRY.

STAY TOO LONG AND YOU'LL DIE!

TO DIE LIVING, THERE'S NO TRAGEDY IN THAT.

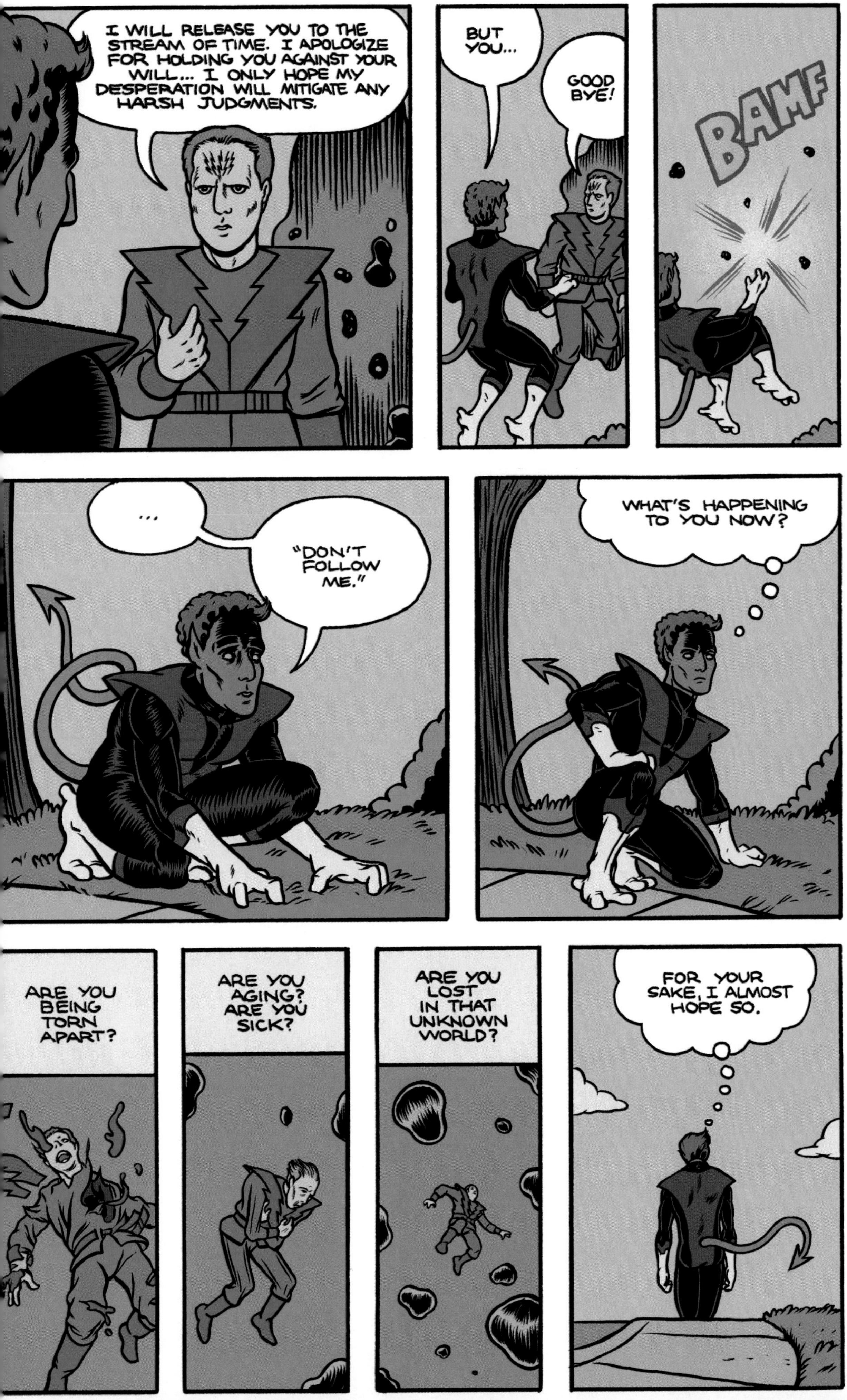
I WILL RELEASE YOU TO THE STREAM OF TIME. I APOLOGIZE FOR HOLDING YOU AGAINST YOUR WILL... I ONLY HOPE MY DESPERATION WILL MITIGATE ANY HARSH JUDGMENTS.
BUT YOU...
GOOD BYE!
BAMF
...
"DON'T FOLLOW ME."
WHAT'S HAPPENING TO YOU NOW?
ARE YOU BEING TORN APART?
ARE YOU AGING? ARE YOU SICK?
ARE YOU LOST IN THAT UNKNOWN WORLD?
FOR YOUR SAKE, I ALMOST HOPE SO.

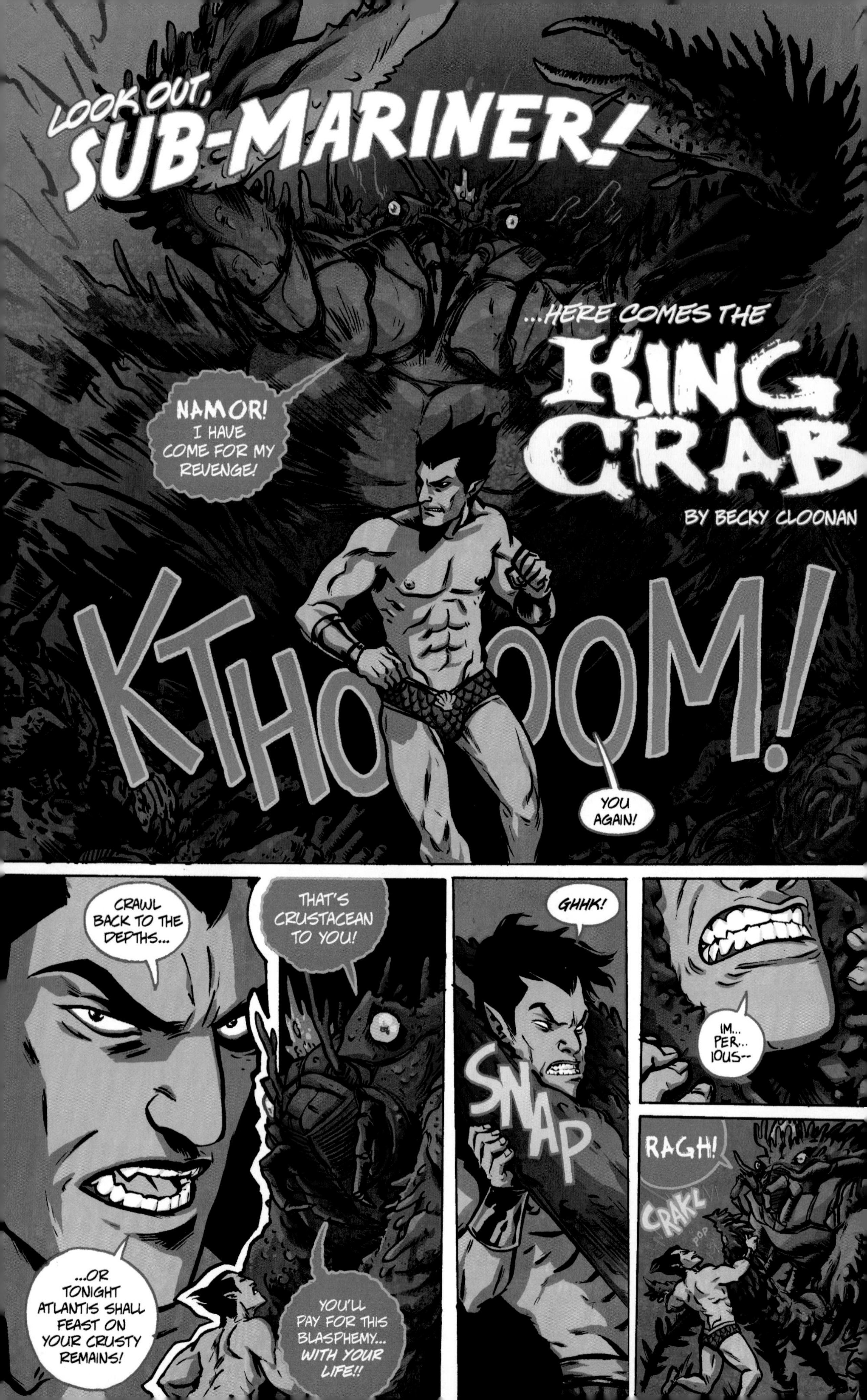

LOOK OUT, SUB-MARINER!
...HERE COMES THE KING CRAB
BY BECKY CLOONAN
NAMOR! I HAVE COME FOR MY REVENGE!
KTHOOOM!
YOU AGAIN!
CRAWL BACK TO THE DEPTHS...
THAT'S CRUSTACEAN TO YOU!
...OR TONIGHT ATLANTIS SHALL FEAST ON YOUR CRUSTY REMAINS!
YOU'LL PAY FOR THIS BLASPHEMY... WITH YOUR LIFE!!
GHHK!
SNAP
IM... PER... IOUS--
RAGH!
CRAKL
POP

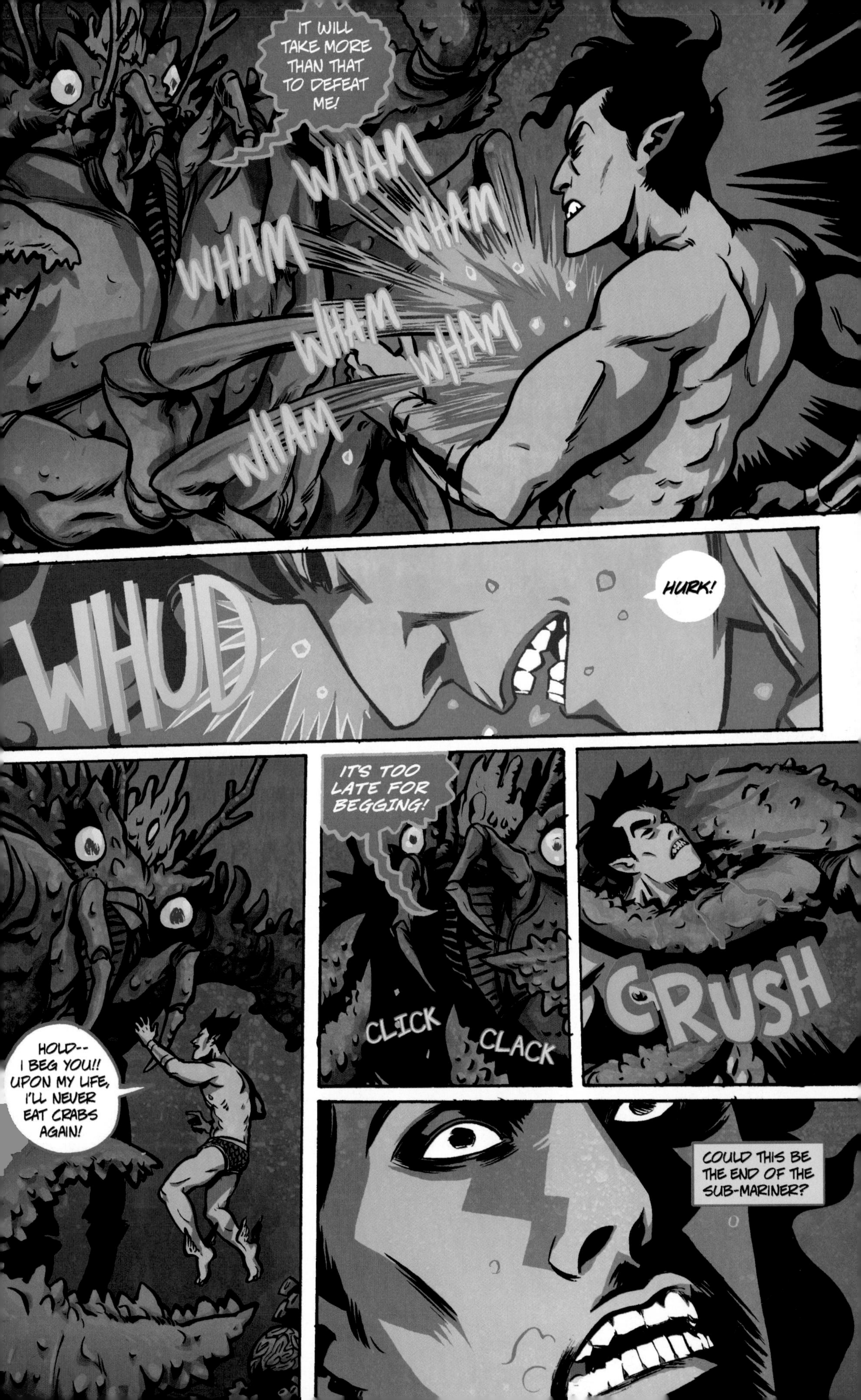
IT WILL TAKE MORE THAN THAT TO DEFEAT ME!
WHAM
WHAM
WHAM
WHAM
WHAM
WHAM
WHAM
WHUD
HURK!
HOLD-- I BEG YOU!! UPON MY LIFE, I'LL NEVER EAT CRABS AGAIN!
IT'S TOO LATE FOR BEGGING!
CLICK
CLACK
CRUSH
COULD THIS BE THE END OF THE SUB-MARINER?

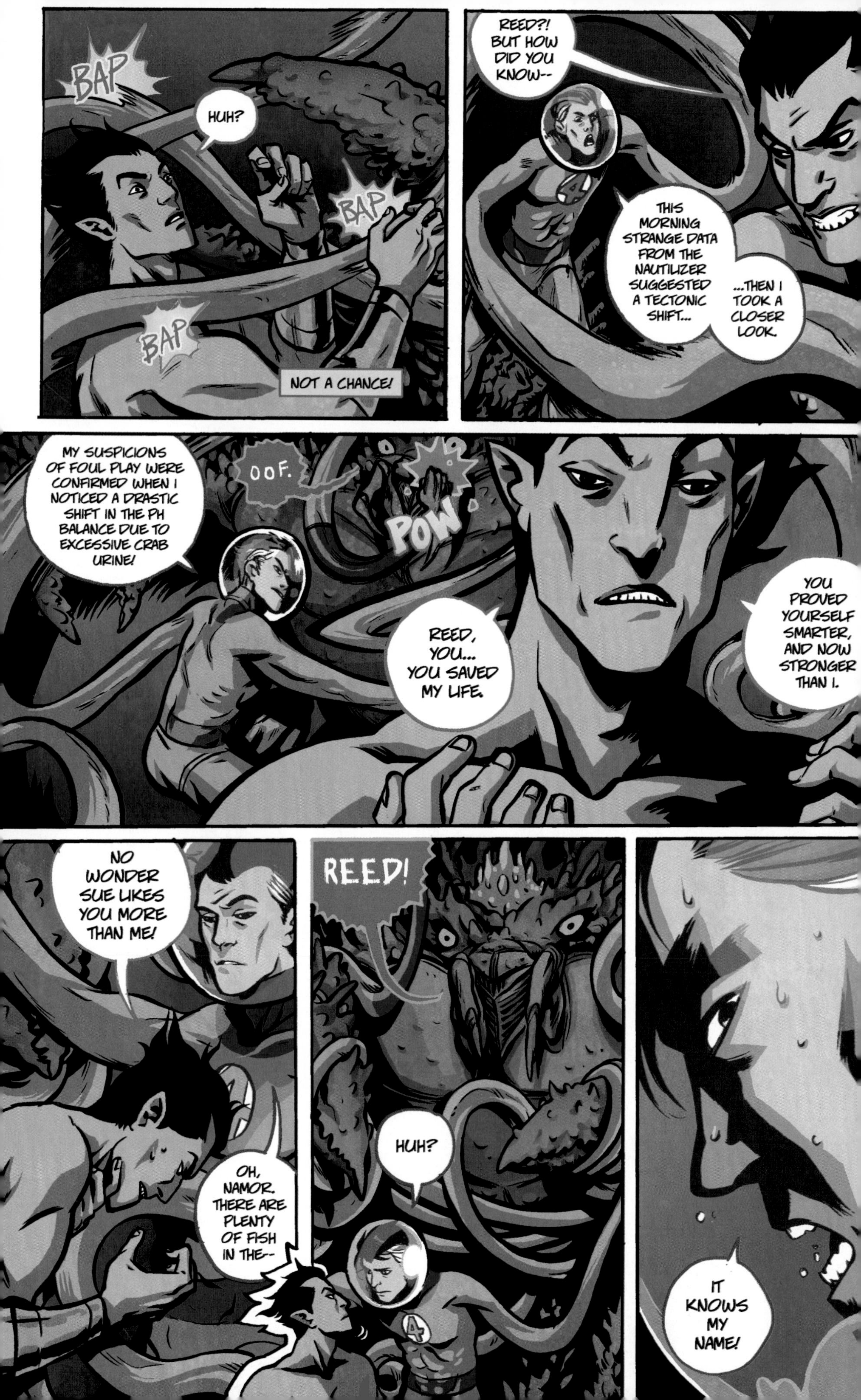
BAP
HUH?
BAP
BAP
NOT A CHANCE!
REED?! BUT HOW DID YOU KNOW--
THIS MORNING STRANGE DATA FROM THE NAUTILIZER SUGGESTED A TECTONIC SHIFT...
...THEN I TOOK A CLOSER LOOK.
MY SUSPICIONS OF FOUL PLAY WERE CONFIRMED WHEN I NOTICED A DRASTIC SHIFT IN THE PH BALANCE DUE TO EXCESSIVE CRAB URINE!
OOF.
POW
REED, YOU... YOU SAVED MY LIFE.
YOU PROVED YOURSELF SMARTER, AND NOW STRONGER THAN I.
NO WONDER SUE LIKES YOU MORE THAN ME!
OH, NAMOR. THERE ARE PLENTY OF FISH IN THE--
REED!
HUH?
IT KNOWS MY NAME!

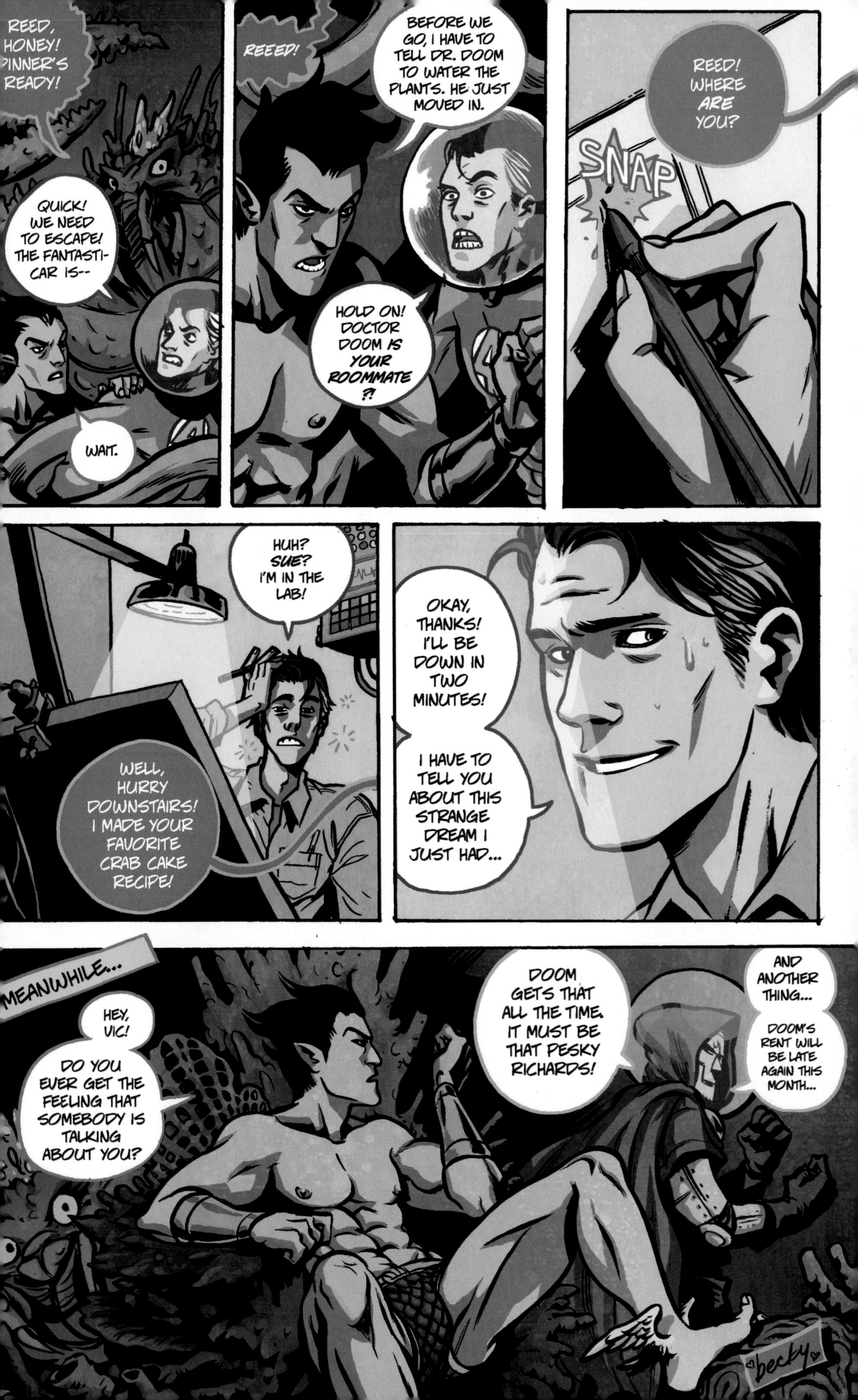
REED, HONEY! DINNER'S READY!
QUICK! WE NEED TO ESCAPE! THE FANTASTI-CAR IS--
WAIT.
REEED!
BEFORE WE GO, I HAVE TO TELL DR. DOOM TO WATER THE PLANTS. HE JUST MOVED IN.
HOLD ON! DOCTOR DOOM IS YOUR ROOMMATE?!
REED! WHERE ARE YOU?
SNAP
HUH? SUE? I'M IN THE LAB!
WELL, HURRY DOWNSTAIRS! I MADE YOUR FAVORITE CRAB CAKE RECIPE!
OKAY, THANKS! I'LL BE DOWN IN TWO MINUTES!
I HAVE TO TELL YOU ABOUT THIS STRANGE DREAM I JUST HAD...
MEANWHILE...
HEY, VIC!
DO YOU EVER GET THE FEELING THAT SOMEBODY IS TALKING ABOUT YOU?
DOOM GETS THAT ALL THE TIME. IT MUST BE THAT PESKY RICHARDS!
AND ANOTHER THING...
DOOM'S RENT WILL BE LATE AGAIN THIS MONTH...
becky

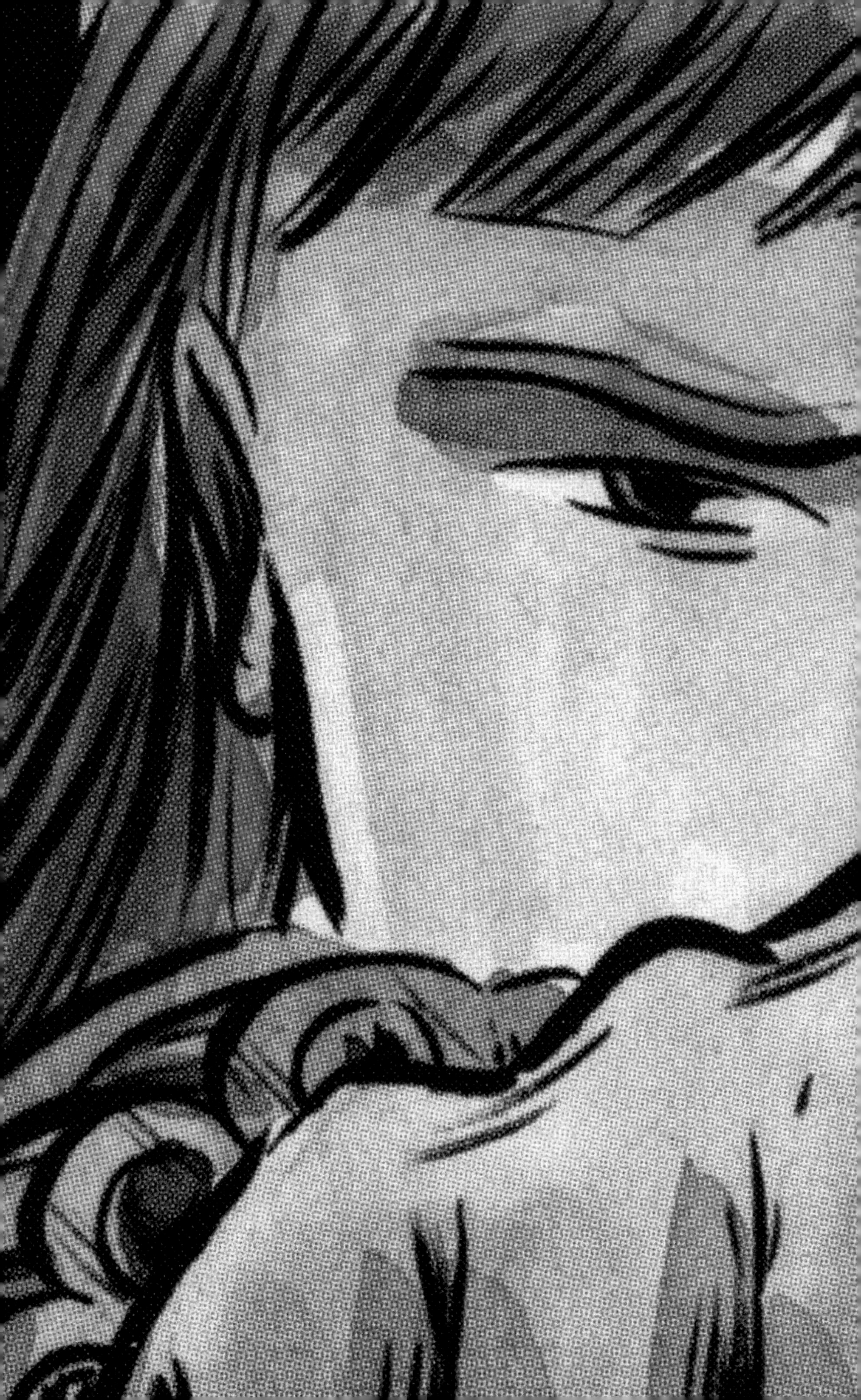

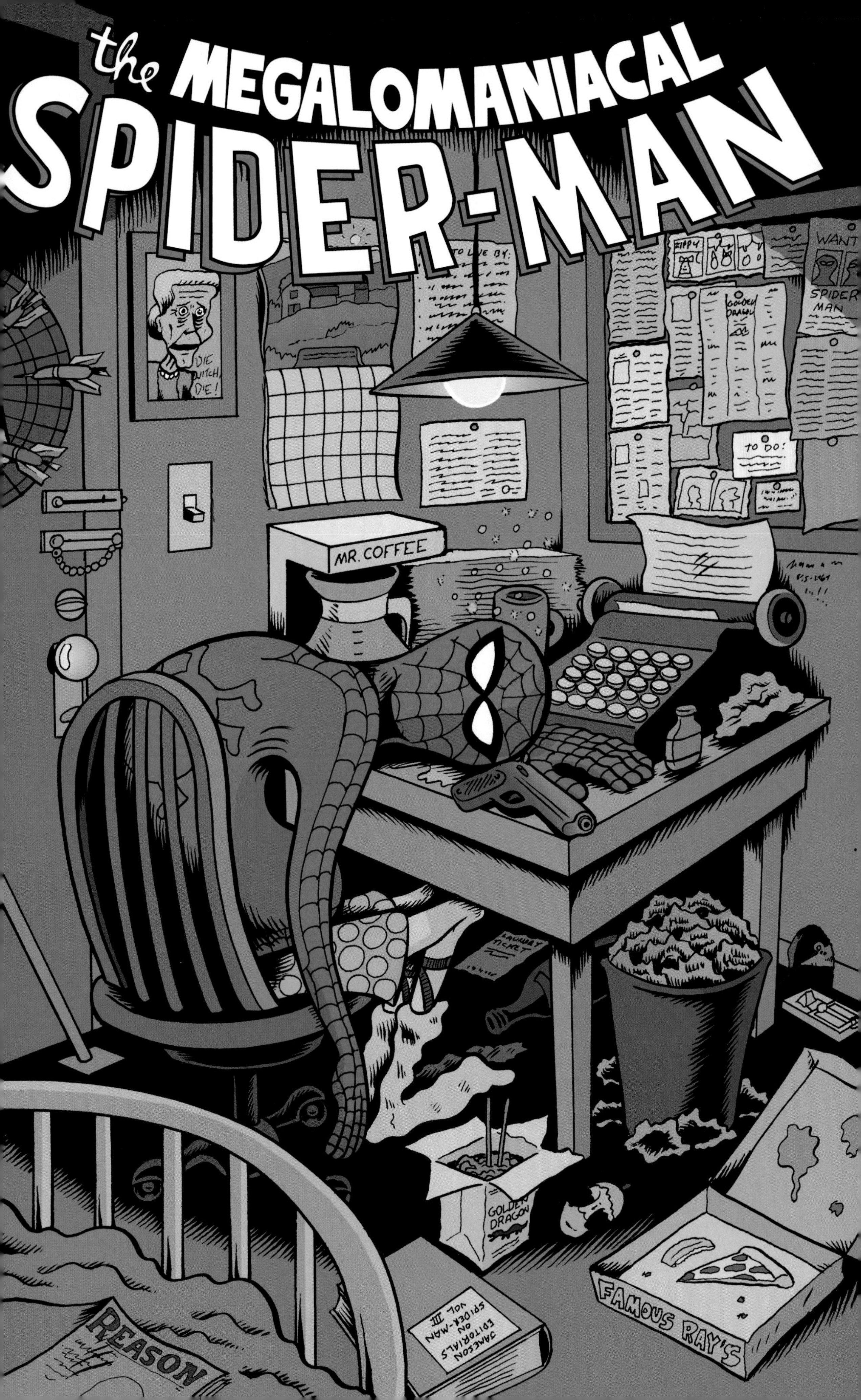
the MEGALOMANIACAL
SPIDER-MAN
DIE WITCH, DIE!
TO LIVE BY:
ZIPPY
GOLDEN DRAGON
SPIDER MAN
TO DO:
MR. COFFEE
LAUNDRY TICKET
GOLDEN DRAGON
JAMESON EDITORIALS ON SPIDER-MAN VOL. III
FAMOUS RAY'S
REASON

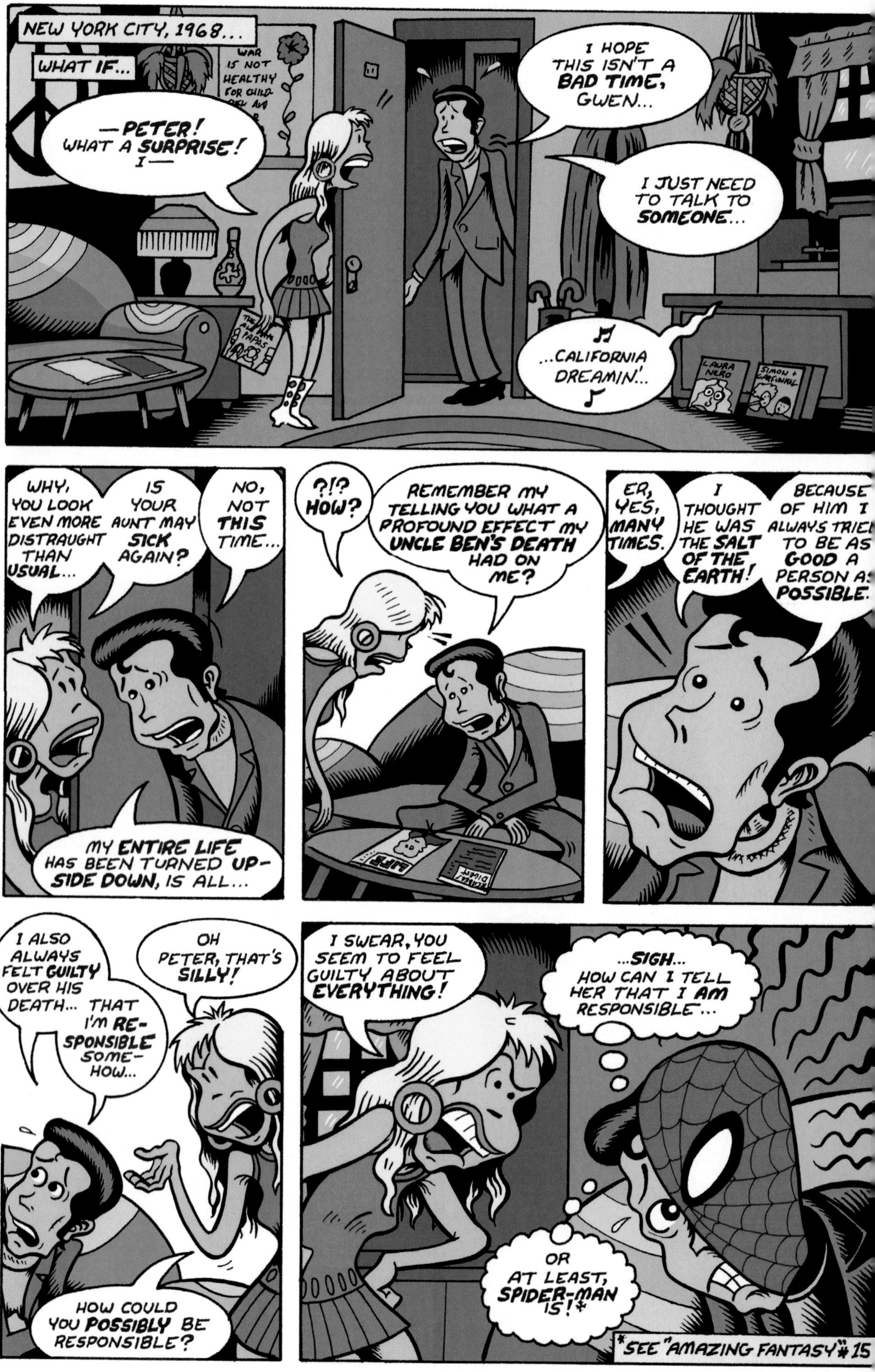
NEW YORK CITY, 1968...
WHAT IF...
WAR IS NOT HEALTHY FOR CHILD-
—PETER! WHAT A SURPRISE! I—
I HOPE THIS ISN'T A BAD TIME, GWEN...
I JUST NEED TO TALK TO SOMEONE...
...CALIFORNIA DREAMIN'...
LAURA NERO
SIMON + GARFUNKEL
WHY, YOU LOOK EVEN MORE DISTRAUGHT THAN USUAL...
IS YOUR AUNT MAY SICK AGAIN?
NO, NOT THIS TIME...
MY ENTIRE LIFE HAS BEEN TURNED UP-SIDE DOWN, IS ALL...
?!? HOW?
REMEMBER MY TELLING YOU WHAT A PROFOUND EFFECT MY UNCLE BEN'S DEATH HAD ON ME?
LIFE
ER, YES, MANY TIMES.
I THOUGHT HE WAS THE SALT OF THE EARTH!
BECAUSE OF HIM I ALWAYS TRIED TO BE AS GOOD A PERSON AS POSSIBLE.
I ALSO ALWAYS FELT GUILTY OVER HIS DEATH... THAT I'M RE-SPONSIBLE SOME-HOW...
OH PETER, THAT'S SILLY!
HOW COULD YOU POSSIBLY BE RESPONSIBLE?
I SWEAR, YOU SEEM TO FEEL GUILTY ABOUT EVERYTHING!
...SIGH... HOW CAN I TELL HER THAT I AM RESPONSIBLE...
OR AT LEAST, SPIDER-MAN IS!*
*SEE "AMAZING FANTASY" #15

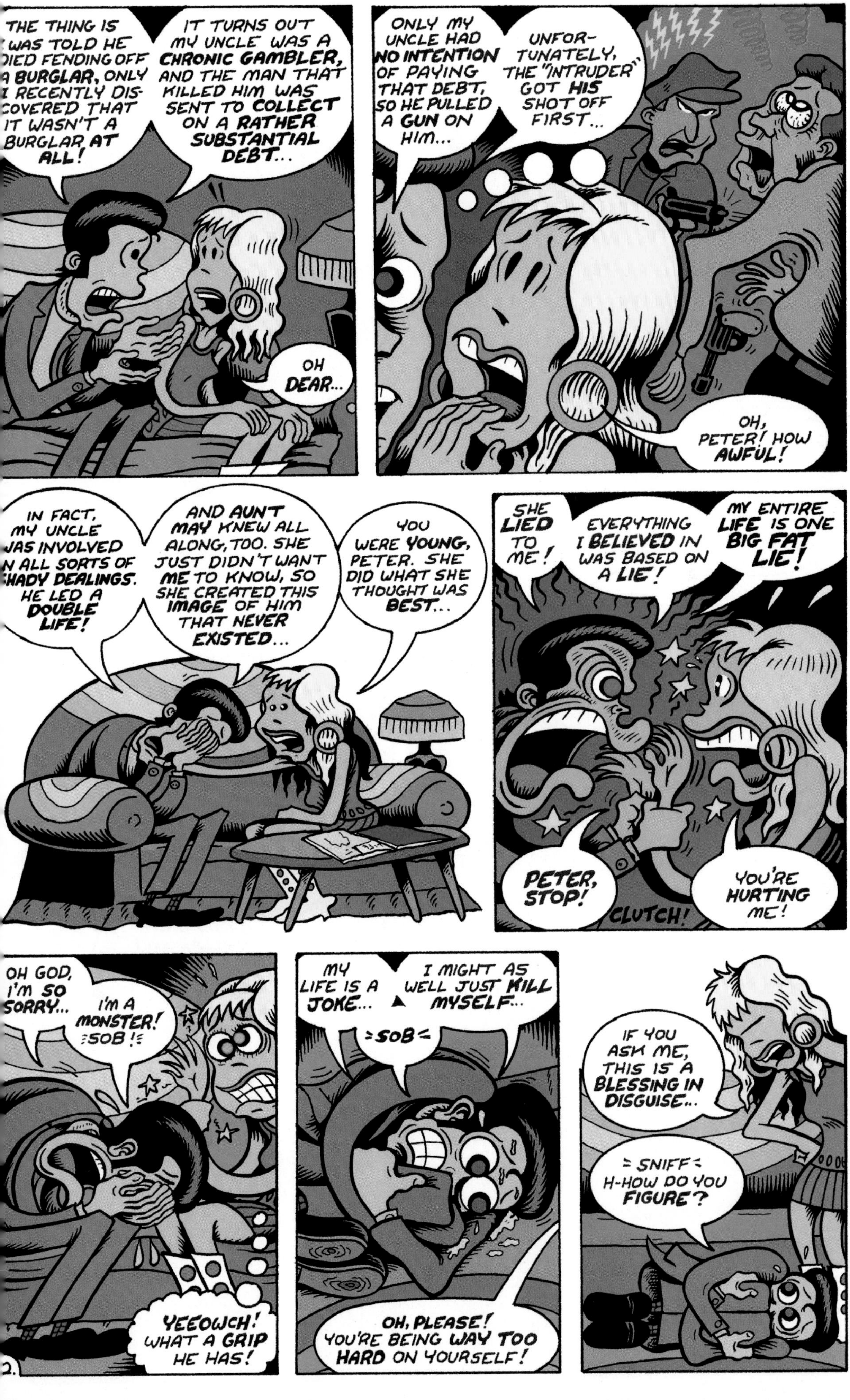
THE THING IS I WAS TOLD HE DIED FENDING OFF A BURGLAR, ONLY I RECENTLY DISCOVERED THAT IT WASN'T A BURGLAR AT ALL!
IT TURNS OUT MY UNCLE WAS A CHRONIC GAMBLER, AND THE MAN THAT KILLED HIM WAS SENT TO COLLECT ON A RATHER SUBSTANTIAL DEBT...
OH DEAR...
ONLY MY UNCLE HAD NO INTENTION OF PAYING THAT DEBT, SO HE PULLED A GUN ON HIM...
UNFORTUNATELY, THE "INTRUDER" GOT HIS SHOT OFF FIRST...
OH, PETER! HOW AWFUL!
IN FACT, MY UNCLE WAS INVOLVED IN ALL SORTS OF SHADY DEALINGS. HE LED A DOUBLE LIFE!
AND AUNT MAY KNEW ALL ALONG, TOO. SHE JUST DIDN'T WANT ME TO KNOW, SO SHE CREATED THIS IMAGE OF HIM THAT NEVER EXISTED...
YOU WERE YOUNG, PETER. SHE DID WHAT SHE THOUGHT WAS BEST...
SHE LIED TO ME!
EVERYTHING I BELIEVED IN WAS BASED ON A LIE!
MY ENTIRE LIFE IS ONE BIG FAT LIE!
PETER, STOP!
CLUTCH!
YOU'RE HURTING ME!
OH GOD, I'M SO SORRY...
I'M A MONSTER! SOB!
YEEOWCH! WHAT A GRIP HE HAS!
MY LIFE IS A JOKE...
I MIGHT AS WELL JUST KILL MYSELF...
SOB
OH, PLEASE! YOU'RE BEING WAY TOO HARD ON YOURSELF!
IF YOU ASK ME, THIS IS A BLESSING IN DISGUISE...
SNIFF
H-HOW DO YOU FIGURE?
2.

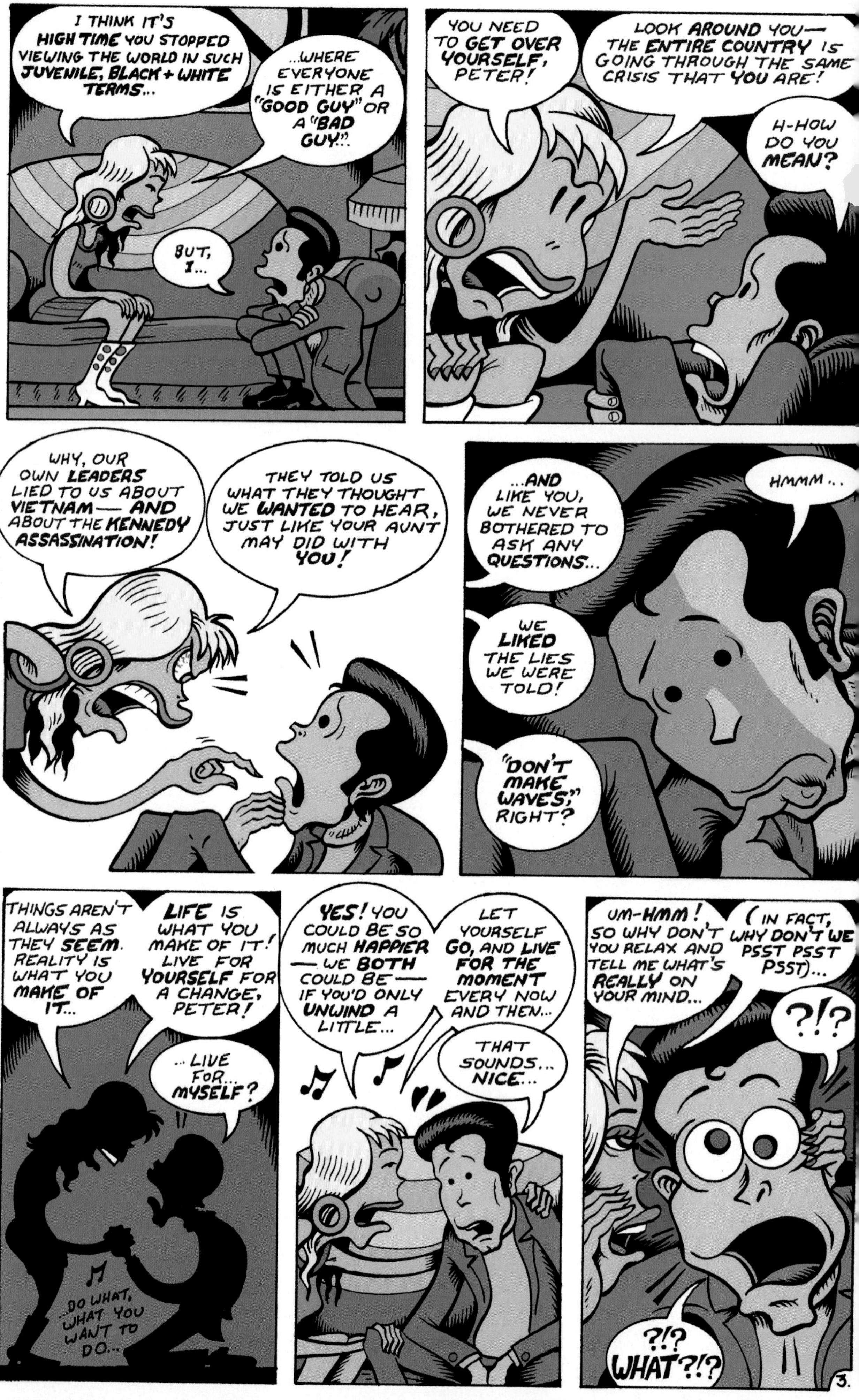
I THINK IT'S HIGH TIME YOU STOPPED VIEWING THE WORLD IN SUCH JUVENILE, BLACK + WHITE TERMS...
...WHERE EVERYONE IS EITHER A "GOOD GUY" OR A "BAD GUY."
BUT, I...
YOU NEED TO GET OVER YOURSELF, PETER!
LOOK AROUND YOU— THE ENTIRE COUNTRY IS GOING THROUGH THE SAME CRISIS THAT YOU ARE!
H-HOW DO YOU MEAN?
WHY, OUR OWN LEADERS LIED TO US ABOUT VIETNAM— AND ABOUT THE KENNEDY ASSASSINATION!
THEY TOLD US WHAT THEY THOUGHT WE WANTED TO HEAR, JUST LIKE YOUR AUNT MAY DID WITH YOU!
...AND LIKE YOU, WE NEVER BOTHERED TO ASK ANY QUESTIONS...
HMMM...
WE LIKED THE LIES WE WERE TOLD!
"DON'T MAKE WAVES," RIGHT?
THINGS AREN'T ALWAYS AS THEY SEEM. REALITY IS WHAT YOU MAKE OF IT...
LIFE IS WHAT YOU MAKE OF IT! LIVE FOR YOURSELF FOR A CHANGE, PETER!
...LIVE FOR... MYSELF?
...DO WHAT, WHAT YOU WANT TO DO...
YES! YOU COULD BE SO MUCH HAPPIER —WE BOTH COULD BE— IF YOU'D ONLY UNWIND A LITTLE...
LET YOURSELF GO, AND LIVE FOR THE MOMENT EVERY NOW AND THEN...
THAT SOUNDS... NICE...
UM-HMM! SO WHY DON'T YOU RELAX AND TELL ME WHAT'S REALLY ON YOUR MIND...
(IN FACT, WHY DON'T WE PSST PSST PSST)...
?!?
?!? WHAT?!?

GET AWAY FROM ME, YOU VIXEN!
I'M ON TO YOUR GAME!
?!? WHAT "GAME"? WHAT ARE YOU TALKING ABOUT?
LEAP!
DON'T PLAY DUMB WITH ME, SISTER! I WASN'T BORN YESTERDAY!
FIRST YOU SEDUCE ME WITH YOUR FEMININE WILES, AND THEN YOU'LL FILL MY SOFTENED HEAD WITH ALL SORTS OF RADICAL NOTIONS YOU PICKED UP FROM THOSE PROTESTER TYPES YOU HANG OUT WITH ON CAMPUS!
"RADICAL NOTIONS"? "PROTESTER TYPES"?
PETER, YOU'RE TALKING CRAZY!
"CRAZY," EH? WELL, I FOR ONE AM NOT GONNA SIT AROUND AND WATCH WHILE THE COUNTRY GOES TO THE COMMIE DOGS!
WHO ARE YOU CALLING A COMMIE?
AND GET DOWN FROM THERE THIS INSTANT!
WAIT A MINUTE —YOU'RE WORKING FOR MYSTERIO NOW, AREN'T YOU? OR DOCTOR OCTOPUS, PERHAPS?
I SHOULD'VE SUSPECTED AS MUCH ALL ALONG!
I'M OUTTA HERE!
OMIGOSH, YOU'VE COMPLETELY LOST YOUR MIND, HAVEN'T YOU?
PLEASE COME BACK INSIDE...
I ONLY WANT TO HELP...
...SIGH... HE'S GONE...
HE IS WITHOUT A DOUBT THE MOST MENTALLY DISTURBED PERSON I'VE EVER MET...
YET HE'S ALSO AS CUTE AS THE DICKENS...
AM I HOPELESSLY ATTRACTED TO HIM BECAUSE HE'S SUCH A MESS?
IF SO, I MUST BE AS CRAZY AS HE IS...
...SIGH...
I HOPE HE ISN'T GAY...

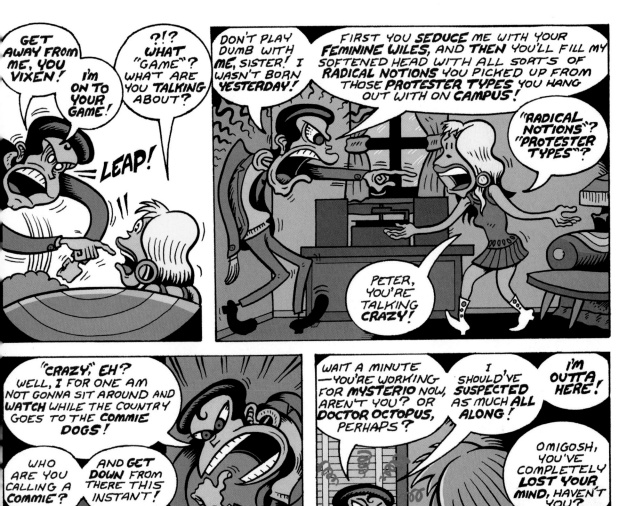

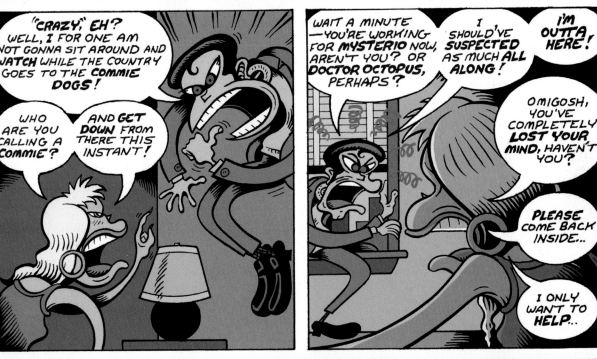

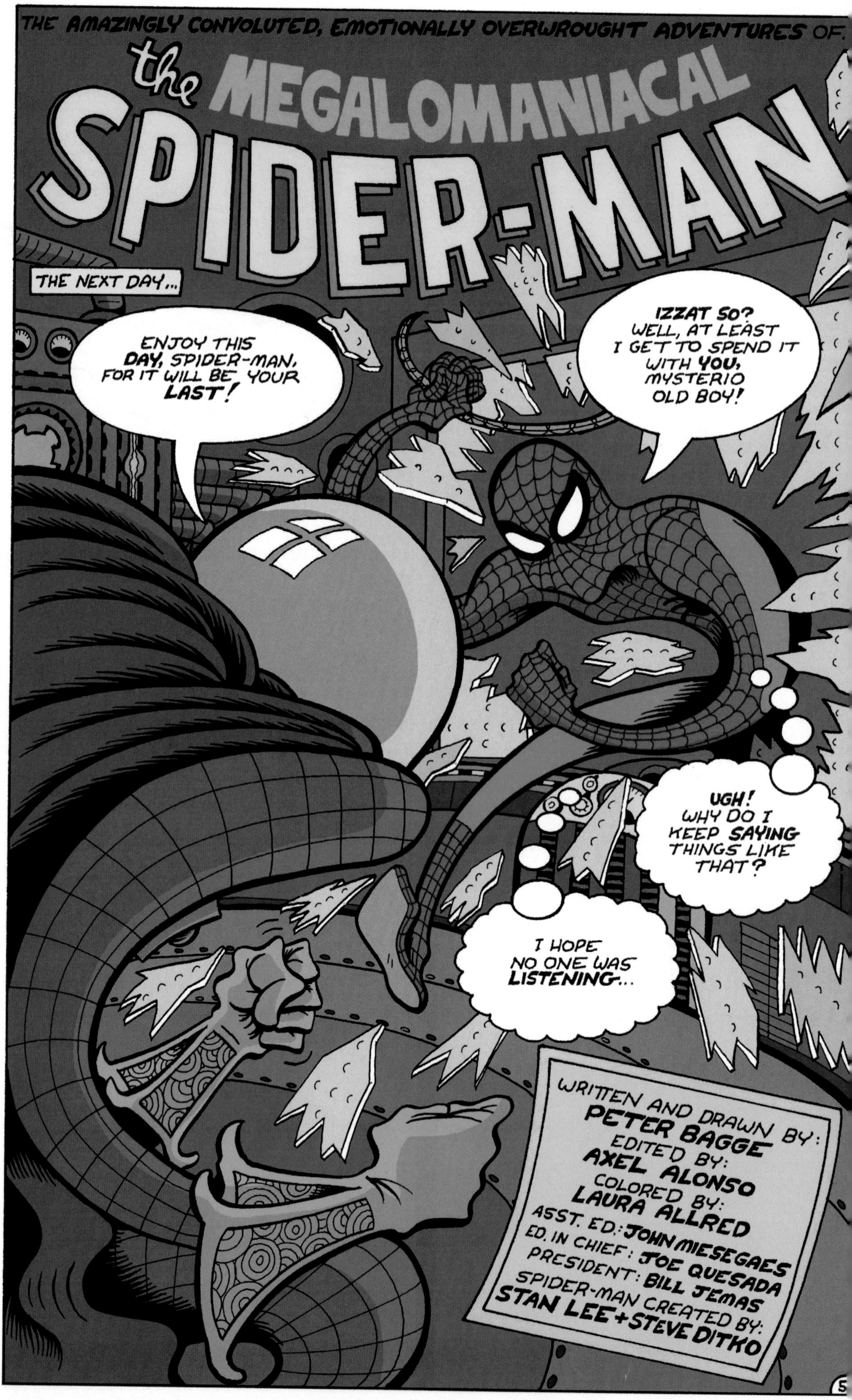
THE AMAZINGLY CONVOLUTED, EMOTIONALLY OVERWROUGHT ADVENTURES OF:
the MEGALOMANIACAL SPIDER-MAN
THE NEXT DAY...
ENJOY THIS DAY, SPIDER-MAN, FOR IT WILL BE YOUR LAST!
IZZAT SO? WELL, AT LEAST I GET TO SPEND IT WITH YOU, MYSTERIO OLD BOY!
UGH! WHY DO I KEEP SAYING THINGS LIKE THAT?
I HOPE NO ONE WAS LISTENING...
WRITTEN AND DRAWN BY: PETER BAGGE
EDITED BY: AXEL ALONSO
COLORED BY: LAURA ALLRED
ASST. ED: JOHN MIESEGAES
ED. IN CHIEF: JOE QUESADA
PRESIDENT: BILL JEMAS
SPIDER-MAN CREATED BY: STAN LEE + STEVE DITKO

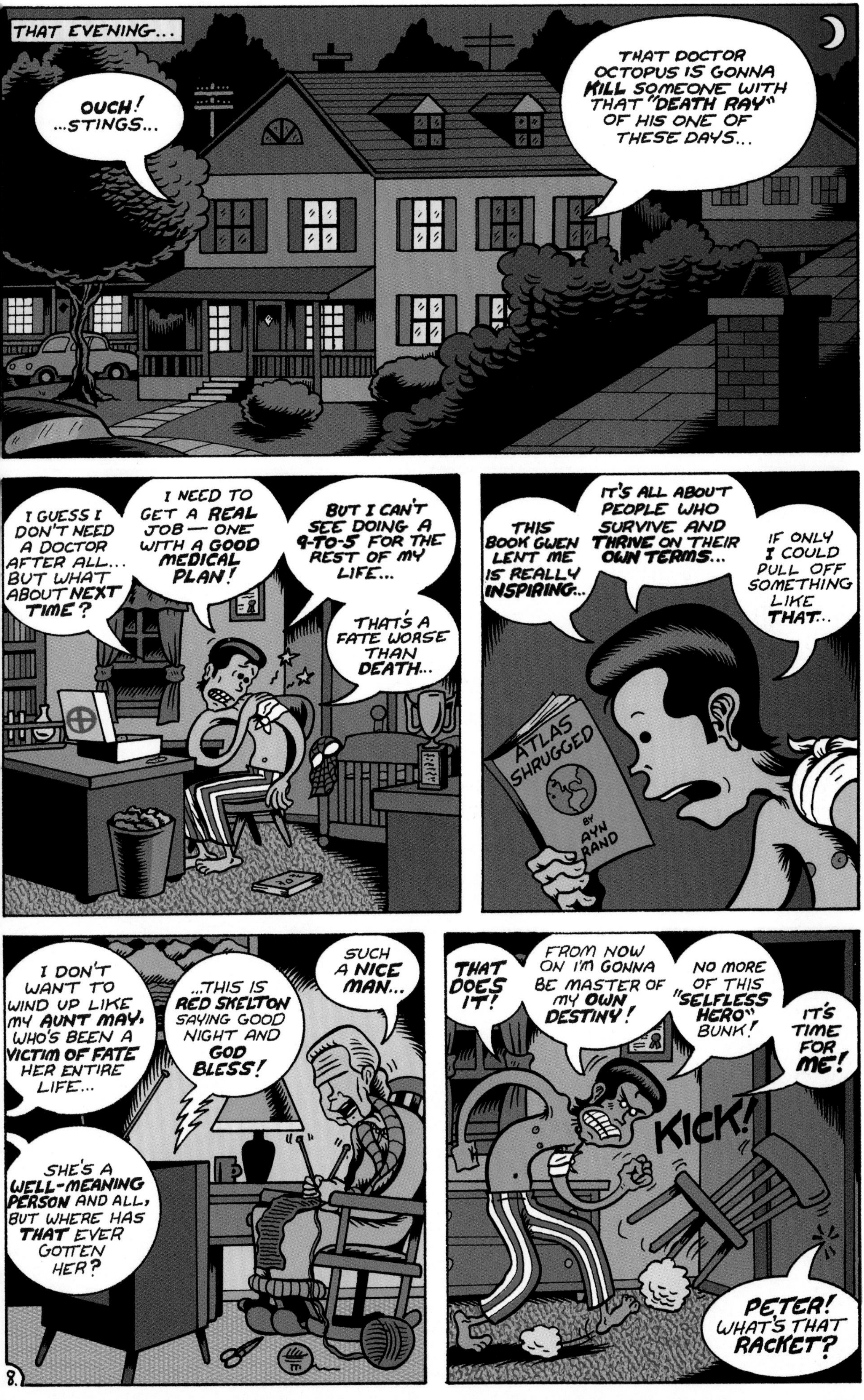
THAT EVENING...
OUCH! ...STINGS...
THAT DOCTOR OCTOPUS IS GONNA KILL SOMEONE WITH THAT "DEATH RAY" OF HIS ONE OF THESE DAYS...
I GUESS I DON'T NEED A DOCTOR AFTER ALL... BUT WHAT ABOUT NEXT TIME?
I NEED TO GET A REAL JOB — ONE WITH A GOOD MEDICAL PLAN!
BUT I CAN'T SEE DOING A 9-TO-5 FOR THE REST OF MY LIFE...
THAT'S A FATE WORSE THAN DEATH...
THIS BOOK GWEN LENT ME IS REALLY INSPIRING...
IT'S ALL ABOUT PEOPLE WHO SURVIVE AND THRIVE ON THEIR OWN TERMS...
IF ONLY I COULD PULL OFF SOMETHING LIKE THAT...
ATLAS SHRUGGED BY AYN RAND
I DON'T WANT TO WIND UP LIKE MY AUNT MAY, WHO'S BEEN A VICTIM OF FATE HER ENTIRE LIFE...
...THIS IS RED SKELTON SAYING GOOD NIGHT AND GOD BLESS!
SUCH A NICE MAN...
SHE'S A WELL-MEANING PERSON AND ALL, BUT WHERE HAS THAT EVER GOTTEN HER?
THAT DOES IT!
FROM NOW ON I'M GONNA BE MASTER OF MY OWN DESTINY!
NO MORE OF THIS "SELFLESS HERO" BUNK!
IT'S TIME FOR ME!
KICK!
PETER! WHAT'S THAT RACKET?

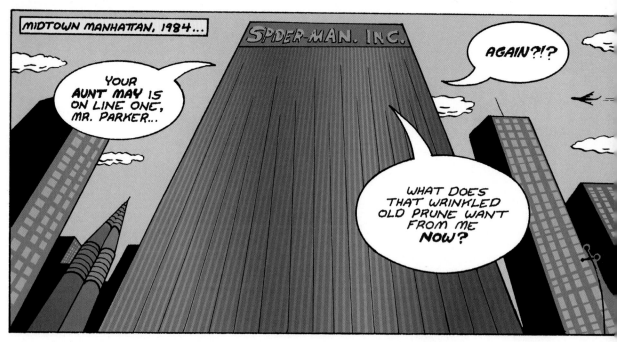

MIDTOWN MANHATTAN, 1984...

SPIDER-MAN. INC.

YOUR **AUNT MAY** IS ON LINE ONE, MR. PARKER...

AGAIN?!?

WHAT DOES THAT WRINKLED OLD PRUNE WANT FROM ME **NOW**?

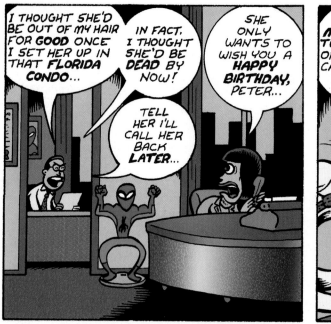

I THOUGHT SHE'D BE OUT OF MY HAIR FOR **GOOD** ONCE I SET HER UP IN THAT **FLORIDA CONDO**...

IN FACT, I THOUGHT SHE'D BE **DEAD** BY NOW!

TELL HER I'LL CALL HER BACK **LATER**...

SHE ONLY WANTS TO WISH YOU A **HAPPY BIRTHDAY**, PETER...

THAT'S **MR. PARKER** TO YOU, BETTY— OR SHOULD I CALL YOU "**MS. BRANT**"?

THAT'S WHAT YOU **FEMINIST TYPES** WANT TO BE CALLED NOW, RIGHT? "**MZZZZ**"?

AND PLEASE REMIND MY AUNT BIDDY TO **NEVER** CALL ME AT WORK AGAIN!

Y-YES, MR. PARKER...

ACTUALLY, "MR. PARKER **SIR**" HAS A **BETTER** RING TO IT...

IT ADDS AN AIR OF **DIGNITY** AND **RESPECT** THAT MY POSITION **DESERVES**...

OR BETTER YET, HOW ABOUT "**YOUR EXCELLENCY**"? HA-HA!

I'M **SORRY**, MAY...

I KNOW, HE'S BEEN **IMPOSSIBLE** LATELY...

≶SNIFF!≶

GET **JAMESON** IN HERE, MZZZ BRANT...

I WANT TO HEAR HOW MY NEW TITLE SOUNDS COMING OUT OF THAT **MEALY MOUTH** OF HIS...

YES, SIR...

OH GOD, I WISH HE'D LEAVE THAT POOR MAN **ALONE**...

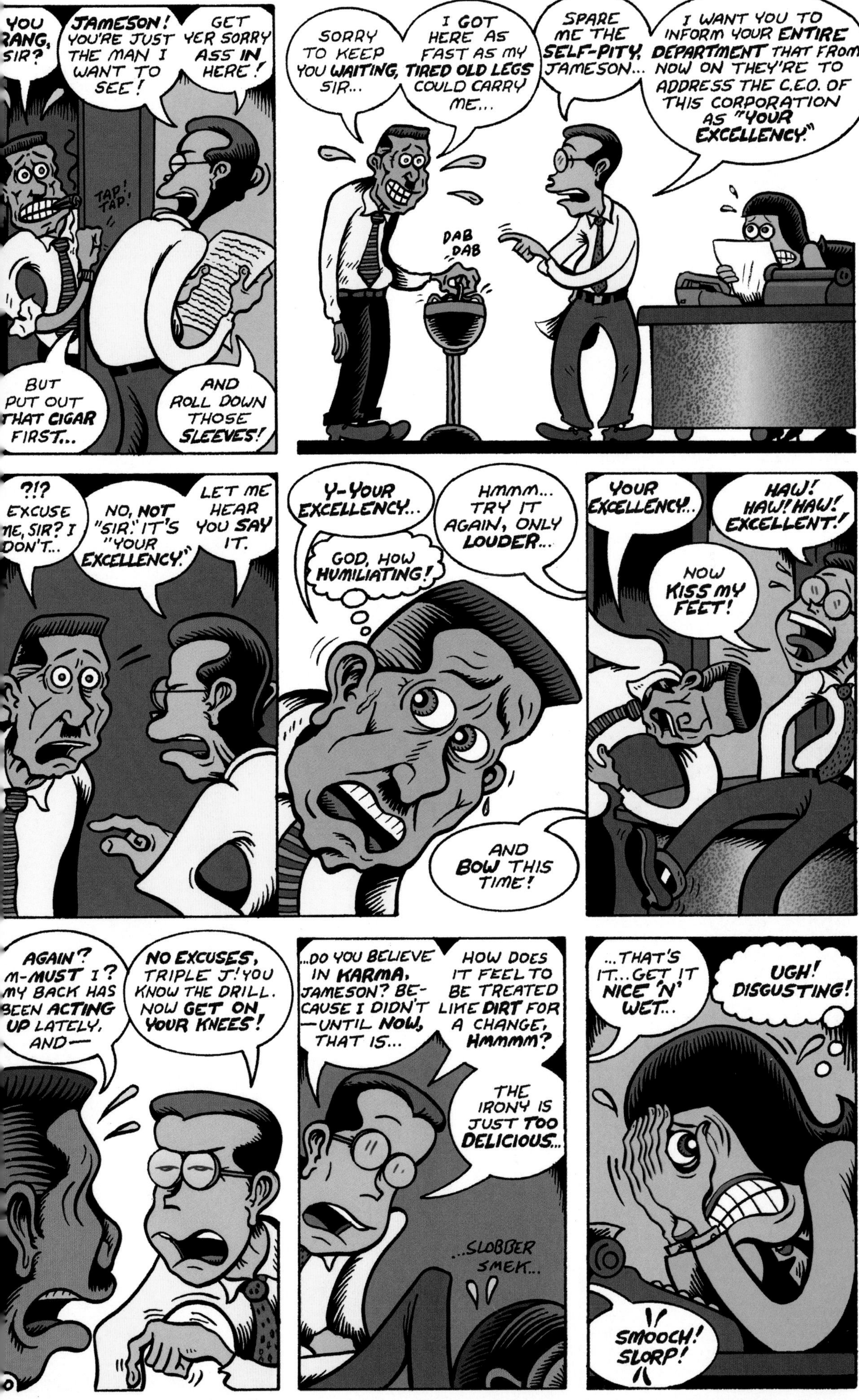
YOU RANG, SIR?
JAMESON! YOU'RE JUST THE MAN I WANT TO SEE!
GET YER SORRY ASS IN HERE!
TAP! TAP!
BUT PUT OUT THAT CIGAR FIRST...
AND ROLL DOWN THOSE SLEEVES!
SORRY TO KEEP YOU WAITING, SIR...
I GOT HERE AS FAST AS MY TIRED OLD LEGS COULD CARRY ME...
DAB DAB
SPARE ME THE SELF-PITY, JAMESON...
I WANT YOU TO INFORM YOUR ENTIRE DEPARTMENT THAT FROM NOW ON THEY'RE TO ADDRESS THE C.E.O. OF THIS CORPORATION AS "YOUR EXCELLENCY."
?!? EXCUSE ME, SIR? I DON'T...
NO, NOT "SIR." IT'S "YOUR EXCELLENCY."
LET ME HEAR YOU SAY IT.
Y-YOUR EXCELLENCY...
GOD, HOW HUMILIATING!
HMMM... TRY IT AGAIN, ONLY LOUDER...
YOUR EXCELLENCY...
HAW! HAW! HAW! EXCELLENT!
NOW KISS MY FEET!
AND BOW THIS TIME!
AGAIN? M-MUST I? MY BACK HAS BEEN ACTING UP LATELY, AND—
NO EXCUSES, TRIPLE J! YOU KNOW THE DRILL. NOW GET ON YOUR KNEES!
...DO YOU BELIEVE IN KARMA, JAMESON? BECAUSE I DIDN'T —UNTIL NOW, THAT IS...
HOW DOES IT FEEL TO BE TREATED LIKE DIRT FOR A CHANGE, HMMMM?
THE IRONY IS JUST TOO DELICIOUS...
...SLOBBER SMEK...
...THAT'S IT...GET IT NICE 'N' WET...
UGH! DISGUSTING!
SMOOCH! SLORP!

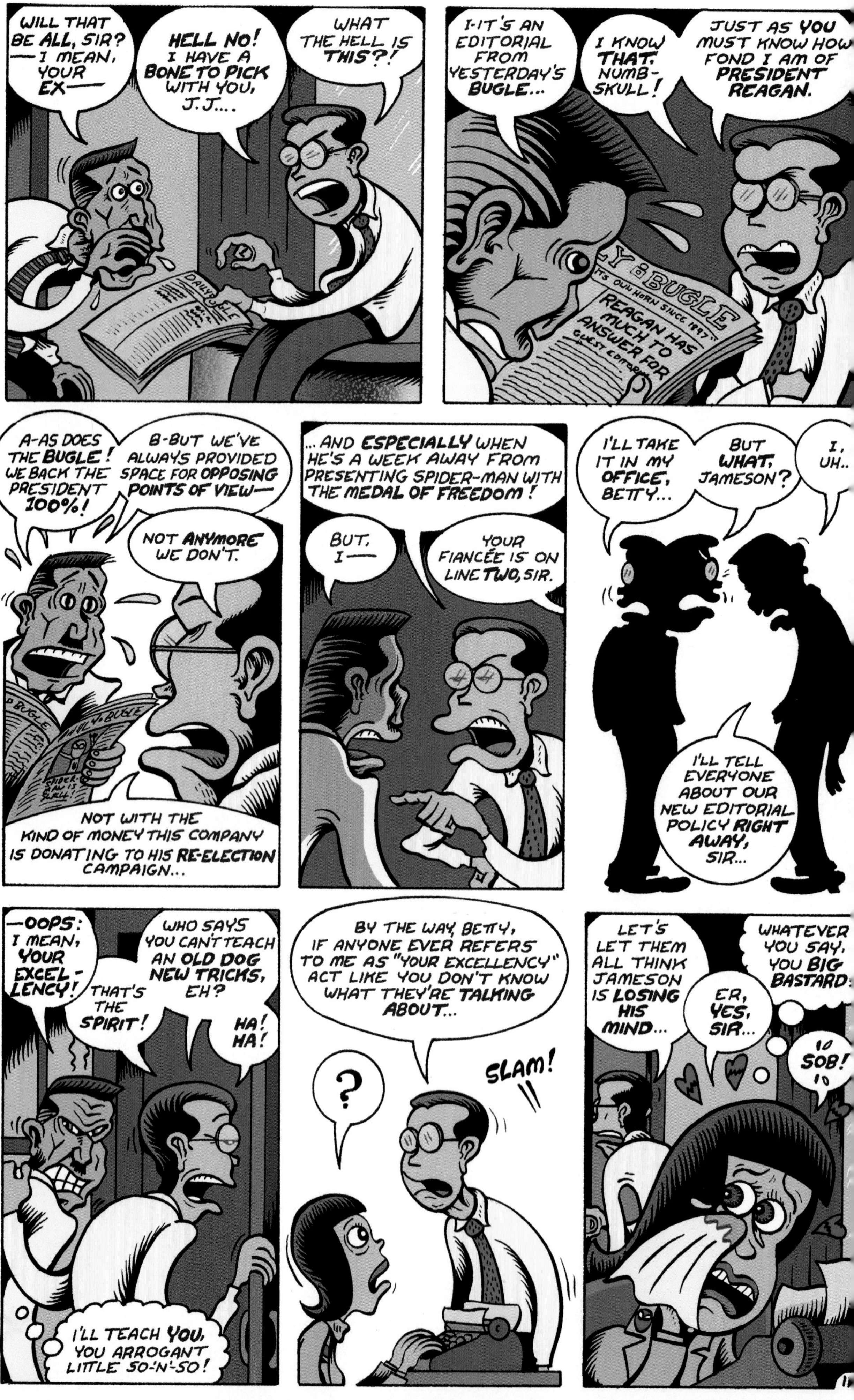
WILL THAT BE ALL, SIR? —I MEAN, YOUR EX—
HELL NO! I HAVE A BONE TO PICK WITH YOU, J.J....
WHAT THE HELL IS THIS?!
DAILY BUGLE
I-IT'S AN EDITORIAL FROM YESTERDAY'S BUGLE...
I KNOW THAT, NUMB-SKULL!
JUST AS YOU MUST KNOW HOW FOND I AM OF PRESIDENT REAGAN.
BUGLE
ITS OWN HORN SINCE 1897
REAGAN HAS MUCH TO ANSWER FOR
GUEST EDITORIAL
A-AS DOES THE BUGLE! WE BACK THE PRESIDENT 100%!
B-BUT WE'VE ALWAYS PROVIDED SPACE FOR OPPOSING POINTS OF VIEW—
NOT ANYMORE WE DON'T.
NOT WITH THE KIND OF MONEY THIS COMPANY IS DONATING TO HIS RE-ELECTION CAMPAIGN...
...AND ESPECIALLY WHEN HE'S A WEEK AWAY FROM PRESENTING SPIDER-MAN WITH THE MEDAL OF FREEDOM!
BUT, I—
YOUR FIANCÉE IS ON LINE TWO, SIR.
I'LL TAKE IT IN MY OFFICE, BETTY...
BUT WHAT, JAMESON?
I, UH..
I'LL TELL EVERYONE ABOUT OUR NEW EDITORIAL POLICY RIGHT AWAY, SIR...
—OOPS: I MEAN, YOUR EXCEL-LENCY!
WHO SAYS YOU CAN'T TEACH AN OLD DOG NEW TRICKS, EH?
THAT'S THE SPIRIT!
HA! HA!
I'LL TEACH YOU, YOU ARROGANT LITTLE SO-'N'-SO!
BY THE WAY, BETTY, IF ANYONE EVER REFERS TO ME AS "YOUR EXCELLENCY" ACT LIKE YOU DON'T KNOW WHAT THEY'RE TALKING ABOUT...
?
SLAM!
LET'S LET THEM ALL THINK JAMESON IS LOSING HIS MIND...
ER, YES, SIR...
WHATEVER YOU SAY, YOU BIG BASTARD.
SOB!

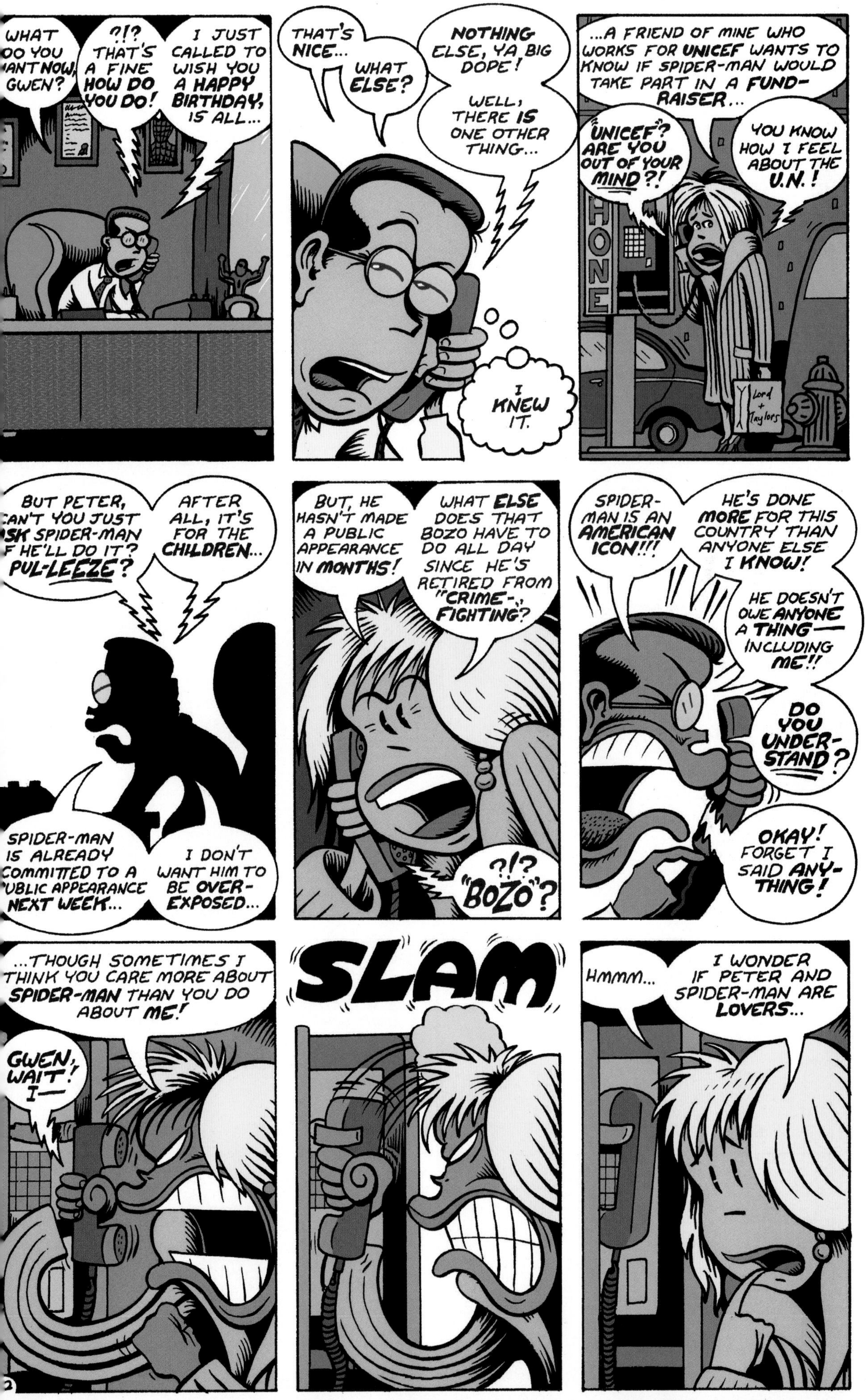
WHAT DO YOU WANT NOW, GWEN?
?!? THAT'S A FINE HOW DO YOU DO!
I JUST CALLED TO WISH YOU A HAPPY BIRTHDAY, IS ALL...
THAT'S NICE...
WHAT ELSE?
NOTHING ELSE, YA BIG DOPE!
WELL, THERE IS ONE OTHER THING...
I KNEW IT.
...A FRIEND OF MINE WHO WORKS FOR UNICEF WANTS TO KNOW IF SPIDER-MAN WOULD TAKE PART IN A FUND-RAISER...
UNICEF? ARE YOU OUT OF YOUR MIND?!
YOU KNOW HOW I FEEL ABOUT THE U.N.!
HONE
Lord + Taylors
BUT PETER, CAN'T YOU JUST ASK SPIDER-MAN IF HE'LL DO IT? PUL-LEEZE?
AFTER ALL, IT'S FOR THE CHILDREN...
SPIDER-MAN IS ALREADY COMMITTED TO A PUBLIC APPEARANCE NEXT WEEK...
I DON'T WANT HIM TO BE OVER-EXPOSED...
BUT, HE HASN'T MADE A PUBLIC APPEARANCE IN MONTHS!
WHAT ELSE DOES THAT BOZO HAVE TO DO ALL DAY SINCE HE'S RETIRED FROM "CRIME-FIGHTING"?
?!? "BOZO"?
SPIDER-MAN IS AN AMERICAN ICON!!!
HE'S DONE MORE FOR THIS COUNTRY THAN ANYONE ELSE I KNOW!
HE DOESN'T OWE ANYONE A THING— INCLUDING ME!!
DO YOU UNDERSTAND?
OKAY! FORGET I SAID ANYTHING!
...THOUGH SOMETIMES I THINK YOU CARE MORE ABOUT SPIDER-MAN THAN YOU DO ABOUT ME!
GWEN, WAIT! I—
SLAM
HMMM...
I WONDER IF PETER AND SPIDER-MAN ARE LOVERS...

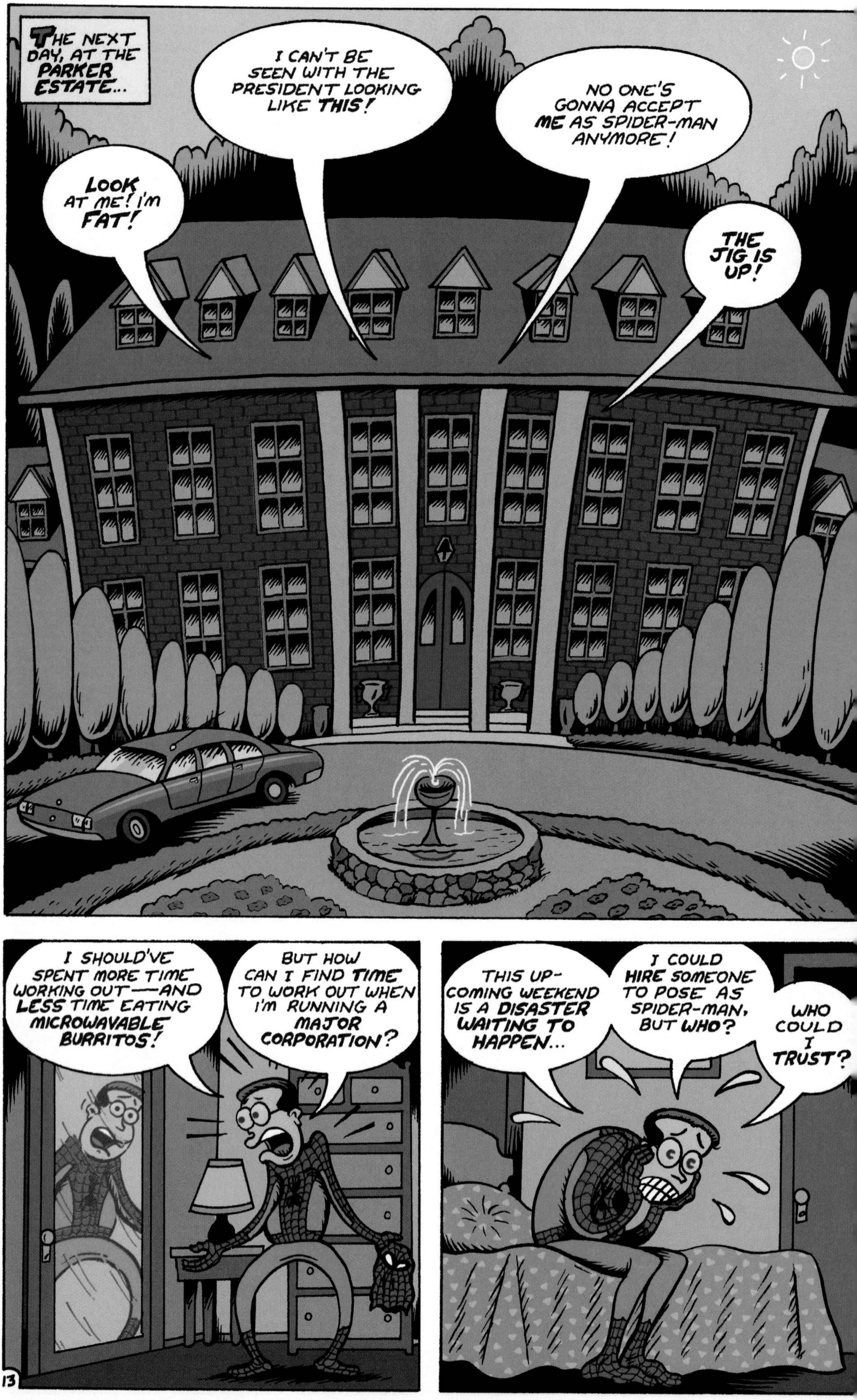
THE NEXT DAY, AT THE PARKER ESTATE...
LOOK AT ME! I'M FAT!
I CAN'T BE SEEN WITH THE PRESIDENT LOOKING LIKE THIS!
NO ONE'S GONNA ACCEPT ME AS SPIDER-MAN ANYMORE!
THE JIG IS UP!
I SHOULD'VE SPENT MORE TIME WORKING OUT--AND LESS TIME EATING MICROWAVABLE BURRITOS!
BUT HOW CAN I FIND TIME TO WORK OUT WHEN I'M RUNNING A MAJOR CORPORATION?
THIS UP-COMING WEEKEND IS A DISASTER WAITING TO HAPPEN...
I COULD HIRE SOMEONE TO POSE AS SPIDER-MAN, BUT WHO?
WHO COULD I TRUST?

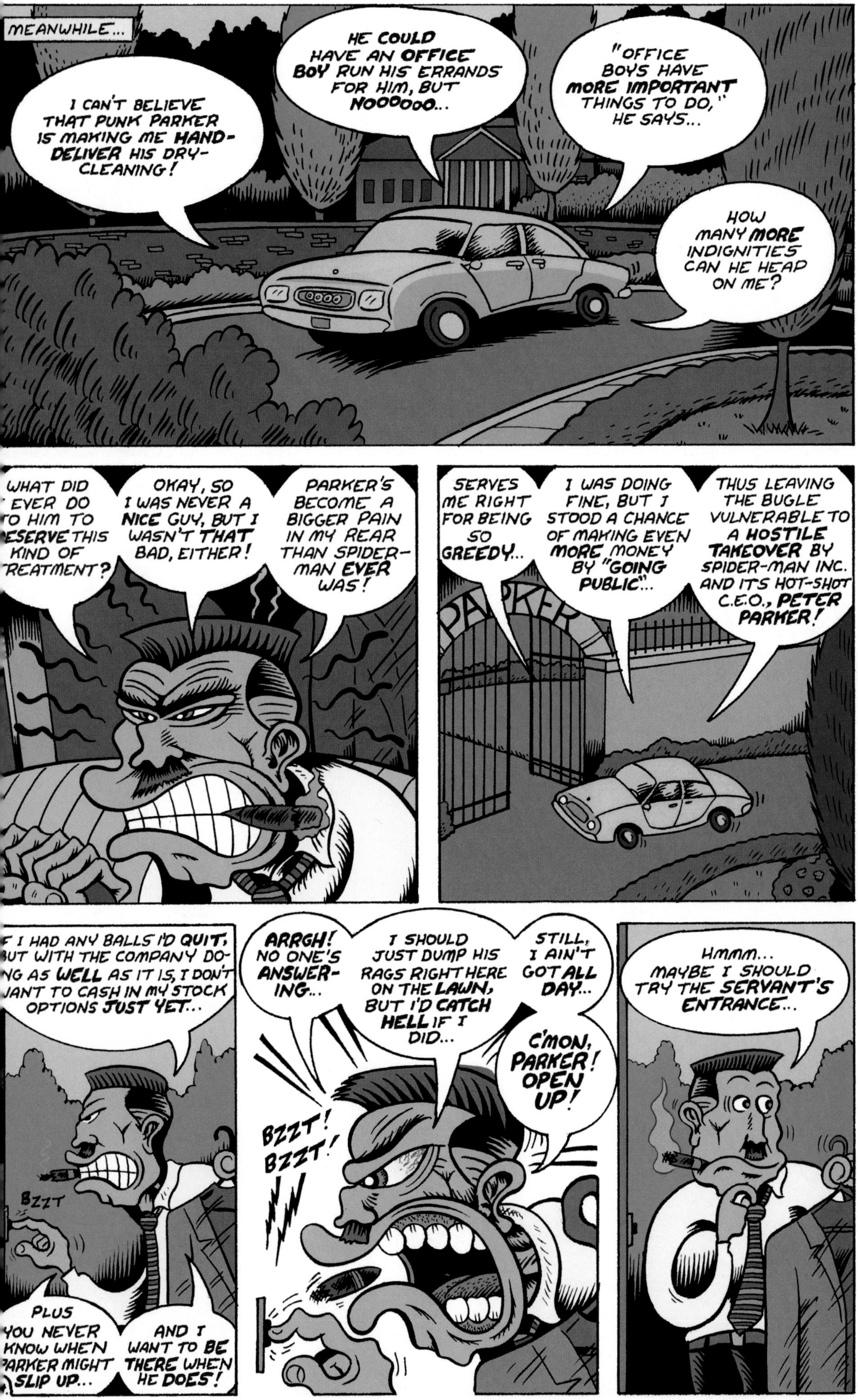
MEANWHILE...
I CAN'T BELIEVE THAT PUNK PARKER IS MAKING ME HAND-DELIVER HIS DRY-CLEANING!
HE COULD HAVE AN OFFICE BOY RUN HIS ERRANDS FOR HIM, BUT NOOOOOO...
"OFFICE BOYS HAVE MORE IMPORTANT THINGS TO DO," HE SAYS...
HOW MANY MORE INDIGNITIES CAN HE HEAP ON ME?
WHAT DID I EVER DO TO HIM TO DESERVE THIS KIND OF TREATMENT?
OKAY, SO I WAS NEVER A NICE GUY, BUT I WASN'T THAT BAD, EITHER!
PARKER'S BECOME A BIGGER PAIN IN MY REAR THAN SPIDER-MAN EVER WAS!
SERVES ME RIGHT FOR BEING SO GREEDY...
I WAS DOING FINE, BUT I STOOD A CHANCE OF MAKING EVEN MORE MONEY BY "GOING PUBLIC"...
THUS LEAVING THE BUGLE VULNERABLE TO A HOSTILE TAKEOVER BY SPIDER-MAN INC. AND ITS HOT-SHOT C.E.O., PETER PARKER!
PARKER
IF I HAD ANY BALLS I'D QUIT, BUT WITH THE COMPANY DOING AS WELL AS IT IS, I DON'T WANT TO CASH IN MY STOCK OPTIONS JUST YET...
BZZT
PLUS YOU NEVER KNOW WHEN PARKER MIGHT SLIP UP...
AND I WANT TO BE THERE WHEN HE DOES!
ARRGH! NO ONE'S ANSWERING...
I SHOULD JUST DUMP HIS RAGS RIGHT HERE ON THE LAWN, BUT I'D CATCH HELL IF I DID...
STILL, I AIN'T GOT ALL DAY...
C'MON, PARKER! OPEN UP!
BZZT! BZZT!
HMMM... MAYBE I SHOULD TRY THE SERVANT'S ENTRANCE...

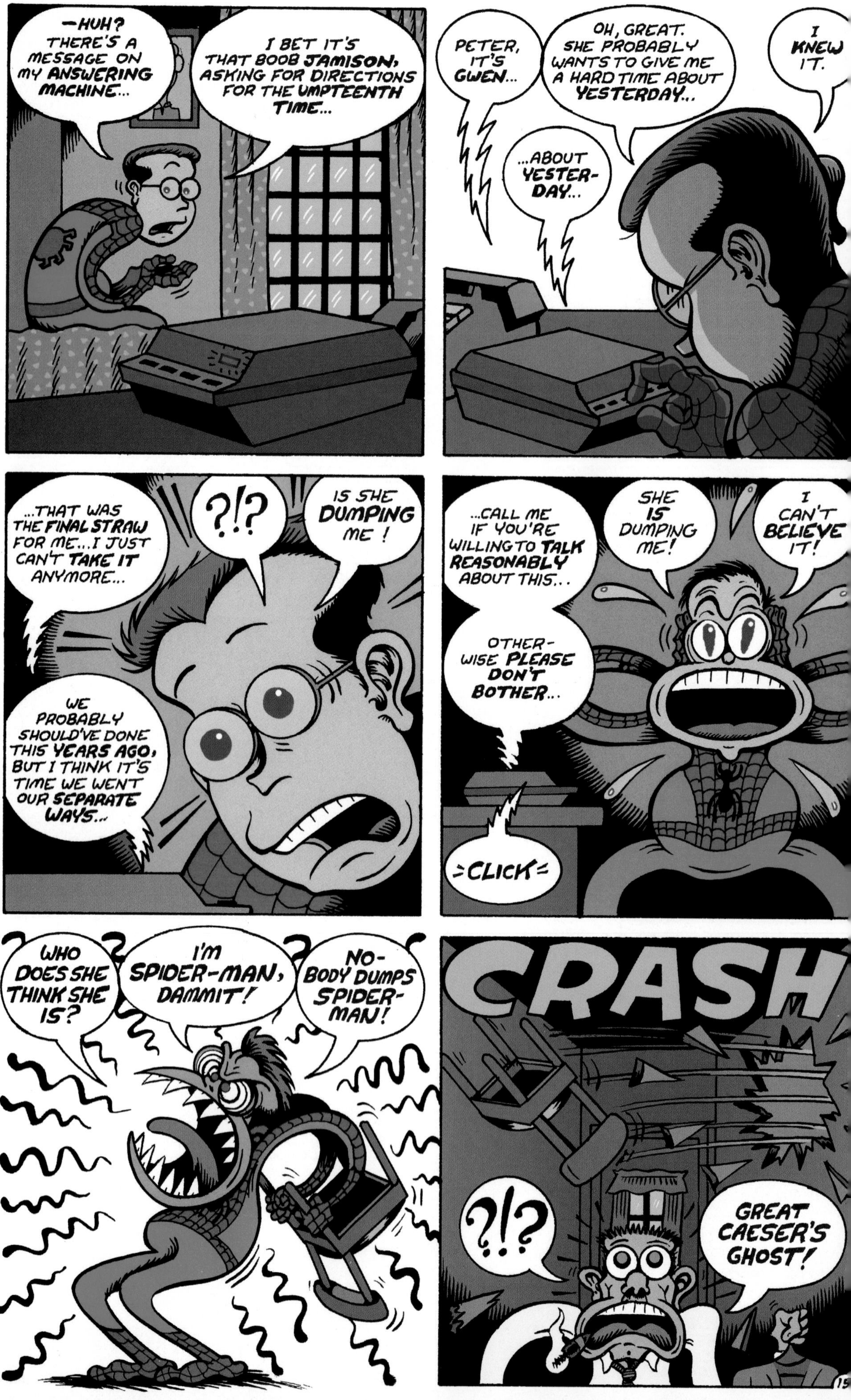

—HUH? THERE'S A MESSAGE ON MY ANSWERING MACHINE...
I BET IT'S THAT BOOB JAMISON, ASKING FOR DIRECTIONS FOR THE UMPTEENTH TIME...
PETER, IT'S GWEN...
OH, GREAT. SHE PROBABLY WANTS TO GIVE ME A HARD TIME ABOUT YESTERDAY...
...ABOUT YESTER-DAY...
I KNEW IT.
...THAT WAS THE FINAL STRAW FOR ME...I JUST CAN'T TAKE IT ANYMORE...
?!?
IS SHE DUMPING ME!
WE PROBABLY SHOULD'VE DONE THIS YEARS AGO, BUT I THINK IT'S TIME WE WENT OUR SEPARATE WAYS...
...CALL ME IF YOU'RE WILLING TO TALK REASONABLY ABOUT THIS...
SHE IS DUMPING ME!
I CAN'T BELIEVE IT!
OTHER-WISE PLEASE DON'T BOTHER...
=CLICK=
WHO DOES SHE THINK SHE IS?
I'M SPIDER-MAN, DAMMIT!
NO-BODY DUMPS SPIDER-MAN!
CRASH
?!?
GREAT CAESER'S GHOST!

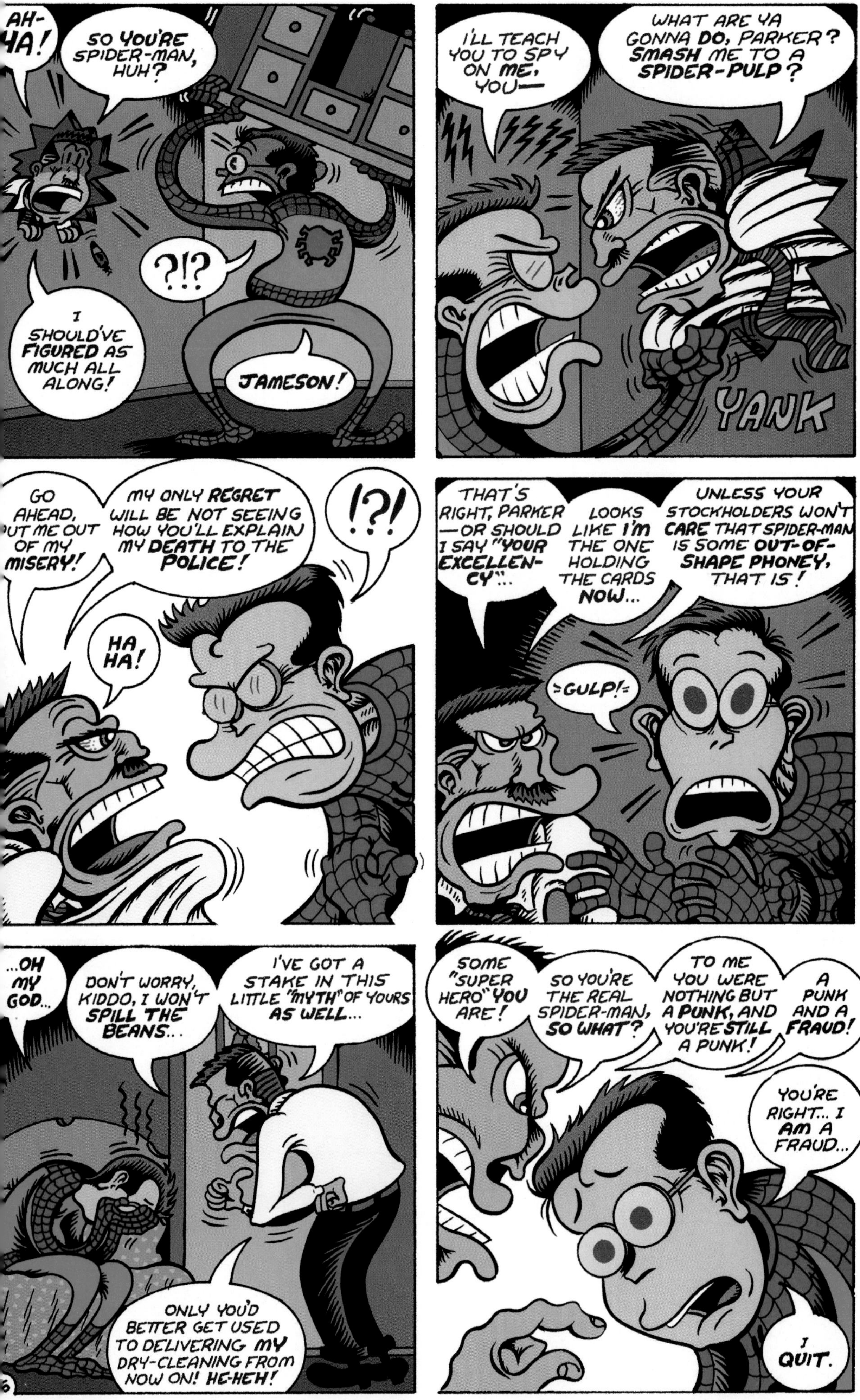
AH-
HA!
SO YOU'RE SPIDER-MAN, HUH?
?!?
I SHOULD'VE FIGURED AS MUCH ALL ALONG!
JAMESON!
I'LL TEACH YOU TO SPY ON ME, YOU—
WHAT ARE YA GONNA DO, PARKER? SMASH ME TO A SPIDER-PULP?
YANK
GO AHEAD,
UT ME OUT
OF MY MISERY!
MY ONLY REGRET WILL BE NOT SEEING HOW YOU'LL EXPLAIN MY DEATH TO THE POLICE!
!?!
HA HA!
THAT'S RIGHT, PARKER —OR SHOULD I SAY "YOUR EXCELLENCY"...
LOOKS LIKE I'M THE ONE HOLDING THE CARDS NOW...
UNLESS YOUR STOCKHOLDERS WON'T CARE THAT SPIDER-MAN IS SOME OUT-OF-SHAPE PHONEY, THAT IS!
=GULP!=
...OH MY GOD...
DON'T WORRY, KIDDO, I WON'T SPILL THE BEANS...
I'VE GOT A STAKE IN THIS LITTLE "MYTH" OF YOURS AS WELL...
ONLY YOU'D BETTER GET USED TO DELIVERING MY DRY-CLEANING FROM NOW ON! HE-HEH!
SOME "SUPER HERO" YOU ARE!
SO YOU'RE THE REAL SPIDER-MAN, SO WHAT?
TO ME YOU WERE NOTHING BUT A PUNK, AND YOU'RE STILL A PUNK!
A PUNK AND A FRAUD!
YOU'RE RIGHT... I AM A FRAUD...
I QUIT.

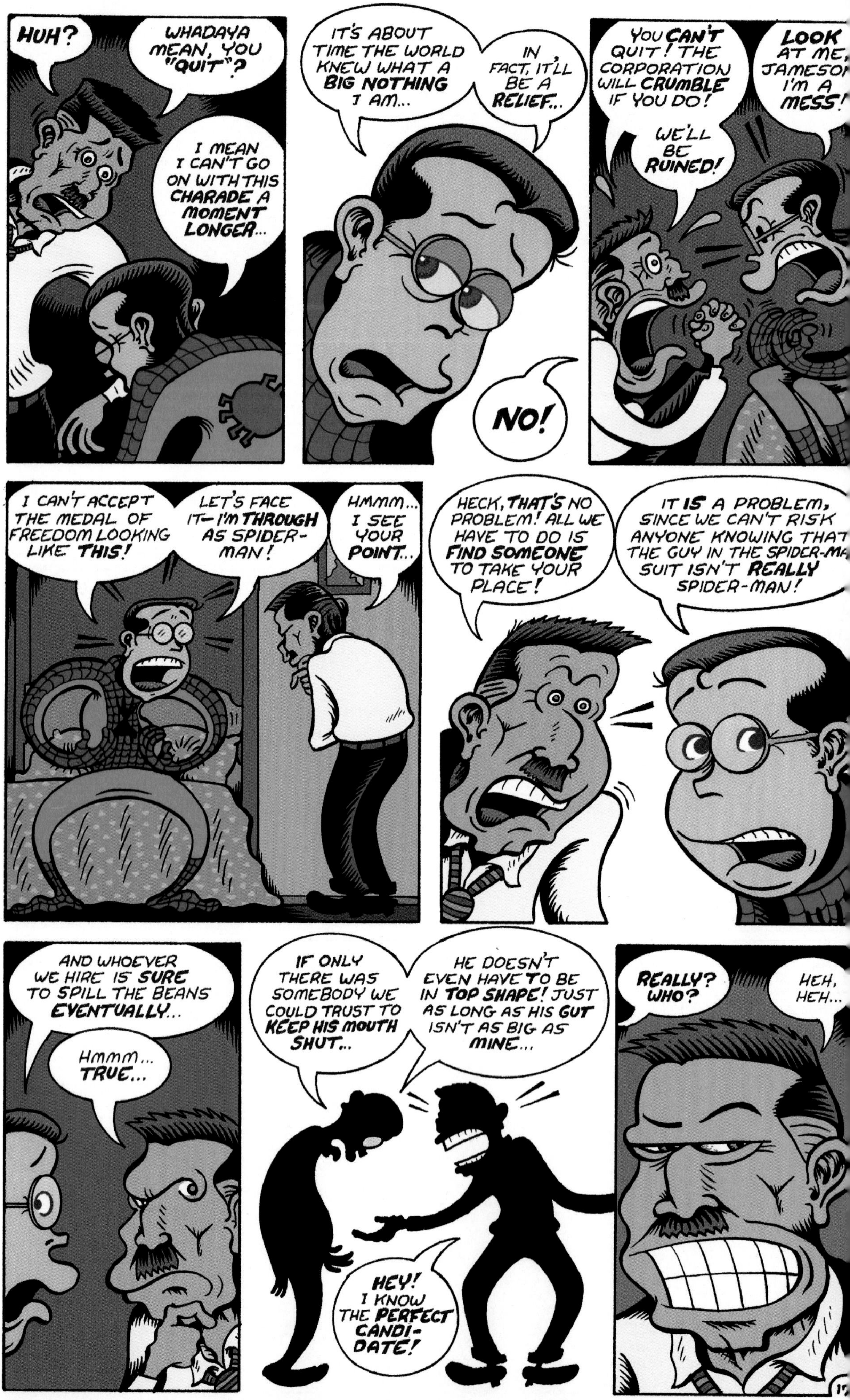
HUH?
WHADAYA MEAN, YOU "QUIT"?
I MEAN I CAN'T GO ON WITH THIS CHARADE A MOMENT LONGER...
IT'S ABOUT TIME THE WORLD KNEW WHAT A BIG NOTHING I AM...
IN FACT, IT'LL BE A RELIEF...
NO!
YOU CAN'T QUIT! THE CORPORATION WILL CRUMBLE IF YOU DO!
WE'LL BE RUINED!
LOOK AT ME, JAMESON! I'M A MESS!
I CAN'T ACCEPT THE MEDAL OF FREEDOM LOOKING LIKE THIS!
LET'S FACE IT— I'M THROUGH AS SPIDER-MAN!
HMMM... I SEE YOUR POINT...
HECK, THAT'S NO PROBLEM! ALL WE HAVE TO DO IS FIND SOMEONE TO TAKE YOUR PLACE!
IT IS A PROBLEM, SINCE WE CAN'T RISK ANYONE KNOWING THAT THE GUY IN THE SPIDER-MAN SUIT ISN'T REALLY SPIDER-MAN!
AND WHOEVER WE HIRE IS SURE TO SPILL THE BEANS EVENTUALLY...
HMMM... TRUE...
IF ONLY THERE WAS SOMEBODY WE COULD TRUST TO KEEP HIS MOUTH SHUT...
HE DOESN'T EVEN HAVE TO BE IN TOP SHAPE! JUST AS LONG AS HIS GUT ISN'T AS BIG AS MINE...
HEY! I KNOW THE PERFECT CANDI-DATE!
REALLY? WHO?
HEH, HEH...

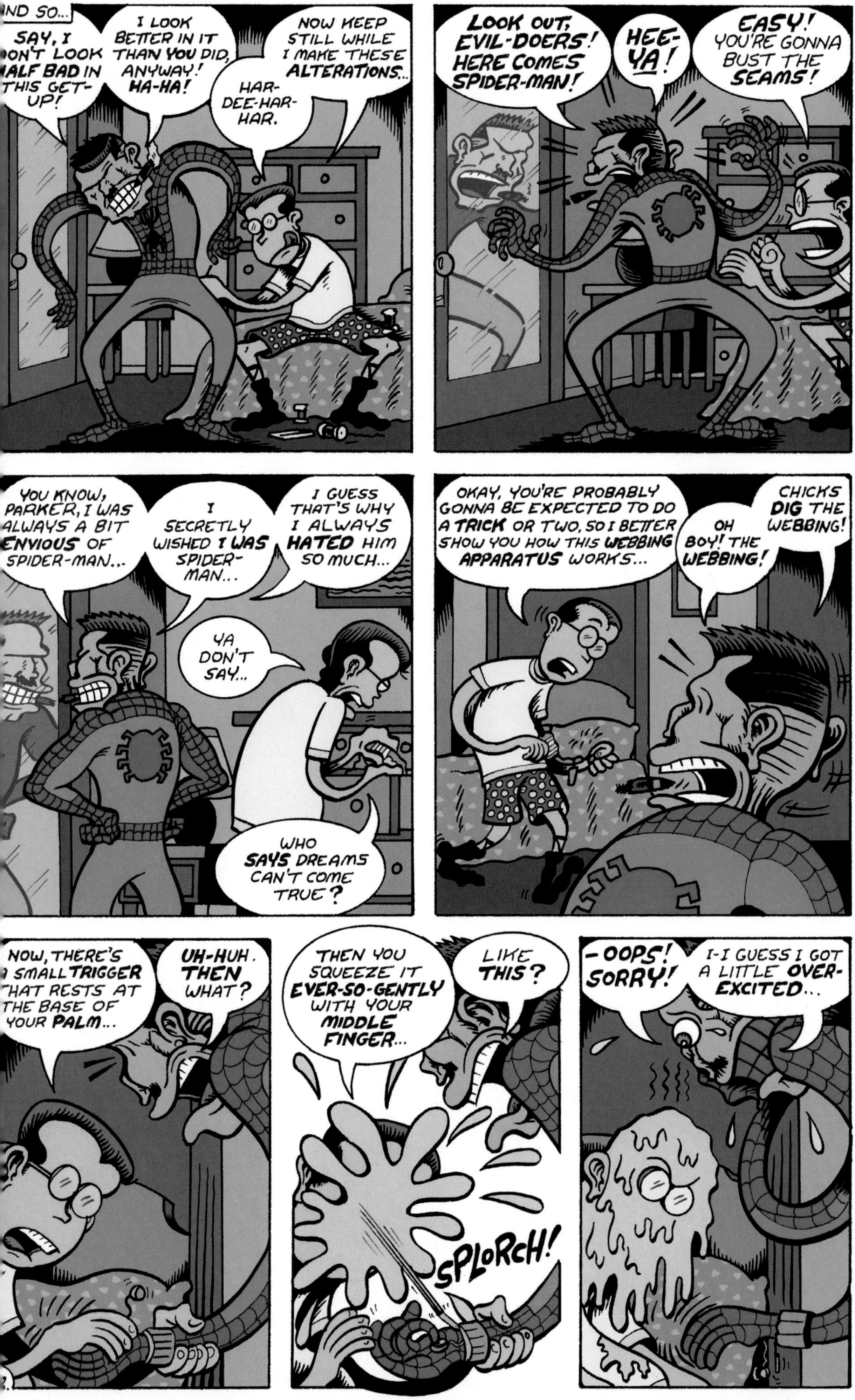

ND SO...
SAY, I ON'T LOOK ALF BAD IN THIS GET-UP!
I LOOK BETTER IN IT THAN YOU DID, ANYWAY! HA-HA!
HAR-DEE-HAR-HAR.
NOW KEEP STILL WHILE I MAKE THESE ALTERATIONS...
LOOK OUT, EVIL-DOERS! HERE COMES SPIDER-MAN!
HEE-YA!
EASY! YOU'RE GONNA BUST THE SEAMS!
YOU KNOW, PARKER, I WAS ALWAYS A BIT ENVIOUS OF SPIDER-MAN...
I SECRETLY WISHED I WAS SPIDER-MAN...
I GUESS THAT'S WHY I ALWAYS HATED HIM SO MUCH...
YA DON'T SAY...
WHO SAYS DREAMS CAN'T COME TRUE?
OKAY, YOU'RE PROBABLY GONNA BE EXPECTED TO DO A TRICK OR TWO, SO I BETTER SHOW YOU HOW THIS WEBBING APPARATUS WORKS...
OH BOY! THE WEBBING!
CHICKS DIG THE WEBBING!
NOW, THERE'S SMALL TRIGGER THAT RESTS AT THE BASE OF YOUR PALM...
UH-HUH. THEN WHAT?
THEN YOU SQUEEZE IT EVER-SO-GENTLY WITH YOUR MIDDLE FINGER...
LIKE THIS?
SPLORCH!
-OOPS! SORRY!
I-I GUESS I GOT A LITTLE OVER-EXCITED...

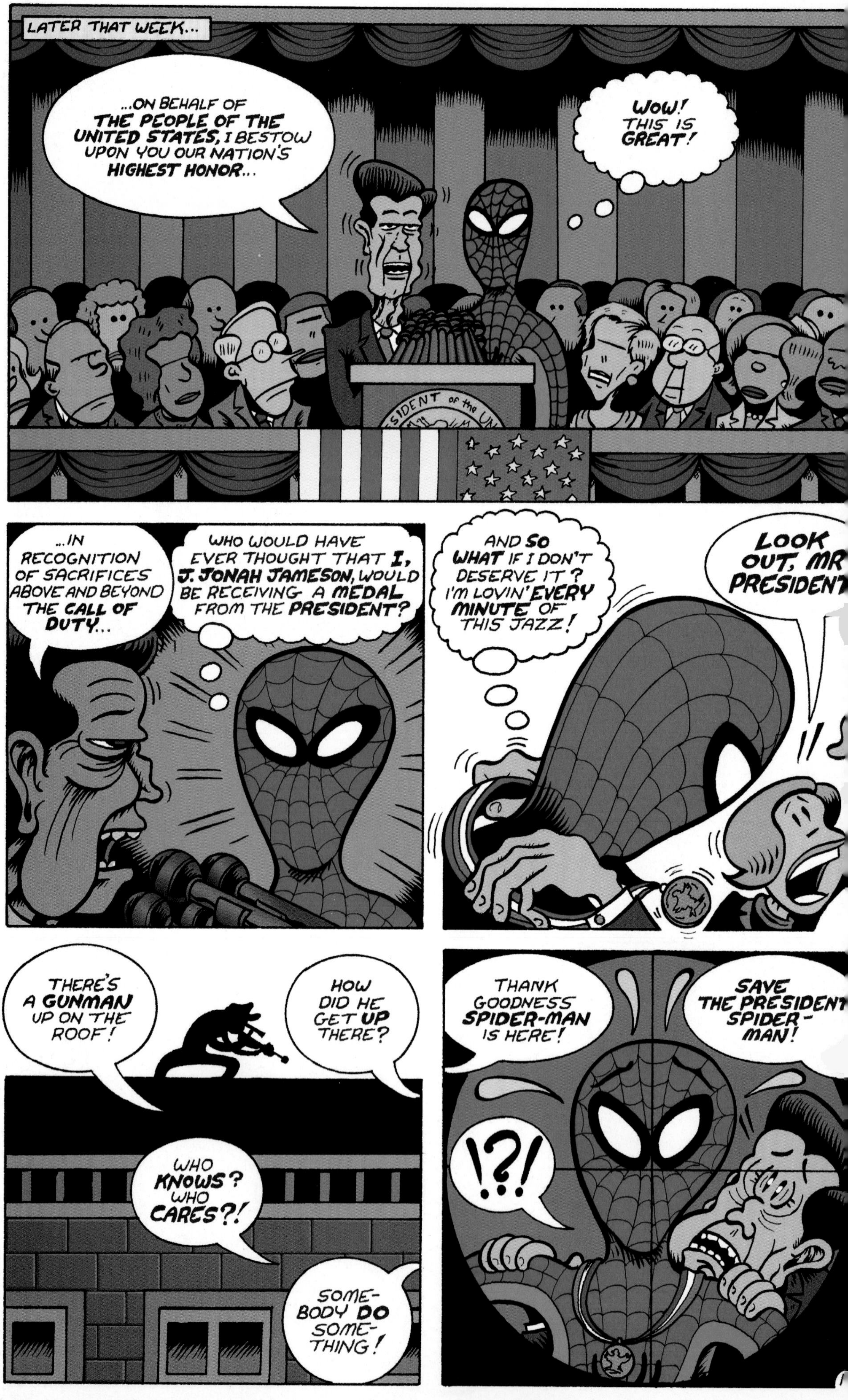
LATER THAT WEEK...
...ON BEHALF OF THE PEOPLE OF THE UNITED STATES, I BESTOW UPON YOU OUR NATION'S HIGHEST HONOR...
WOW! THIS IS GREAT!
...IN RECOGNITION OF SACRIFICES ABOVE AND BEYOND THE CALL OF DUTY...
WHO WOULD HAVE EVER THOUGHT THAT I, J. JONAH JAMESON, WOULD BE RECEIVING A MEDAL FROM THE PRESIDENT?
AND SO WHAT IF I DON'T DESERVE IT? I'M LOVIN' EVERY MINUTE OF THIS JAZZ!
LOOK OUT, MR PRESIDENT
THERE'S A GUNMAN UP ON THE ROOF!
HOW DID HE GET UP THERE?
WHO KNOWS? WHO CARES?!
SOME-BODY DO SOME-THING!
THANK GOODNESS SPIDER-MAN IS HERE!
SAVE THE PRESIDENT SPIDER-MAN!
!?!

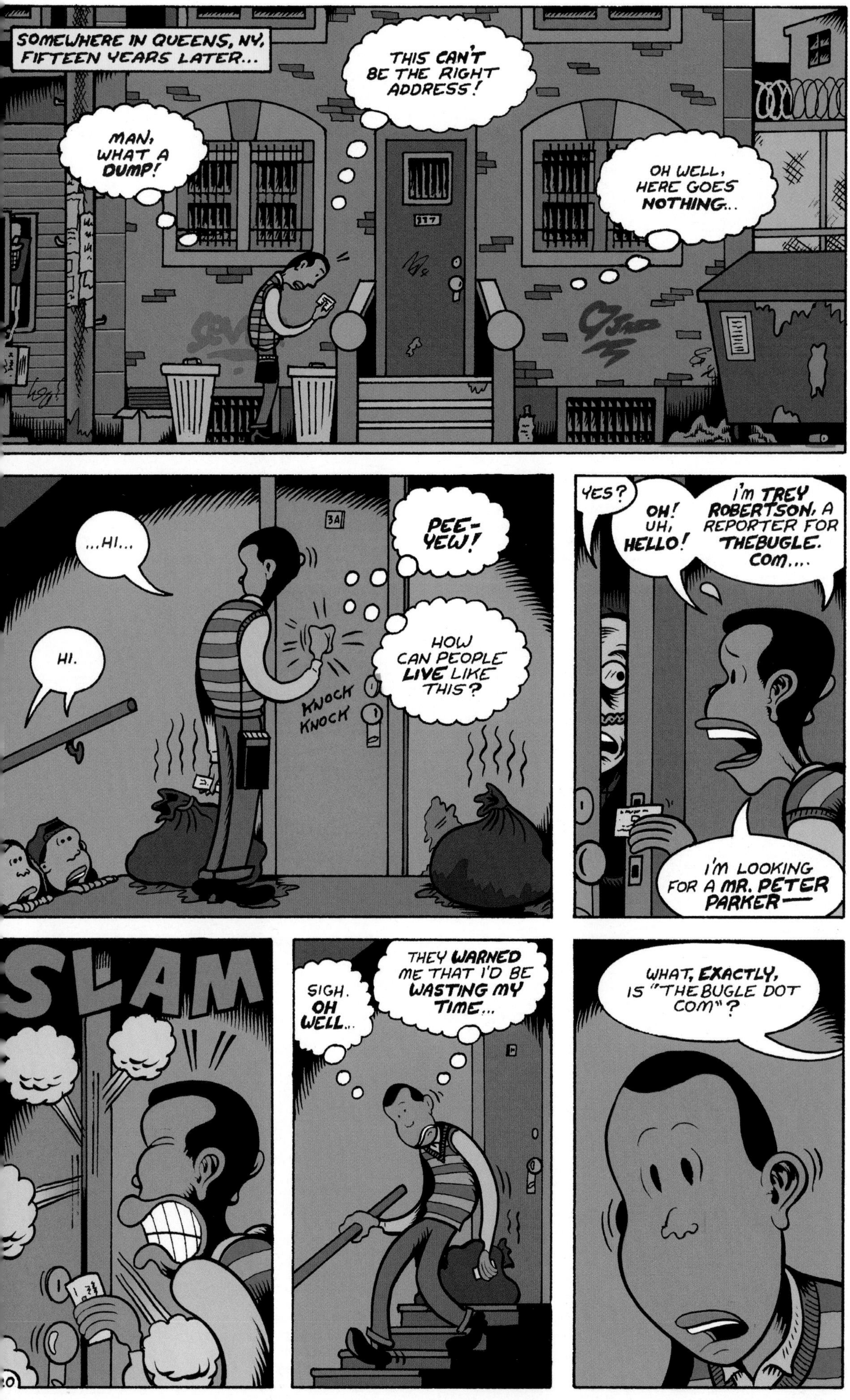
SOMEWHERE IN QUEENS, NY, FIFTEEN YEARS LATER...
MAN, WHAT A DUMP!
THIS CAN'T BE THE RIGHT ADDRESS!
OH WELL, HERE GOES NOTHING...
...HI...
HI.
PEE-YEW!
KNOCK KNOCK
HOW CAN PEOPLE LIVE LIKE THIS?
YES?
OH! UH, HELLO!
I'M TREY ROBERTSON, A REPORTER FOR THEBUGLE.COM....
I'M LOOKING FOR A MR. PETER PARKER—
SLAM
SIGH. OH WELL...
THEY WARNED ME THAT I'D BE WASTING MY TIME...
WHAT, EXACTLY, IS "THEBUGLE DOT COM"?

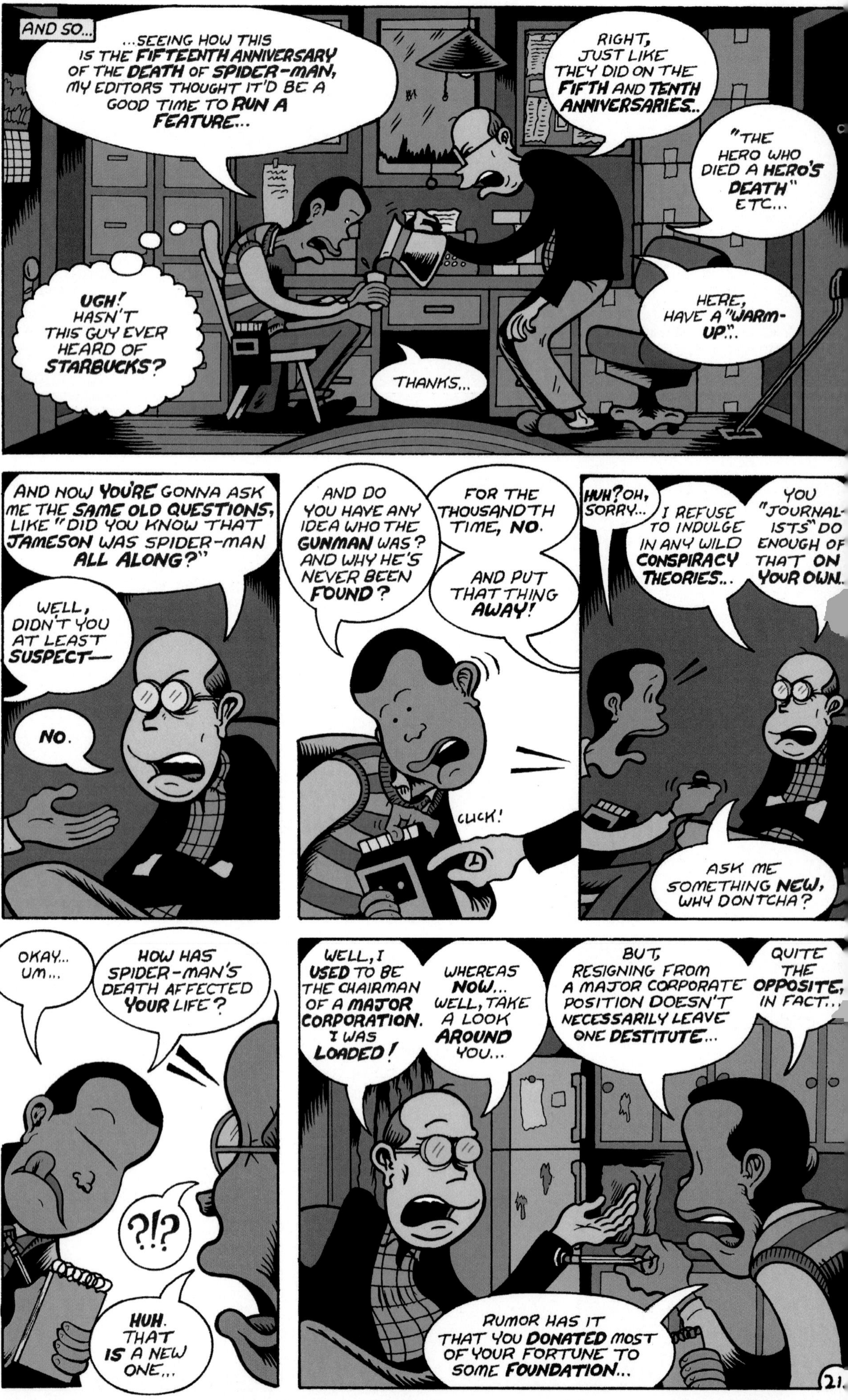
AND SO...
...SEEING HOW THIS IS THE FIFTEENTH ANNIVERSARY OF THE DEATH OF SPIDER-MAN, MY EDITORS THOUGHT IT'D BE A GOOD TIME TO RUN A FEATURE...
RIGHT, JUST LIKE THEY DID ON THE FIFTH AND TENTH ANNIVERSARIES...
"THE HERO WHO DIED A HERO'S DEATH" ETC...
UGH! HASN'T THIS GUY EVER HEARD OF STARBUCKS?
HERE, HAVE A "WARM-UP"...
THANKS...
AND NOW YOU'RE GONNA ASK ME THE SAME OLD QUESTIONS, LIKE "DID YOU KNOW THAT JAMESON WAS SPIDER-MAN ALL ALONG?"
WELL, DIDN'T YOU AT LEAST SUSPECT—
NO.
AND DO YOU HAVE ANY IDEA WHO THE GUNMAN WAS? AND WHY HE'S NEVER BEEN FOUND?
FOR THE THOUSANDTH TIME, NO.
AND PUT THAT THING AWAY!
CLICK!
HUH? OH, SORRY...
I REFUSE TO INDULGE IN ANY WILD CONSPIRACY THEORIES...
YOU "JOURNALISTS" DO ENOUGH OF THAT ON YOUR OWN.
ASK ME SOMETHING NEW, WHY DONTCHA?
OKAY... UM...
HOW HAS SPIDER-MAN'S DEATH AFFECTED YOUR LIFE?
?!?
HUH. THAT IS A NEW ONE...
WELL, I USED TO BE THE CHAIRMAN OF A MAJOR CORPORATION. I WAS LOADED!
WHEREAS NOW... WELL, TAKE A LOOK AROUND YOU...
BUT, RESIGNING FROM A MAJOR CORPORATE POSITION DOESN'T NECESSARILY LEAVE ONE DESTITUTE...
QUITE THE OPPOSITE, IN FACT...
RUMOR HAS IT THAT YOU DONATED MOST OF YOUR FORTUNE TO SOME FOUNDATION...
21

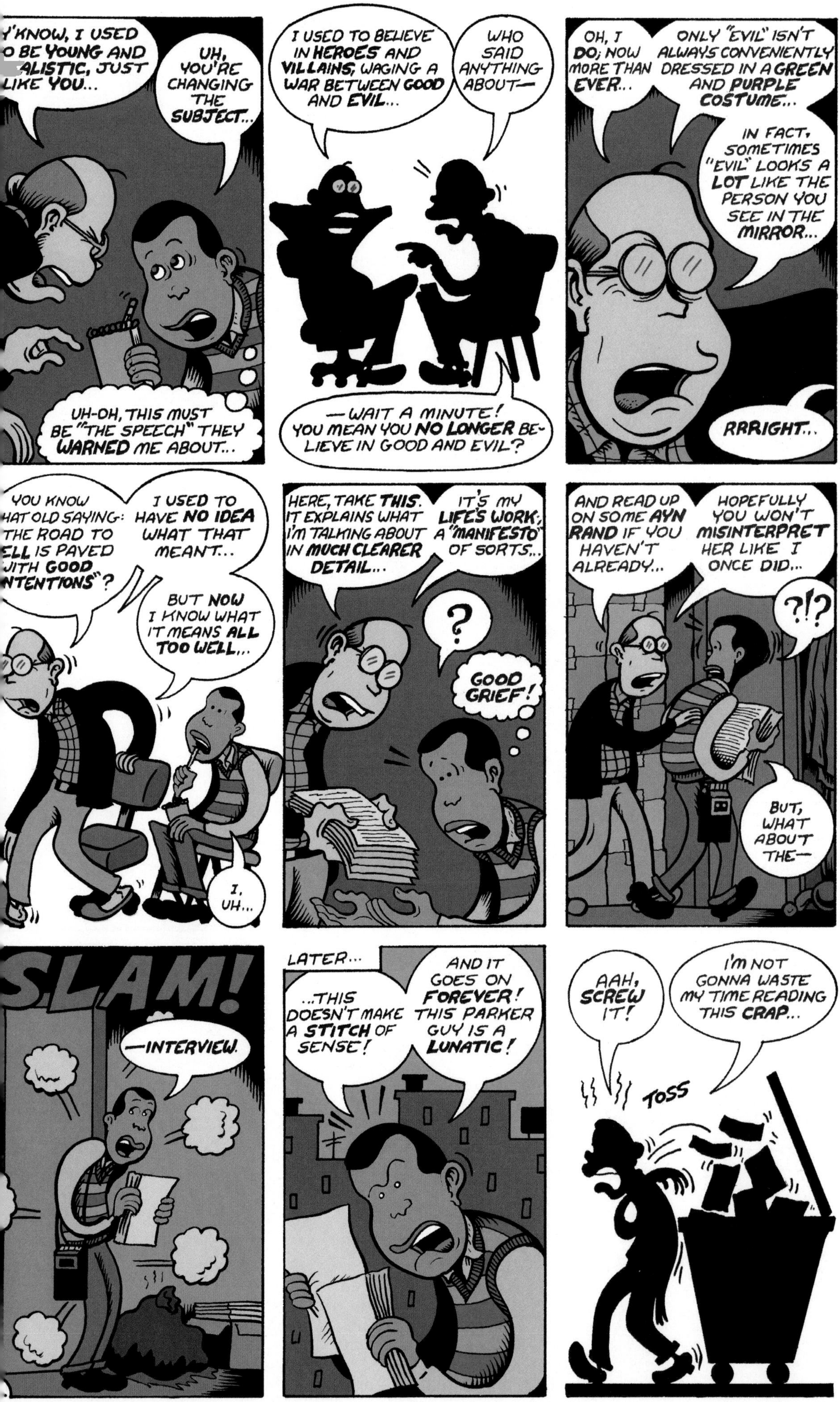
Y'KNOW, I USED O BE YOUNG AND ALISTIC, JUST LIKE YOU...
UH, YOU'RE CHANGING THE SUBJECT...
UH-OH, THIS MUST BE "THE SPEECH" THEY WARNED ME ABOUT...
I USED TO BELIEVE IN HEROES AND VILLAINS, WAGING A WAR BETWEEN GOOD AND EVIL...
WHO SAID ANYTHING ABOUT—
—WAIT A MINUTE! YOU MEAN YOU NO LONGER BE-LIEVE IN GOOD AND EVIL?
OH, I DO; NOW MORE THAN EVER...
ONLY "EVIL" ISN'T ALWAYS CONVENIENTLY DRESSED IN A GREEN AND PURPLE COSTUME...
IN FACT, SOMETIMES "EVIL" LOOKS A LOT LIKE THE PERSON YOU SEE IN THE MIRROR...
RRRIGHT...
YOU KNOW HAT OLD SAYING: THE ROAD TO ELL IS PAVED WITH GOOD NTENTIONS"?
I USED TO HAVE NO IDEA WHAT THAT MEANT...
BUT NOW I KNOW WHAT IT MEANS ALL TOO WELL...
I, UH...
HERE, TAKE THIS. IT EXPLAINS WHAT I'M TALKING ABOUT IN MUCH CLEARER DETAIL...
IT'S MY LIFE'S WORK; A "MANIFESTO" OF SORTS...
?
GOOD GRIEF!
AND READ UP ON SOME AYN RAND IF YOU HAVEN'T ALREADY...
HOPEFULLY YOU WON'T MISINTERPRET HER LIKE I ONCE DID...
?!?
BUT, WHAT ABOUT THE—
SLAM!
—INTERVIEW.
LATER...
...THIS DOESN'T MAKE A STITCH OF SENSE!
AND IT GOES ON FOREVER! THIS PARKER GUY IS A LUNATIC!
AAH, SCREW IT!
I'M NOT GONNA WASTE MY TIME READING THIS CRAP...
TOSS

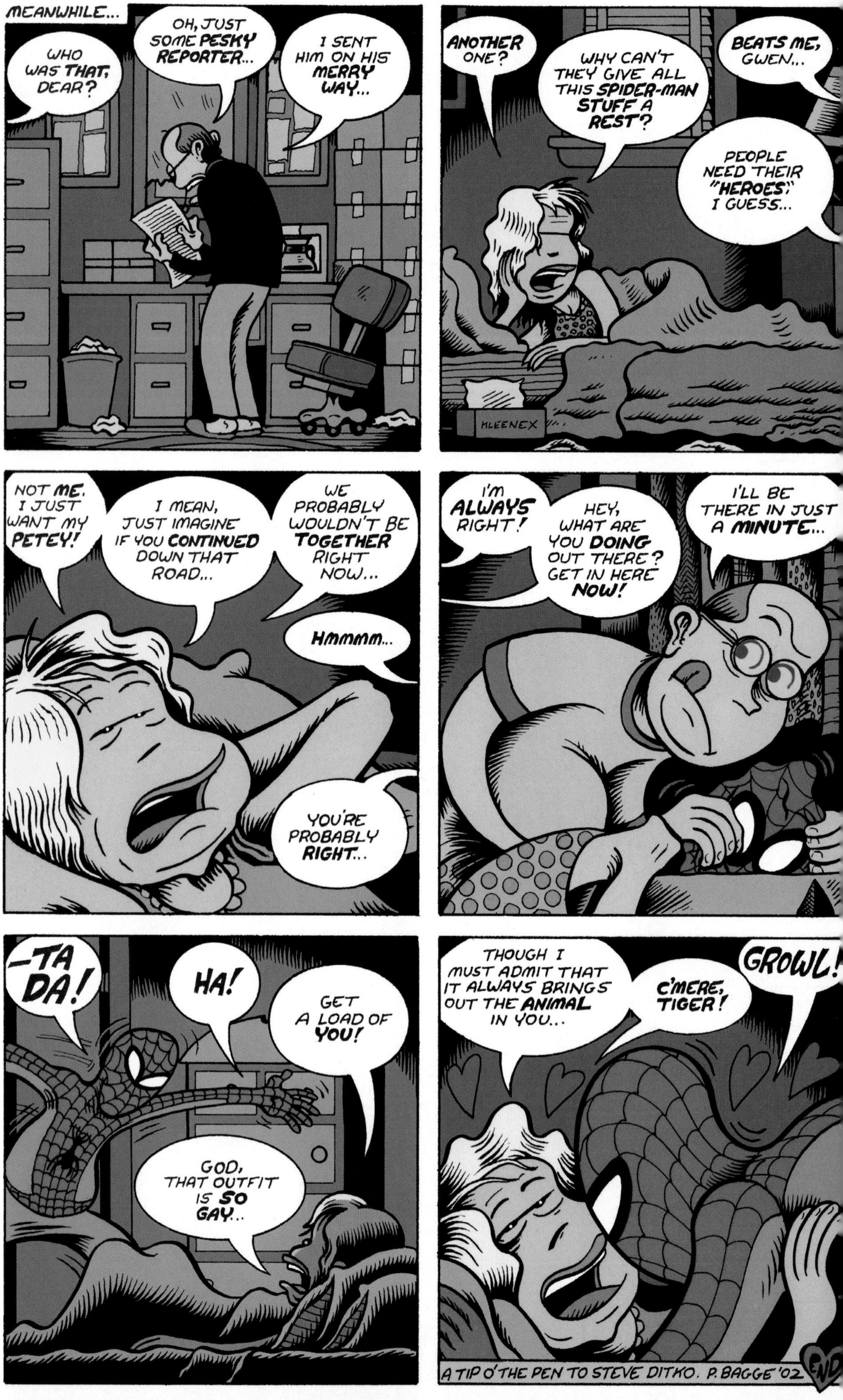
MEANWHILE...
WHO WAS THAT, DEAR?
OH, JUST SOME PESKY REPORTER...
I SENT HIM ON HIS MERRY WAY...
ANOTHER ONE?
WHY CAN'T THEY GIVE ALL THIS SPIDER-MAN STUFF A REST?
BEATS ME, GWEN...
PEOPLE NEED THEIR "HEROES," I GUESS...
KLEENEX
NOT ME. I JUST WANT MY PETEY!
I MEAN, JUST IMAGINE IF YOU CONTINUED DOWN THAT ROAD...
WE PROBABLY WOULDN'T BE TOGETHER RIGHT NOW...
HMMMM...
YOU'RE PROBABLY RIGHT...
I'M ALWAYS RIGHT!
HEY, WHAT ARE YOU DOING OUT THERE? GET IN HERE NOW!
I'LL BE THERE IN JUST A MINUTE...
—TA DA!
HA!
GET A LOAD OF YOU!
GOD, THAT OUTFIT IS SO GAY...
THOUGH I MUST ADMIT THAT IT ALWAYS BRINGS OUT THE ANIMAL IN YOU...
C'MERE, TIGER!
GROWL!
A TIP O' THE PEN TO STEVE DITKO. P. BAGGE '02
END

THE INCORRIGIBLE
HULK
YOURS, Bruce
HULK SHOES HURT.
?!?
Be mine
BAGGE '03

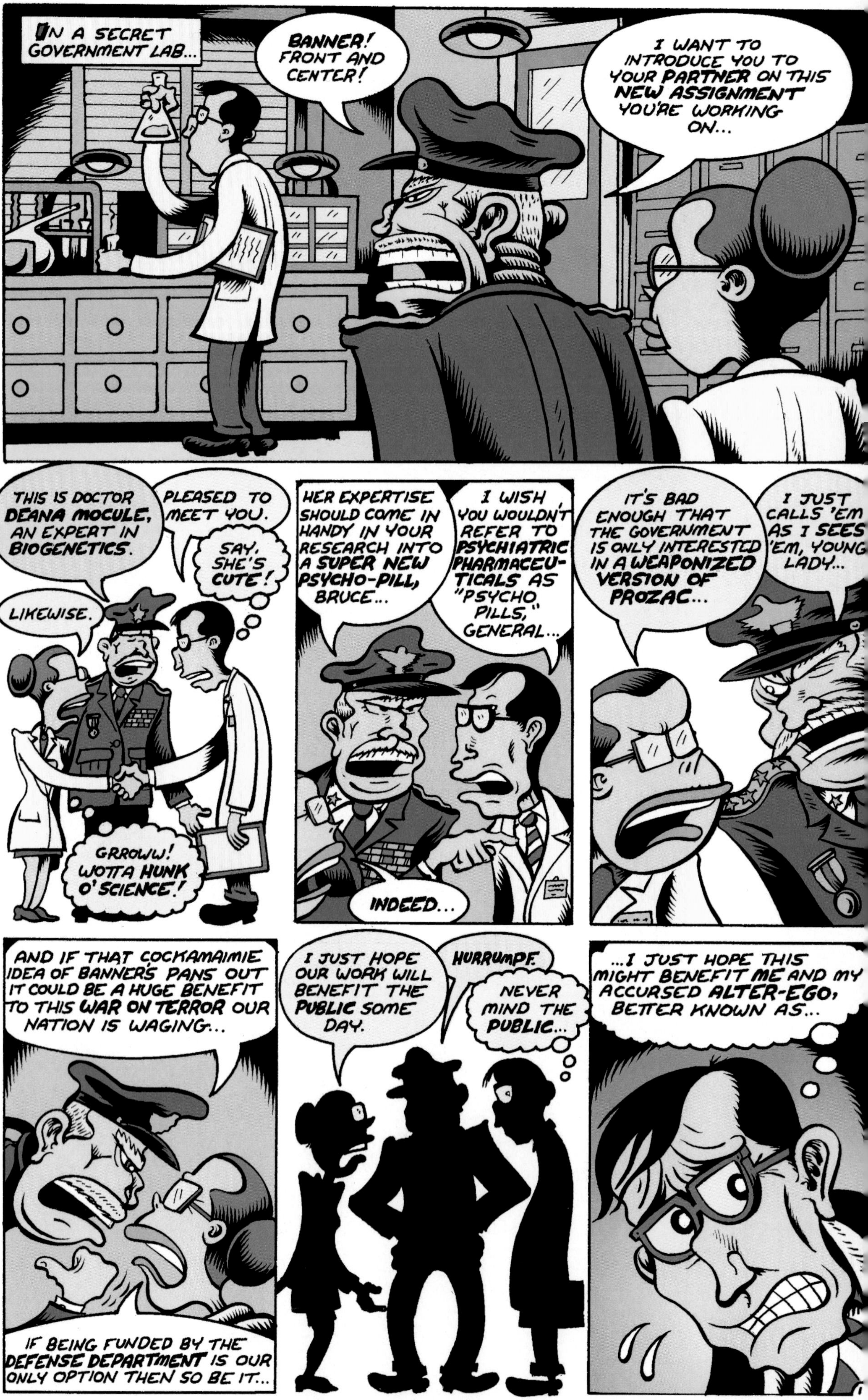
IN A SECRET GOVERNMENT LAB...
BANNER! FRONT AND CENTER!
I WANT TO INTRODUCE YOU TO YOUR PARTNER ON THIS NEW ASSIGNMENT YOU'RE WORKING ON...
THIS IS DOCTOR DEANA MOCULE, AN EXPERT IN BIOGENETICS.
PLEASED TO MEET YOU.
SAY, SHE'S CUTE!
LIKEWISE.
GRROWW! WOTTA HUNK O' SCIENCE!
HER EXPERTISE SHOULD COME IN HANDY IN YOUR RESEARCH INTO A SUPER NEW PSYCHO-PILL, BRUCE...
I WISH YOU WOULDN'T REFER TO PSYCHIATRIC PHARMACEU-TICALS AS "PSYCHO PILLS," GENERAL...
INDEED...
IT'S BAD ENOUGH THAT THE GOVERNMENT IS ONLY INTERESTED IN A WEAPONIZED VERSION OF PROZAC...
I JUST CALLS 'EM AS I SEES 'EM, YOUNG LADY...
AND IF THAT COCKAMAIMIE IDEA OF BANNER'S PANS OUT IT COULD BE A HUGE BENEFIT TO THIS WAR ON TERROR OUR NATION IS WAGING...
IF BEING FUNDED BY THE DEFENSE DEPARTMENT IS OUR ONLY OPTION THEN SO BE IT...
I JUST HOPE OUR WORK WILL BENEFIT THE PUBLIC SOME DAY.
HURRUMPF.
NEVER MIND THE PUBLIC...
...I JUST HOPE THIS MIGHT BENEFIT ME AND MY ACCURSED ALTER-EGO, BETTER KNOWN AS...

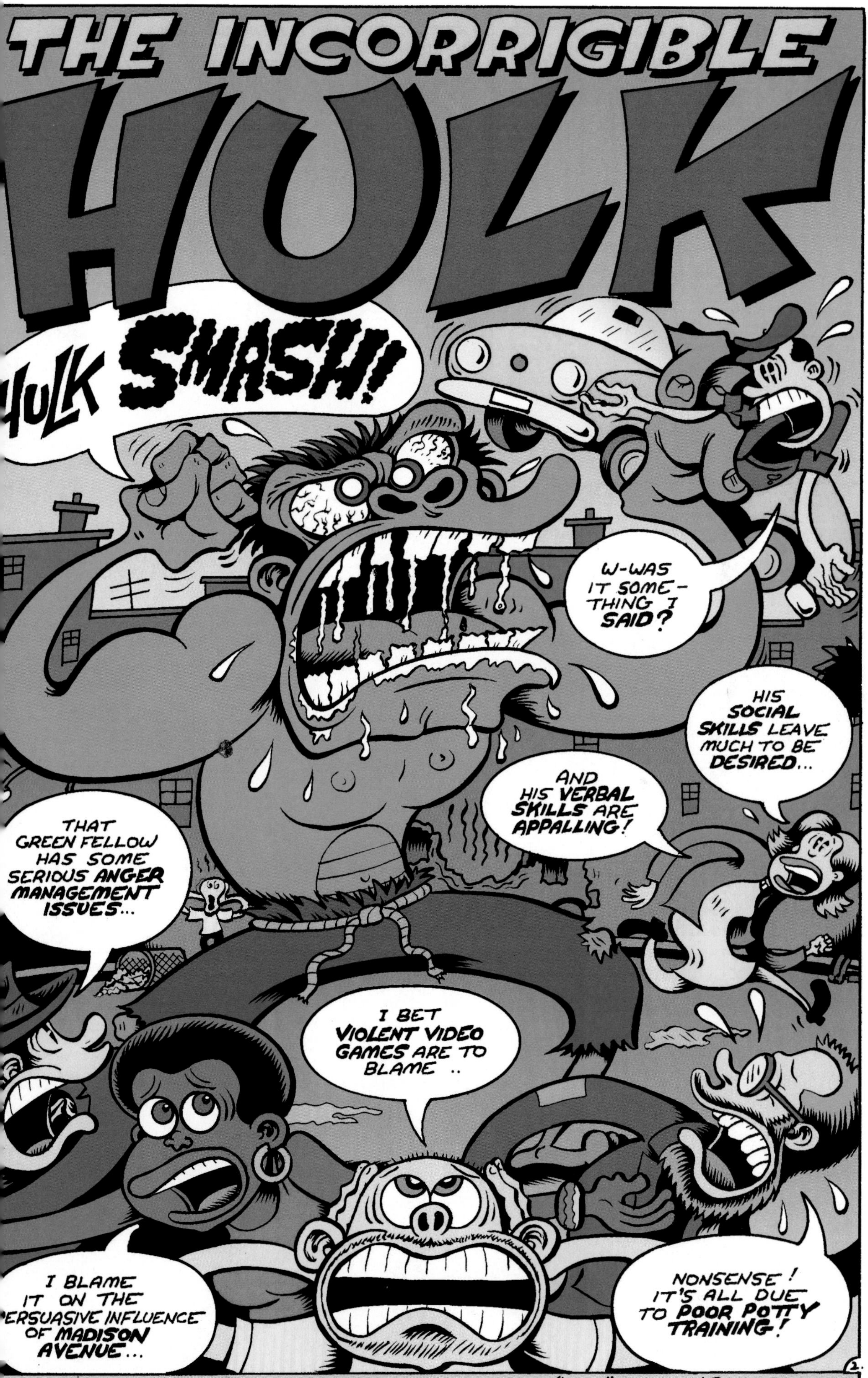
THE INCORRIGIBLE
HULK
HULK SMASH!
W-WAS IT SOMETHING I SAID?
HIS SOCIAL SKILLS LEAVE MUCH TO BE DESIRED...
AND HIS VERBAL SKILLS ARE APPALLING!
THAT GREEN FELLOW HAS SOME SERIOUS ANGER MANAGEMENT ISSUES...
I BET VIOLENT VIDEO GAMES ARE TO BLAME ..
I BLAME IT ON THE ERSUASIVE INFLUENCE OF MADISON AVENUE...
NONSENSE! IT'S ALL DUE TO POOR POTTY TRAINING!
2.

RITTEN + DRAWN BY P. BAGGE • COLOR: J. BAGGE • EDITOR: A. ALONZO • "HULK" CREATED BY S. LEE + J. KIRBY

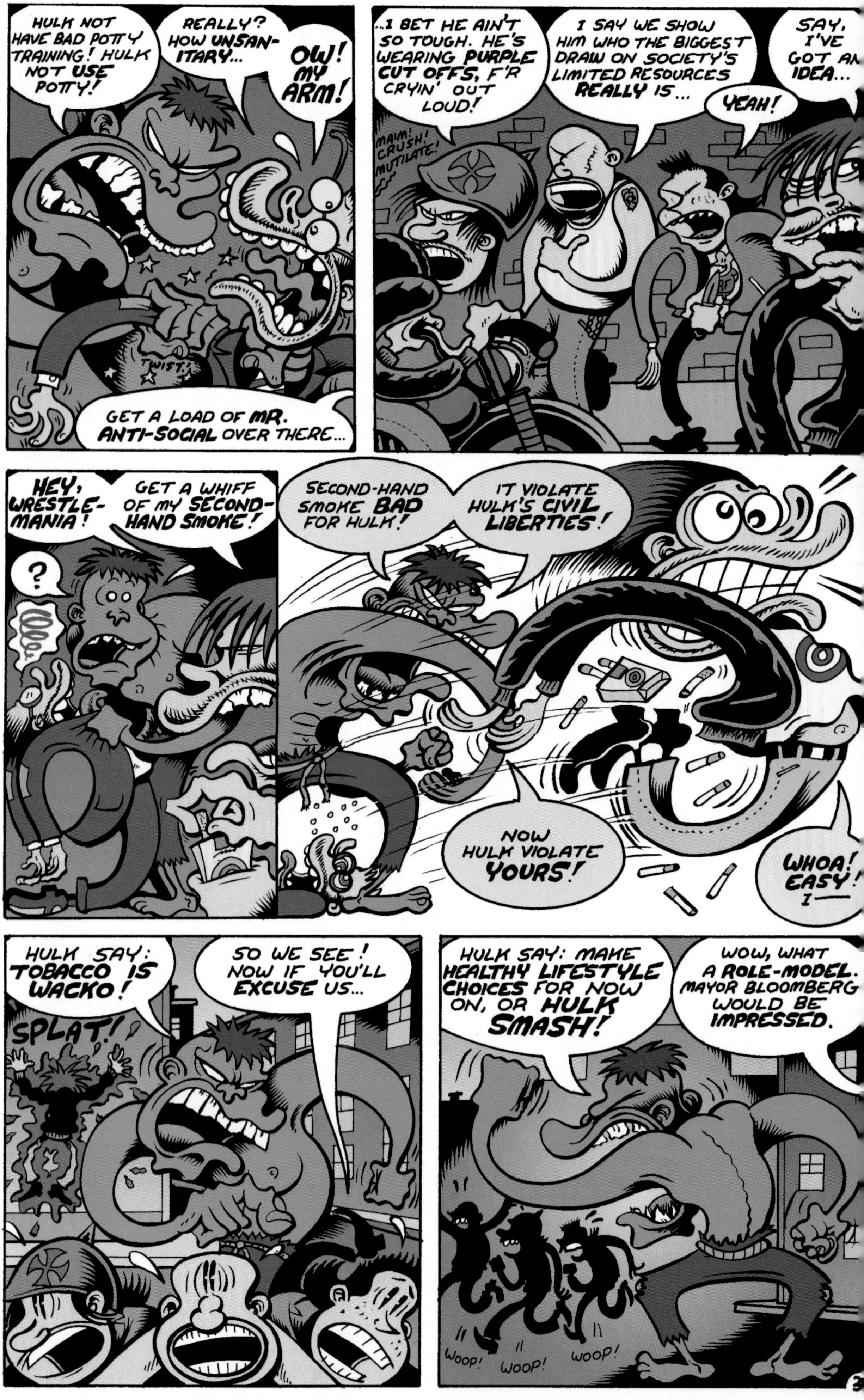
HULK NOT HAVE BAD POTTY TRAINING! HULK NOT USE POTTY!
REALLY? HOW UNSAN-ITARY...
OW! MY ARM!
TWIST!
GET A LOAD OF MR. ANTI-SOCIAL OVER THERE...
..I BET HE AIN'T SO TOUGH. HE'S WEARING PURPLE CUT OFFS, F'R CRYIN' OUT LOUD!
MAIM! CRUSH! MUTILATE!
I SAY WE SHOW HIM WHO THE BIGGEST DRAW ON SOCIETY'S LIMITED RESOURCES REALLY IS...
YEAH!
SAY, I'VE GOT AN IDEA...
HEY, WRESTLE-MANIA!
GET A WHIFF OF MY SECOND-HAND SMOKE!
?
SECOND-HAND SMOKE BAD FOR HULK!
IT VIOLATE HULK'S CIVIL LIBERTIES!
NOW HULK VIOLATE YOURS!
WHOA! EASY! I—
HULK SAY: TOBACCO IS WACKO!
SO WE SEE! NOW IF YOU'LL EXCUSE US...
SPLAT!
HULK SAY: MAKE HEALTHY LIFESTYLE CHOICES FOR NOW ON, OR HULK SMASH!
WOW, WHAT A ROLE-MODEL. MAYOR BLOOMBERG WOULD BE IMPRESSED.
WOOP!
WOOP!
WOOP!

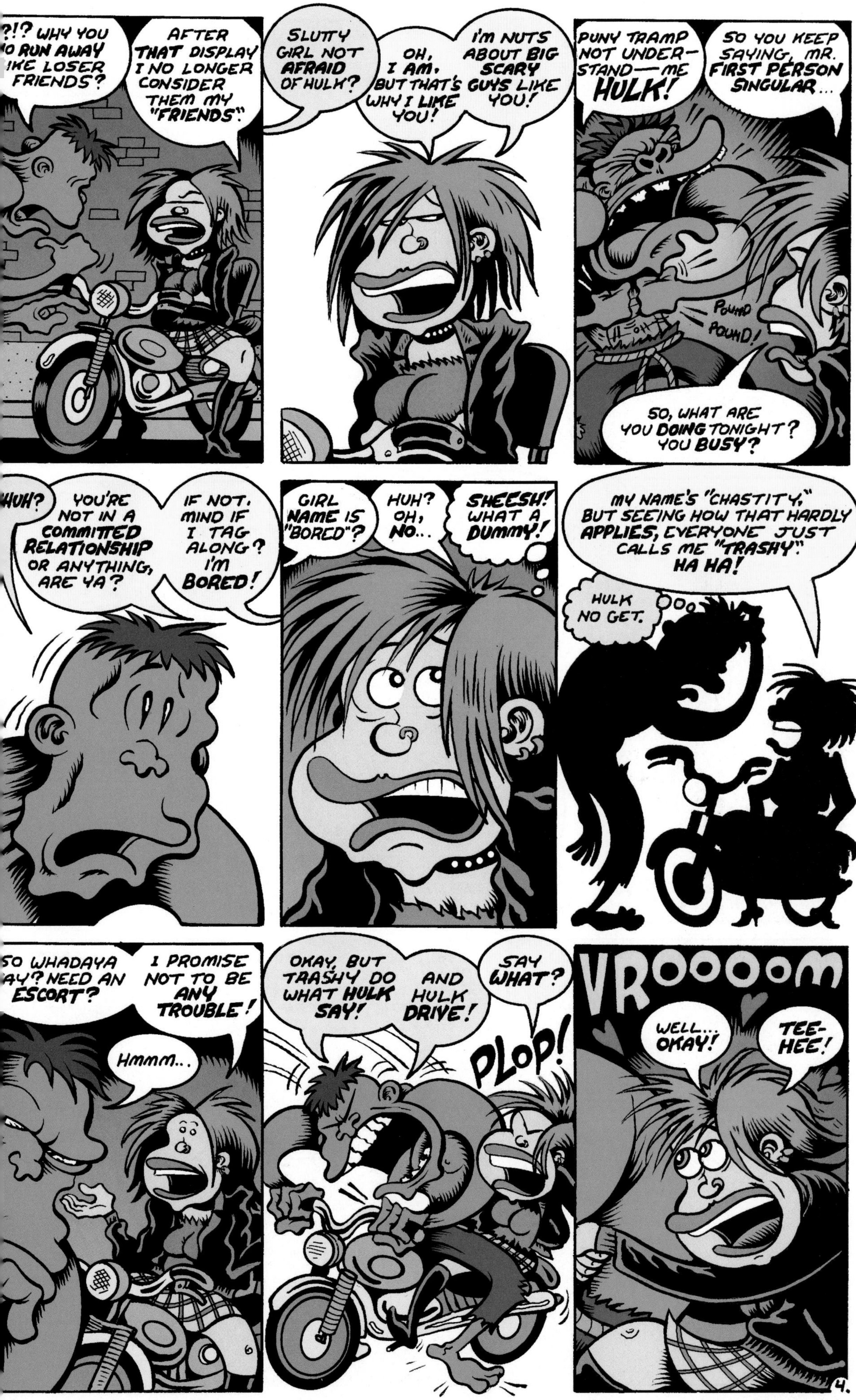
?!? WHY YOU
O RUN AWAY
IKE LOSER
FRIENDS?
AFTER THAT DISPLAY I NO LONGER CONSIDER THEM MY "FRIENDS".
SLUTTY GIRL NOT AFRAID OF HULK?
OH, I AM, BUT THAT'S WHY I LIKE YOU!
I'M NUTS ABOUT BIG SCARY GUYS LIKE YOU!
PUNY TRAMP NOT UNDER-STAND—ME HULK!
SO YOU KEEP SAYING, MR. FIRST PERSON SINGULAR...
POUND POUND!
SO, WHAT ARE YOU DOING TONIGHT? YOU BUSY?
HUH?
YOU'RE NOT IN A COMMITTED RELATIONSHIP OR ANYTHING, ARE YA?
IF NOT, MIND IF I TAG ALONG? I'M BORED!
GIRL NAME IS "BORED"?
HUH? OH, NO...
SHEESH! WHAT A DUMMY!
MY NAME'S "CHASTITY," BUT SEEING HOW THAT HARDLY APPLIES, EVERYONE JUST CALLS ME "TRASHY". HA HA!
HULK NO GET.
SO WHADAYA
AY? NEED AN
ESCORT?
I PROMISE NOT TO BE ANY TROUBLE!
HMMM...
OKAY, BUT TRASHY DO WHAT HULK SAY!
AND HULK DRIVE!
SAY WHAT?
PLOP!
VROOOOM
WELL... OKAY!
TEE-HEE!

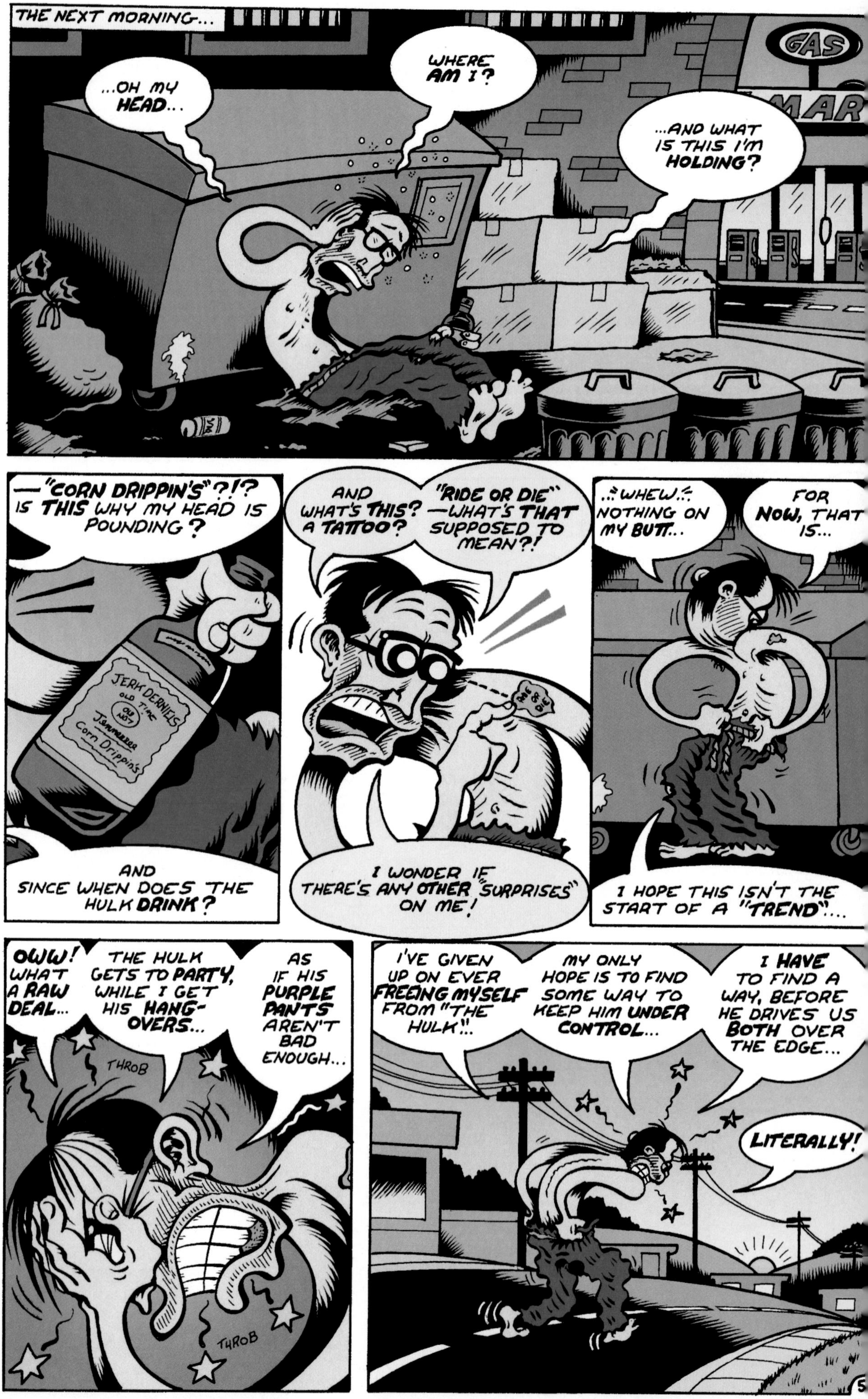
THE NEXT MORNING...
GAS
...OH MY HEAD...
WHERE AM I?
...AND WHAT IS THIS I'M HOLDING?
—"CORN DRIPPIN'S"?!? IS THIS WHY MY HEAD IS POUNDING?
Corn Drippin's
AND SINCE WHEN DOES THE HULK DRINK?
AND WHAT'S THIS? A TATTOO?
"RIDE OR DIE" —WHAT'S THAT SUPPOSED TO MEAN?!
I WONDER IF THERE'S ANY OTHER "SURPRISES" ON ME!
...WHEW... NOTHING ON MY BUTT...
FOR NOW, THAT IS...
I HOPE THIS ISN'T THE START OF A "TREND"...
OWW! WHAT A RAW DEAL...
THE HULK GETS TO PARTY, WHILE I GET HIS HANG-OVERS...
AS IF HIS PURPLE PANTS AREN'T BAD ENOUGH...
THROB
THROB
I'VE GIVEN UP ON EVER FREEING MYSELF FROM "THE HULK"...
MY ONLY HOPE IS TO FIND SOME WAY TO KEEP HIM UNDER CONTROL...
I HAVE TO FIND A WAY, BEFORE HE DRIVES US BOTH OVER THE EDGE...
LITERALLY!

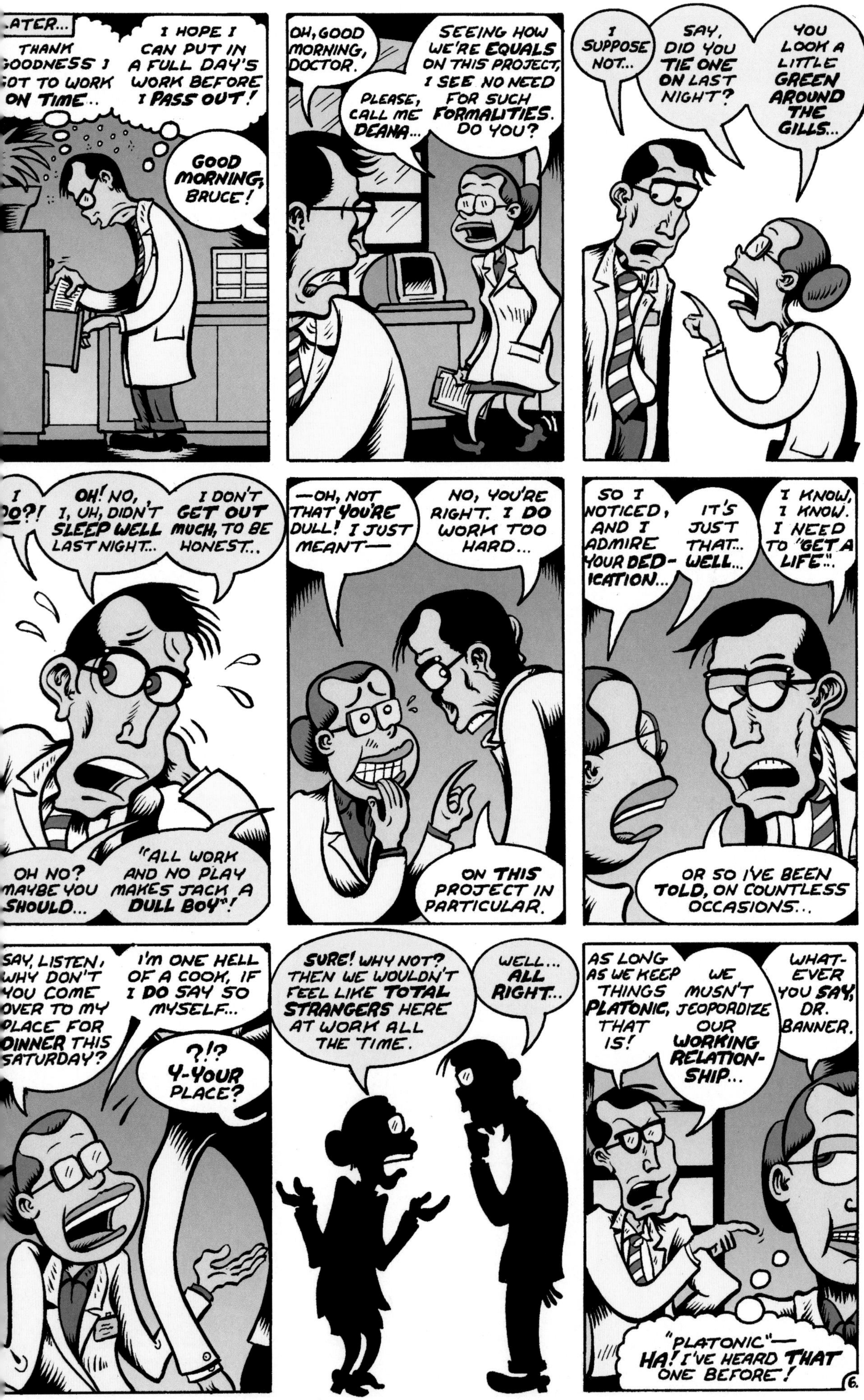
LATER...
THANK GOODNESS I GOT TO WORK ON TIME...
I HOPE I CAN PUT IN A FULL DAY'S WORK BEFORE I PASS OUT!
GOOD MORNING, BRUCE!
OH, GOOD MORNING, DOCTOR.
PLEASE, CALL ME DEANA...
SEEING HOW WE'RE EQUALS ON THIS PROJECT, I SEE NO NEED FOR SUCH FORMALITIES. DO YOU?
I SUPPOSE NOT...
SAY, DID YOU TIE ONE ON LAST NIGHT?
YOU LOOK A LITTLE GREEN AROUND THE GILLS...
I DO?!
OH! NO, I, UH, DIDN'T SLEEP WELL LAST NIGHT...
I DON'T GET OUT MUCH, TO BE HONEST...
OH NO? MAYBE YOU SHOULD...
"ALL WORK AND NO PLAY MAKES JACK A DULL BOY"!
—OH, NOT THAT YOU'RE DULL! I JUST MEANT—
NO, YOU'RE RIGHT. I DO WORK TOO HARD...
ON THIS PROJECT IN PARTICULAR.
SO I NOTICED, AND I ADMIRE YOUR DEDICATION...
IT'S JUST THAT... WELL...
I KNOW, I KNOW. I NEED TO "GET A LIFE"...
OR SO I'VE BEEN TOLD, ON COUNTLESS OCCASIONS...
SAY, LISTEN, WHY DON'T YOU COME OVER TO MY PLACE FOR DINNER THIS SATURDAY?
I'M ONE HELL OF A COOK, IF I DO SAY SO MYSELF...
?!? Y-YOUR PLACE?
SURE! WHY NOT? THEN WE WOULDN'T FEEL LIKE TOTAL STRANGERS HERE AT WORK ALL THE TIME.
WELL... ALL RIGHT...
AS LONG AS WE KEEP THINGS PLATONIC, THAT IS!
WE MUSN'T JEOPORDIZE OUR WORKING RELATIONSHIP...
WHATEVER YOU SAY, DR. BANNER.
"PLATONIC"— HA! I'VE HEARD THAT ONE BEFORE!
6.

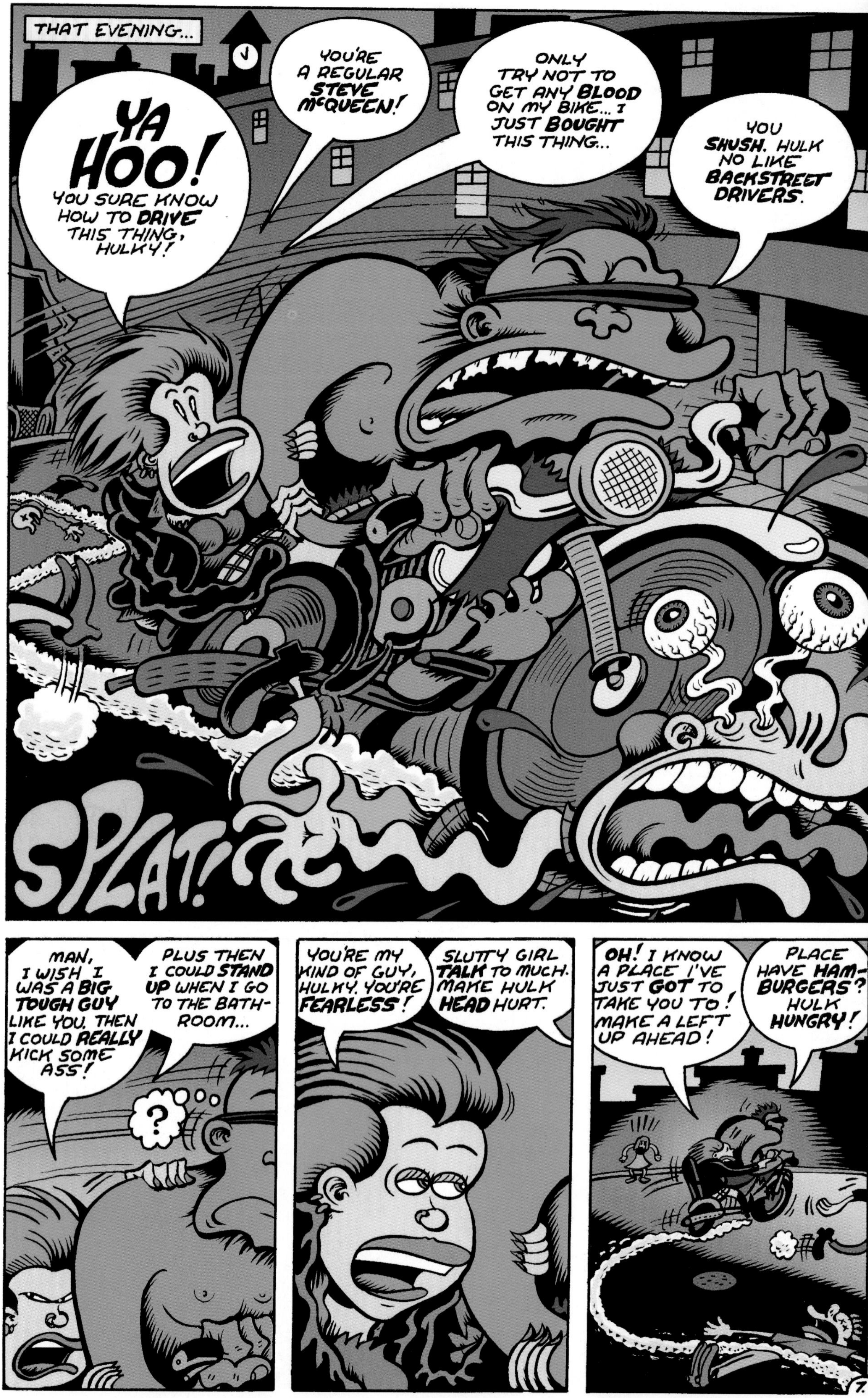
THAT EVENING...
YA HOO! YOU SURE KNOW HOW TO DRIVE THIS THING, HULKY!
YOU'RE A REGULAR STEVE McQUEEN!
ONLY TRY NOT TO GET ANY BLOOD ON MY BIKE... I JUST BOUGHT THIS THING...
YOU SHUSH. HULK NO LIKE BACKSTREET DRIVERS.
SPLAT!
MAN, I WISH I WAS A BIG TOUGH GUY LIKE YOU. THEN I COULD REALLY KICK SOME ASS!
PLUS THEN I COULD STAND UP WHEN I GO TO THE BATH-ROOM...
?
YOU'RE MY KIND OF GUY, HULKY. YOU'RE FEARLESS!
SLUTTY GIRL TALK TO MUCH. MAKE HULK HEAD HURT.
OH! I KNOW A PLACE I'VE JUST GOT TO TAKE YOU TO! MAKE A LEFT UP AHEAD!
PLACE HAVE HAM-BURGERS? HULK HUNGRY!

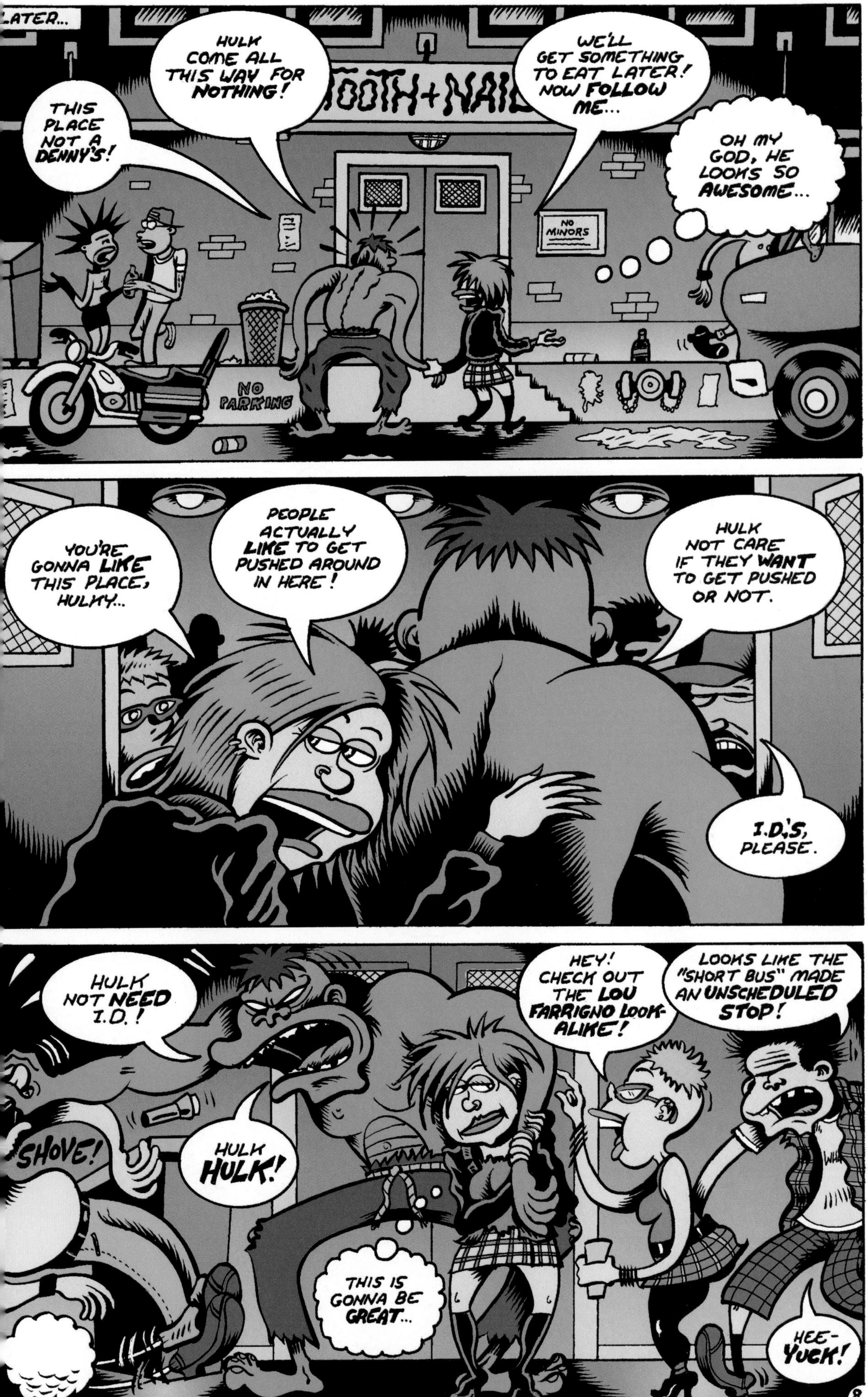
LATER...
THIS PLACE NOT A DENNY'S!
HULK COME ALL THIS WAY FOR NOTHING!
TOOTH + NAIL
WE'LL GET SOMETHING TO EAT LATER! NOW FOLLOW ME...
OH MY GOD, HE LOOKS SO AWESOME...
NO MINORS
NO PARKING
YOU'RE GONNA LIKE THIS PLACE, HULKY...
PEOPLE ACTUALLY LIKE TO GET PUSHED AROUND IN HERE!
HULK NOT CARE IF THEY WANT TO GET PUSHED OR NOT.
I.D.'S, PLEASE.
HULK NOT NEED I.D.!
SHOVE!
HULK HULK!
HEY! CHECK OUT THE LOU FARRIGNO LOOK-ALIKE!
LOOKS LIKE THE "SHORT BUS" MADE AN UNSCHEDULED STOP!
THIS IS GONNA BE GREAT...
HEE-YUCK!

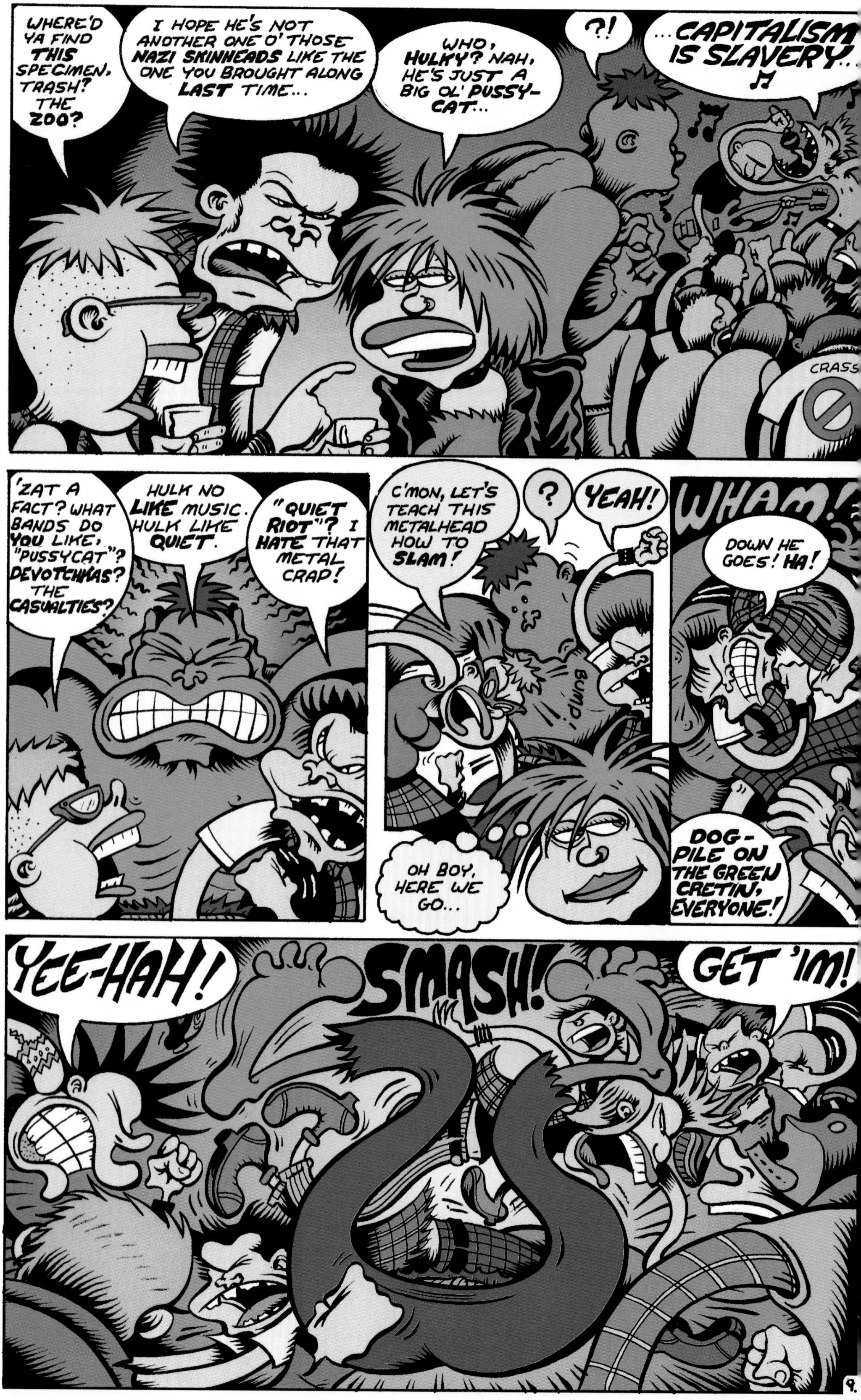
WHERE'D YA FIND THIS SPECIMEN, TRASH? THE ZOO?
I HOPE HE'S NOT ANOTHER ONE O' THOSE NAZI SKINHEADS LIKE THE ONE YOU BROUGHT ALONG LAST TIME...
WHO, HULKY? NAH, HE'S JUST A BIG OL' PUSSY-CAT...
?!
...CAPITALISM IS SLAVERY...
CRASS
'ZAT A FACT? WHAT BANDS DO YOU LIKE, "PUSSYCAT"? DEVOTCHKAS? THE CASUALTIES?
HULK NO LIKE MUSIC. HULK LIKE QUIET.
"QUIET RIOT"? I HATE THAT METAL CRAP!
C'MON, LET'S TEACH THIS METALHEAD HOW TO SLAM!
?
YEAH!
BUMP!
OH BOY, HERE WE GO...
WHAM!
DOWN HE GOES! HA!
DOG-PILE ON THE GREEN CRETIN, EVERYONE!
YEE-HAH!
SMASH!
GET 'IM!

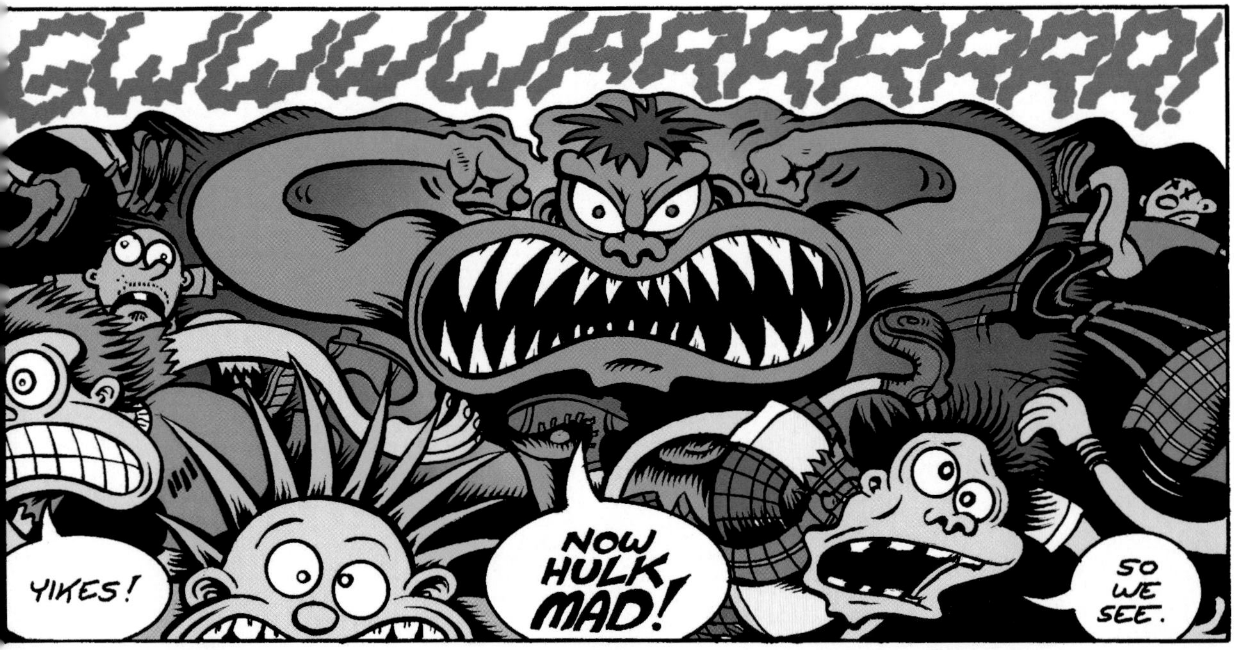
GWWWWARRRRRRR!
YIKES!
NOW HULK MAD!
SO WE SEE.

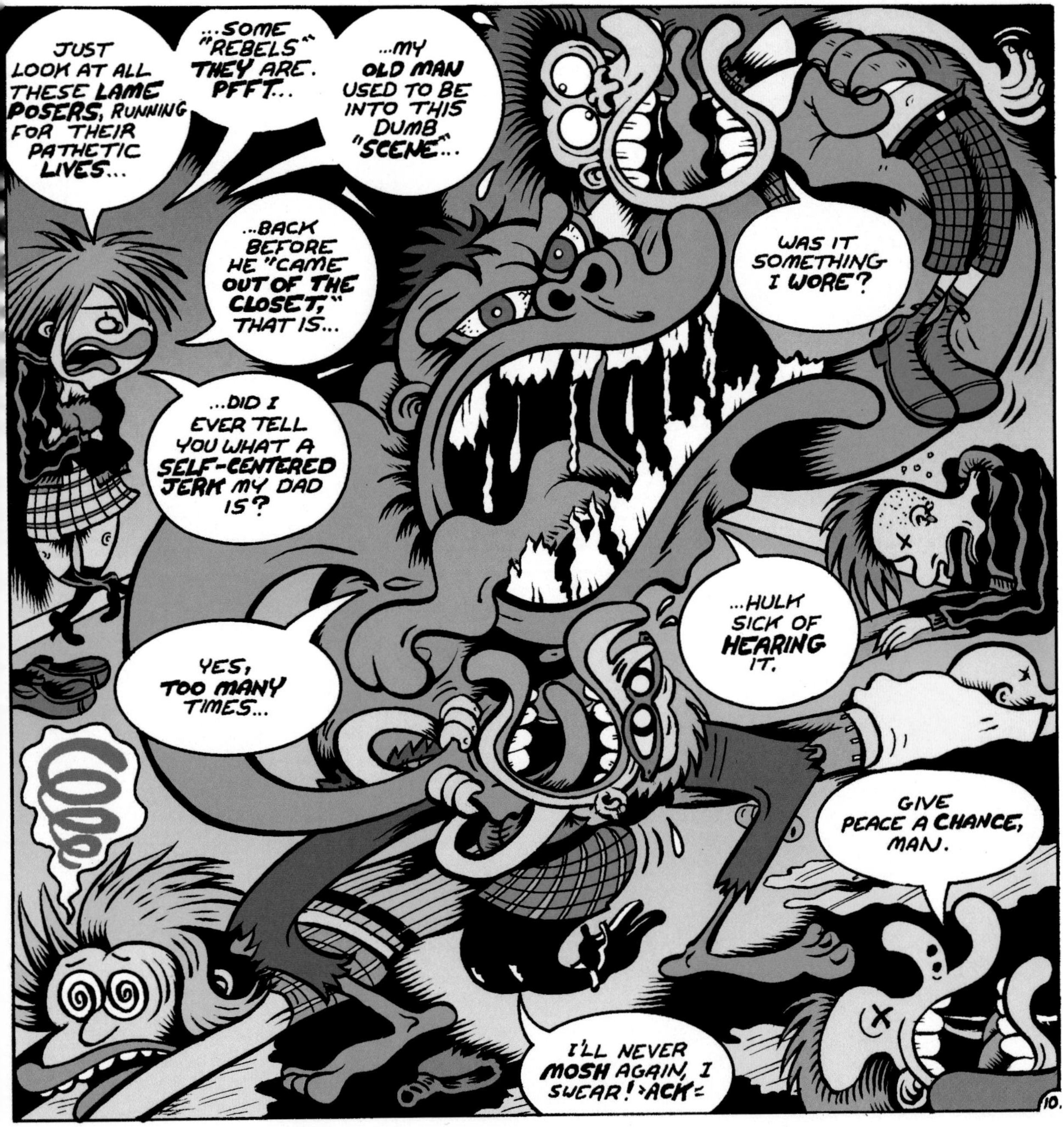
JUST LOOK AT ALL THESE LAME POSERS, RUNNING FOR THEIR PATHETIC LIVES...
...SOME "REBELS" THEY ARE. PFFT...
...MY OLD MAN USED TO BE INTO THIS DUMB "SCENE"...
...BACK BEFORE HE "CAME OUT OF THE CLOSET," THAT IS...
...DID I EVER TELL YOU WHAT A SELF-CENTERED JERK MY DAD IS?
YES, TOO MANY TIMES...
WAS IT SOMETHING I WORE?
...HULK SICK OF HEARING IT.
GIVE PEACE A CHANCE, MAN.
I'LL NEVER MOSH AGAIN, I SWEAR! >ACK<

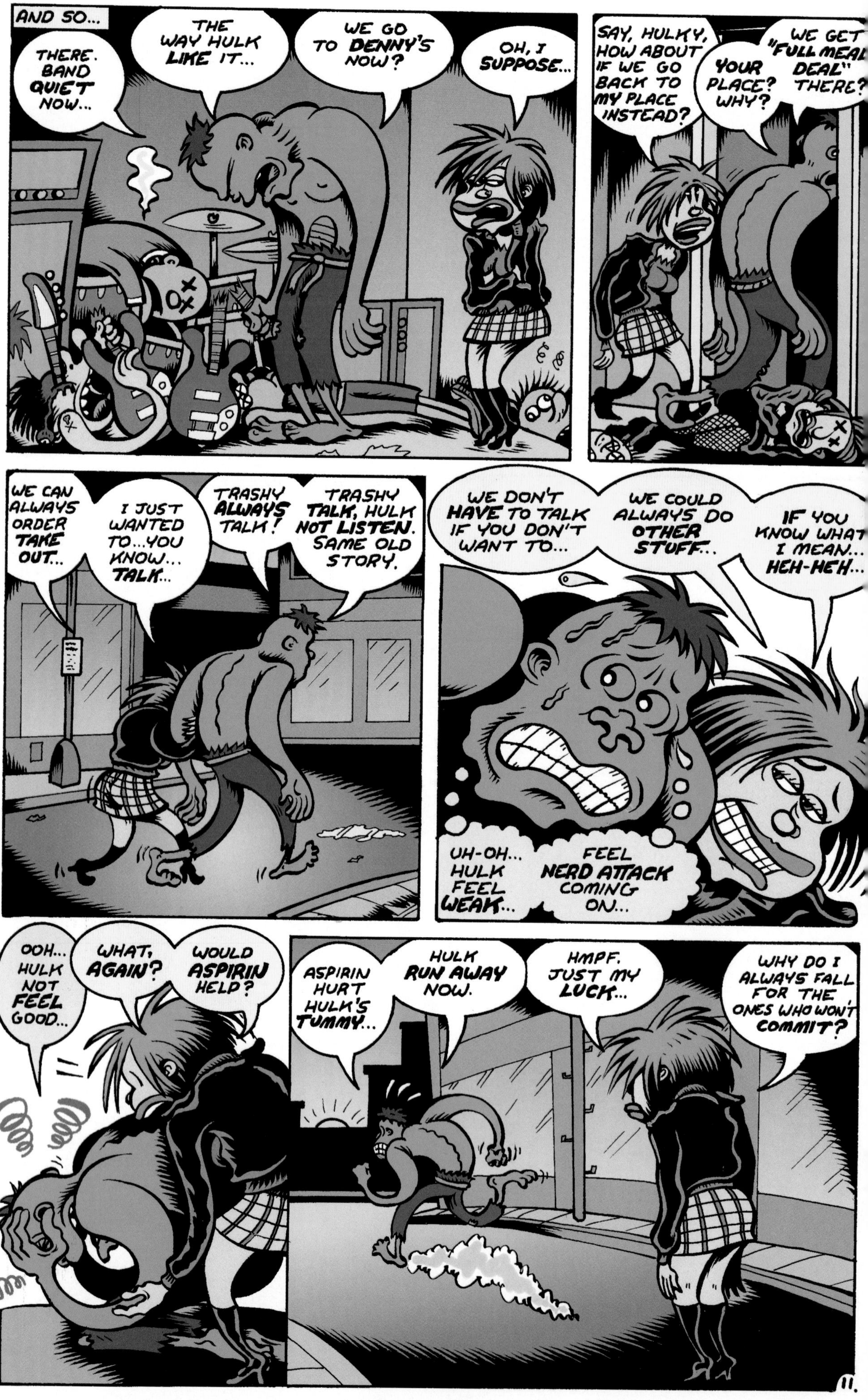

AND SO...
THERE. BAND QUIET NOW...
THE WAY HULK LIKE IT...
WE GO TO DENNY'S NOW?
OH, I SUPPOSE...
SAY, HULKY, HOW ABOUT IF WE GO BACK TO MY PLACE INSTEAD?
YOUR PLACE? WHY?
WE GET "FULL MEAL DEAL" THERE?
WE CAN ALWAYS ORDER TAKE OUT...
I JUST WANTED TO...YOU KNOW... TALK...
TRASHY ALWAYS TALK!
TRASHY TALK, HULK NOT LISTEN. SAME OLD STORY.
WE DON'T HAVE TO TALK IF YOU DON'T WANT TO...
WE COULD ALWAYS DO OTHER STUFF...
IF YOU KNOW WHAT I MEAN... HEH-HEH...
UH-OH... HULK FEEL WEAK...
FEEL NERD ATTACK COMING ON...
OOH... HULK NOT FEEL GOOD...
WHAT, AGAIN?
WOULD ASPIRIN HELP?
ASPIRIN HURT HULK'S TUMMY...
HULK RUN AWAY NOW.
HMPF. JUST MY LUCK...
WHY DO I ALWAYS FALL FOR THE ONES WHO WON'T COMMIT?

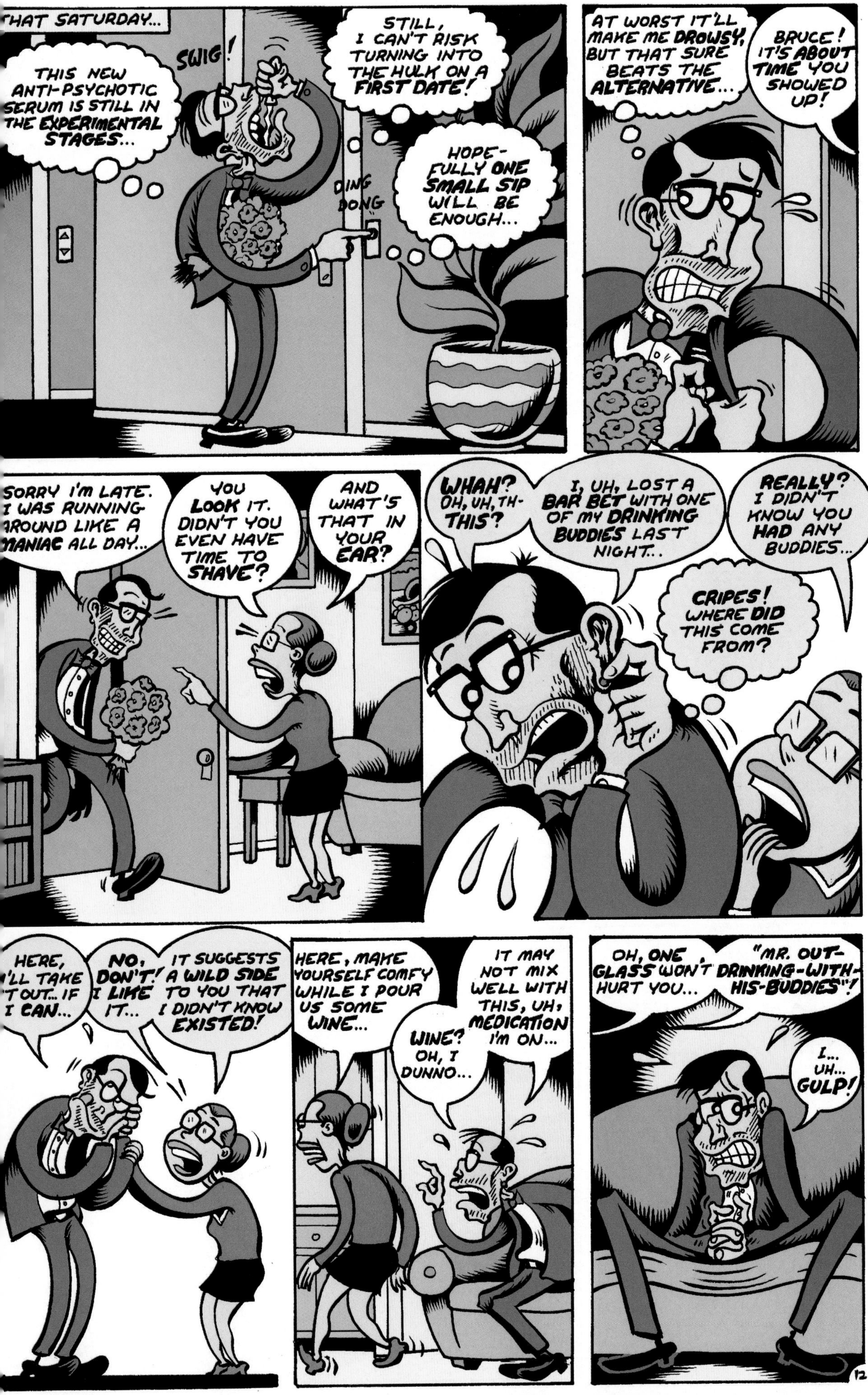
THAT SATURDAY...
THIS NEW ANTI-PSYCHOTIC SERUM IS STILL IN THE EXPERIMENTAL STAGES...
SWIG!
STILL, I CAN'T RISK TURNING INTO THE HULK ON A FIRST DATE!
DING DONG
HOPE-FULLY ONE SMALL SIP WILL BE ENOUGH...
AT WORST IT'LL MAKE ME DROWSY, BUT THAT SURE BEATS THE ALTERNATIVE...
BRUCE! IT'S ABOUT TIME YOU SHOWED UP!
SORRY I'M LATE. I WAS RUNNING AROUND LIKE A MANIAC ALL DAY...
YOU LOOK IT. DIDN'T YOU EVEN HAVE TIME TO SHAVE?
AND WHAT'S THAT IN YOUR EAR?
WHAH? OH, UH, TH- THIS?
I, UH, LOST A BAR BET WITH ONE OF MY DRINKING BUDDIES LAST NIGHT...
REALLY? I DIDN'T KNOW YOU HAD ANY BUDDIES...
CRIPES! WHERE DID THIS COME FROM?
HERE, I'LL TAKE IT OUT... IF I CAN...
NO, DON'T! I LIKE IT...
IT SUGGESTS A WILD SIDE TO YOU THAT I DIDN'T KNOW EXISTED!
HERE, MAKE YOURSELF COMFY WHILE I POUR US SOME WINE...
WINE? OH, I DUNNO...
IT MAY NOT MIX WELL WITH THIS, UH, MEDICATION I'M ON...
OH, ONE GLASS WON'T HURT YOU...
"MR. OUT-DRINKING-WITH-HIS-BUDDIES"!
I... UH... GULP!

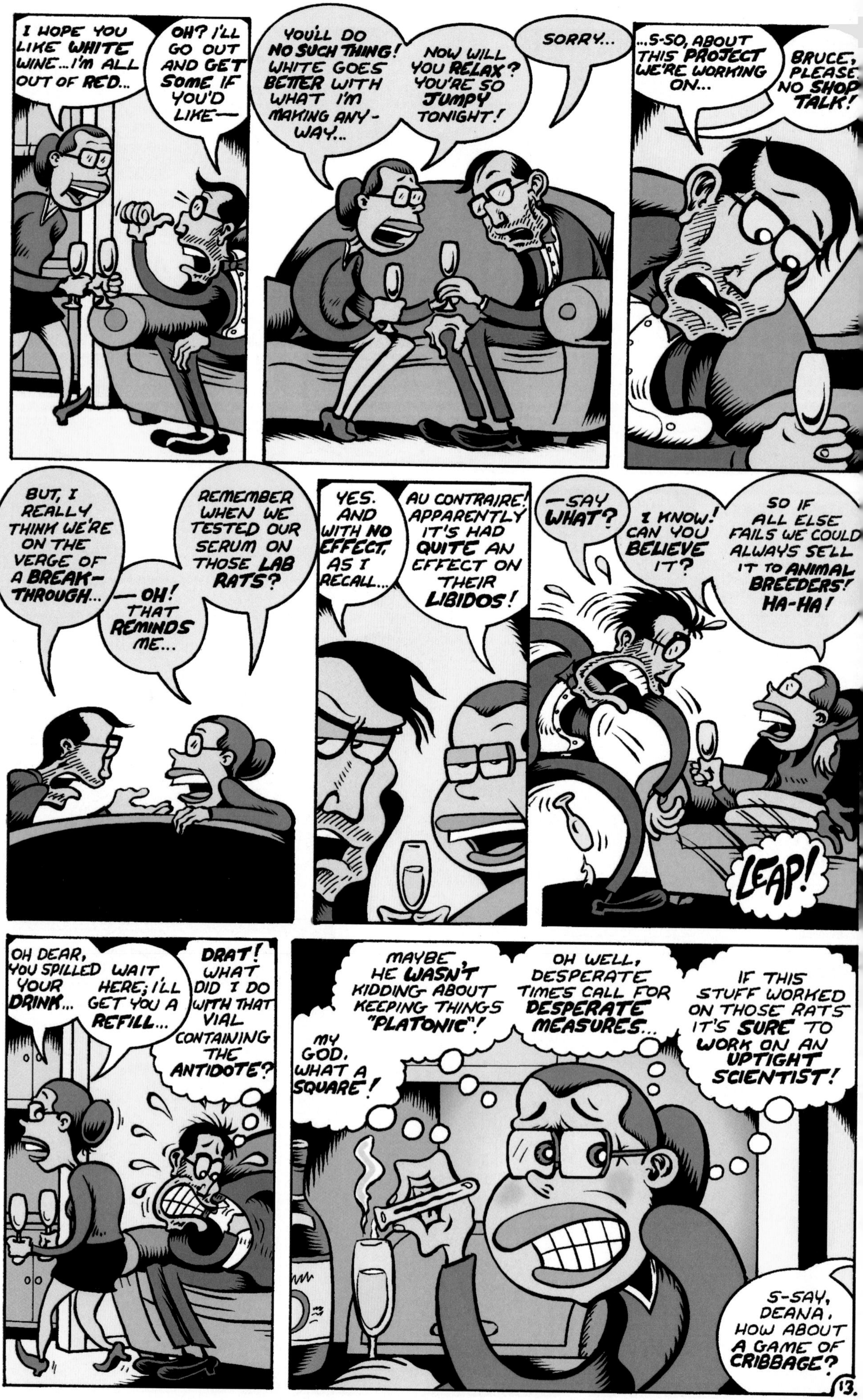

I HOPE YOU LIKE WHITE WINE...I'M ALL OUT OF RED...
OH? I'LL GO OUT AND GET SOME IF YOU'D LIKE—
YOU'LL DO NO SUCH THING! WHITE GOES BETTER WITH WHAT I'M MAKING ANY-WAY...
NOW WILL YOU RELAX? YOU'RE SO JUMPY TONIGHT!
SORRY...
...S-SO, ABOUT THIS PROJECT WE'RE WORKING ON...
BRUCE, PLEASE NO SHOP TALK!
BUT, I REALLY THINK WE'RE ON THE VERGE OF A BREAK-THROUGH...
—OH! THAT REMINDS ME...
REMEMBER WHEN WE TESTED OUR SERUM ON THOSE LAB RATS?
YES. AND WITH NO EFFECT, AS I RECALL...
AU CONTRAIRE! APPARENTLY IT'S HAD QUITE AN EFFECT ON THEIR LIBIDOS!
—SAY WHAT?
I KNOW! CAN YOU BELIEVE IT?
SO IF ALL ELSE FAILS WE COULD ALWAYS SELL IT TO ANIMAL BREEDERS! HA-HA!
LEAP!
OH DEAR, YOU SPILLED YOUR DRINK...
WAIT HERE; I'LL GET YOU A REFILL...
DRAT! WHAT DID I DO WITH THAT VIAL CONTAINING THE ANTIDOTE?
MY GOD. WHAT A SQUARE!
MAYBE HE WASN'T KIDDING ABOUT KEEPING THINGS "PLATONIC"!
OH WELL, DESPERATE TIMES CALL FOR DESPERATE MEASURES...
IF THIS STUFF WORKED ON THOSE RATS IT'S SURE TO WORK ON AN UPTIGHT SCIENTIST!
S-SAY, DEANA, HOW ABOUT A GAME OF CRIBBAGE?

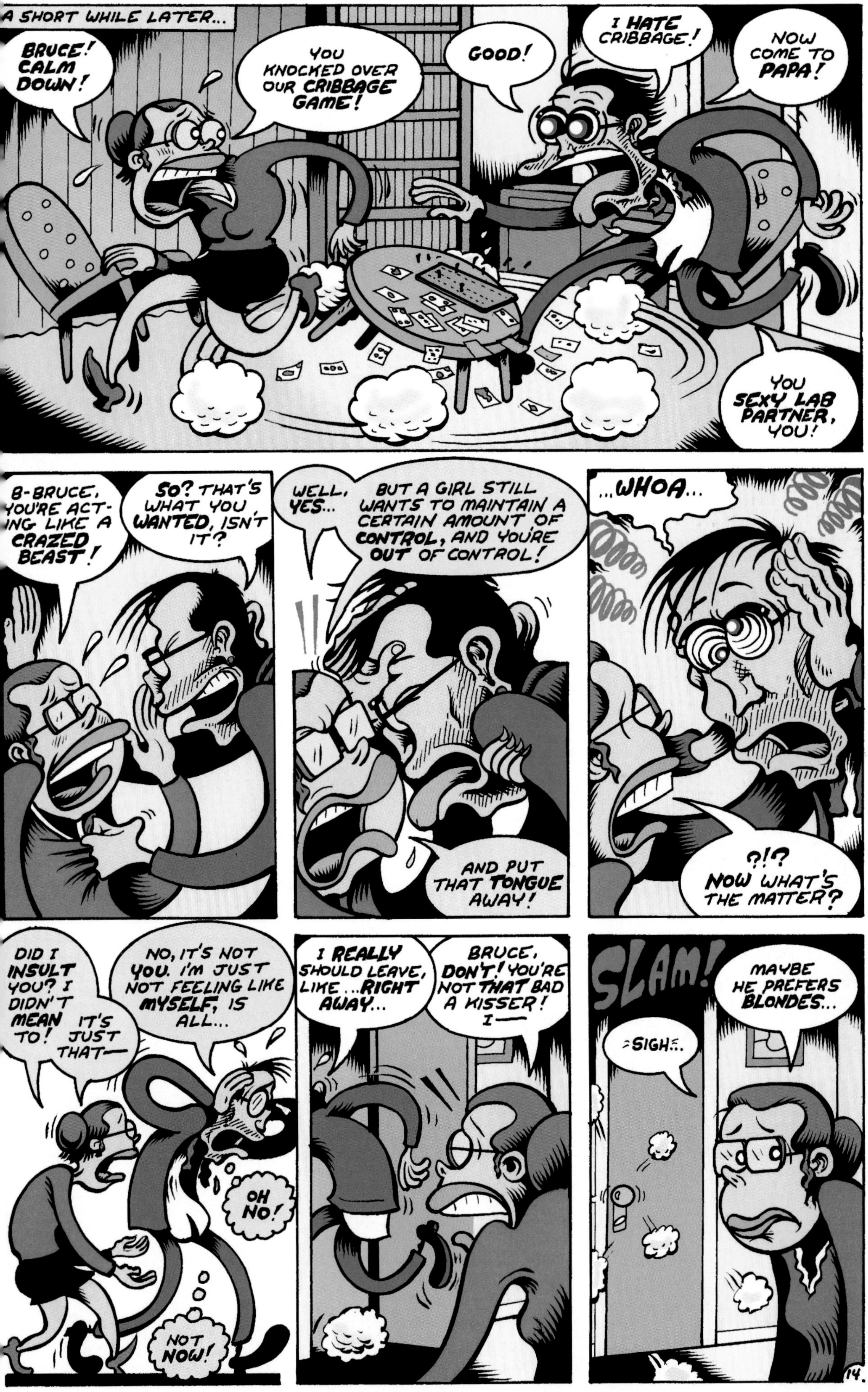
A SHORT WHILE LATER...
BRUCE! CALM DOWN!
YOU KNOCKED OVER OUR CRIBBAGE GAME!
GOOD!
I HATE CRIBBAGE!
NOW COME TO PAPA!
YOU SEXY LAB PARTNER, YOU!
B-BRUCE, YOU'RE ACTING LIKE A CRAZED BEAST!
SO? THAT'S WHAT YOU WANTED, ISN'T IT?
WELL, YES...
BUT A GIRL STILL WANTS TO MAINTAIN A CERTAIN AMOUNT OF CONTROL, AND YOU'RE OUT OF CONTROL!
AND PUT THAT TONGUE AWAY!
...WHOA...
?!? NOW WHAT'S THE MATTER?
DID I INSULT YOU? I DIDN'T MEAN TO!
IT'S JUST THAT—
NO, IT'S NOT YOU. I'M JUST NOT FEELING LIKE MYSELF, IS ALL...
OH NO!
NOT NOW!
I REALLY SHOULD LEAVE, LIKE...RIGHT AWAY...
BRUCE, DON'T! YOU'RE NOT THAT BAD A KISSER! I—
SLAM!
MAYBE HE PREFERS BLONDES...
:SIGH:
14.

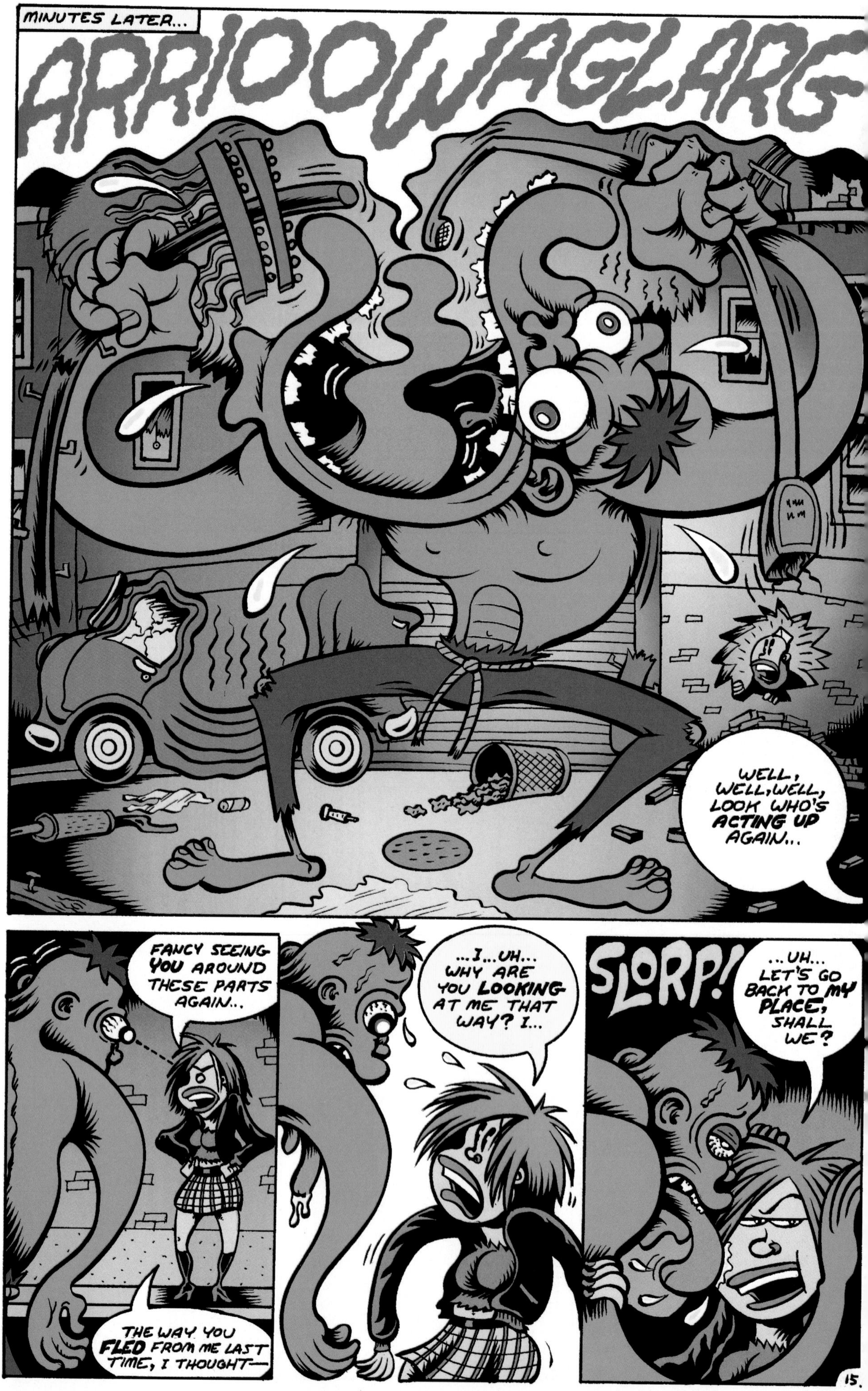
MINUTES LATER...
ARRIOOWAGLARG
WELL, WELL, WELL, LOOK WHO'S ACTING UP AGAIN...
FANCY SEEING YOU AROUND THESE PARTS AGAIN...
THE WAY YOU FLED FROM ME LAST TIME, I THOUGHT—
...I...UH... WHY ARE YOU LOOKING AT ME THAT WAY? I...
SLORP!
...UH... LET'S GO BACK TO MY PLACE, SHALL WE?

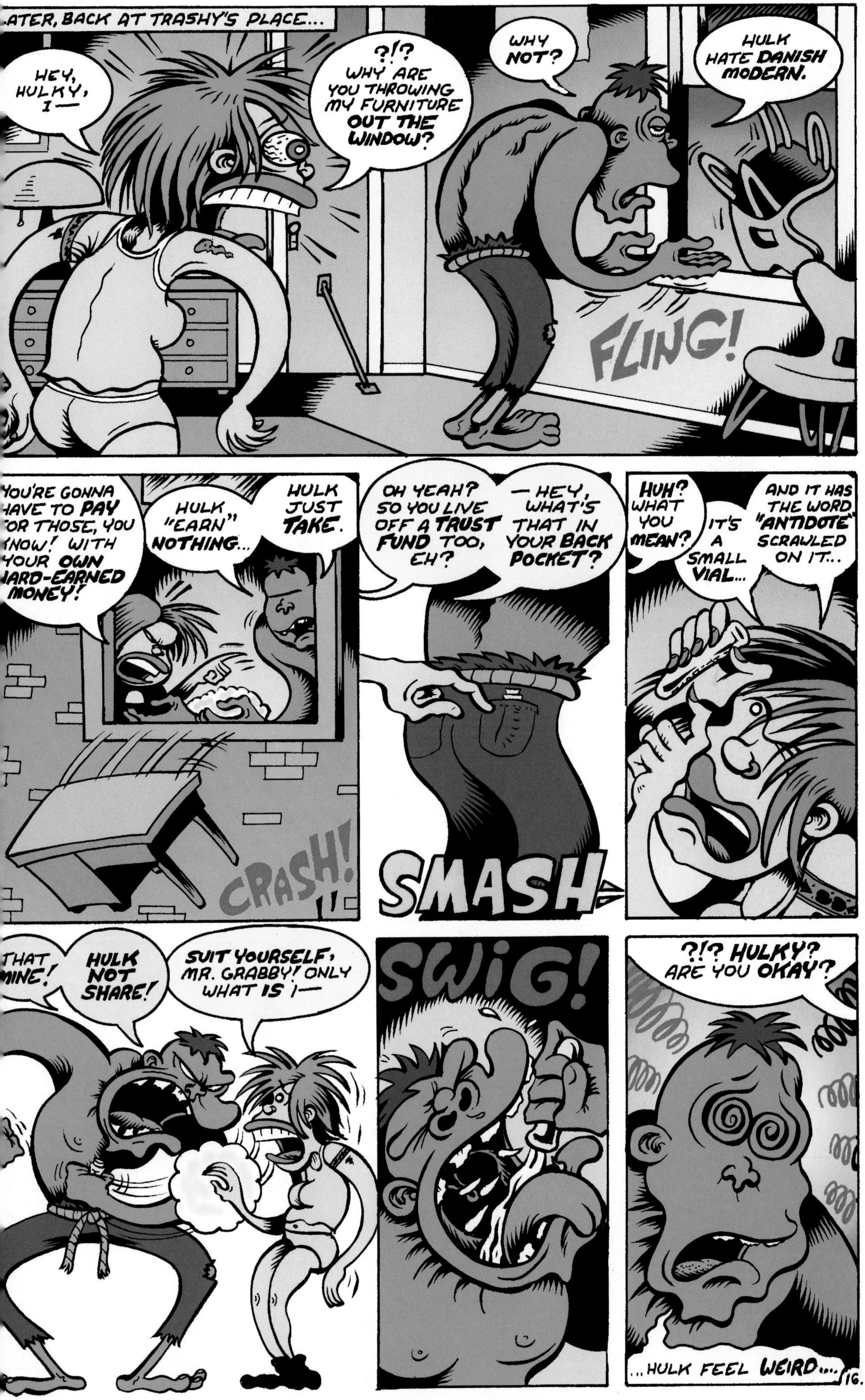

LATER, BACK AT TRASHY'S PLACE...
HEY, HULKY, I—
?!? WHY ARE YOU THROWING MY FURNITURE OUT THE WINDOW?
WHY NOT?
HULK HATE DANISH MODERN.
FLING!
YOU'RE GONNA HAVE TO PAY FOR THOSE, YOU KNOW! WITH YOUR OWN HARD-EARNED MONEY!
HULK "EARN" NOTHING...
HULK JUST TAKE.
CRASH!
OH YEAH? SO YOU LIVE OFF A TRUST FUND TOO, EH?
—HEY, WHAT'S THAT IN YOUR BACK POCKET?
SMASH
HUH? WHAT YOU MEAN?
IT'S A SMALL VIAL...
AND IT HAS THE WORD "ANTIDOTE" SCRAWLED ON IT...
THAT MINE!
HULK NOT SHARE!
SUIT YOURSELF, MR. GRABBY! ONLY WHAT IS I—
SWIG!
?!? HULKY? ARE YOU OKAY?
...HULK FEEL WEIRD...

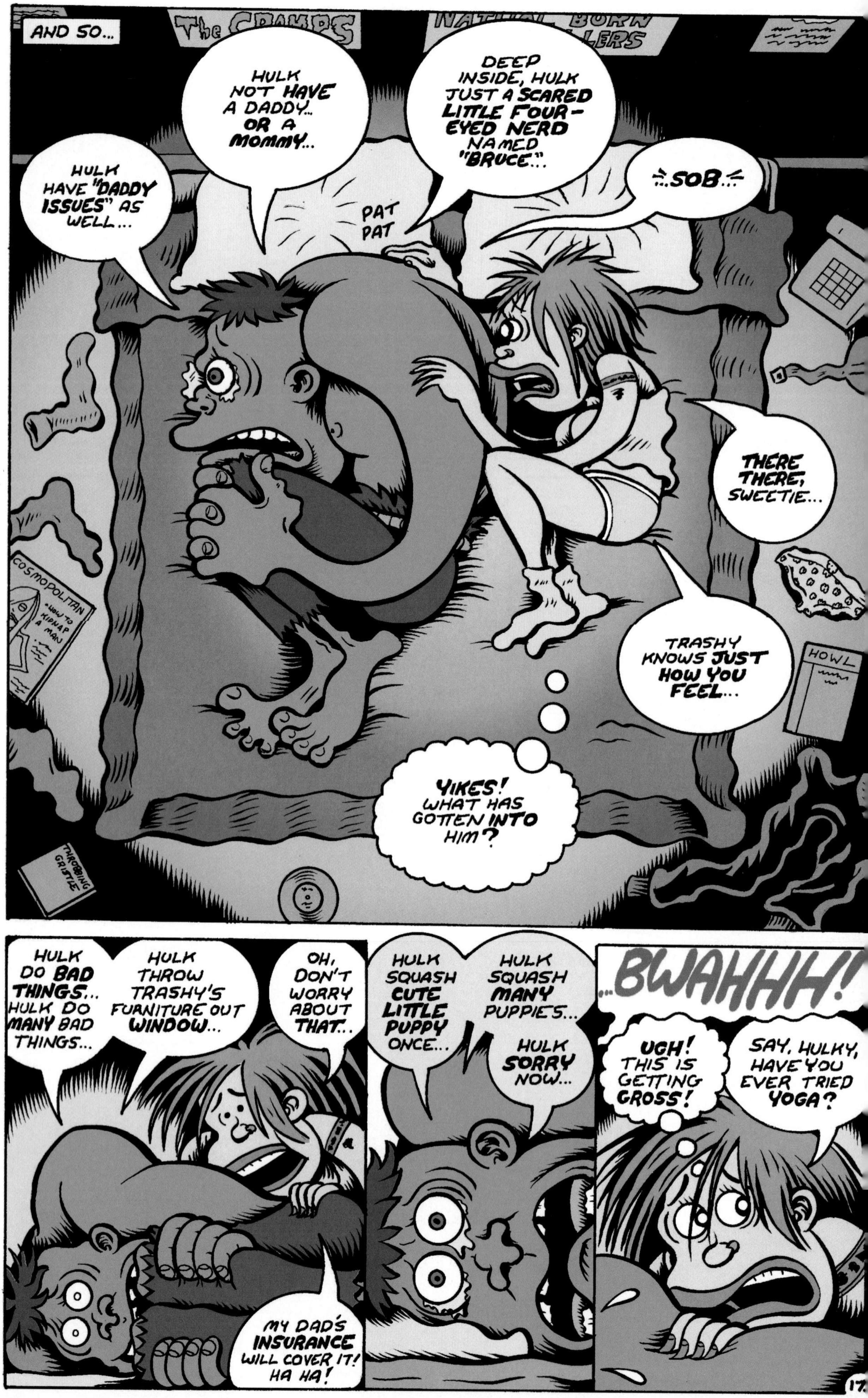
AND SO...
HULK HAVE "DADDY ISSUES" AS WELL...
HULK NOT HAVE A DADDY... OR A MOMMY...
PAT PAT
DEEP INSIDE, HULK JUST A SCARED LITTLE FOUR-EYED NERD NAMED "BRUCE"...
SOB
THERE THERE, SWEETIE...
TRASHY KNOWS JUST HOW YOU FEEL...
YIKES! WHAT HAS GOTTEN INTO HIM?
COSMOPOLITAN
HOW TO KIDNAP A MAN
HOWL
THROBBING GRISTLE
HULK DO BAD THINGS... HULK DO MANY BAD THINGS...
HULK THROW TRASHY'S FURNITURE OUT WINDOW...
OH, DON'T WORRY ABOUT THAT...
MY DAD'S INSURANCE WILL COVER IT! HA HA!
HULK SQUASH CUTE LITTLE PUPPY ONCE...
HULK SQUASH MANY PUPPIES...
HULK SORRY NOW...
...BWAHHH!
UGH! THIS IS GETTING GROSS!
SAY, HULKY, HAVE YOU EVER TRIED YOGA?

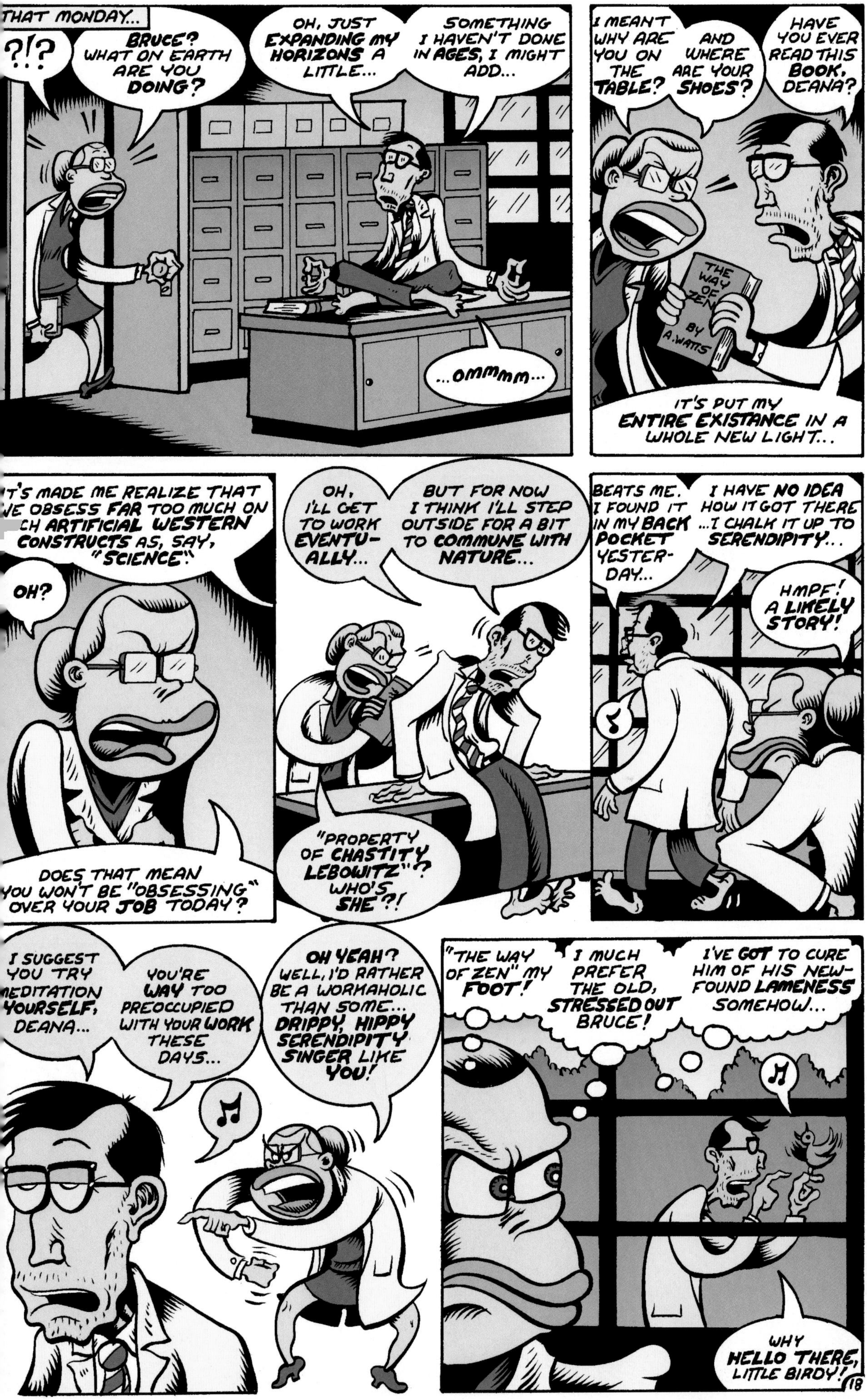
THAT MONDAY...
?!?
BRUCE? WHAT ON EARTH ARE YOU DOING?
OH, JUST EXPANDING MY HORIZONS A LITTLE...
SOMETHING I HAVEN'T DONE IN AGES, I MIGHT ADD...
...OMMMM...
I MEANT WHY ARE YOU ON THE TABLE?
AND WHERE ARE YOUR SHOES?
HAVE YOU EVER READ THIS BOOK, DEANA?
THE WAY OF ZEN BY A. WATTS
IT'S PUT MY ENTIRE EXISTANCE IN A WHOLE NEW LIGHT...
IT'S MADE ME REALIZE THAT WE OBSESS FAR TOO MUCH ON SUCH ARTIFICIAL WESTERN CONSTRUCTS AS, SAY, "SCIENCE".
OH?
DOES THAT MEAN YOU WON'T BE "OBSESSING" OVER YOUR JOB TODAY?
OH, I'LL GET TO WORK EVENTUALLY...
BUT FOR NOW I THINK I'LL STEP OUTSIDE FOR A BIT TO COMMUNE WITH NATURE...
"PROPERTY OF CHASTITY LEBOWITZ"? WHO'S SHE?!
BEATS ME. I FOUND IT IN MY BACK POCKET YESTERDAY...
I HAVE NO IDEA HOW IT GOT THERE ...I CHALK IT UP TO SERENDIPITY...
HMPF! A LIKELY STORY!
I SUGGEST YOU TRY MEDITATION YOURSELF, DEANA...
YOU'RE WAY TOO PREOCCUPIED WITH YOUR WORK THESE DAYS...
OH YEAH? WELL, I'D RATHER BE A WORKAHOLIC THAN SOME... DRIPPY, HIPPY SERENDIPITY SINGER LIKE YOU!
"THE WAY OF ZEN" MY FOOT!
I MUCH PREFER THE OLD, STRESSED OUT BRUCE!
I'VE GOT TO CURE HIM OF HIS NEW-FOUND LAMENESS SOMEHOW...
WHY HELLO THERE, LITTLE BIRDY!

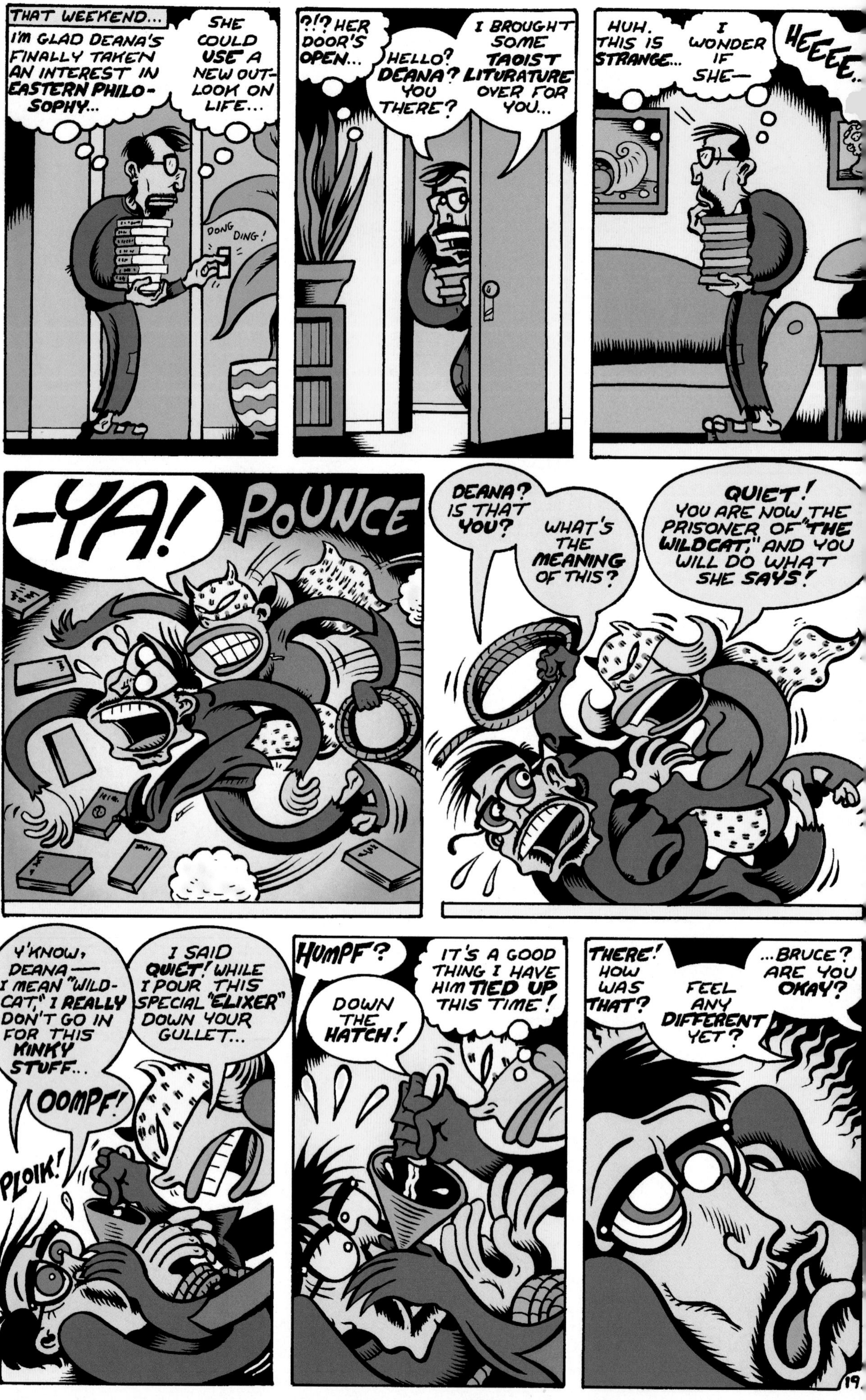
THAT WEEKEND...
I'M GLAD DEANA'S FINALLY TAKEN AN INTEREST IN EASTERN PHILO-SOPHY...
SHE COULD USE A NEW OUT-LOOK ON LIFE...
DONG DING!
?!? HER DOOR'S OPEN...
HELLO? DEANA? YOU THERE?
I BROUGHT SOME TAOIST LITURATURE OVER FOR YOU...
HUH. THIS IS STRANGE...
I WONDER IF SHE—
HEEEE...
-YA!
POUNCE
DEANA? IS THAT YOU?
WHAT'S THE MEANING OF THIS?
QUIET! YOU ARE NOW THE PRISONER OF "THE WILDCAT," AND YOU WILL DO WHAT SHE SAYS!
Y'KNOW, DEANA— I MEAN "WILD-CAT," I REALLY DON'T GO IN FOR THIS KINKY STUFF...
I SAID QUIET! WHILE I POUR THIS SPECIAL "ELIXER" DOWN YOUR GULLET...
OOMPF!
PLOIK!
HUMPF?
DOWN THE HATCH!
IT'S A GOOD THING I HAVE HIM TIED UP THIS TIME!
THERE! HOW WAS THAT?
FEEL ANY DIFFERENT YET?
...BRUCE? ARE YOU OKAY?

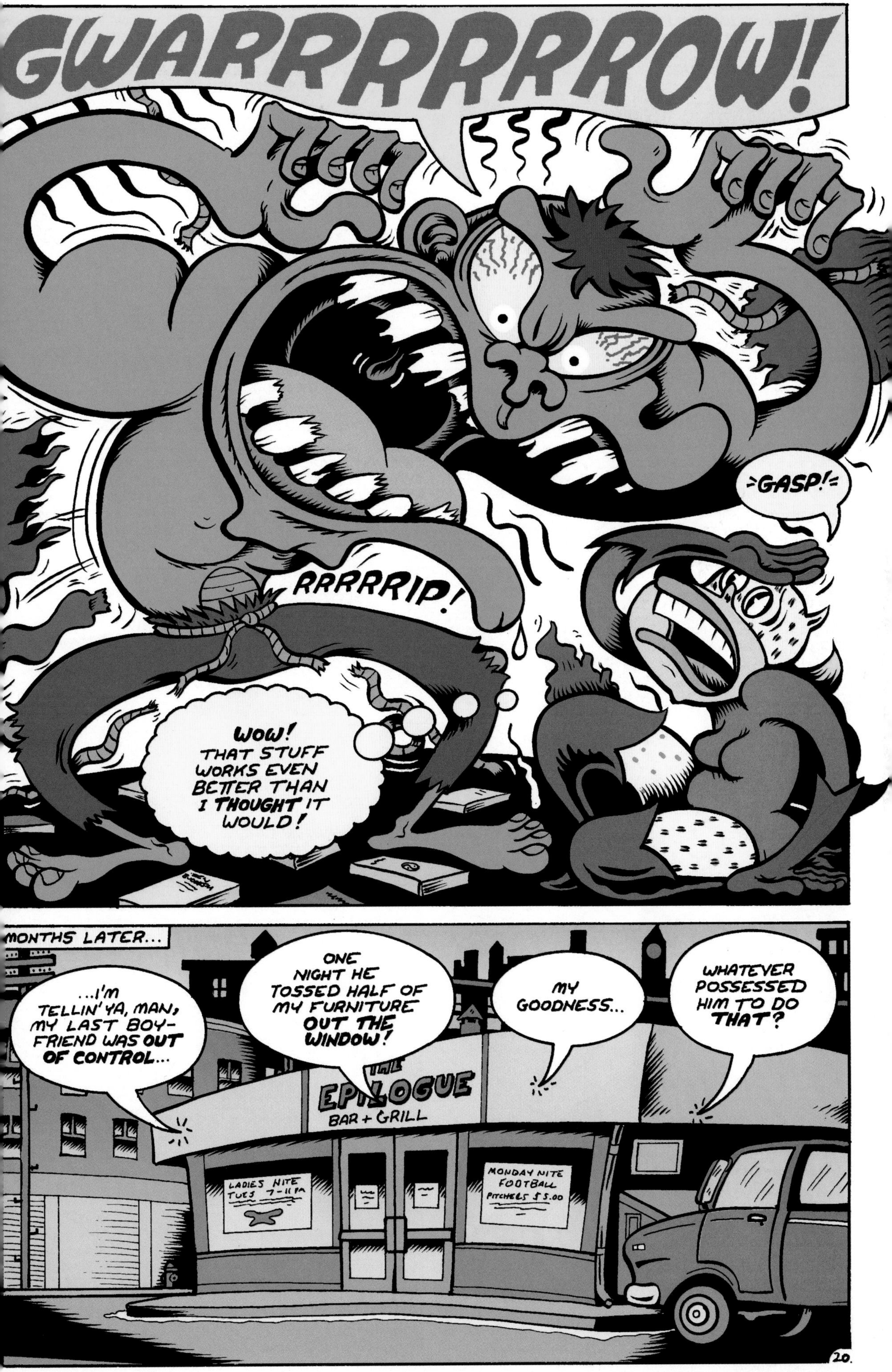
GWARRRRRROW!
>GASP!<
RRRRRIP!
WOW! THAT STUFF WORKS EVEN BETTER THAN I THOUGHT IT WOULD!
MONTHS LATER...
...I'M TELLIN' YA, MAN, MY LAST BOY-FRIEND WAS OUT OF CONTROL...
ONE NIGHT HE TOSSED HALF OF MY FURNITURE OUT THE WINDOW!
MY GOODNESS...
WHATEVER POSSESSED HIM TO DO THAT?
THE EPILOGUE BAR + GRILL
LADIES NITE TUES 7-11 PM
MONDAY NITE FOOTBALL PITCHERS $5.00

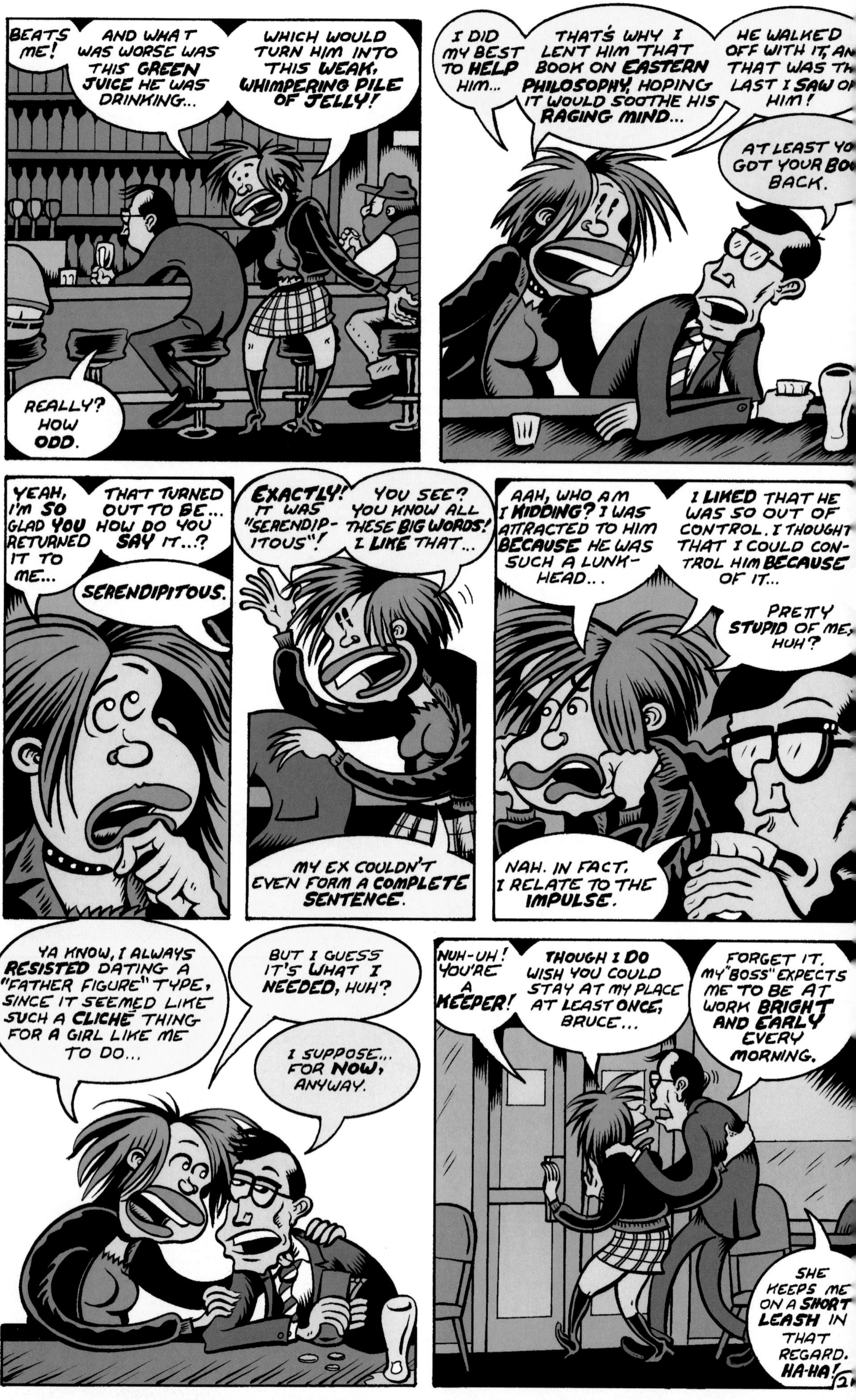
BEATS ME!
AND WHAT WAS WORSE WAS THIS GREEN JUICE HE WAS DRINKING...
WHICH WOULD TURN HIM INTO THIS WEAK, WHIMPERING PILE OF JELLY!
REALLY? HOW ODD.
I DID MY BEST TO HELP HIM...
THAT'S WHY I LENT HIM THAT BOOK ON EASTERN PHILOSOPHY, HOPING IT WOULD SOOTHE HIS RAGING MIND...
HE WALKED OFF WITH IT, AN THAT WAS TH LAST I SAW O HIM!
AT LEAST YO GOT YOUR BO BACK.
YEAH, I'M SO GLAD YOU RETURNED IT TO ME...
THAT TURNED OUT TO BE... HOW DO YOU SAY IT...?
SERENDIPITOUS.
EXACTLY! IT WAS "SERENDIP-ITOUS"!
YOU SEE? YOU KNOW ALL THESE BIG WORDS! I LIKE THAT...
MY EX COULDN'T EVEN FORM A COMPLETE SENTENCE.
AAH, WHO AM I KIDDING? I WAS ATTRACTED TO HIM BECAUSE HE WAS SUCH A LUNK-HEAD...
I LIKED THAT HE WAS SO OUT OF CONTROL. I THOUGHT THAT I COULD CON-TROL HIM BECAUSE OF IT...
PRETTY STUPID OF ME, HUH?
NAH. IN FACT, I RELATE TO THE IMPULSE.
YA KNOW, I ALWAYS RESISTED DATING A "FATHER FIGURE" TYPE, SINCE IT SEEMED LIKE SUCH A CLICHÉ THING FOR A GIRL LIKE ME TO DO...
BUT I GUESS IT'S WHAT I NEEDED, HUH?
I SUPPOSE... FOR NOW, ANYWAY.
NUH-UH! YOU'RE A KEEPER!
THOUGH I DO WISH YOU COULD STAY AT MY PLACE AT LEAST ONCE, BRUCE...
FORGET IT. MY "BOSS" EXPECTS ME TO BE AT WORK BRIGHT AND EARLY EVERY MORNING.
SHE KEEPS ME ON A SHORT LEASH IN THAT REGARD. HA-HA!

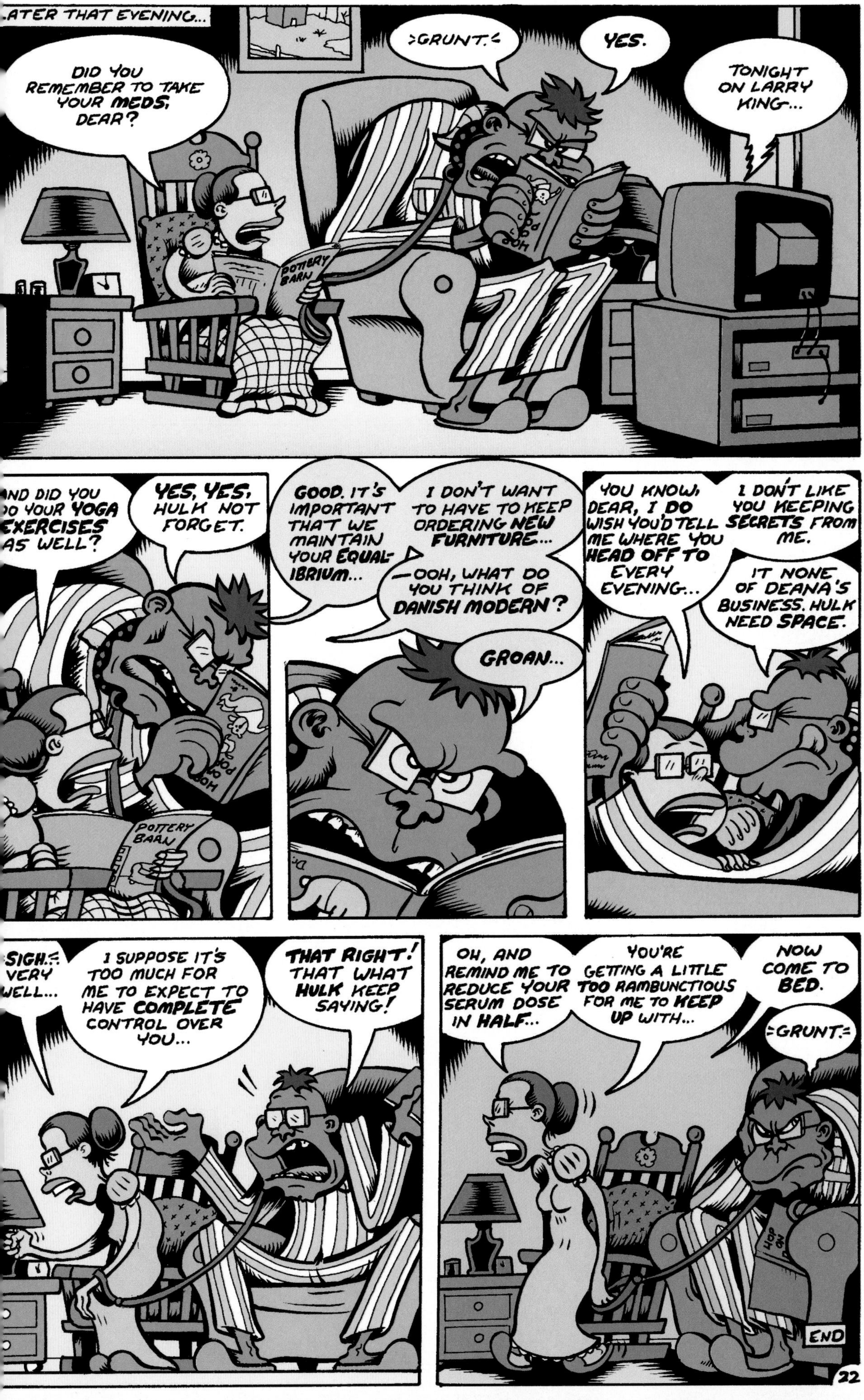
LATER THAT EVENING...
DID YOU REMEMBER TO TAKE YOUR MEDS, DEAR?
>GRUNT.<
YES.
TONIGHT ON LARRY KING...
POTTERY BARN
AND DID YOU DO YOUR YOGA EXERCISES AS WELL?
YES, YES, HULK NOT FORGET.
GOOD. IT'S IMPORTANT THAT WE MAINTAIN YOUR EQUAL-IBRIUM...
I DON'T WANT TO HAVE TO KEEP ORDERING NEW FURNITURE...
—OOH, WHAT DO YOU THINK OF DANISH MODERN?
GROAN...
YOU KNOW, DEAR, I DO WISH YOU'D TELL ME WHERE YOU HEAD OFF TO EVERY EVENING...
I DON'T LIKE YOU KEEPING SECRETS FROM ME.
IT NONE OF DEANA'S BUSINESS. HULK NEED SPACE.
SIGH. VERY WELL...
I SUPPOSE IT'S TOO MUCH FOR ME TO EXPECT TO HAVE COMPLETE CONTROL OVER YOU...
THAT RIGHT! THAT WHAT HULK KEEP SAYING!
OH, AND REMIND ME TO REDUCE YOUR SERUM DOSE IN HALF...
YOU'RE GETTING A LITTLE TOO RAMBUNCTIOUS FOR ME TO KEEP UP WITH...
NOW COME TO BED.
GRUNT.
END

CREATOR BIOGRAPHIES

Peter Bagge's long-running Fantagraphics series *Neat Stuff* and *Hate* chronicled the life of his alienated antihero Buddy Bradley, whose adventures are collected in *Buddy Does Seattle* and *Buddy Does Jersey*. His political comics for *Reason* magazine were recently collected in *Everybody Is Stupid Except for Me*. His first book for Marvel was *The Megalomaniacal Spider-Man*.

Nick Bertozzi is the Ignatz Award, Harvey Award, and Xeric Grant-winning writer/artist of *Rubber Necker* and *The Masochists* (Alternative Comics) and *The Salon* (St. Martin's). He has collaborated with writer Jason Little on *Houdini: The Handcuff King* (Hyperion) and Colbert Report writer Glenn Eichler on the recently released *Stuffed!* (First Second).

Molly Crabapple and **John Leavitt** are the co-founders of Dr. Sketchy's Anti-Art School, an ongoing series burlesque life-drawing classes. Their comics collaborations include *Scarlett Takes Manhattan* from Fugu Press and the webcomic *Backstage* at *Act-I-Vate.com*. Both are sought-after illustrators as well.

Nicholas Gurewitch is the Ignatz, Eisner, and Web Cartoonist's Choice Award-winning writer/artist of *The Perry Bible Fellowship*, a gag-strip webcomic at *pbfcomics.com*. The entire run of the strip has been collected in *The Perry Bible Fellowship Almanack* from Dark Horse.

Jason is the Eisner Award-winning writer/artist of *The Last Musketeer*, *I Killed Adolf Hitler*, *Hey, Wait...* and many other graphic novels and collections from Fantagraphics. The Norwegian cartoonist's most recent book is *Low Moon*, which collects the strip of the same name that ran in *The New York Times*. His upcoming book *Werewolves of Montpellier* will be released by Fantagraphics in 2010.

James Kochalka pioneered the diary comic w[ith] his daily "sketchbook diary" webcomic *Americ[an] Elf*, which has since been collected by Top Shelf. H[is] comic series include *SuperF*ckers*, *Johnny Boo* a[nd] *Monkey vs. Robot*. He is also the lead singer of t[he] band James Kochalka Superstar. His first work [for] Marvel appeared in the 2001 *Incredible H[ulk] Annual*.

Michael Kupperman is the writer/artist of t[he] humor comic *Tales Designed to Thrizzle* fro[m] Fantagraphics. His first book, *Snake 'n' Baco[n] Cartoon Cabaret*, was released by HarperCollin[s]. His work has been adapted into animated for[m] for Robert Smigel's *TV Funhouse* and the Ad[ult] Swim pilot *Snake 'n' Bacon*. His first work [for] Marvel appeared in *All Select Comics 7[0th] Anniversary Special #1*.

Junko Mizuno is a renowned manga-ka who[se] adaptations of fairy tales such as *Cinderella* a[nd] *Hansel & Gretel* have been published by Viz. H[er] debut graphic novel, *Pure Trance*, was released [in] America by Last Gasp. She has created illustratio[ns] for *Shojo Beat*, and her art book *Flare: The Art [of] Junko Mizuno* is available from Edition Treville.

Paul Pope is the Eisner Award-winning write[r/] artist of *Batman: Year 100*, *Heavy Liquid*, a[nd] *100%* for DC/Vertigo, as well as the art bo[ok] *PulpHope: The Art of Paul Pope* from AdHouse. H[is] self-published science-fiction series *THB* will so[on] be collected by First Second, which will also relea[se] his upcoming graphic novel *Battling Boy*. He h[as] collaborated on projects with the clothing compani[es] Diesel and DKNY.

Johnny Ryan is the humor cartoonist behi[nd] Fantagraphics' *Angry Youth Comix* and the com[ic] strip *Blecky Yuckerella*, seen in the pages of *Vi[ce]* magazine. His books include the paro[dy] collections *The Comic Book Holocaust* and *T[...]*

...assic Komix Klub from Buenaventura Press. ...s most recent work is the action/sci-fi Prison ...t Vol. 1 from Fantagraphics.

...ash Shaw's graphic novels include The Mother's ...outh (Alternative Comics), Bottomless Belly ...utton (Fantagraphics) and the forthcoming Body ...orld (Pantheon), collecting his sci-fi webcomic of ...e same name. Shaw is a frequent contributor to ...e Fantagraphics anthology series Mome, and his ...nimation project The Unclothed Man in the 35th ...entury will appear on IFC.com.

...ax Cannon is the writer and artist of the long-...nning gag strip Red Meat, which appears in ...ternative weekly newspapers nationwide, as well ...s The Onion A.V. Club. Three Red Meat collections ...e available from St. Martin's Griffin.

...cob Chabot is the artist of Marvel's X-Babies ...ritten by Gregg Schigiel). He is best known as the ...eator of the humor comic The Mighty Skullboy ...rmy, a collection of which is available from Dark ...orse. Skullboy currently appears as a back-up ...rip in Chris Giarrusso's G-Man: Cape Crisis from ...nage Comics.

...onathan Hickman is the writer of Marvel's ...ecret Warriors (with Brian Michael Bendis) and ...antastic Four. He is the writer and artist of the ...nage Comics miniseries The Nightly News, which ...eceived an Eisner Award nomination for Best ...imited Series in 2008. His other comics include ...ax Romana, Red Mass for Mars and Transhuman, ...ll from Image.

.. Kikuo Johnson received a Harvey Award and a ...uss Manning Promising Newcomer Award in 2006 ...r his debut graphic novel, the coming-of-age tale ...he Night Fisher (Fantagraphics). His comics have ...ppeared in Mome, and he's worked as an illustrator ...r The New Yorker, The New York Times, The Believer ...nd Nickelodeon Magazine.

Matt Kindt is the Harvey Award-winning writer-artist of such espionage/thriller graphic novels as Super Spy, 2 Sisters, and Pistolwhip (Top Shelf). Fall 2009 sees the release of Kindt's 3 Story: The Secret History of the Giant Man from Dark Horse.

Tony Millionaire is the creator of two long-running humor comics: The syndicated gag strip Maakies, collections of which are available from Fantagraphics, and the quirky children's comic Sock Monkey, from Dark Horse. In addition Tony recently won a Best Writer/Artist – Humor Eisner for his graphic novel Billy Hazelnuts from Fantagraphics. Animated versions of his work have appeared on Saturday Night Live and Adult Swim. A deluxe art book of his work, The Art of Tony Millionaire, is available from Dark Horse.

Jim Rugg and Brian Maruca are the co-creators of the street-level heroes Street Angel (SLG) and Afrodisiac, a deluxe collection of which is available from AdHouse in December 2009. Rugg is also the artist of The Plain Janes from DC/Minx, and the writer-artist of the new limited series One Model Nation from Image.

Jhonen Vasquez is the Eisner Award-nominated writer-artist of such comics as Squee!, I Feel Sick, Fillerbunny, and Johnny the Homicidal Maniac, all of which are available from SLG. He is the creator of the cult-favorite cartoon Invader Zim, currently available on DVD.

Jeffrey Brown is widely known as the author of the intimate autobiographical "Girlfriend Trilogy," including Clumsy, Unlikely and AEIOU: Any Easy Intimacy. But he's proven equally adept at action parodies like Bighead, The Incredible Change-Bots, and the ongoing series Sulk. His memoir Funny Misshapen Body is out now from Simon & Schuster.

Chris Chua is a member of Ten Ton Studios (along with Incredible Hercules artist Koi Pham). He is the artist of the sci-fi/action graphic novel *Liquid Fury*. Chris is also an accomplished caricaturist.

Becky Cloonan contributed to the Eisner Award-winning anthology 5 and its horror-themed follow-up *Pixu*. She is the writer-artist of *East Coast Rising*, and her acclaimed collaborations include *Demo* (with Brian Wood), *American Virgin* (with Steven T. Seagle), and the ongoing webcomic *KGB* (with Hwan Cho).

Paul Hornschemeier is the acclaimed writer-artist of the graphic novels *The Three Paradoxes* and *Mother, Come Home* and the comic collections *The Collected Sequential, Let Us Be Perfectly Clear* and *All and Sundry*, released this fall by Fantagraphics. He won an Eisner for coloring Jonathan Lethem and Farel Dalrymple's *Omega the Unknown* for Marvel. His most recent graphic novel, *Life with Mr. Dangerous*, was serialized in *Mome* and will be released in a collected edition by Random House in 2010.

Jonathan Jay Lee is a freelance illustrator who graduated from the Parsons School of Design and whose work has appeared in various publications his native Hong Kong. He is a contributor to t anime book *Neo York*, due out from IdN and Freesty Collective this spring.

Corey Lewis' unique combination of Wester manga, and street-art influences can be seen in h graphic novels *Sharknife* (about a ninja wh defends a restaurant) and *Peng!* (about the wor of kickball). He is also the writer-artist of th webcomic *Seedless*.

Stan Sakai has been writing and drawing h signature series *Usagi Yojimbo*, about a rabb samurai in feudal Japan, for nearly 25 years runnin His latest Usagi book, *Yokai*, hit stores in Novemb 2009 from Dark Horse. Stan also letters the *Spide Man* newspaper strip, written by Stan Lee.

Jay Stephens is an Emmy, Eisner, Harvey, ar Reuben Award-winning artist and animator be known for creating the acclaimed animated seri *Tutenstein* and *The Secret Saturdays*. He is also th author of three instructional drawing book *Monsters!*, *Heroes!* and *Robots!*